GUIDE TO Marine Life

CARIBBEAN ▪ BAHAMAS ▪ FLORIDA

GUIDE TO
Marine Life

CARIBBEAN · BAHAMAS · FLORIDA

MARTY SNYDERMAN

& CLAY WISEMAN

AQUA QUEST PUBLICATIONS · NEW YORK

Library of Congress Cataloging-in-Publication Data

Snyderman, Marty, 1949-
    Guide to marine life : Caribbean, Bahamas, Florida / by Marty Snyderman & Clay Wiseman.
        p.   cm.
    Includes bibliographical references and index.
    ISBN 1-881652-06-8 (alk. paper)
    1. Marine fauna—Caribbean Sea. 2. Marine fauna—Bahamas 3. Marine fauna—Florida. 4. Marine fauna—Habitat—Caribbean Sea. 5. Marine fauna—Habitat—Bahamas.
6. Marine fauna—Habitat—Florida. I. Wiseman, Clay, 1959-   .
II. Title.

QL134.5.S59 1996
591.92'35—dc20   95-26095
                                                    CIP

Cover Photographs
(Left to Right)
Top row:
Brown tube sponge, graysby, painted tunicate
Middle row:
Red night shrimp, white-spotted filefish, loggerhead turtle
Bottom row:
Featherduster worms, manatee, Nassau grouper being cleaned by goby

Printed in Hong Kong
10 9 8 7 6 5 4 3 2 1

Cover design by Dan Smith

ACKNOWLEDGEMENTS

We would like to thank the many people who helped us with this project. At times during the course of working on this book, we weren't so sure we wanted to thank those who encouraged us to start. But now that the work is done, our feelings are more magnanimous. Unfortunately, we can not mention everyone by name and it is not our intent to appear ungrateful to those not mentioned, so please understand.

We do want to express heartfelt thanks to Carl Roessler and the gang at See & Sea Travel, all the folks at Aggressor Fleet, Frank Fennell and the Nikonos gang for asking Marty to be involved in the Nikonos Seminar program which allowed him to meet Captain Clay in the first place, a lot of dive guides who took us to a lot of their favorite places and shared their knowledge, Tony Bliss and all the folks at Aqua Quest Publications who said give us your best shot and we will work with you to publish this book, Mark Conlin and Doug Perrine who helped us research and verify our facts, Dr. Steven Webster of the Monterey Bay Aquarium and Dr. Bob Wisner of the Scripps Institution of Oceanography who read the manuscript for accuracy, Howard Hall, Bob Cranston, and Norbert Wu for good naturedly abusing the authors into finally finishing what they had started, Christie Jurney and Debbie Cecil for running one million and one errands, and to 9-year-old Madison Quartiano who helped us keep it all in perspective. Also thank you to the following photographers who let us use their photographs to fill in some gaps: Bob Cranston, Stephen Frink, Howard Hall, Ken Loyst, Doug Perrine, Peter Pitchard and the Center for Marine Conservation, Courtney Platt, Carl Roessler and Dr. James Spotila.

For all of the rest of you that helped us, and especially to those of you who buy or use this book, we really do want to say a sincere thank you.

All the best in diving!

M.S.
C.W.

 CONTENTS

CHAPTER 16

Phylum: Chordata

Subphylum: Vertebrata

Class: Osteichthyes

BONY FISHES

(Family by Family)

161

CHAPTER 17

Phylum: Chordata

Subphylum: Vertebrata

Class: Reptilia

Order: Testudines

SEA TURTLES

239

CHAPTER 18

Phylum: Chordata

Subphylum: Vertebrata

Class: Mammalia

MARINE MAMMALS:

MANATEES, DOLPHINS AND WHALES

247

SECTION

V

Enjoying The Marine Environment

CHAPTER 19

THE UNTOUCHABLES

261

FOREWORD

Guide to Marine Life of the Caribbean, Bahamas and Florida is written for scuba divers, snorkelers, boaters, and anyone else who is fascinated by the natural wonders of these waters. We emphasize the most interesting aspects of the natural history of animals that range from spectacularly colored sponges to the great whales. The text includes information on how animals adapt to their surroundings, how each species manages to survive, how various animals reproduce, how they capture their food, and what "bag of tricks" they employ in order to avoid being captured by other animals. In many respects this book can be described as a "who lives where and who eats who" guide to the marine life of the Caribbean, Bahamas and Florida.

Together we have more than 40 years experience in diving, underwater photography, and exploring the wonders of the Caribbean and associated waters. While we worked extremely hard to be as complete and scientifically accurate as possible, this book was written to help recreational divers have fun. The text is not written to help scientists pass their doctoral exams. We have used the following operating premise: "If an animal is more likely to be seen during the day or night, or if it changes color, habitat or sex in mid-life, we want our readers to know. We want readers to discover what animals eat, who eats them, where they live, and how they survive. If you have to count dorsal spines to distinguish one very similar species from the next, you probably won't read about it here."

More than 330 of our best color photographs, as well as quick-reference charts and sidebars, help make this book easy to use. To enable you to put your finger on a lot of information quickly, we have included "At A Glance" boxes, which are used as captions for many of the photographs. This information will quickly inform you about the animal's common name or names, its genus and species, typical adult size, preferred habitat, how likely you are to see the animal, and some of the more striking aspects of its natural history.

We have also included numerous "Photo Tip" boxes, in which we share our experiences on how best to photograph a particular animal and what equipment to use. In the appendices you will find a selected bibliography and a glossary which will give you additional explanations of some of the terms used in the text.

If you want information in a hurry, you can find it quickly. On the other hand, if you want a little more information about a variety of marine creatures, it can be found as well. You can use this book as a quick-reference field guide, or as a light-reading text for anyone who marvels at the marine life of the Caribbean, Florida and the Bahamas.

We hope you enjoy this book!

Marty Snyderman
San Diego, California

Clay Wiseman
Santa Cruz, California
January 1996

SECTION

I

The Caribbean, Bahamas and Florida

1

Where in the World Are the Caribbean, Bahamas and Florida

When world travelers think of the Caribbean, images of turquoise water, magnificent sunrises and sunsets, tanned bodies, the peaceful solitude of long walks along isolated beaches, the warm memories of a cool rum punch at sunset, and Reggae music come to mind. For snorkelers and scuba divers, their memories also include the spectacular sights of the underwater world where awe-inspiring reefs and a dazzling array of magnificently colored reef fishes captivate anyone who ever put on a face mask and peered into Neptune's Kingdom. Novice divers often describe the experience as a "thrill of a lifetime." Many well-seasoned divers and snorkelers—people who have spent years exploring oceans around the world—count their Caribbean adventures among their most memorable.

The Caribbean Sea

The Caribbean Sea is located in the western hemisphere, north of the

Opposite page: Idyllic islands with palm trees, sandy beaches, balmy breezes, and clear waters with abundant marine life make the Caribbean region popular with divers, snorkelers and other vacationers.

Section opener: A tiger grouper, commonly seen in the waters of the Caribbean, Bahamas and Florida, opens its mouth at a cleaning station signaling its readiness to be cleaned.

equator and south of the Tropic of Cancer. To members of the scientific community, the Caribbean Sea is known as a suboceanic basin. The term "suboceanic" is derived from the fact that the Caribbean Sea is considered to be part of the Atlantic Ocean.

The prolific waters of the Caribbean are bounded on the north and east by the island nations collectively known as the West Indies; to the south by the northern rim of South America; and on the west by Central America, Mexico's Yucatan Peninsula, and the passageways into the Gulf of Mexico. This expanse of ocean covers just over 1 million square miles. From east to west the Caribbean Sea stretches for close to 1,700 miles, and from north to south the width varies from approximately 500 to 800 miles.

In terms of evolutionary time, the Caribbean is a comparatively young sea. Many geologists subscribe to the theory that the Caribbean was connected to the Mediterranean Sea some 225 to 570 million years ago before the Atlantic was fully formed. Yet it is believed that the Caribbean Sea, as we know it today, is only about 20,000 years old, a mere grain of sand in the hourglass of time that represents planet Earth's history.

The melting of enormous glaciers is believed to have greatly impacted the Caribbean at the end of the last great Ice Age. Compared to the bordering Atlantic and the oceans of the Indo-Pacific, the Caribbean is a shallow sea. As a result, the glaciers altered the physical characteristics of the Caribbean far more than they affected the deeper sea floors of many other seas.

As a younger sea, the Caribbean has significantly fewer species of fishes, corals and other invertebrates than do older seas where species have had considerably more time to branch out and diversify. So, as magnificent as the marine environment of the Caribbean is, the region's wildlife is not as diverse as it is in many other oceans and seas around the world.

The sea floor of the Caribbean is created by five approximately equal-sized elliptical basins that are separated by a number of undersea ridges, rises and mountain ranges. Subsurface waters from the deeper and cooler Atlantic Ocean enter the Caribbean through two deep passages: the Anegada Passage, which lies between the Virgin Islands and the Lesser Antilles; and the Windward Passage, which is located between Cuba and Haiti. The treacherous Anegada Passage is legendary in sea lore as scores of sailing ships foundered here, many plummeting to the bottom as far as 7,700 feet below the surface. The deepest portion of the Windward Passage is 5,350 feet.

But as deep as the Windward Passage is, it is only one fifth as deep as the deepest point in the Caribbean— the Cayman Trench, which is located between Cuba and Jamaica. There, the sea floor plunges almost 5 miles below the surface to a depth of

25,216 feet. However, on the whole the Caribbean is considered to be a rather shallow sea compared to the neighboring Atlantic.

Geographers refer to the Caribbean as a marginal sea, which is technically defined as a large oceanic depression found near a continent (in this case North and South America), and which is separated from the true open ocean (the Atlantic) by deep submarine ridges or islands. If you look at a map of the Caribbean, you will see that the land masses of the West Indies and the arc of islands known as the Antillean chain, which span from Cuba to the Grenadines, separate the Atlantic Ocean from the Caribbean Sea. These islands are, in fact, the tops of great undersea mountains and ridges which effectively divide the waters of the Atlantic and Caribbean.

Collectively, these land masses deflect large, deep, cold water currents from the Atlantic, and at least partially prevent these currents from spilling into the Caribbean.

Due to the combination of geography, the tropical location, and the comparatively shallow nature of the Caribbean basin, the water in the Caribbean is warmer than that in the Atlantic. Surface temperatures typically vary from the low 70's F in the northern sector during late winter and early spring to the low to mid 80's F throughout much of the Caribbean during late summer and early fall. While thermoclines do occur, uniform temperatures in sport diving depths are common. Water temperature is a major factor in determining where many species of marine life prefer to live. Though it is true that many species are common to both the Caribbean and the Atlantic, there are also many significant differences in the marine life found in the two bodies of water.

Compared to many other oceans, tidal flow and the difference in height between tides is very low throughout the Caribbean. Even in the case of the highest spring tides,

the tidal range is only about two feet. Certainly this is one of the feature attractions as far as tourists are concerned because resort facilities can be constructed very close to the water's edge. Less tidal fluctuation also plays a role in minimizing the strength of currents.

By comparison, the difference in height between high and low tide in Southern California is often as much as nine feet, but on a global scale even this difference is considered moderate.

LAND MASSES

According to a strict geological definition, the land masses of the Caribbean include the islands of the Antillean chain and the land masses of Central America and the Yucatan Peninsula which are part of the continent of North America, and the northern rim of the continent of South America. The island groups of the Antillean chain are often separated into two groups, the Greater Antilles and the Lesser Antilles. Located to the northwest, the largest land masses in the Greater Antilles include Cuba, Jamaica, Hispaniola (Haiti and the Dominican Republic) and Puerto Rico. The Lesser Antilles extend from the British Virgin Islands and U.S. Virgin Islands southeast through Grenada and continuing westward to Bonaire, Curacao and Aruba.

The Lesser Antilles is composed of two island groups known as the Windward and Leeward Islands. The Windward Islands are so named because they are exposed to the northeast trade winds which dominate the region's climate. The northeast trades average a speed of 10 to 20 miles per hour. The Windward Islands, known for their wonderful sailing conditions as well as for superb diving, include Martinique, St. Lucia, St. Vincent, the Grenadine chain and Grenada.

Some of the major Leeward Islands, which extend from the Vir-

gin Islands to the top of the Windwards, are Antigua, Barbados, St. Christopher, Anguilla, Montserrat, St. Martin, Dominica and Guadeloupe. The Leewards are generally sheltered from the trade winds, and on the whole, have a much drier climate.

Throughout the Caribbean, the climate is generally tropical with great local variations depending upon elevation, the presence of mountain ranges, currents and trade winds. The average mean temperature in the summer is 80 to 82°F while rainfall varies from as much as 350 inches a year in Dominica to as little as 10 inches annually in Bonaire. As a rule days are hot with some rain and evenings potentially cool and breezy. But don't assume that balmy tropical conditions prevail at all times of year.

Technically speaking, Florida's reefs, like those in the Bahamas, lie outside the boundaries of the Caribbean Sea. However, from a diver's point of view, it is interesting to note that many species of marine life found in both the Bahamas and Florida are the same as those observed in the Caribbean. That is not to say that the mix of marine life in Florida, even in the Florida Keys, is exactly the same as that found in the Bahamas or the Caribbean. Each area has a unique blend, but while some species are found only in small geographic areas, other species are found in all three regions. In many cases, closely related species are found throughout neighboring waters.

In any case, if you can identify the family (such as butterflyfishes or angelfishes) in which a particular fish is described (or the class in which an invertebrate is described), you can often garner some general understanding about the natural history of any animal you encounter. If you see an animal while snorkeling or diving anywhere in the Caribbean, Bahamas or Florida, but you can't find the exact image in this book, try looking for similar species

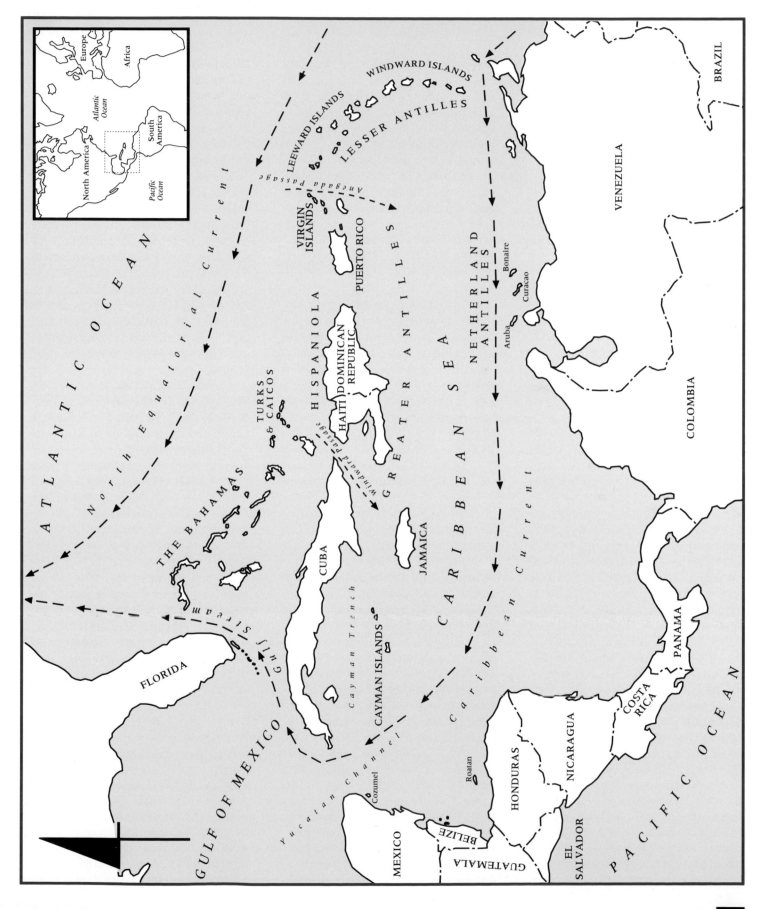

to get an idea of what creature you encountered, and how they live their lives.

THE BAHAMAS

Impressions of the Bahamas are dominated by images of cobalt blue seas, gentle breezes, white sand beaches, a slow, yet colorful life style, and myriad marine creatures. The waters surrounding this island nation teem with life.

While the westernmost islands in the archipelago are less than 50 miles from Miami, Florida, the Bahamas chain stretches southeastward for more than 750 miles, extending well past Cuba before finally ending off the coast of Hispaniola (Haiti and the Dominican Republic). The islands are bordered on the north and east by the Atlantic, to the west by the warming influence of the Gulf Stream, and to the south by the Caribbean.

In the Bahamas, there are 29 major islands and more than 3,000 smaller islands referred to as cays (keys). Only 30 or so of the islands are inhabited, and three-fourths of the population live on Grand Bahama or on New Providence, where the capital city of Nassau is located. The remaining islands are sometimes collectively referred to as the out islands. Most of the land masses are relatively small, encompassing a total of only 5,382 square miles. The tallest point, a mere 206 feet above sea level, is found on Cat Island.

The islands are formed from coralline limestone. Most are long and narrow, with each rising from an eastern shore. Lagoons, mangrove swamps and coral reefs are found along many shorelines.

Astronauts have repeatedly commented that when viewed from space, the islands, which are surrounded by more than 100,000 square miles of water, look like small gray-green gems set in a vast tapestry of azure and turquoise, with breaks created by the sugar-white sand of the legendary Bahama Banks. Columbus named the Bahamas well when he called the region *Bajamar*, "the shallow or shoaling area."

Experiencing only two seasons each year, winter, from roughly December through April, and summer, from approximately May through November, the Bahamas are known for their mild climate and subtropical beauty. Water temperature in the winter dips into the low to mid-70's F, and in the summer it rises to a soothing high 70's to low 80's F. The air temperature is approximately 10°F warmer than the water.

Most of the islands within the chain lie along the outside edges of several expansive, underwater plateaus known as the Bahama Banks. It is the banks that distinguish the Bahamas from so many other diving destinations. On the whole, the white sandy banks are rather shallow, with typical depths being 20 to 30 feet. However, they are separated by deep oceanic trenches which plummet precipitously to depths in excess of 12,000 feet. Sheer walls populated by a diverse group of marine animals are found where the edges of the banks plummet into the depths.

Large coral heads and reefs the size of liveaboard dive boats are found sporadically throughout the open expanses of the banks. The reefs support small marine communities by providing food, shelter and a place for attachment. These shallow banks serve as nurseries for many juvenile fishes, helping to keep the nearby, deeper reefs well populated. The reefs also attract a variety of larger animals including sharks, turtles, southern stingrays, spotted eagle rays, and at times, spotted dolphins.

The flow of nutrients from the deep waters of the surrounding Atlantic and the Gulf Stream also have a significant impact upon life on the Bahama Banks. A variety of large, pelagic animals that reside in the open sea, such as whale sharks, silky sharks and billfish, are known to swim in the cuts between the banks, filling their bellies with treats from the nutrient-rich waters.

Eons ago during the Ice Ages, the plateaus of the Bahama Banks stood far above sea level. Great plateaus surrounded by sheer cliffs and dramatic bluffs made up the landscape of the day. And on the islands, great sinkholes and caverns that we call "blue holes" were formed. But when the last great Ice Age ended approximately 12,000 years ago, sea water rose by more than 300 feet, and even the tops of the plateaus were flooded by the sea. It is these once high and dry plateaus that we know today as the Bahama Banks, and we know the cliffs as the vertical walls that border these once terrestrial plateaus.

Evidence of previous sea levels can be seen by the series of ledges carved out of the sheer walls. Each ledge is indicative of an ancient shoreline created during a period when there was a geological pause in the rise of sea level. Distinct ledges can usually be identified at about 80 feet and 120 feet.

Along the northern end of the Bahamas is the bank known as the Little Bahama Bank. It is bounded on the northeast by the Abacos and to the south by Grand Bahama Island. It is on the Little Bahama Bank where so many snorkelers and divers have enjoyed encounters with Atlantic spotted dolphins.

To the south lies the roughly U-shaped Great Bahama Bank. The westernmost leg forms the base of Bimini, the Berry Islands and Andros. The eastern branch gives rise to New Providence, Eleuthera, the Exumas, Cat Island and Long Island. The smaller Cay Sal Bank lies westward of the Great Bahama Bank. Although from the surface, the Cay Sal Bank seems less striking than her sister banks, with only a number of sand spits and barely exposed rocks and reefs serving as landmarks, underwater, Cay Sal is bounded by a number of fringing reefs and sheer walls, many of which provide superb diving and ideal habitats for marine residents.

The Bahamas chain also includes a number of islands to the south and east which are the exposed tops of isolated undersea mountain peaks. We know these crests as San Salvador, Rum Cay, Conception Island, Little Inagua, Great Inagua, Mayaguana, Plana Cays and Hogsty Reef, the only true atoll in the Atlantic.

The Bahamas are known for their excellent underwater visibility (between 80 and 150 feet) which is due to the combination of several factors. First, there is no runoff from any major rivers, and second, the porous limestone bedrock absorbs the minimal amounts of rainfall, meaning that there is very little sedimentation. If a storm silts up a shallow area, the water is usually washed clear by the flow from the Gulf Stream on the next tide.

FLORIDA

While almost everyone recognizes Florida as the Sunshine State, snorkelers and divers appreciate the southernmost state on the continental mainland for her prolific waters. With more than 1,350 miles of coastline, Florida has more shoreline than any other state in the United States with the exception of Alaska. 580 miles are bounded by the Atlantic, while 770 miles lie along the Gulf of Mexico. If one counts all of Florida's bays, lagoons, estuaries and offshore islands, the number of miles of coastline bordering the Atlantic swell to 3,331 miles and the Gulf coastline reaches approximately 5,095 miles.

Diversity is a term that accurately depicts Florida's marine life and diving conditions. Though the waters bordering much of the state are not what one would normally call tropical, there is a definite tropical feel to some of the southernmost dive

sites along the peninsula, and especially in the Florida Keys. Even Florida's northernmost border lies 120 miles southward of the southernmost point in California.

Adorned with giant oaks and towering pines, the hard-packed beaches of Florida's northeast coast face the waters of the Atlantic Ocean. Further south, the oaks and pines give way to tropical palms, and sandy beaches glisten in the sunlight. The Florida Keys, a diver's paradise, lie south of Miami, reaching toward the Caribbean as they extend to within 90 miles of Havana, Cuba. Key Largo boasts the first underwater park in the United States, John Pennekamp Coral Reef State Park. Within the park's 78 square miles, divers enjoy more than 40 species of corals and a whopping 300-plus species of fishes.

The waters facing the Atlantic Ocean along Florida's northeast coast provide a strong contrast to the protected waters of the panhandle. Instead of big waves and body surfing, beachgoers are more likely to find the water along the panhandle to be calm, blue and fairly shallow for miles. Powder-white sands characterize the panhandle beaches.

Both sides of the Florida peninsula show strong influence from the marine community of the Caribbean. However, as you would probably suspect, the farther north you dive along the Atlantic coast and the further north and west you explore in the Gulf, the less similar the water conditions and marine life are to the Caribbean. For example, while surface water temperature in the Gulf of Mexico often reaches the high 80'sF in late summer, by the end of winter the mercury dips to the mid- to low 60'sF, a figure which is not exactly tropical.

Because water temperature has such a strong influence on where marine animals live, it is in the Florida Keys where the mix of marine creatures is most similar to that found throughout the Caribbean and in the Bahamas.

THE FLORIDA KEYS

The Florida Keys are comprised of a series of more than 200 small, flat islands which in modern times have been stitched together by U.S. Highway 1. These limestone islands stretch over a 150- mile-long arc that reaches from Key Largo in the north to Key West to the southwest.

The Tropic of Cancer is south of the southernmost point in the Keys, but clearly the Florida Keys lie in the confluence of the temperate and tropical regions. Indeed, the tropical influence in the Keys is as strong underwater as it is in the lifestyles exhibited by the locals.

The northbound flow of the Gulf Stream, a major offshore current, brings massive quantities of warm, clear waters past the Keys. Some of the Keys are washed by the Gulf Stream on a regular basis, and some are not.

The Gulf Stream strongly influences the weather as well as the water conditions. Combined with the prevailing tropical trade winds, the Gulf Stream is instrumental in creating balmy conditions year round in the Keys. Unlike the majority of Florida as well as the rest of the continental United States, which both enjoy and endure four seasons throughout the year, residents in the Keys will likely tell you that they have only two seasons, summer and winter.

Daytime highs in winter are typically in the 70's to low 80's F, while the average air temperature is 64°F. At night, the thermometer drops into the 60'sF. Summers, on the other hand, are hot and humid, with air temperatures in the 90's F being common.

At least four times over the course of recent geologic time, the Keys have risen above sea level only to be submerged once more. As recently as 100,000 years ago, the Keys emerged as shallow coral reefs which gradually rose to be exposed to the elements of sun, wind and rain. As the seas receded, the once-living corals perished, leaving their limestone-based skeletons to anchor the soil and vegetation. Seedlings from mangroves were brought to the Keys from distant shores by ocean currents, and over time the mangroves began to form a natural perimeter which protected the emerging shoreline. Then palm trees and the Florida hardwoods found their ecological niche.

Today, a huge system of offshore fringing reefs has developed. The most fully evolved reefs lie between four to six miles off the beaches, and parallel virtually the entire shoreline of the Keys. By far and away, the best diving is enjoyed on these reefs, not along the coastal beaches. Offshore visibility in the Keys averages from 30 to 50 feet throughout the year, but can range as far as 150 feet. The inshore visibility is often less than 20 feet. Water temperature ranges from wintertime lows of 68°F or so, the minimum in which reef-building hard corals can survive, to mid-80's in the summer.

The reefs of the Florida Keys teem with life. Huge schools of snappers and grunts have become synonymous with the region. Many, of course, make a number of shipwrecks their permanent homes. Barracudas, jewfish, squirrelfishes, angelfishes, trumpetfish, tarpon, schools of horse-eye jacks, porkfish and schoolmasters are daily fare. So are parrotfishes, butterflyfishes, groupers, goatfishes, sergeant majors, moray eels, glass minnows and many more species. Divers commonly encounter sea turtles and occasionally see a variety of sharks ranging from nurse sharks to hammerheads.

Myriad invertebrates can be enjoyed by snorkelers and divers alike. A variety of sponges, corals, hydroids, jellyfishes, sea fans, lobsters, shrimps, crabs, flame scallops, colorful feather duster worms, ornate Christmas tree worms, snails, squids and octopuses can be filmed or simply observed in an average dive.

THE GULF STREAM

One of the major influences in terms of climate, water conditions, the circulation of oceanic nutrients and wastes, and economics is the presence of a generally northeastward moving current known as the Gulf Stream, which flows along the western edge of the Caribbean. The swift-moving Gulf Stream forms the northwestern boundary of a large system of generally clockwise-moving currents in the north Atlantic. Generated by the combination of the westward-flowing North Equatorial Current, which originates off of the north coast of Africa, and of the Caribbean Current, which flows westward along the north coast of South America, the Gulf Stream forms in the western Caribbean. It then flows into the Gulf of Mexico through the Yucatan Channel, between Cuba and Mexico's Yucatan Peninsula, before turning sharply to the northeast as the current flows out the Straits of Florida between the Florida Keys and Cuba.

A number of important counter currents which flow in the opposite direction of the Gulf Stream help to ensure a constant mixing of nutrients. A major ocean current, the Gulf Stream penetrates to a depth of as much as 2,600 feet in places. In some regions the flow of the Gulf Stream averages as much as 4 miles per hour and contains hundreds of times the volume of water that is carried by the Mississippi River. Most of the Gulf Stream lies outside the strict definition of the Caribbean, but the presence of the current strongly influences the prevailing weather and water conditions found in the Caribbean region.

Amazingly, constant winds in the Gulf of Mexico, and between the southern tip of Florida, Cuba, and the Yucatan, pile surface water up as high as 9 to 18 inches above sea level. The flow of this "high water" toward sea level helps power the fast-moving Gulf Stream.

HURRICANES

Hurricanes are one of the most interesting and awesome forces in the Caribbean. The hurricane season extends from June to November. These incredibly powerful storms are seasonally common, and the Caribbean region endures an annual average of eight storms per year. September is considered to be the height of the hurricane season. Most hurricanes occur in the northern Caribbean and the Gulf of Mexico, only rarely occurring in the southern Caribbean.

Hurricanes are typically borne from long, narrow regions of low pressure toward the eastern edge of the Caribbean. As the storms increase in intensity, they develop from tropical depressions into hurricanes. Winds in hurricanes swirl in a counterclockwise direction. Hurricanes tend to move westward when they first develop, following the arc-like path of the trade winds into the Gulf of Mexico, but most turn east after reaching the temperate latitudes to the north.

The storms are usually 200 to 300 miles in diameter and the winds just outside the center whip about at a minimum of 75 miles per hour. Violent winds of 140 miles per hour or even higher are not uncommon in strong hurricanes.

The wind, rain, swell and surge generated by hurricanes can have great impact on the marine environment. Often entire coral reefs are destroyed either by literally being broken apart or by sand, mud and other debris burying or otherwise suffocating corals.

While seeing a once-pristine reef reduced to shambles by a powerful storm is a humbling and saddening experience, it is helpful to realize that hurricanes are part of the natural cycle. It usually doesn't take long before a variety of plants and animals begin to utilize the newly formed coral rubble for shelter, food and habitat.

SECTION
II
Marine Habitats

LIFE ON THE REEF

2

Gaze downward through your face mask toward a colorful Caribbean reef below, and you can't help but be filled with wonderment. Brightly colored fishes perform their eye catching dances in perpetuity over a stunning array of sun dappled corals, sponges and sea fans. Almost everywhere you look, brilliant flashes of color command your attention. Nearly every nook and cranny teems with a diversified mix of fascinating invertebrates. Well armored crabs, shrimps and lobsters, as well as strikingly patterned cowries, snails, dazzling nudibranchs, delicate looking worms, sea stars, octopuses and sea anemones add to the spectacular tapestry of the reef.

Together, the myriad organisms that are part of the ecosystem of a coral reef community form one of the most complex and productive living systems in the world.

CORALS: BUILDING BLOCKS OF REEF SYSTEMS

More than 70 species of corals occur in the reefs of the Caribbean, Baha-

Opposite page: Large schools of silversides attract a host of predators including this giant jewfish. The jewfish may also be feeding on other fishes higher up in the food chain that also feed on the silversides. The reefs of the Caribbean, Bahamas and Florida are resplendent with fish life.

Section opener: Caribbean reefs sparkle with colors. Here, in a common Caribbean scene, a schoolmaster snapper cruises along a shallow reef.

mas and Florida. These corals are commonly divided into two categories: the **hard** or **reef-building corals**, and the **soft** or **non-reef-building corals**. The reef-building corals are responsible for laying down the structural foundation of the reef. It is the deposits of limestone (calcium carbonate) left from the skeletal remains of tiny hard-coral polyps that collectively create the habitat we know as coral reefs. These hardened corals provide structure for the reef and create countless living quarters and hiding places for the residents of the reef.

The soft, or non-reef-building, corals play an important role in the reef ecosystem during their lifetime by providing habitat and food for many animals. However, soft corals are considerably different from hard corals in that the skeletons of soft corals lack the calcium carbonate found in the spicules of the hard corals. It is calcium carbonate which provides hard corals with the ability to create coral reefs that can exist for millions of years. The impact of the hard reef-building corals is long lasting while that of the soft corals is more temporary.

Important reef-building corals in the Caribbean include **staghorn coral**, **elkhorn coral**, and two species of **star coral**. To a lesser extent a variety of other species also contribute to the long-standing physical structure of Caribbean reefs. These other reef-building species include several types of corals commonly known as **brain coral**, **pitted coral**, **finger coral** and **pillar coral,** to name a few. Like all hard corals, these species secrete a stony calcium

carbonate skeleton as part of their natural metabolic process.

Individual coral animals are referred to as polyps. A colony of polyps is commonly referred to as a coral head. Coral heads are built of anywhere from a dozen to as many as a thousand or more polyps, while coral reefs are created by a number of coral heads. Small reefs may consist of only a handful of coral heads, while large reef systems are made up of thousands of coral heads and can extend for miles. In the final analysis, a coral reef is built by billions upon billions of individual coral polyps.

The creation of a reef is a constantly ongoing process. When old coral heads die, new polyps often settle or bud out to recolonize the surface areas of dead areas. Generations of once living hard corals form the foundation upon which countless currently living corals flourish. Their subsequent demise will add even more limestone to the reef, providing a place for future generations of hard corals to attach.

Violent storms destroy some reefs. Further, many animals like parrotfishes transform hard corals into sand as they feed. Given the opportunity, competitive plants and animals will reduce the area available to corals by moving in and taking over the territory. This process continually repeats itself as the geological clock of the reef ticks away.

The reef-building process is not one that is perfectly uniform. Reef building forces are constantly being challenged by destructive forces. Whenever a coral head dies, it is very likely that some areas will not be

All animals that attach to the reef compete for valuable space. Various species of corals, both soft and hard, are constantly fighting a silent, but intense, war for places to attach and grow.

immediately recolonized by new polyps. However, this space is not likely to go unused for long. A variety of algae and a host of invertebrates aggressively compete in the vital and constant struggle for space on the reef. The ability to attach to the sea floor or to other organisms is a life-or-death priority for many animals that live in a coral reef ecosystem. Recognizing the critical nature of the ongoing competition for space in a coral reef, and understanding the various survival strategies employed by different species, is fundamental to truly comprehending what life on the reef is all about.

CORAL ZONATION IN A TYPICAL CARIBBEAN REEF

Exactly where each species of coral can be found within a typical Caribbean reef ecosystem is not a matter of happenstance—not by any stretch of the imagination. Competition bet-

ween the species is fierce, and each species must find its own niche where it can be successful. In nature, success is defined as the survival of the species, while failure brings death.

All reef-building species of coral require a lot of sunlight. As a result these species tend to require shallow, clean water which affords maximum light penetration. Shallow water typically means rougher water, and the corals that live in comparatively shallow water must be able to withstand the forces of pounding surf and constant wave action. Other corals are better adapted for the slightly calmer living conditions found in water a little deeper, while still other species are best suited for life along the walls and drop-offs.

Several of the more common species of corals are indicative of specific areas, or zones, within a reef system. For example, immediately under and just seaward of the breakers elkhorn coral is typically the most commonly found species. Elkhorn coral is a hardy and fast growing species whose sturdy, branching structure helps it endure and dissipate the continuous pounding of the surf. Immediately seaward of the elkhorn zone you will encounter large quantities of coral rubble, the result of the relentless surf breaking down various species of living corals and the remains of their skeletal ancestors.

Small separated colonies of star corals and a variety of soft gorgonian corals may thrive around the rubble. The flexible soft corals tend to gently sway back and forth as they keep time with the sea's ebb and flow. Hard corals, because of their calcium carbonate structure, lack flexibility.

As you swim toward deeper water, extensive sand patches soon appear. These stretches of sand are the end product of the ever present surf which batters and degrades a variety of corals and shells. Springing up from the sand are patches of reef

comprised of **star corals, brain corals, pitted corals**, and a variety of gorgonians including those eye catching sea fans. These so called "patch reefs" are oases for small fishes and a wide variety of invertebrates, especially crustaceans.

Further seaward of the patch reefs, you are likely to discover fingers of continuous reef running perpendicular to the drop-off and parallel to one another. These fingers are separated by sand patches running from the shallows to the reef buttress or edge of the wall. Commonly included in the group of corals which comprise these fingers are the star corals, brain corals, finger corals, lettuce coral, pillar coral and staghorn coral. These reefs are often occupied by various species of soft corals such as **sea fans**, **sea whips** and **sea plumes** which sway back and forth with the surge.

In some locations thickets of fast-growing staghorn coral form shallow to moderately deep reefs. Colonies of this coral, which form dense latticework-like forests, can often be found seaward of the reef flat, as well as in protected shallows along some shorelines and in protected lagoons. The area of the forest nearest the sea floor is often occupied by dead staghorn that has been colonized by sponges, tunicates and algae. And almost always, opportunistic damselfishes are quick to take advantage of the presence of the algae as they move in to "cultivate and farm" their own highly treasured algal crop which they vigorously protect as they stake out their territories.

A topographical overview of a typical Caribbean reef as seen from above reveals a series of sand strips interrupted by coral fingers which extend from the shallows all the way to the top of the drop-off. This arrangement, often called a "spur and groove" formation, is common to most bank-barrier reefs of the Caribbean. From a bird's-eye view high above the reef and sand, the configuration resembles a flexible ladder

These commonly seen and highly reflective spheres are actually the egg sacs of a type of marine algae!

surrounding the islands with the uprights being the shallow, near-shore breaker-zone corals on one side and the deeper reef buttress, or wall, on the other. The rungs of this ladder are the coral fingers which stretch between the uprights. The spaces between the uprights represent the sand channels.

The upper edge of the reef buttress and the top portion of a wall is often occupied by several species of large and colorful sea fans, also known as deep-water gorgonians. Their fan shaped superstructures bear countless polyps which flourish in areas where currents flow. The polyps of sea fans form a stinging net that sweeps nutrient rich particles from the flowing waters.

Large star coral, *Montastrea cavernosa*, is the most predominant coral on many reefs between depths of 40 and 100 feet. As you descend down the wall along the reef escarpment, you will notice that the star corals begin to grow in thin layers called "plates". These corals are said to "plate out" rather than form large rounded heads as they do on top of the wall. It is believed that the plating out is an adaptation intended to increase the surface area of the coral which is exposed to sunlight. Obviously, the amount of sunlight received decreases with depth, and the increased surface area allows the vitally important symbiotic algae known as **zooxanthellae,** which live within the tissues of the corals, to continue to photosynthesize and therefore provide food for the coral polyps.

The algae zooxanthellae may be small but not because of any lack of biological significance. Quite the contrary! Zooxanthellae are actually the fundamental building blocks of all coral reef systems. These algae use the natural waste products of the coral polyps as fertilizer for their own photosynthetic processes. In return for the nutrients supplied and for a place to live, the algae provide vital food in the form of simple sugars to the coral polyps. The algae also enhance the coral's abiliy to utilize calcium.

This symbiotic relationship between reef-building corals and zooxanthellae is the single most important relationship between any two life forms in the reef environment. Amazingly, it was not until after World War II that the existence of the zooxanthellae was established. The presence of the tiny algae solved a great mystery. All food chains are built on a foundation of plants which produce energy and food for the animal kingdom. However, plant life was thought to be lacking in tropical reef communities. Without the availability of plentiful food for organisms on the lower end of the food chain, scientists were unable to explain how coral reef ecosystems supported themselves. The discovery of enormous quantities of the microscopic zooxanthellae, which live inside the tissues of living coral polyps, enabled scientists to understand how coral reef ecosystems are able to flourish.

As you continue to descend, the variety and quantity of hard corals diminish considerably. However, there are some notable exceptions. Various brain corals often remain abundant, while plate corals and lettuce corals tend to become even more numerous. **Giant polyp coral, green coral** and **flower coral** are also common along the reef escarpment. Many soft corals, such as the variety of species commonly called **black coral** and **wire coral,** tend to flourish at depth. **Deep-water orange gorgonians** are sometimes still common at depths that exceed sport diving limits.

Real estate is a precious commodity in reef communities. On and around the large basket, or barrel, sponge (foreground) are the echinoderms known as golden crinoids, sea rods (a type of cnidarian), red encrusting sponges and algae. All are competing with each other as well as with the sponge for living space.

The giant Caribbean anemone, cleverly disguised as a harmless looking, "undersea flower" is actually a deadly predator whose tentacles are packed with batteries of powerful stinging cells. Fish that get too close often end up as a meal for the anemone.

CREATURES OF THE REEF COMMUNITY

Coral reefs are built from a variety of coral heads, and each coral head is composed of a colony of coral polyps. The number of polyps in any one coral head typically ranges from a dozen to several thousand or more. Each coral polyp is equipped with a centrally located mouth, which is surrounded by a ring of tentacles. Batteries of potent stinging cells called nematoblasts arm the tentacles. The system acts like a net which traps food floating by in the current. Once captured, the food is quickly passed to the mouth of the coral polyp.

In most species of corals, the potent tentacles are extended only after dark, however, there are some notable exceptions. Pillar corals, for example, often feed during the day, and the extended tentacles are readily apparent when the corals feed. Of course, the food provided by symbiotic algae by day also plays a vital role in sustaining the polyps.

The possession of stinging cells, which are used as a means of capturing food and providing defense, is a characteristic that is shared by a variety of commonly encountered residents of Caribbean reef communities. Collectively, these animals are described in the phylum Cnidaria. The cnidarians include a wide variety of corals, anemones, zoanthids, hydroids and jellyfishes.

Many divers are familiar with the painful stings of a variety of species commonly referred to as **fire corals**. While fire "corals" are cnidarians, they are not really types of coral. These animals are actually colonial hydroids, but in the common language used by divers, these species are almost always referred to as corals. The same is true for the species known as **branching corals**.

Anemones, such as the **giant Caribbean anemone**, the **corkscrew anemone** and the **knobby anemone**, commonly provide a home for a variety of animals that have developed an immunity to their potentially deadly sting. Included in this select group are the **Pederson's cleaning shrimp**, the **anemone shrimp**, the **anemone crab**, and a handsome and often curious fish known as the **diamond blenny**.

The presence of Pederson's cleaning shrimp amongst the tentacles of a giant Caribbean anemone marks this location as an area where a variety of fishes may go to be preened by the shrimp and by a variety of small fishes. Such an area is known as a **cleaning station**. Studies have shown that in some reefs, cleaning stations are extremely important in sustaining the long term health of the many species of reef fishes. The bodies and gills of the fishes being

A gang of gobies provide cleaning services for this Nassau grouper. Cleaning helps rid reef fishes of external parasites, dead tissue and bacteria, and thereby promotes their healthy existence.

cleaned are often infested by debilitating skin parasites (ectoparasites, such as sea lice and some isopods). The cleaners remove many of these parasites. Experiments in which the cleaning stations have been removed from the environment have shown that in many instances the dependent fishes soon become sick or die.

When being cleaned, many fishes will change colors and darken their skin (an act called flushing) in order to make the lightly colored parasites more conspicuous and easier for cleaners to find. If you see a fish that appears to be a darker color than normal, consider pausing for a few moments as you watch from a distance. Odds are in your favor that you will be able to watch a cleaning station in service. A number of fishes, including a variety of gobies, juvenile angelfishes and juvenile hogfishes are also active cleaners.

Once satisfied, the fish being cleaned will often flash colors, or change back to a lighter hue as a means of communicating with the cleaners that their services are no longer needed.

The abundant coral formations of the reefs create a series of flat surfaces, ledges, overhangs, underhangs, caves and crevices which are often used as a place of attachment for the extraordinary variety of **sponges** that occur in the Caribbean. It comes as a surprise to many to learn that sponges are actually animals. In fact, they are the simplest of all multicellular animals.

Sponges are omnipresent on Caribbean reefs and include the largest found anywhere in the world. Sponges occur in a wide range of colors and shapes that are sure to catch your eye. Some are shaped like tubes, baskets, ropes, fingers, barrels and vases. Others look like miniature volcanoes, while still others are encrusting and take on the shape of the substrate to which they attach.

To the eye of the underwater photographer, few subjects provide more opportunity. Colorful sponges make wonderful foreground sub-

Like many fishes which congregate around cleaning stations, this Nassau grouper will flare its gills and "open wide" as it requests the cleaning services of neon gobies, cleaner shrimp and other cleaner species.

jects that give photographs life. And as far as the residents of Caribbean reef communities are concerned, sponges create ideal living quarters and places of refuge and hiding. Brittle stars, zoanthids, arrow crabs, shrimps, and a variety of gobies and other fishes utilize selected sponges.

Sponges are great filter feeders and are often credited with creating the phenomenal water clarity associated with Caribbean diving. While it is true that sponges filter amazing quantities of water, the wonderful underwater visibility that we enjoy in the Caribbean and associated waters is primarily due to the lack of nutrients in the water compared

to temperate and polar seas where the visibility is commonly much more limited.

Microscopic hairs that line the cells of the chamber walls of a sponge constantly beat back and forth, generating currents that circulate water through the walls of the animal. A maze of fine silica spicules secreted by the cells of the sponge intermesh to strain bacteria and other minute food from the water.

The filtered water carries some waste as it exits the sponge through a large central opening called the osculum, but on the whole sponges remove far more particulate matter than they create. It is amazing that sponges are able to coordinate their filtering activity so efficiently even though they possess no organs, muscles, or specialized tissues.

Some of the more common species of sponges that occur in Caribbean waters include the **giant barrel sponge**, the **yellow tube sponge**, the **azure vase sponge**, the **purple tube sponge** and the **red rope sponge**. Typically found in quieter, deeper waters, giant barrel sponges are known to stand 12 feet high off the sea floor, a dimension that makes this species the world's largest sponge. A specimen that size is likely to be hundreds of years old! Please be careful around these enormous sponges, for despite their size, they are surprisingly fragile.

Both yellow tube sponges and azure vase sponges, along with a number of other species of sponges, exhibit a natural iridescence, a characteristic which makes these species glow as if they are being artificially lit. Red rope sponges may grow upward or hang downward in formations that reach six feet or longer.

Sponges often have their walls infiltrated with many tiny, anemone-like animals called **zoanthids**. For years it was thought that these small, yellow-to-green zoanthids were parasites that preyed on sponges, but recent studies have demonstrated that the zoanthids actually discourage some fishes from feeding on the sponges. In effect, the zoanthids serve as a valuable repellent to predators.

It is somewhat surprising that given the incredible variety and sheer biomass of sponges found in the Caribbean, only two families of fishes commonly feed on sponges. They are the angelfishes and the filefishes. Evidence indicates that it is probably the combination of noxious chemicals, sharp silica spicules and zooanthids that make sponges poor fodder for most reef fishes.

However, sponges themselves are known to parasitize various reef building corals. The **boring sponge** serves as a classic case in point. This

Caribbean sponges, such as this yellow tube sponge, occur in a wide variety of forms and stunning colors.

sponge actually bores its way into coral heads by secreting powerful acids. In doing so, boring sponges find protection and a place of attachment. However, an overly aggressive community of boring sponges can so weaken their host coral head that it tumbles down the wall into the abyss, sponges and all! But soon afterwards new organisms will occupy the vacated space. Before too long the coral will again rise and proliferate only to create the ideal place of attachment for a boring sponge.

Understanding this cycle of competition, parasitism, demise and rebirth provides valuable insight into the natural cycles of the marine environment.

While we often tend to think of the various creatures of the reef as separate from one another, in real life they are highly interdependent. The relationships between the species are complex and varied, and each plays a vital role in the overall inner workings of a reef community.

A variety of crabs, shrimps and lobsters play prominent roles in Caribbean reef communities. These spe-

cies are commonly known as crustaceans, in reference to their class, Crustacea. Nature has provided crabs, shrimps and lobsters with a hard, protective body armor called an exoskeleton. This armament has helped make them successful, but it also imposes some severe limitations. Crustaceans must shed their exoskeletons temporarily during periods of growth and reproduction. They are especially vulnerable to predators during these times.

Although many species of crustaceans such as **cleaning shrimps**, **anemone crabs** and **anemone shrimps** can be seen during the day, nighttime is unquestionably the best time to see the majority of reef dwelling crustaceans. Most crabs, shrimps and lobsters are nocturnal scavengers, and they tend to hide in the protective confines of the reef during the day.

The **red-banded coral shrimp** is an example. Certainly it is not unheard of for divers to see these shrimp actively cleaning fishes or foraging along the reef during the day, but it is far more common to see just their long white antennae protruding out of a crevice while the sun is high. At night these magnificently colored shrimp can easily be found in many reef communities.

Clawless **spiny lobster** emerge from the caves and crevices in the hours between sunset and sunrise. The same is true for the giant **Caribbean king crabs**, animals whose claw-to-claw measurements commonly exceed three feet! Strange looking slipper lobsters also leave their daytime hiding places to forage at night. **Slipper lobster** have a stubby, well-armored body and short antennae. Their color varies from drab brown to richer hues of red, purple, orange and yellow.

A variety of **hermit crabs** feed mostly at night, but observant divers can commonly find these crabs scurrying about on the reef during the day. Hermit crabs tow their pilfered snail shells from place to place so that they have a safe place to hide if

At night the reef community is alive with a host of creatures that are not often seen during the day. Here, a spider crab (also known as a king crab and as a channel clinging crab) takes an evening stroll.

and when danger threatens.

Among the strangest looking of all the crustaceans are the **arrow crabs.** They possess what appear to be oversized, long, thin legs and a long nose, giving them some resemblance to the common spiders we know as daddy long legs. Arrow crabs can sometimes be seen during the day if you look under ledges, and at night they often climb high atop gorgonians and sponges to forage.

Another seldom noticed, but very significant crustacean found in Caribbean reef communities is the species commonly known as **sea lice.** These tiny crustaceans feed on the mucus and skin of the many reef fishes which they parasitize. If left unchecked, sea lice can quickly debilitate their hosts. One of the subtle joys that can be experienced by observant divers is to hover close to a cleaning station and watch as cleaner gobies and shrimps chase frantic sea lice over the skin of some unfor-

tunate to be infested, but soon to be cleaned, moray eel or grouper.

Many additional species of invertebrates reside on the reef surfaces or inhabit the cracks and crevices of Caribbean reefs. Included in this list are a variety of mollusks (**snails, nudibranchs, oysters, squids, octopuses,** etc.), a variety of echinoderms (**sea stars, brittle stars, sea cucumbers, sea urchins,** etc.), and an array of colorful **marine worms.** With the exception of octopuses and squids, these invertebrates in their adult stage are either comparatively slow moving, or they are attached to the substrate and completely immobile. As a result, many of these animals are filter feeders. They use extremely efficient ciliated gills to extract both food and oxygen from the water. Some reef residents such as the **giant basket starfish** utilize sticky mucus on outstretched arms to trap bits of food that float past in the current. Basket stars often seek shelter like so many other invertebrates, or they tuck themselves into tight balls during the day. These echinoderms emerge to feed at night under the cover of darkness, a time when the amount of available planktonic food is highest. Simply put, the need to seek shelter during the day is part of the price to be paid for a lack of speed. If you can't flee quickly, it is best not to make yourself too obvious.

Only the nimble squid is quick enough to trap small fishes, but their dexterity is closely matched by that of the quick and wily octopus. Octopuses, too, are primarily nocturnal predators. They paralyze crabs, snails, and other invertebrates with their venomous bite.

Some nocturnal creatures are quick to react to a dive light and they will do what they can to escape the beam. Some retract into shells, others into crevices, but others tend not to react at all. It is often best to illuminate nocturnal animals with the periphery of your dive light rather than the main beam. The lower intensity of the edge of the beam will

Shy and reclusive during the light of day, brittle stars emerge at night to search for food. They are often seen on sponges.

not spook some animals that are quick to seek cover if directly lit.

One of the prettiest of all the reef mollusks is the **flamingo tongue snail** (commonly referred to as the flamingo tongue cowrie). These one-to three-inch-long mollusks are often seen at night when they are out feeding on gorgonians, especially the purple sea fan.

Another stunning mollusk of the reef is the **flame scallop**. Rarely seen during the day, flame scallops emerge at night from the cracks and crevices of coral heads to filter the water for food.

Flame scallops have a brilliant crimson colored mantle that is fringed by a number of white tentacles. The mantle is particularly noteworthy because of its glowing crimson color, a characteristic which is attributed to the presence of hemoglobin in the blood. This is rare in the world of mollusks since most contain a colorless pigment known as hemocyanin in their blood.

Sea urchins are grazers and they feed on a variety of algae and organic debris along the reef and sea floor. The algae serve an important function in the creation of oxygen, but if left unchecked they will overgrow a reef to the detriment of corals. While **sharp-spined urchins** are often cursed by divers, in some instances when sea urchins are absent from a reef community, once-colorful reefs are quickly overgrown by a variety of drably colored algae. On the whole, sea urchins play a fundamental role in keeping algae populations in balance with the rest of the reef community.

Sea urchins are well protected from most fishes by their long, sharp spines. It is those same spines that make many divers categorize urchins as a complete nuisance. Avoiding urchins during the day is relatively easy, but like so many reef invertebrates most sea urchins emerge to feed at night. Rest assured, they won't stick you just for fun, but you do need to be careful where you place your hands, feet, knees and

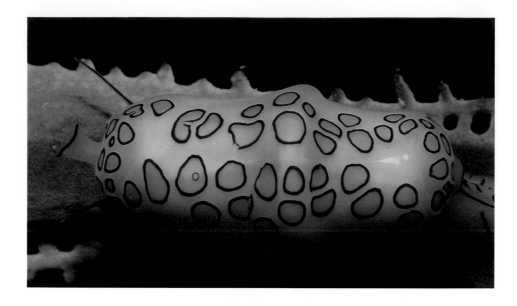

The lovely leopard pattern, which is often thought to be the pattern of the shell of a flamingo toungue snail, is actually on soft tissue that covers the hard shell. This tissue is called the mantle (or mantle flap) and is responsible for secreting and maintaining the shell of this snail, and of all snails in general. The possession of a mantle is a characteristic that is commonly shared by all classes of mollusks. If a flamingo tongue snail becomes disturbed, it is likely to quickly withdraw the mantle into the shell.

other parts of your body during night dives.

In contrast to their terrestrial relatives, many species of marine worms are quite stunning in their appearance. A common characteristic shared by many marine worms, including the colorful and often admired **Christmas tree worm**, is that most of the body is hidden from our view by a protective tube. We see only the gill whorl which is exposed to the water column. The rest of the animal is burrowed into the reef.

The gill whorls are used to filter food and to extract oxygen from the water. The gills possess giant nerve cells called axons which help detect any local disturbance in the water. Blocking sunlight and casting a shadow or any movement which causes even the slightest current will often cause these worms, as well as many other species of marine worms, to instantly withdraw their gills into their protective tubes.

A noteworthy exception to the tube-dwelling theme demonstrated by many marine worms is that of the

flatworms and **bristle worms**. Flatworms are often confused with nudibranchs because of their stunning colors, but it is easy to tell the species apart with only a little practice. Flatworms are exactly that—flat! Nudibranchs have thicker bodies, and it is usually easy to find the gill tufts of nudibranchs, but not of flatworms. They are usually seen crawling around in coral rubble. Flatworms demonstrate remarkable regenerative properties, and torn body segments that have been completely removed from the rest of the worm are often capable of developing into whole animals!

Bristle worms are free-living worms that crawl about the reef feeding on the tissues of a variety of other corals and gorgonians. Their bright orange, red or green coloration is often eye-catching, but beware! The bodies of bristle worms are covered with glass-like venomous spines that will easily penetrate the most callused of hands, causing an intense burning sensation.

More than 400 species of fishes

are found in Caribbean waters. It is beyond the scope of this introduction to address each species, and you can find far greater detail in the chapters devoted to various families of fish in Section IV. However, certain species of fish demonstrate behaviors which provide valuable insight into the inner workings of Caribbean reef communities. These behaviors include feeding models, fascinating symbiotic relationships with other species, and the use of interesting survival strategies.

Often the most noticeable animal in any habitat is the largest one. In Caribbean reef communities, this honor goes to the grouper family! The largest member of the family of sea basses and groupers is the **jewfish**, a species that often exceeds six feet in length. **Black grouper** can be almost as large. The groupers are ambush predators. They lay in wait or sneak up within close range of their prey. When the predators are within striking distance, sea basses and groupers quickly open their enormous mouths and actually suck in their unsuspecting victims. Many small, backward pointing teeth ensure that the prey does not escape.

Spiny lobster are one of the preferred foods of the larger members of the sea bass family. Imagine the digestive system of a fish that can swallow a whole lobster, shell and all! Groupers, like many other fishes, have pharyngeal grinding teeth that enable them to crush and swallow a lobster.

Jewfish are opportunistic feeders, and they will readily feed upon a variety of fishes given the chance. In fact, most groupers prefer fish as their main course.

If you are especially curious and patient, you might try stopping if you see a **Nassau grouper** hiding behind a sea fan some distance away. Often, if a parade of creole wrasse swim close to the grouper, a well-timed lunge by the hiding hunter will result in a meal of surprised wrasse.

Usually it is the spectacular array of stunningly colorful reef fishes that mesmerize us during our dive. None are more captivating than the dazzling **angelfishes** and **butterflyfishes**. For many years these species were considered to be members of a single family, but now they have been separated because of distinct anatomical differences. Their flittering and often stately swimming styles and patterns have given rise to their common family names. As adults, the males and females of both families sometimes pair up for life. In other instances they only pair up when they encounter each other within a given territory.

Small mouths, located on the very end of the face, enable both butterflyfishes and angelfishes to feed on a mix of tiny invertebrates that seek cover within the crevices of the reef. This feeding method is taken to extremes by the **longsnout butterflyfish**, a resident of some deep reefs, which has a small mouth positioned on the far end of elongated jaws. Using this adaptation, longsnout butterflyfish are able to probe deep into cracks where other species cannot reach.

The feeding preferences and behavior of a variety of **parrotfishes** make them prominent members of most Caribbean reef communities. Parrotfishes use powerful fused teeth to grate at the reef's surface as they ingest living coral polyps, the calcium carbonate deposits of the skeletal remains of once living corals, and the symbiotic algae that live within the tissues of living corals. It is generally believed that the parrotfishes are primarily seeking out the algae for its food value and the rest of the coral is part of the price that must be paid to get the algae.

Intermittently, parrotfishes can be seen to excrete huge clouds of waste which settle to the bottom to be called sand. The sand created by the maceration of coral skeletons adds significantly to the quantity of sand on and around the reefs.

As darkness falls, parrotfishes go into a sleep-like state called torpor.

Parrotfishes have developed the unique ability to secrete a mucous cocoon around themselves when they rest at night. It is thought that the cocoon helps to mask the scent of the parrotfish, helping to protect them from moray eels whose nocturnal feeding behavior and keen sense of smell helps make eels extremely capable predators.

TROPHIC LEVELS IN A FOOD CHAIN

The paths through which energy is transferred in nature are called food chains. Plants form the foundation of all major food chains. In a given food chain, there may be several animals linked between the plants and the chain's top-end, or apex, predator. For example, in the ocean tiny animals called zooplankton feed on small plants called phytoplankton. Small fish like silversides feed on zooplankton. Groupers prey upon silversides and Caribbean reef sharks feed on groupers.

Each of the groups just mentioned represents a level in the chain called trophic level. The flow of energy in all food chains is from sunlight toward the trophic level of the top-end predators. The transfer of energy from one trophic level to the next is not very efficient, usually ranging only between 6 percent and 20 percent. The point being, it takes six to ten ounces of plant to produce one ounce of animal that eats the plants, and it takes six to ten ounces of small animals to produce one ounce of a larger animal that is higher up the chain.

During this dormant period, they are often seen enshrouded within a protective mucous cocoon of their own making. Some authorities maintain that the cocoon helps to mask the scent of the parrotfish, and therefore lessens the chance that parrotfish might fall prey to moray eels, which are primarily nocturnal feeders.

Several species of moray eels play important roles as reef predators. These moray species include the **green**, **spotted**, **jewel**, **purple-mouth**, **goldentail** and **chain**. Many fishes use a pair of hardened gill covers called opercula to pump oxygenated water over their gills. The disadvantage of possessing gill covers is that if a fish tries to move backwards when the opercula are flared, the fish is likely to get hung up in the reef. In fact, many fishes are incapable of rapidly swimming backwards. Morays lack gill covers; instead they use their mouths to pump oxygen-rich water over their gills. This adaptation makes it easy for morays to go forwards and backwards, a huge advantage when trying to sneak up on and corner prey.

In addition, morays lack the heavy scales found in many fishes. Morays possess very fine scales and their bodies are covered with a layer of mucus, another characteristic which helps them maneuver within the tight confines of the reef.

Surgeonfishes are the vegetarians of the reefs. They are often seen swimming in tight schools as they move over the reefs looking for areas that are covered with a rich crop of algae. Once the algae have been located, surgeonfishes are quick to settle and begin a massive nibbling session during which they often appear oblivious to their surroundings.

Areas with a lot of dead staghorn coral are particularly fruitful for surgeonfishes as filamentous algae are often quick to overgrow the once

The reef is home to a great diversity of schooling fishes such as the grunts pictured here.

towering staghorn. **Threespot damselfish**, often referred to as "the farmers of the sea," commonly cultivate plots of this algae, and the comparatively small damsels vigorously defend their realms from all intruders. However, as a rule the damsels are no match for the onslaught of several hundred surgeonfish that have their minds set on this rich crop of algae!

One of the oddest looking fishes on the reef is the species known as the **trumpetfish.** These fish have extremely thin bodies, elongated jaws and tiny mouths. Trumpetfish often try to hide amongst tall stands of gorgonians and in clusters of staghorn coral by hanging in a head-down vertical position. They blend in so well that small fishes are often oblivious to their presence until the strong suction caused by the long, straw-like mouth of the trumpetfish overwhelms the small prey.

Trumpetfish are occasionally seen swimming immediately next to, above, or below a grouper. When swimming in this position, a trumpetfish is said to be shadowing a grouper. Exactly why they shadow groupers is a question that is still being debated. One reason the trumpetfish are thought to do so is for the protection which is probably unintentionally supplied by the grouper bodyguard. Another suspected reason is so that an unseen trumpetfish can surprise prey that allow the grouper to come close. It is likely that the prey, mostly other fishes, allow the grouper to get close when they don't suspect that the grouper is in a feeding mode. Trumpetfish are not fast swimmers, but they are capable of surprising unsuspecting prey with quick bursts of speed before the prey can escape. The trumpetfish is also in position to clean up after the grouper should the hunter be messy with its meal and leave leftovers.

The various **cleaner gobies** and some small juvenile reef fishes, most notably the **juvenile Spanish hogfish, bluehead wrasse** and several

Once quite common in the reef communities of the Caribbean, Florida and the Bahamas, turtles have been dangerously overfished and their nesting sites have been taken away by human intervention. It is hoped that the ongoing efforts to help turtle populations will once again make them common sights.

angelfishes, take advantage of an ever-present, although somewhat surprising, food source on the reefs. These fishes concentrate their feeding activities on the ectoparasite crustaceans that infest other reef fishes. So tolerated in their cleaning activities are these cleaner species that they can occasionally be seen passing directly into the gills and mouths of even the most potentially dangerous predators of all, such as the **great barracuda**. These cleaners always seem to be able to depart the encounter unscathed, yet well fed.

Of course, that is not always the case for many other species that catch the eye of the swift-swimming and well-armed barracudas. Barracudas are important reef predators whose menacing appearance makes wonderful subject matter for adventuresome photographers. "Cudas," as they are often called, prefer to feed on small, schooling reef fishes, but they often shadow divers throughout the dive. One look at their mouthful of long, sharp teeth can set imaginations free, but in real life barracudas are far less threatening than they are in the tales of sea lore.

A variety of **pufferfishes** make up another of the stranger-looking fish families. When alarmed, the common **spiny puffer** will swallow water into its greatly expandable stomach, a feat which enables it to grossly inflate its body. The inflation erects a number of long, sharp, protective spines that cover the body, making this species far less palatable for would-be predators!

Hundreds of other species, ranging from the vividly colored **fairy basslets** to **coneys, grasbys, hamlets, triggerfishes** and **blennies,** also have a significant role in the reef community.

Sometimes fortunate divers enjoy encounters with majestic **spotted eagle rays** that glide over the reef top, or forage in the sand adjacent to the reefs. Few animals in nature, appear more graceful than these rays as they ripple their dark wings which are covered with small white spots or rings. These rays occasionally gather in squadrons of a half-dozen or more.

Sharks, too, play a role in the reef communities of the Caribbean and associated waters. **Nurse sharks** are among the most commonly encountered reef sharks. Though most specimens are 3 to 5 feet long, it is not unheard of for divers to round a reef only to find themselves looking at a nurse shark that is well over 10 feet long. Nurse sharks, like other sharks, are generally quite happy to leave well enough alone, and often the sight of a diver causes them to rapidly flee into the distance. Opportunistic feeders, nurse sharks prey upon small fishes, mollusks, echinoderms and crustaceans.

Other sharks that lucky divers sometimes get to see include **Caribbean reef sharks, bull sharks, blacktip sharks, lemon sharks** and **hammerheads**. Caribbean reef sharks are handsome animals, and make spectacular photographic subjects. The same is true of bull and lemon sharks.

Blacktips tend to be noticeably smaller than Caribbean reef sharks, bull sharks and lemon sharks, but just the same, an encounter with a blacktip will make the dive a memorable one. The black tips on their dorsal and tail fins provide an excellent means of making a positive identification.

In real life, sharks are far different than they are portrayed to be on television and in Hollywood thrillers. Each species plays an important role in the environmental niche into which it fits.

Fishes known as **remoras**, which attach themselves to the host sharks, can often be seen. The relationship between remoras and other animals is not completely understood. Some authorities suspect that the remoras

FASCINATING RELATIONSHIPS AMONG MARINE ANIMALS

Marine animals share a variety of relationships. Perhaps the most obvious is that of predator and prey. Not all of the shared relationships are as immediately obvious, and some are quite surprising in nature. Collectively, scientists refer to the entire body of relationships as symbiotic relationships. The organisms involved are called symbionts or hosts, depending upon their role in the relationship.

Laymen commonly use the term symbiotic relationship to describe only the relationships which are mutually beneficial to both organisms involved, but symbiosis encompasses a variety of relationships, not all of which are mutually beneficial. Symbiosis is defined as a relationship in which two organisms that are members of different species live in intimate association with one another in a way that allows at least one party to benefit. The benefit is usually food. Depending upon the nature of their interaction, the relationship is classified as commensalism, mutualism, parasitism or phoresis.

In a commensal relationship, members of two different species live together in a manner in which one, the commensal or symbiont, which is usually physically smaller, benefits without seriously affecting the host in any way. The relationship between a Portuguese man-of-war and the symbiont man-of-war fish provides an excellent example of commensalism. The potent tentacles of the Portuguese man-of-war provide a protected retreat for the small man-of-war fish without altering the behavior of the Portuguese man-of-war. Several species of shrimps and fishes utilize the protective spines of long-spined sea urchins in a similar manner.

Mutualism is defined as a form of symbiosis in which members of two different species live together in a manner so that both benefit and neither is harmed. Mutualism is exhibited in the relationships between cleaner shrimps and the fishes which benefit from their services. The cleaners remove parasites, bacteria and dead tissue from the fish they are servicing, and in the process the cleaners receive food.

In parasitic relationships, one member of the relationship, the parasite or symbiont, depends on the other, the host, for food which is taken from the body or eggs of the host. Isopods have a parasitic relationship with soldierfish, and parasitic copepods are often seen attached to the fins of mako sharks and other species.

Phoresis is a form of symbiotic relationship in which a host provides transportation for the symbiont. Remoras riding on manta rays and turtles provide classic examples of phoresis as does the scenario of barnacles attached to the bodies of humpback whales.

In perfect position to strike at unsuspecting prey, a pair of trumpetfish shadow a tiger grouper.

clean the hosts by ridding them of parasites which the remoras gladly consume. It is also thought by some that the remoras gain some protection by being so close to a large predator. However, it must be noted that remoras are commonly found in the stomach-content analyses of sharks that have been captured not long after the sharks have taken a meal of their own. Obviously, there is no such thing as a free lunch in the ocean either! Remoras are often seen accompanying barracudas, jewfish, turtles, dolphins, whales and some other animals.

Several species of air breathers play important roles on the reef. These animals include a variety of **sea turtles**, **dolphins** and **whales**. Evolution has favored these species by providing them with the ability to spend extended periods below the surface of the sea.

Almost all of us feel a special thrill at catching even the slightest glimpse of a turtle, dolphin or whale. Perhaps it is our shared characteristic of being air breathers that amplifies our experience. And in the case of dolphins and whales, certainly many people share a sense of

appreciation for the higher intelligence shown by these species. In additon, these animals have shared an evolutionary pathway back to the sea. It is well accepted among the scientific community that the ancestors of sea turtles, as well as many dolphins and whales, were terrestrial beings. Just as the organisms that make up a coral reef community are interdependent, they are not isolated from the rest of planet Earth. Instead, the reef habitat and all the creatures found within are inexorably linked with all other creatures on earth.

3

LIFE IN THE SAND AND RUBBLE

Throughout the areas which are generally referred to as coral reefs are expanses of sand. In some cases, fragments of dead coral and other debris are mixed with the sand. These are typically called rubble zones. Some of the patches are only a few square yards while others stretch on much farther than you can swim in a single dive. In any case, the species found in these areas are often considerably different from the creatures that reside in the nearby reefs. Keen observers will likely notice that some animals are found in both the sand and rubble zone, while other species show a distinct preference for one area or the other.

As you make your descent toward the sand it might not be immediately apparent that there is much life and activity in this habitat. Subconsciously we may associate the sand biome with that of the terrestrial sand biome, the desert. However, while a desert often appears to be devoid of life to the casual observer, specialists know that life abounds. So too, is the case with the sand patches between the coral heads.

Typically, we do not plan to spend an entire dive exploring a sand bottom or a rubble one, yet these environments contain distinctive and diversified communities. It is while exploring these habitats that many of us will enjoy some of our most fascinating moments.

Especially after sunset, the sand can be alive with creatures of the night. The list of animals includes a wide variety of fishes, **crabs**, **octopuses**, **squids**, **clams**, **sea stars**, **brittle stars**, **sea cucumbers**, **sea urchins**, **sand dollars** and **snake eels**. Of course, there aren't always that many animals to be seen, but in many locations keen eyes and patience will pay off, and in almost every place you look you will discover a pair of eyes looking back at you. During these times you are likely to see a variety of animals and behaviors that you have not seen before. And yet, at other times there is simply "no one home."

Most species that choose to live in the sand have extremely low profiles. A major difference between a crevice-filled reef habitat and the sand is that while a reef is a latticework of hiding places, there are very few places to hide on the sand. As a result, most animals that inhabit the sand must be excellent burrowers, able to rebury themselves rapidly if they are exposed, able to stabilize the substrate around them in some way, or be superbly camouflaged if they are to successfully survive.

As examples, many species of clams and crabs are excellent diggers. Clams spend a considerable amount of time buried in the sand with only their paired, tube-like siphons exposed. The siphons enable clams to take in oxygenated water, feed, and eliminate wastes without ever exposing their bodies to potential danger. Creatures like **tube anemones** often appear uninteresting when seen during the day, but at night their long, flowing tentacles, which are used to paralyze and capture their prey, become more obvious. If uncovered, these anemones can quickly rebury, as can **heart urchins**, many species of sand-dwelling **shrimps**, and a variety of other sand residents.

In some sites, groups of sand dollars and brittle stars are so thick that the association works to stabilize the sand. The same is true for several species of **worms**. Flatfish, such as **peacock flounders**, use their ability to alter the appearance of their skin to match that of their surroundings in order to blend in and avoid being too obvious to both potential predators and prey. Masters of cam-

Peacock flounders are masters of camouflage. Their ability to change colors to match their background makes them almost ghost-like. Often we wouldn't even see them if they didn't move.

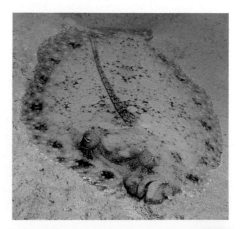

Tiny dancers of the sand community, yellowhead jawfish flutter vertically over their sand burrows. They lunge toward tiny particles of food that drift past in the current, and then race back to the protection of their holes. Strangely, the males of the species brood their eggs in their mouths. It is not uncommon to see a male yellowhead jawfish, jaws agape, with the dark eggs being held gently in his mouth.

ouflage, peacock flounders are often overlooked unless they are on the move. Look closely and you will notice the presence of a number of handsome light blue circular patterns on the topside of the flounder.

Flounders, like other flatfishes such as halibut, turbot, sole and sand dabs, undergo exceptional morphological changes as they mature through their larval stages. Larval flounders live out in the open sea, and like most other fishes have one eye on either side of their head. As the young flounders mature, one eye actually migrates from one side of the head to the other so that as adults both eyes end up on one side of the head. Once they settle to the sea floor as adults, flounders spend the rest of their lives swimming with one side facing up toward the surface

Sea cucumbers creep across the sea floor adjacent to the coral reefs as they vacuum up the sand to extract nutrients with their elaborate feeding mechanism.

and the other side facing down toward the sea floor.

In every sea you can find the vacuum cleaners commonly known as **sea cucumbers**. These sausage-shaped echinoderms are close relatives to sea stars, brittle stars, sand dollars and sea urchins. Sea cucumbers remove organic material (food) from the sand as it passes through their digestive tract, and they elim-

inate the remaining debris, leaving long trails of waste.

Like all members of the phylum of echinoderms, sea cucumbers posses sucker-like tube feet which allow them to move slowly about.

While some animals permanently inhabit the sand, others are transients and use the sand only as a feeding ground and place of refuge.

While still far above the sandy bottom, you might notice some of the larger animals associated with this habitat. The angular outlines of partially buried **southern stingrays** often stand out. When the rays are active, you might see them grubbing through the sand in search of mollusks and crustaceans for their palate. Often one or more bar jacks

Southern stingrays are common inhabitants of the sand biome. Sometimes they bury themselves in the sand, exposing only their eyes, and their spiracles which are used in respiration. They are often accompanied by bar jacks which are believed to pick up unwanted or overlooked food uncovered by the stingray as it feeds.

Spotted eagle rays are often seen cruising along a wall which is adjacent to deep water, but these majestic rays also commonly hunt in areas with sandy bottoms by grubbing through the sand in search of mollusks, crustaceans and other prey items.

closely follow a feeding southern stingray. The jacks try to take advantage of the ray's grubbing activity by feeding upon food items overlooked or unwanted by the ray.

If luck is with you, you might see a **spotted eagle ray** cruise in from the wall to grub through the sand for food, their favorite prey being of mollusks, echinoderms and crustaceans. Spotted eagle rays are easy to distinguish from southern stingrays as the eagle rays have a number of prominent yellow to white spots on their brown to black backs. The dark gray to black backs of southern stingrays are solid in color. In addition, spotted eagle rays have a very long tail with two long spines positioned at the base. The tail of southern stingrays is much shorter and has only one barb.

Though very well equipped to inflict a painful sting, neither species is aggressive toward divers. However, it is wise to keep in mind that both species can inflict a painful wound if harassed or stepped on.

Diving or swimming with any species of **dolphin** is always a great thrill. Dolphins are often wary of their human counterparts, but encounters with pods of Atlantic spotted dolphins are common in the shallow, crystal-clear waters of the Little Bahama Bank. The sugar-white, sandy sea floor is only 20 to 30 feet deep. Most people snorkel or free dive when the dolphins decide to pay a visit. Sometimes the encounters last only for a few minutes, but other times the meetings last for an hour or more, and divers

are left with a memory that will last a lifetime.

Hogfish are often observed hanging in a head-down, near vertical orientation as they blow powerful jets of water into the sand in order to try to uncover food. Adult male hogfish can readily be distinguished from mature females by noting the larger size of the male, and by his oversized lips and angular forehead. Schools of **goatfishes** may be seen using their whisker-like sensory barbels to detect prey that is hidden beneath the top layer of sand.

Sand tilefish, common residents of bottoms that are composed of sand and coral rubble, are both builders and excavators. These attractive fish can be identified by their cigar-shaped white bodies and the captivating ripple of their dorsal fin. Sand tilefish transport bits of coral debris to their lair, often forming a circular rubble area that is four feet or more in diameter. Each piece of rubble is neatly arranged until these fish are

satisfied that they have built a safe hiding place equipped with both an entry and an exit.

Sand tilefish can often be seen hovering near their burrow as they anticipate potential danger. Once frightened they will instantly disappear into the safety of their burrow.

If you are lucky and have a keen eye, you might see an unusual fish commonly called a **flying gurnard**. Members of this species dig through the sand in search of food by using the tough anterior parts of their pectoral fins. If alarmed, flying gurnards will unfold the oversized posterior ends of its wing-like pectoral fins which resemble the vibrant feathers of a peacock.

Another oddball of the sand community is the **shortnosed batfish**. Observed from above, this typically stationary fish appears more like a limestone rock than a fish, but at eye level you can see the orange lips, foot-like fins and a stump-like bump on its head.

Seemingly random trails through the sand are created by **queen conchs**, the largest of the gastropod mollusks found in the Caribbean. Although camouflaged on the outside of its shell by strings of attached filamentous algae, the actual shells of queen conchs exhibit a handsome pinkish-orange underside. Look closely under the shell of a live conch and you will probably be able to see the stalked eyes of this shy snail. You are also likely to see its

Goatfishes taste their way along the sandy bottom by using the barbels located underneath their chins. The barbels house extremely sensitive chemoreceptors. When swimming faster, goatfishes retract these "whiskers" to create a more streamlined profile.

Swaying back and forth while rising out of their burrows in areas of fine sand are delicate-looking garden eels. Garden eels rise from their holes to feed on small particles delivered by the current. As you move closer to them you will notice that they synchronously descend into their protective lairs.

horny operculum, a plate which it uses to seal off the opening in its shell should danger present itself.

With its muscular foot, queen conchs pull themselves over the sand and graze on a layer of diatomaceous algae that commonly grows on the grains of sand on the sea floor. Occasionally you will discover a small conchfish living around or within the refuge provided by the queen conch's shell.

When resting on a sand bottom, look closely at what appears to be strands of eel grass swaying in the distance. Soon you will notice that each blade shortens in length as you approach. Suddenly you realize that what you thought was eel grass is actually a colony of shy **garden eels**. You are not the first diver to fall victim to this natural deceit.

Garden eels burrow into the sand bottom and they rise up to feed by plucking small particles out of the water column. Their shy and secretive nature causes them to disappear into their sand burrows if you swim too close. Keep a low profile and don't expect to get too close.

Surprising to many, the inquisitive fish known as the **harlequin bass** is actually a member of the grouper family. Harlequin bass get their common name from their clown-like pattern and coloration. Though they are only a few inches long, these bold groupers will often hold their ground even as you approach to within inches. **Tobacco-fish** possess similar disposition but without quite as much nerve. Tobaccofish tend to perpetually scurry about in short bursts of haste.

Handsome juvenile **coneys** can often be seen amongst the sand rubble as they feed and chase one another in displays of territoriality. Coneys are also members of the family of sea basses and groupers.

Colonies of **yellowhead jawfish** provide entertainment that will fascinate many divers for an entire dive. These fish live in elaborately constructed burrows which they build in the flats of the sand/rubble interface. When feeding, yellowhead jawfish rise out of their burrows to gracefully pluck minute planktonic organisms out of the water column.

If you pay close attention, you will likely see **bridled gobies** and **colon gobies** resting on the rubble as they sit propped up on their pectoral fins. These translucent species blend in very well with the surrounding sand and rubble. Once you see one, you are likely to begin to see them quite often despite their well-camouflaged design. Both species are extremely wary of intruders and they are quick to flee if you approach too closely, but they are likely to settle a few feet away.

Laterally compressed **razorfish** can be seen hovering, tail cocked, over the sand and in eel grass beds,

TURTLE GRASS BEDS

Turtle grass is an important seed-bearing plant inhabiting the shallow waters of lagoons and estuaries throughout the Caribbean and associated waters. Rooted in a bottom of sand or coral rubble, turtle grass is commonly found in quiet lagoons that are protected from the wind, current and surge by bordering coral reefs. The plants possess broad leaves which partially restrict the flow of current, thus helping to create an ideal habitat for a wide variety of algae as well as encrusting sponges, hydroids, bryozoans and other small invertebrates that live on the blades of grass. Their presence attracts many fishes and other predators to the lagoons. In addition, many animals such as sea cucumbers and sea urchins feed on the decaying blades of turtle grass that settle to the bottom after the grass dies.

In essence, turtle grass serves as the foundation of a very important ecosystem within the Caribbean, as a great many species depend upon the existence of turtle grass for food, shelter and habitat.

Scuba divers and snorkelers rarely, if ever, visit the turtle grass beds and shallow lagoons, but their importance as a breeding ground and a habitat for young to grow, and as a feeding area for many species, should not be underestimated or undervalued.

Construction projects and commercial development throughout the Caribbean have eliminated and threatened many turtle grass beds, but in recent years scientists, governments and developers have been working together more closely to protect the beds.

ready to dart away when intruders approach. They bury themselves in the sandy seabed so quickly that it is often impossible to follow their rapid movement. If, however, you wait patiently and watch the sand directly on top of the area into which you think the razorfish disappeared, odds are that in just a few minutes the fish will cautiously emerge and resume its activities.

Yellowface pikeblennies and **bluethroat pikeblennies** are residents of the sand/rubble zone that often go unnoticed. As you swim over the sand, keep your eyes open for tiny (two- to five-inch long) eel-like fish that live in sand tubes. Like many blennies, the males of these species are highly territorial. Male bluethroat pikeblennies put on amazing displays to ward off intruders. The male will rise out of its burrow, open its mouth and flare its

Bluethroat pikeblennies live in sand burrows with only their heads projecting. The behavior of the highly territorial males can best be described as demonstrative and aggressive when another male of the species invades their realm. The display by the male pictured here is intended to ward off territorial intruders.

The water over the sugar-white sands of the Little Bahama Bank is home to pods of Atlantic spotted dolphins. The banks are quite shallow, and most people prefer to snorkel, around the dolphins instead of using scuba.

huge dorsal fin in an attempt to make itself look imposing.

Scientific studies have shown that the displays are enough to prevent actual physical confrontations as much as 90 percent of the time. The intruder simply finds it easier to move on and establish his own territory instead of risking injury or death while trying to invade the realm of another male.

Small, volcano-shaped mounds in the sand will often tip off the presence of **red heart urchins** which are burrowing through the sand as they search for food. Small, whitish-colored **pea crabs** enjoy a symbiotic relationship with red heart urchins, and the crabs can often be found underneath the urchins.

Seemingly unoccupied 3/4-inch-diameter holes in the sand often prove to harbor lightning-quick **mantis shrimp.** These shrimp are renowned for their highly specialized, razor-sharp claws which can cut other shrimp in half with a single blow, and bash open the shells of crustaceans and mollusks which they prey upon. These shrimp have also been known to sever the finger of unfortunate fishermen who tried to remove them from their nets.

When exploring the area where the reef meets the sand, and where coral rubble and sand mix together, you are likely to discover **corkscrew anemones.** These anemones can be identified by their translucent spiral tentacles. They look harmless, but beware—the stinging cells in their tentacles pack a potent punch!

Corkscrew anemones are often home for several **Pederson's cleaning shrimp.** As their name implies, these translucent purple shrimp are active cleaners, animals that play a vital role in maintaining the health of a variety of reef fish.

If you see a corkscrew anemone, you might not want to rush in immediately to look for the shrimp. Instead, hang back for a few moments and look for fish that are lined up waiting to be serviced by the cleaner shrimp.

Clearly the macro environment associated with the sand biome is filled with a fascinating array of diverse creatures. Most residents of the sand community are not the kind of animals that jump out and demand your attention, yet the time spent in the sand biome may offer some of the most educational and enjoyable moments of any dive.

4

LIFE ALONG THE WALL

For any diver that cruises along the top of a Caribbean wall there is always the incredible temptation to swim over the edge and descend down its face. With just one kick of your fins you can find yourself hovering over a bottom that is hundreds, if not thousands, of feet below you. Seaward of the coral reefs, it is a deep blue which eventually darkens past the point of twilight.

Somehow it feels more comfortable to turn and face the sheer wall even though it plummets sharply into the abyss. There is a sense of familiarity and comfort with the wall, but if you are at all like many divers, just knowing that a great expanse of open ocean lies immediately to your back often puts a little knot in your stomach or sends chills up and down your spine.

However, as soon as you become oriented with the wall you are likely to become comfortable. Then, you can't help but be moved by the stunning beauty of the scene that lies before you. In many areas, the walls slope gently as they gradually disappear into the blue-black water below. In other places the walls are absolutely vertical and even undercut. Prominent outcroppings accentuate the sheerness.

Many walls are laced with caves that skewer the reef. The thought of exploring the caves is both alluring and a bit unsettling. But almost all divers are drawn to the walls where

These brown tube sponges are one of many sponges that adorn the walls of the Caribbean, Bahamas and Florida.

they are soon introduced to another community of marine animals.

Perpetually facing toward the open sea is a unique community of animals which inhabit the drop-offs of the coral reefs. The Caribbean is known to members of the international diving community for the splendid colors and sheer walls that surround many of the islands, banks, shores and seamounts. Some of the residents of the drop-offs can be seen on or around the reefs of the shallows. Other wall visitors, like tuna and big jacks, spend the majority of their lives in the open sea and invade the walls only when on the hunt. And still other animals live their entire adult lives only in, on, or around the face of the drop-offs.

Living conditions, such as exposure to food-bearing currents, light penetration, surfaces for attachment, and the amount of shelter, are significantly different along a wall than they are in the shallows and out in the open sea. In some cases the differences are obvious even to laymen, and in other instances they are far more subtle. These differences play a vital role in the evolutionary decision-making processes which cause some animals to seek out the walls or choose to live elsewhere.

As you explore the walls, keep in mind that the animals you encounter are there for a reason. In their own struggle for survival, the members of the wall community are best equipped for the living conditions found along the drop-offs. Mobile animals take advantage of each nook and cranny on the wall, using these recesses as places to hide and feed. Animals that visit the walls from

time to time go there to find food, shelter or other benefits offered along the drop-offs.

The top lip of a wall, often called the reef buttress, denotes the beginning of the wall proper. From the reef buttress down to the safe limits of sport diving and beyond, there lives a diversified community of animals that is unique to the wall biome. Inhabitants of the wall cling tenaciously and often compete rather viciously for the limited space and habitat. A place of attachment is critical to many wall dwellers, and they are well adapted to take advantage of any open space that can be found. Marine algae and invertebrates are amazingly quick to colonize vacant areas. These vacancies might be created by natural cycles such as storm surges. Other times some organisms perish due to a careless boater that drags an anchor, or because a diver inadvertently kicks a sponge or coral head loose from its place of attachment.

Access to nutrient-rich currents make the walls the ideal habitat for a variety of animals that use stinging cells to trap floating food particles. These stinging animals are all members of the phylum Cnidaria. Included in this grouping are **corals, sea anemones, jellyfishes** and **hydroids.** As adults, these creatures are comparatively immobile. Many are attached to the reef, and those that are not are poor swimmers that tend to go wherever the currents take them. In any case, corals, sea anemones, jellyfishes and hydroids all depend upon the potency of the numerous stinging cells located in their deadly tentacles to capture

Divers are commonly awestruck by the magnificence of the seascape along the sheer vertical walls where the variety of sponges often appear like brilliant paint strokes in a blue world. This image of a photographer and sponges was recorded along Little Cayman's famous Bloody Bay Wall.

maximize their surface area exposed to the weakening sunlight. The expanded surface area allows the vitally important symbiotic algae known as zooxanthellae to produce even more food for the host corals thru photosynthesis. More food means faster growth, a greater opportunity to create more calcium carbonate, and a better chance to dominate the competitive scene.

Typically the most common species of reef-building corals found along a wall are **star corals**. They tend to take on a mound shape toward the top of the wall, but grow in flatter plate-like structures with depth. The star corals are the most important reef-building corals along the walls, and as such are responsible for laying down much of the long-standing structure of the reef and wall. Eons ago, however, when sea level was far lower than it is today, the corals described in the genus *Aeroporas* were responsible for creating the foundation of the reefs.

Staghorn coral is another species that is common along the top edge of walls. It is sometimes confused with the species commonly called **elkhorn coral**, but distinguishing between the two is very easy. Elkhorn coral typically occurs in shallow water near the windward side of islands and reefs. The tannish-colored branches of elkhorn are flat and wide. The upright branches of staghorn coral are comparatively thin and often look entangled or interwoven in a design that looks like latticework. Staghorn is often found in the shallows as well as along the upper edges of walls.

Due to its delicate structure, staghorn coral is often one of the first coral species to suffer from severe storm damage. As a result, it is quite common to see staghorn rubble at the bottom of a thicket of living staghorn. This coral is prone to diver-induced damage as well.

Fortunately, staghorn is also one of the faster growing corals, meaning that its delicate nature is compensated for by its ability to replace

their prey. As a result, the cnidarians are highly dependent on food-bearing currents to bring them their meals.

Competition for space amongst the corals is often extremely intense, and battles that can easily go unnoticed rage on as the various species use an array of strategies to try to dominate areas along the walls. Some corals are extremely fast-growing and will out-colonize others simply by their ability to lay down tissues, or biomass, faster than other species. Other corals simply overgrow existing species using their more virulent tentacles to sting their competitors into submission. In still other battles, some corals form broad plates along the walls rather than growing in rounded coral head formations in order to

devastated colonies with rapid regrowth. In addition, many animals find the staghorn rubble a desirable habitat.

Along many drop-offs, several species of stony **brain corals** play an important role. Brain corals are so named because of their hemispherical shape and the convoluted arrangement of the polyps. **Finger coral** is another commonly encountered hard coral associated with the reef buttress and wall outcroppings, but this species does not typically attach to vertical surfaces. Stands of finger coral form countless hiding places for a variety of small invertebrates and fishes.

Further down the wall, **plate coral** often grows in abundance. Plate coral is named due to its obvious plate-like appearance. As is the case with star corals, colonies of plate coral spread out as they grow to allow more of the diffused rays of sunlight that penetrate into deeper waters to reach the symbiotic zooxanthellae within their tissues.

Other species of corals common to the wall include **flower coral**, **orange cup coral**, **solitary coral**, **green coral** and **pink hydrocoral**. These corals are not important in terms of being reef builders, but they are part of many wall communities.

Along some walls, **deep-water gorgonians** form fan-shaped colonies, and bushy feather-like stands of **black coral** extend outward from the wall, enhancing an already stunning scene. Black coral belongs to a group of non-reef-building corals called antipatharians. This group includes the long, thin **wire corals**. Wire corals are usually greenish in color and project from the wall like enormous strands of coiled or kinked wire.

The term black coral is somewhat deceiving. It is the polished jewelry made from black corals that takes on a glistening deep black appearance, but in the wild, black coral trees vary from tan to yellow, orange and green. All antipatharian corals are extremely slow growers, making the use of black coral in jewelry more and more questionable as stocks are depleted.

The species that is commonly called **branching coral** is not a true reef-building coral, and is actually more closely related to hydroids than to corals. However, branching coral is commonly found along walls, and provides ideal hiding places for a variety of creatures in the community of the wall. The same is true of the animals commonly referred to as **fire corals**.

Notorious for their virulent stinging cells, fire corals have raised many a welt on the skin of divers! These colonial hydrozoans are extremely opportunistic and aggressive, and they commonly overgrow sea fans and gorgonians, causing their demise.

Corkscrew anemones, knobby anemones and **Caribbean anemones** are usually found on the outcroppings and ledges of walls. Discovering an anemone often means that you will also discover a host of symbiotic inhabitants including **Pederson's cleaning shrimps**, **anemone crabs** and **diamond blennies**.

The beautiful **orange ball anemone** is typically found only at night as it reaches out from under ledges along vertical walls. Exposure to bright dive lights will quickly cause these sensitive anemones to retract.

A variety of species of sponges stand out prominently on almost all walls. Sponges thrive in the wall environment because their efficient filter feeding system is augmented by the food-bearing currents associated with the drop-offs, and by the fact that at night many planktonic organisms migrate upward toward the shallower portions of walls.

Many of these same species of sponges are also common to the shallower reef flats, but some are typically limited to the wall biome. For example, **red vase sponges** often overgrow black coral trees and deep-water gorgonians. Without the

Colorful sea fans, like this deep-water gorgonian, are a feature attraction on many walls. Colonial animals, sea fans are soft corals and do not add significantly to the long term structure of the reef.

aid of an artificial light, a red vase sponge actually appears to be black at depth because of the selective filtration of light by seawater. Your dive light will bring out the brilliant crimson color of this wall inhabitant.

The inside (lumen) of this species is a favorite hideout for **brittle stars** which by day use the sponge as a place to hide. The onset of darkness prompts the brittle stars to move to the outer surface of the sponges where they can feed and be less susceptible to predation by fishes which hunt by the light of day and rest at night. It is truly amazing just how many brittle stars are often associated with a single sponge at night and how well they can hide during the day.

The **giant verongia sponge** is common to many walls and may readily be recognized by its stubby tube formations that are a mottled combination of yellow and green. Like the reef-building corals, this large sponge harbors symbiotic algae within its tissues. Often the outer surface of the giant verongia is encrusted with a host of invertebrates intent on their struggle for a place of attachment.

Elephant ear sponges can easily be as large as divers. Once you see the size and shape of one specimen you will immediately understand why this orange colored species has the common name elephant ear. Their large, flat surfaces are often colonized by small, blue **sea squirts** which parasitize the sponge for space. Many other sponge species are invaded by thousands of **zoanthids**. These examples are just two of the hundreds of possible classic cases of the competition for living space and the ability many animals demonstrate to adapt to the available options.

The **boring sponge** is a noteworthy species because its strategy for securing space along a crowded wall is to secrete acids that bore into the limestone of the true reef-building corals with relative ease. That strat-

egy is sound until the limestone becomes so honeycombed that the whole complex is overcome by gravity and tumbles into the abyss. The result is catastrophic to the sponge and its coral host, but the event opens up a new area which is quickly colonized by aggressive species of algae and invertebrates.

Other prominent sponge species associated with the walls include the hanging **red rope sponge**, **purple tube sponge**, **brown tube sponge**, and **yellow tube sponge**. All of these species help give the walls a distinct appearance.

While the corals and sponges include the most prominent attached members of the wall community, there is a host of additional invertebrates that also play key roles. Many of these creatures are not nearly as obvious during the day as they are at night.

Red night shrimp provide a classic case in point. During the day they are nowhere to be seen, but at night you will often find a pair of their highly reflective, bright red eyes everywhere you point your dive light. **Arrow crabs** climb atop deepwater gorgonians to take advantage of the food trapped within a gorgonian's stinging net. **Banded coral shrimp** forage about the reef or participate in cleaning activities which at night usually center around resting fishes or eels that take a break from the rigors of active predation. Under the cover of darkness, **spiny lobsters** roam freely about the walls and outcroppings, and **Caribbean king crabs** emerge from their dark daytime recesses to forage.

When a variety of crabs, shrimp, snails and other potential items of prey emerge from their daytime hiding places, expect to see **octopuses** on the prowl as they search the wall for these favorite foods. During the day you must consider yourself lucky if you get a glimpse of an octopus hiding in its den, but at night they are often seen scouring the faces of walls while on the hunt.

Prominent outcroppings along

The Caribbean is home to the largest and most diversified mixture of sponges in the world. Sponges filter the water, provide food and refuge for many animals, and supply a splash of color to many eye-catching images of the Caribbean's underwater world.

walls are particularly well suited to the needs of filter feeding bivalve mollusks such as **oysters** and the brilliantly colored cherry red **flame scallops**. The outcroppings provide the maximum exposure to food bearing currents. **Frons oysters** live their adult lives attached to the higher branches of a variety of gorgonians and black corals. From these lofty positions the oysters take full advantage of food-rich currents. Adult **Atlantic thorny oysters** attach to vertical walls where they, too, gain access to food-laden currents. Being extremely sensitive to both movement and changes in light levels, thorny oysters are quick to close up if you carelessly approach.

With the cover of darkness many sea fans and sponges become adorned with the aptly named **basket stars**. Members of the phylum of echinoderms, basket stars possess an intricate network of branching arms that serve as a water filtering mechanism. When a basket star feeds its arms unfurl, giving the animal a basket-like appearance. However, when the arms are withdrawn, basket stars are said to look like a human brain or a ball of entangled yarn. Large specimens may reach diameters of three feet or more!

A close relative of the basket stars, the nocturnal **brittle star** is another creature of the night as its common name suggests. Nocturnal brittle stars remain mostly hidden even at night as they project their serpent-like arms out through small holes in the wall in an effort to capture prey.

Crinoids, other echinoderms that are members of the community of the wall, also extend their arms out into the water column at night as they feed. Also referred to as feather stars, crinoids actively feed along the wall and reef buttress throughout the day. However, at night they tend to crawl farther out from the confines of the reef as they perch atop coral heads and sea fans in order to reach out into the water column in search of food.

As any experienced diver is well aware, fishes abound along the walls. Several species of plankton-feeding fishes take advantage of the currents associated with the walls. **Creole wrasse** school along the top of the drop-offs in many areas, stopping to feed in places where the current has delivered an abundant supply of plankton. The jaws of creole wrasse have evolved to be able to telescope outward and intercept current-borne particles of food.

Both **blue chromis** and **brown chromis** also hover near the wall's ledges waiting for the current to kick up and bring them their next meal. When the current does come up, both of these species readily swim out into the current to feed on a variety of planktonic delicacies that drift by.

Sunshinefish normally hover close to the protection of the wall, but when feeding they become intensely involved and seem to drop their guard, making them considerably easier to approach. Typically found down the face of a wall and not near the reef buttress, sunshinefish tend to be found in deeper water than creole wrasse, blue chromis and brown chromis. Sunshinefish prey upon plankton.

The magnificently colored yellow and purple **fairy basslets** are considered by many to be among the most beautiful of all Caribbean fishes, and fortunately for us, fairy basslets are quite common. Also known as **royal grammas** and **purple grammas**, fairy basslets tend

A grasby peers from his perch in a pink vase sponge near the top of Little Cayman's spectacular Bloody Bay Wall.

THE BLUE HOLE OF BELIZE

A feature attraction of diving in Belize, especially for divers with an appreciation of geological phenomena, is the opportunity to explore the famed Blue Hole. Part of the Lighthouse Reef system, it lies approximately 60 miles off the mainland out of Belize City.

The diameter of the circular reef area stretches for about 1,000 feet and provides an ideal habitat for corals to attach and flourish. The coral actually breaks the surface in many sections at low tide. Except for two narrow channels, the reef surrounds the hole. The hole itself is the opening to a system of caves and passageways that penetrate this undersea mountain. In various places, massive limestone stalactites hang down from what was once the ceiling of air-filled caves before the end of the last Ice Age. When the ice melted the sea level rose, flooding the caves.

For all practical purposes the over 400-foot depth makes the Blue Hole a bottomless pit. The walls are sheer from the surface until a depth of approximately 110 feet where you will begin to encounter stalactite formations which actually angle back, allowing you to dive underneath monstrous overhangs. Hovering amongst the stalactites, you can't help but feel humbled by the knowledge that the massive formations before you once stood high and dry above the surface of the sea eons ago. The feeling is enhanced by the dizzying effects of nitrogen breathed at depths. The water is motionless and the visibility often approaches 200 feet as you break a very noticeable thermocline.

In the deeper waters of the Blue Hole itself, you might see a curious blacktip, tiger or hammerhead shark, but on most dives you won't see anyone except your dive buddy. Little light reaches the depths of the Hole and water does not circulate freely. As a result, the deeper areas inside the Blue Hole just don't have the profusion of life associated with most drop-offs. But as you venture into the shallows around the rim of the Blue Hole to off-gas after your dive, you will discover a wonderful area filled with life.

Pederson's cleaning shrimp are everywhere inhabiting the ringed and knobby anemones. With the frantic waving of their antennae, these shrimp invite you, along with passing fishes, to be cleaned. Neon gobies also advertise their cleaning services from the various coral heads. Angelfishes, butterflyfishes, hamlets and small groupers are also commonly seen.

Elkhorn coral grows to the surface and purple sea fans, resplendent in their rich hues, sweep at the calm surface waters. If you look up, you will double your pleasure as you catch the reflections of sea fans in the aquamarine mirror of the calm water.

For anyone who wants to dive into the geologic past, exploring the Blue Hole is guaranteed to be a rewarding experience.

Above: An aerial view provides a great look at the surrounding shallow reefs and the deep-blue water of the Blue Hole. Right: Before the end of the last Ice Age, this massive stalactite hung from the ceiling of a terrestrial cave. When the polar ice caps melted, seawater rose and flooded the cave system.

to hover close to the wall, utilizing the many hiding places to escape potential danger. When the strength of currents increase, bringing more food, these normally wary plankton feeders often become easier to approach.

Strange as it might seem to us, fairy basslets appear to be just as comfortable upside down as rightside up. Or perhaps it is more accurate to say that there is no such thing as upside down and rightside up to a fairy basslet. These fish tend to orient to the nearest ledge or wall. If they are swimming under an overhang, their belly tends to face the overhang. When on top of a reef, their belly faces toward the reef, and when swimming up a wall, they tend to swim belly to the wall. In essence, fairy basslets are not restricted to the orientational requirements imposed by gravitational pull, and therefore, have no sense of "up and down" as we do.

Blackcap basslets, close relatives of the fairy basslets, are another of the more stunning wall species. Their vivid purple bodies are real eye catchers, but they often go unseen by divers who remain near the top of the reef buttress. Blackcap basslets are most common below depths of 60 to 70 feet where they tend to replace fairy basslets.

Outcroppings along the walls are often temporary homes for **tiger groupers**, a species which truly seems to love to be cleaned and preened by a variety of cleaner shrimps and fishes. If you see a tiger grouper hovering above an outcropping, do not approach too quickly. Instead, you might want to stop and see if you can observe the cleaning ritual. If you are patient and move slowly and deliberately, you can often close to within a few feet without interfering.

In search of a meal, **Nassau groupers** often roam along the edge of the wall hoping to surprise a creole wrasse or chromis that has become a little too involved in its own feeding activity. While Nassau groupers,

like many other members of their family, might appear to be slow swimmers, they are capable of astonishing bursts of speed which they use to capture unsuspecting prey. In fact, studies have demonstrated that some groupers can go from a dead stop to full speed within 1/40th of a second.

Ocean triggerfish are commonly associated with the walls. These large, grayish colored triggers normally hang near the walls, passing over the reefs and sand only to build and tend their nests. Ocean triggerfish swim by using their dorsal and anal fins, rather than their tail. These triggers scull awkwardly along as their bodies tend to lay over sideways with each stroke. Ocean triggerfish tend to be wary and difficult to approach, a survival instinct that makes a lot of sense for fish that don't swim or hide very well.

Interstitial spaces in the walls are often occupied by a number of **glass gobies** and **masked gobies**. Because of their diminutive size these species are often overlooked by divers. **Arrow blennies** are commonly found swimming out in the water column, and in the same niches in the reef where you find glass gobies and masked gobies. Challenging

Swirling schools of jacks are common sights along the tops of many Caribbean walls. Jacks are active hunters and often elicit a harried flight response from other fishes when they appear, especially if the jacks are perceived to be in a hunting mode.

photographic subjects, arrow blennies are easy to overlook as well. However, once seen, they are easy to identify due to their tail-cocked body posture and elongated mouth. Once you see one arrow blenny, you are likely to see them on a regular basis along many walls.

Of the butterflyfishes, the **longsnout butterflyfish** is the species that seems most restricted to living along a wall. Their extended mouth allows them to probe deeply into the cracks and crevices of the wall as they search for food. Compared to other butterflyfishes, longsnout butterflyfish tend to be secretive, and they tend to inhabit deeper water as they are not commonly found at depths shallower than 60 to 70 feet.

Two species of parrotfish stand out among the fishes of the wall community. These are the dark blue **midnight parrotfish** and the **rainbow parrotfish**. Easily recognized by their size as well as their coloration, these species are also the largest of the Caribbean parrotfishes. Both midnight parrotfish and rainbow parrotfish commonly forage in loosely organized schools as they graze upon algae that is attached to or living within the tissues of corals.

By day, tight schools of silver colored **horse-eye jacks** are commonly seen as they sweep along the top of a wall. They are only one of many species of highly predatory fishes that often visit the walls in search of smaller fishes to satisfy their voracious appetites. Powerful-looking predators, horse-eye jacks are equipped with large eyes which are indicative of the fact that they commonly feed at night, though these fish will readily take advantage of daytime feeding opportunities.

Barracudas and a variety of **sharks** commonly cruise many walls, but while it is quite common to encounter barracudas at close range, such an opportunity is rare with most of the Caribbean sharks that cruise the walls. When hunt-

Predators along the wall, scalloped hammerhead sharks are only seen on rare occasions, but just a passing glimpse of one of these powerful predators will make any dive a memorable one.

ing along the face of a wall, barracudas often change their coloration from bright silver to dark gray or black in an effort to better blend in with their surroundings. During the hunt they will often settle down toward the bottom and nestle in nooks and crannies where they wait for unsuspecting prey (mostly small fishes) which they quickly snare.

Among the sharks that are occasionally sighted along the faces of walls, the most commonly seen are the **Caribbean reef shark, bull shark, blacktip,** and **scalloped hammerhead.** Like many sharks, these animals tend to be wary and somewhat difficult to approach. And while they might give your heart a bit of a start when you first spot them, it is only the very fortunate diver that gets close enough to take a coveted full-frame photograph.

Spotted eagle rays and **manta rays** are also members of the community of wall animals that are com-

monly seen from a distance. Getting a close look at these rays is possible, but doing so usually requires both luck and patience, and the discipline to resist the urge to charge right at them full speed ahead.

Spotted eagle rays are unmistakable in appearance due to their long tails, black backs covered with white to yellow spots, and their massive heads. They tend to hug the walls as they glide along at a rate just a little faster than you can comfortably swim on scuba. But if you get a little too close for their liking, spotted eagle rays can really scoot.

Manta rays are closely related to eagle rays, but there are some significant anatomical differences. The most notable are that manta rays lack the barbs found at the base of the tail of eagle rays, and the heads of manta rays are equipped with a pair of extensions commonly referred to as rostrums which eagle rays don't

have. The manta's cephalic lobes, or rostrums, are extended when they feed, but are often retracted at other times. They are used by mantas to help scoop plankton toward the mouth when they feed. The presence of the horn-like rostrums gave rise to the ancient term devilfish, a name that led to many commonly accepted myths of sea lore depicting manta rays as ill-tempered sea monsters.

Spotted eagle rays have much thicker heads equipped with thick, powerful jaws used to crush a variety of mollusks, crustaceans and echinoderms which they uncover when grubbing through sand.

Certainly, many other species of fishes are associated with the walls, and many of these are often found in the reef flats and over sand patches. The species mentioned in this chapter are commonly seen along the drop-offs, and may be considered to be representative of the wall biome.

SECTION
III

Marine Life: The Invertebrates
Phylum By Phylum

5

CLASSIFICATION OF MARINE ANIMALS: WHO CARES AND WHY

Many of us remember at least some of the basic principles we learned in our high school biology classes concerning the classification of plants and animals. For example, most of us are aware that plants and animals are given scientific names called genus and species. Those are the all-too-often ridiculously long, all but impossible to pronounce, Latin and Greek italicized words we had to memorize for tests. These names really do serve an important purpose as they provide a precise classification used worldwide to distinctly label every living organism ever described by scientists. Knowing the genus and species of an animal allows both scientists and lay persons

Opposite page: Scientists classify plants and animals according to a variety of commonly shared characteristics. The common octopus is a type of mollusk, one of the many animals described in the phylum Mollusca. Octopuses are also often referred to as cephalopods because within their phylum they are described in the class Cepholopoda. This animal's scientific name, or genus and species, is Octopus vulgaris.

Section opener: Myriad marine creatures, from the great filter-feeding whales to tiny invertebrates like this spotted cleaner shrimp on a giant anemone, fascinate divers throughout the Caribbean, Bahamas and Florida.

to speak with certainty and avoid confusion.

For the exactness required within the scientific community, the use of scientific names is often critical in order to prevent even the slightest misunderstandings.

The use of common names is usually acceptable in conversations between divers, and those who use the genus and species names are sometimes perceived by others as being a bit "high brow" or condescending. Upon further consideration, however, others soon realize that the use of scientific names is really intended to help communicate without misunderstanding.

For example, at least three species of sharks are occasionally called white sharks. They are the great white shark (*Carcharodon carcharius*), oceanic whitetip sharks (*Carcharodon longimanus*) and whitetip reef sharks (*Triaenodon obesus*). Whitetip reef sharks are a comparatively docile species found throughout the tropical Indo-Pacific. Oceanic whitetips, animals that are usually seen in mid-ocean, are often large enough to eat whitetip reef sharks for snacks, and they have a reputation for being a bit more aggresive around divers. The third species, the great white shark, is by far the largest of these three species attaining a maximum documented size of 21 feet long and 7,000 pounds. In casual conversation, divers often refer to these species collectively as white sharks.

Imagine the range of emotions and potential for miscommunication if someone tells you they just saw a white shark under the boat, and asks if you would like to go for a dive and photograph the animal. Anyone with an IQ as high as water temperature will surely ask for a clarification before they leap into the water, camera in hand.

Not only is there a distinct lack of standardization of common names, but many species have been given several common names. For example, the sponge scientifically named *Cliona delitrix* is commonly called red boring sponge and orange boring sponge. Because this species appears in different colors, some divers believe different specimens of this sponge to be two different species, but that is not the case. You can imagine the confusion that might result in a conversation when one diver referred to an obviously orange colored sponge as a red boring sponge. Another example is the lettuce leaf nudibranch (*Tridachia crispata*) which is also called a saccoglossan.

In other cases, the same common name is used in different areas to refer to more than one species. As an example, the name "red crab" is often used to describe totally different animals found in the waters off California. One species is highly valued as a food source while the other is much smaller, and of little or no commercial value. The smaller species is also referred to as a pelagic red crab, tuna crab and squat lobster.

It is easy to understand the potential for confusion and miscommunication caused by the use of common names. And despite the grief it caused us all in high school, we must concede that at least in some situations there really is some benefit to be gained by using scientific nomenclature. However, if you are like many divers, you have long since forgotten much of the information about phyla, classes, orders, families, genera, species, etc. you once had to memorize. If you fit into this group but you really would like to be able to recall at least some of the basics, the information in the remainder of this chapter will prove to be especially helpful. It will enable you to identify the animals you see, and help you gain at least a fundamental understanding of the natural history of most of the animals you are likely to encounter in the marine wilderness of the Caribbean, Bahamas and Florida. In many cases, positive identification by species will be possible.

In cases where the exact species remains unknown, perhaps because a lab analysis is necessary, you will find an "sp." following the genus name.

SCIENTIFIC CLASSIFICATION: A QUICK REVIEW

Nearly two million currently living species of plants and animals have been described and classified by the scientific community. In order to study them, specialists have grouped these organisms together into various categories according to commonly shared traits. This system of organization is referred to as taxonomic classification. Ever since its introduction by a Swedish scientist, Carolus Linnaeus, in 1758, this system has been accepted as the scientific standard.

You are probably more familiar with the system of taxonomic classification than you realize. Surely you have heard human beings referred to by our genus and species names, *Homo sapiens*. The name *Homo sapiens*, derived from the Latin "same wise," is the name used in the taxonomic system. As a matter of standard practice the genus (*Homo*) is capitalized while the species (*sapiens*) is written in the lower case. Both words are italicized.

The taxonomic system is designed as a hierarchy in which organisms are grouped together with one another according to commonly shared anatomical, or morphological, traits. The plants and animals that are grouped together are separated from other plants and animals that have different characteristics.

The first major division is that of kingdoms. These were once believed to be only two kingdoms, the kingdom of plants and the kingdom of animals. Today, however, scientists have identified at least five kingdoms. For the practical purposes of this book, we are primarily concerned with marine animals. Within the kingdom of animals, various species are classified, or grouped, according to the following hierarchy:

Phylum
(Subphylum)
Class
Order
(Suborder)
Family
Genus
species

Beginning with its kingdom, scientists classify an organism all the way down to its species. The animal kingdom consists of approximately 35 phyla, and many animals are described within the same phylum. Each phylum is subdivided into classes, which are divided into orders, the orders into families, the families into genera, and finally each animal in every genus is given its own species name.

In many instances there are subcategories, such as subphylum, suborder and subspecies. As a rule, only specialists really need to know all of the intricacies of classifying an animal, but once in a while you are likely to encounter the subdivision terms. Animals that are grouped together in a subcategory are a little more closely related to each other than they are to other animals in the main category.

The chart on the following page provides a detailed example of the taxonomic classification of three animals whose common names are the spiny lobster, dog snapper and the schoolmaster.

It is easy to see from this chart that the fishes commonly known as the dog snapper and schoolmaster are very closely related. They are described in the same kingdom, phylum, subphylum, class, order, family and genus. The only difference is that they are separate species.

Spiny lobster, on the other hand, are not as closely related to dog snappers as are schoolmasters. While all of these species are included in the animal kingdom, fishes are described in a completely different phylum than lobsters. It logically follows that other fishes are more closely related to dog snappers and schoolmasters than they are to lobsters, and that crabs, shrimps and other creatures described in the class Crustacea within the phylum Arthropoda are more closely related to each other and to spiny lobsters than they are to fishes.

Some generalizations about an animal's natural history can be made about any given animal just by knowing its genus, family, class, etc. For instance, fishes in the family Acanthuridae (surgeonfishes), can easily be identified anywhere in the world by taking note of the lateral slits which ensheathe knife-like spines on either side of the caudal peduncle (tale base). It is these that gave this family its name. The lateral spines are used defensively and are characteristic of this family. In some cases the spines are hidden within the slits and in others they are very prominent, a clear deterrent to any species wanting to get too close to the "surgeons of the reef."

Once you have identified the fish as a surgeonfish you can expect to observe behavior associated with this family as a whole. For example, surgeonfishes are primarily vegetarians and are commonly seen preening algae from the reefs.

Often you will be satisfied just by knowing more or less where an animal fits into nature's overall grand scheme. That seems to be especially true in the case of any number of small, similar-looking invertebrates such as worms, snails and many shrimps. The same is also true in the case of many small reef fishes. Being able to group various animals with similar characteristics even to the family level gives us a handle on how and where animals fit into the animal kingdom.

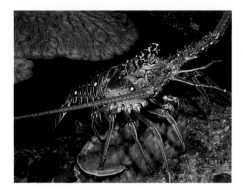

Spiny lobster.

Dog snapper.

Schoolmaster.

Taxonomic Classification of Three Animals			
Common Name	Spiny Lobster	Dog Snapper	Schoolmaster
Kingdom	Animalia	Animalia	Animalia
Phylum	Arthropoda	Chordata	Chordata
Subphylum	Malacostraca	Vertebrata	Vertebrata
Class	Crustacea	Osteichthyes	Osteichthyes
Order	Decopoda	Perciformes	Perciformes
Suborder	Palinura	Percoidei	Percoidei
Family	Palinuridae	Lutjanidae	Lutjanidae
Genus	*Panulirus*	*Lutjanus*	*Lutjanus*
Species	*argus*	*jocu*	*apodus*

6

Phylum: *Porifera*

SPONGES

*O*ccuring in a wide variety of captivating shapes and dazzling colors, sponges play an integral part in creating many of the most awe-inspiring Caribbean seascapes. Sponges inhabit all seas. Along with approximately 5,000 species of fossilized, extinct sponges, there are more than 5,000 currently living species. Yet, nowhere in the world are sponges more spectacular than in the Caribbean!

Sponges are the most primitive of all multicellular animals. Lacking specialized tissues, organs and muscles, the cells of sponges are only loosely associated with one another. No matter how large and elaborate, or how small, the bodies of sponges consist of little more than masses of cells among which there is very little coordination. Strange as it might seem, the contribution by individual cells to the entire sponge is considered to be a matter of pure coincidence. In essence, the cells are collectively embedded in a gelatinous mass and called a sponge. It is amazing that such simple animals can be so varied, so well adapted for life underwater, and so incredibly beautiful.

Sponges are the only members of the phylum Porifera. The name

When spawning, giant barrel sponges are often called "smoking sponges" due to their appearance. A single spawning sponge can start a chain reaction during which many barrel sponges simultaneously spawn, an event which can reduce visibility to near zero. A barrel sponge like the one pictured here may be three hundred years old or older.

The variety of shapes, textures and colors found in the world of sponges is truly astonishing. Several species of sponges are often crowded into formations as they compete for the precious real estate of the reef. Competition for a place of attachment is a fundamental part of life in a crowded reef community.

Porifera stems from the system of pores that perforate the bodies of sponges. These passageways are quite evident in the adult stage of sponges. As adults, sponges are usually attached to the reef, but they may also become attached to the shells of hermit crabs, decorator crabs and other animals.

It is believed that no other organisms have evolved as an offshoot of sponges. As a result, scientists consider sponges to be a dead end on the road of evolution. This conclusion may seem surprising considering that the fossil record of sponges indicate that sponges have lived in the seas of planet earth for at least 550 million years. However, sci-

entists point out that there are plenty of dead ends on the path of evolution.

The large opening in upright sponges is called an osculum. Tiny needles of silica called spicules and stringy fibers of protein called spongin help create an internal skeleton. The skeleton adds strength and helps sponges maintain their shape. Some species of sponges possess both spicules and spongin, while other species have only one or the other.

In laymen's terms, sponges are usually distinguished from one another in name by some reference to their color or shape, or by a combination of the two. For example,

AT A GLANCE

ELEPHANT EAR SPONGE

Scientific name
Agelas clathrodes
Habitat
Reef. Usually on deeper walls.
Typical Adult Size
5 feet in diameter, but varies greatly.
Sightings
Commonly seen in some areas, seldom seen in others.
Natural History
Forms flat encrusting sheets, curved sheets and mounds.

AT A GLANCE

BROWN TUBE SPONGE

Scientific name
Agelas sp.
Habitat
Reef.
Typical Adult Size
2.5 feet long.
Sightings
Commonly seen.
Natural History
Their built-in filtering mechanism is sophisticated enough to filter bacteria out of seawater, a factor which contributes to some degree to the excellent water visibility in the Caribbean. Brown tube sponges are home to various animals including cleaner gobies.

depends primarily upon the configuration of the bottom to which they conform. Encrusting sponges are often found wedged between coral heads, beneath the edges of coral plates, and at the bases of hard coral colonies. Encrusting sponges are believed to protect some corals by preventing boring organisms such as worms from digging into the corals. Common species of encrusting sponges include the tan to green colored **variable sponge**, the bright **orange encrusting sponge**, and the orange **fire sponge** which is often found in piles of coral rubble. Fire sponge, along with several other species, can be highly irritating to

human skin.

Other species such as **barrel sponges**, **tube sponges**, **finger sponges** and **rope sponges** have far more definite shapes than do encrusting sponges. Barrel sponges and tube sponges stand out prominently on many reefs. Commonly attaining heights of five feet or more, barrel sponges are the largest of the sponges. They are typically found in quiet water below 40 feet, and the largest specimens usually occur in the deep water along the forward slope of a reef.

Making a positive identification of the various sponges from their shape, size or color can be very chal-

some notable Caribbean species are referred to as **red rope sponges**, **green rope sponges**, **azure vase sponges** or **elephant ear sponges**. As a general rule, the use of common names allows for casual conversation without significant misunderstandings.

Sponges vary widely in terms of their shape, size and color. They are generally shaped like barrels, baskets, tubes, vases, cups or bowls, or they are flattened and encrusting. The shape of encrusting sponges

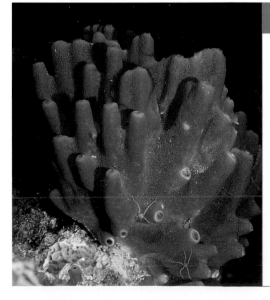

AT A GLANCE

BROWN VOLCANO SPONGE

Scientific Name
Hemectyon sp.
Habitat
Reef.
Typical Adult Size
3 feet in diameter.
Sightings
Occasionally seen.
Natural History
Forms encrusting mats with raised osculae (openings) that look like miniature volcanoes. Do not touch! Can be extremely irritating to skin.

lenging to say the least. Both shape and color can be useful identification keys in distinguishing between the various species of sponges. However, both characteristics can also be misleading since these traits often vary considerably between individual sponges of the same species.

Red cup sponges often appear in small clusters of a few inches to two feet across. Like many sponges, they appear to be drably colored at

AT A GLANCE

YELLOW TUBE SPONGE

Scientific Name
Aplysina fistularis
Habitat
Reef.
Typical Adult Size
3 feet, but some are considerably larger.
Sightings
Commonly seen.
Natural History
In shallow water yellow tube sponges often have antler-like protrusions. In deeper waters the tubes usually lack protrusions and are longer. Contain fluorescent pigments which makes them glow yellow.

AT A GLANCE

STRAWBERRY VASE SPONGE, RED VASE SPONGE, RED CUP SPONGE

Scientific Name
Mycale laxissima
Habitat
Typically in clusters on walls, especially on moderate and deep fore reefs, attached to bottom. Also found in shallow flats, often attached to coral rubble.
Typical Adult Size
5 to 12 inches long.
Sightings
Occasionally seen over range, but a featured attraction for photographers on many walls.
Natural History
Without an artificial light to bring out colors, this sponge usually appears dark black to drab purple. Often see brittle stars on these sponges.

PHOTO TIP

It is amazing what strobe light will do to a cluster of red cup sponges. When your flash hits these drab-looking sponges, the burst of light can turn an otherwise average scene into a most memorable seascape. And when you later project these images, they seem to jump off the screen and earn you "ooohs and ahhhs" from your audience! Be careful, however, to give red cup sponges plenty of light as they are easy to underexpose. Get close with your strobe and really blast them, and of course, bracket your exposures whenever possible.

depth without the use of an artificial light source, but use a dive light or strobe, and bingo! These drab sponges are suddenly transformed into hues of brilliant cherry and scar-

let red. Be sure to hold your light within a few feet or closer to really bring out the punchier colors.

Without artificial light, the colors of many other types of sponges go unnoticed, so bringing your dive light to paint in the true colors of **orange cup sponges**, **red rope sponges**, **orange elephant ear sponges**, **orange boring sponges** and **yellow calcareous sponges** is often a way to spice up your dives.

Even at depth, **yellow tube sponges** retain some of their bright coloration due to fluorescent pigments contained within the body of the sponge. These pigments actually alter the wavelength of the sunlight that strikes them, and as a result they appear yellow even at depth. Yellow tube sponges are common at medium depths, along the tops and edges of walls, and in the deeper water along the drop-offs. A variety of gobies and cardinalfishes are often associated with yellow tube sponges.

Despite the fact that sponges are considered to be very simple animals, they demonstrate some remarkable regenerative properties. For example, experiments with one species revealed that if a mature sponge is broken apart into very small bits by being forced through a sieve made from silk cloth, the parts will soon settle and reorganize themselves into a near replica of the original adult. That seems to be a rather remarkable feat for an animal that lacks any specialized tissues!

Some common bath and household sponges are made from the skeletons of sponges which have had the living tissue removed. But today, the majority of household and industrial sponges are synthetic. Exciting developments in the field of medical research have also made it possible for some sponges to be used to produce a variety of antibiotics and other medicines.

How Sponges Fit into Life on the Reef

Sponges contribute to the ecology of reef systems in a variety of ways. Sponges feed by filtering diatoms, bacteria, protozoans and other tiny organisms out of the water. Studies have demonstrated that a high percentage of the food of many sponges is so small that it cannot be seen without the aid of a microscope. However, only a small percentage of the food used by those sponges is eaten by other organisms. This means that many sponges have found a niche in which there is relatively little competition for food. This niche is of great value to an organism that lives its life attached to the sea floor and is unable to move about to capture its food. In addition, many species of sponges benefit from the presence of symbiotic algae known as zooxanthellae in

PHOTO TIP

Many sponges make wonderful photographic subjects, and they also provide superb negative space for other subjects that are framed against their complimentary colors. In addition, many animals live on, in, and around sponges. So when you see an interesting-looking sponge, stop and take your time. There is probably a great shot waiting to be taken. Consider the potential for (1) a close-focus wide-angle shot with a colorful sponge in the foreground and a silhouetted diver or boat in the background, (2) a portrait of a sponge, or (3) an opportunity to film some interesting reef creature that lives in association with the sponge.

their tissues. The photosynthesis conducted by the algae provides food for these sponges.

Experiments have shown that .061 cubic inch of a variety of sponges can filter up to 5 gallons of water per day, meaning that many sponges can easily filter more than 50 gallons of water a day! Where sponges are prevalent, they are partially responsible for adding to the water clarity.

Sponges have a rather unique form of feeding. It centers around the creation of a current of water which flows through a system of tiny pores and canals. The basic body plan and feeding strategy of sponges is designed around this ability to create currents and filter water. The outside wall of all sponges is filled with tiny pores. An incoming current of water is forced through the passageway of pores and canals where oxygen and food are removed from the water. The filtered water passes out through a series of small passageways which in some species eventually merge into one large excurrent opening known as the osculum. In other species, numerous oscula can easily be seen with the naked eye. The incoming current is created by the frantic and constant beating of numerous, tiny,

hair-like flagella which line the passageway walls. In some sponges the incoming current can be detected more than three feet away from the sponge.

Many sponges provide excellent hiding places for a wide variety of small fishes as well as shrimps, brittle stars, nudibranchs, hermit crabs, juvenile lobsters and other invertebrates. In fact, many species of tunicates, mollusks, echinoderms, worms, crustaceans and fishes actually live the vast majority of their lives inside sponges.

Divers who take their time to carefully examine sponges are often rewarded with the discovery of some creature that is resting on or moving very slowly across the surface of the sponge. Some of the inhabitants are very obvious while others are well camouflaged. A number of species of gobies and blennies can commonly be seen swimming along the edge of tube sponges and barrel sponges. If frightened, these tiny fishes are quick to seek safety inside the sponge. Cardinalfishes, royal grammas and blackcap basslets commonly hide inside vase sponges at night.

During the day, if you look carefully at the base of a sponge or between its lobes and branches, you are likely to discover a variety of tiny animals that roam over the surface of the sponge and nearby reef at night. Brittle stars, hermit crabs and shrimps are especially common.

Although angelfishes, filefishes, and some invertebrates such as sea slugs and bristle worms (also called fire worms) feed directly on sponges, most reef residents consider sponges to be inedible. This provides a much needed form of defense for sponges since they are permanently attached to the bottom and cannot flee from potential predators.

Some species of sponges are parasitic and they bore their way into a variety of corals. These sponges may weaken and eventually topple large coral heads. Other sponges actually

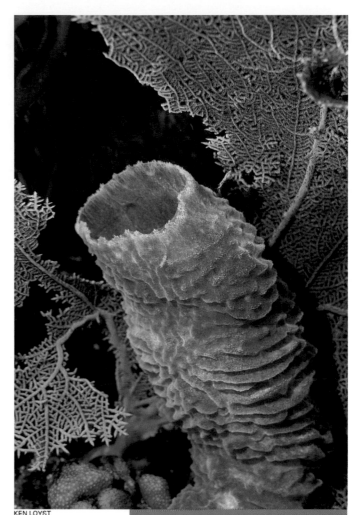

KEN LOYST

AT A GLANCE

ORANGE BORING SPONGE

Scientific Name
Cliona delitrix
Habitat
Reef.
Typical Adult Size
1-foot diameter at coral surface.
Sightings
Commonly seen.
Natural History
Parasitizes coral heads by growing into the skeleton.

AT A GLANCE

AZURE VASE SPONGE

Scientific Name
Callyspongia plicifera
Habitat
Reef.
Typical Adult Size
1 foot.
Sightings
Commonly seen.
Natural History
Glows with a natural iridescence.

PHOTO TIP

The azure vase sponge is a favorite of underwater photographers. In both wide-angle and macro photographs the iridescent purple color adds stunning color. Exposure can be tricky, so be sure to bracket.

When filming sponges, many photographers fall into the trap of trying to photograph the largest specimen they can find. Usually these sponges are older and imperfectly shaped in one way or another. Try looking for smaller, more perfectly shaped specimens and make them appear large in your frame by forcing the perspective with your lens. In other words, use a wide-angle lens, and be sure to get close enough to the sponge so that it fills a pleasing percentage of your frame.

help protect the coral by encrusting the edge of the coral head and creating a barrier to boring sponges.

HOW SPONGES REPRODUCE

As adults, sponges are immobile. So,

how in the world do they reproduce? As is the case with many invertebrates, sponges reproduce both asexually and sexually. In the asexual reproduction found in many species, the sponges reproduce by dividing themselves up into fragments which soon develop into complete individuals. Another com-

AT A GLANCE

RED ROPE SPONGE, SMOOTH RED FINGER SPONGE

Scientific Name
Haliclona rubens
Habitat
Walls.
Typical Adult Size
3 to 5 feet, but some are considerably larger.
Sightings
Commonly seen.
Natural History
Especially common along current-swept walls.

AT A GLANCE

PINK VASE SPONGE

Scientific Name
Dasychalina cyathina
Habitat
Reef.
Typical Adult Size
2 feet long.
Sightings
Commonly seen.
Natural History
Brittle stars often found on this species. Semi-transparent membrane borders the top of the sponge.

AT A GLANCE

LEATHERY BARREL SPONGE

Scientific Name
Geodia neptuni
Habitat
Reefs.
Typical Adult Size
1.5 to 3 feet.
Sightings
Commonly seen.
Natural History
Often inhabits areas where it becomes covered with algae and debris.

AT A GLANCE

GREEN FINGER SPONGE

Scientific Name
Iotrochota birotulata
Habitat
Reef and walls to moderate depths.
Typical Adult Size
1 to 3 feet.
Sightings
Occasionally to commonly seen.
Natural History
Branching sponge that is irregular in shape. Almost always accompanied by yellow zoanthids. Favorite food of rock beauties.

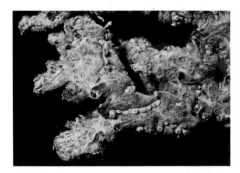

Zoanthids, described in the phylum Cnidaria, are tiny anemone-like animals once thought to parasitize the tissue of many sponges. Their presence, however, may actually benefit the sponge by deterring fishes from preying upon the host sponge. Some fish such as rock beauties are not put off by the zoanthids, and readily feed upon green finger sponges.

AT A GLANCE

PURPLE TUBE SPONGE

Scientific Name
Aplysina lacunosa
Habitat
Reef.
Typical Adult Size
*3 to 5 feet long, some consider-
ably larger.*
Sightings
Commonly seen in some areas.
Natural History
*Similar in overall appearance to
yellow tube sponges, but tubes
are generally thinner and they
are purple. Large clusters with
10 or more tubes can be more
than 6 feet across. Outer surface
covered with wart-like bumps.*

AT A GLANCE

BRANCHING TUBE SPONGE

Scientific Name
Pseudoceratina crassa
Habitat
Reefs and walls.
Typical Adult Size
1.5 to 3 feet.
Sightings
*Commonly seen in the Carib-
bean and Bahamas, occasionally
seen in southern Florida.*
Natural History
*Color of tubes varies consider-
ably from green to purple to
yellow to orange.*

AT A GLANCE

ENCRUSTING SPONGE

Scientific Name
Diplastrella sp.
Habitat
*Protected areas on reefs and
walls with low light. Base of
coral heads, under ledges.*
Typical Adult Size
8 to 20 inches.
Sightings
Occasionally seen.
Natural History
*Protected areas with low light
levels. Under ledges, in caves.*

mon form of asexual reproduction in sponges is through the formation of buds. These buds break off from the parent sponge and float away with the current. Exactly where the buds settle is a matter of happenstance, but if the bottom is favorable, the buds will soon develop into whole new sponges. In other species, the buds remain attached to the parent sponge, giving rise to the formation of a colony of sponges.

Sponges utilize several methods of sexual reproduction. Many are hermaphroditic, meaning that the same individual possesses both male and female reproductive capa-

bilities. However, when these sponges spawn they usually only produce sperm or eggs. In some species of sponges the sexes are fully separate. And some species reproduce through external fertilization by producing enormous quantities of sperm and eggs which are released into the water column where fertilization occurs. The newly formed larval sponges drift with the rest of the plankton and are heavily preyed upon, leaving only a handful of survivors to settle to the bottom.

Most sponges reproduce through a process defined as internal fertili-

AT A GLANCE

BROWN CLUSTERED TUBE SPONGE

Scientific Name
Agelas wiedenmyeri
Habitat
Reefs, often around base of corals.
Typical Adult Size
Tubes, 1 to 4 inches tall.
Sightings
Occasionally seen.
Natural History
Their built-in filtering mechanism is sophisticated enough to filter bacteria out of seawater. Oscular opening is smaller than diameter of tube.

zation, although the use of the term internal can lead to some confusion. In internal reproduction in sponges, large, milky clouds of sperm are first released externally into the water column through the osculum of the donor sponge. The sperm are soon taken in by a recipient sponge where they are united with ripened eggs. At times the density of released sperm is so thick that the water takes on a milky color and visibility is greatly reduced. In fact, at times spawning sponges can reduce visibility to only a few feet or less. Divers occasionally see **barrel sponges** billowing out smoke-like clouds of sperm, and often call these sponges "smoking sponges."

AT A GLANCE

NETTED BARREL SPONGE, BARREL SPONGE

Scientific Name
Verongula gigantea
Habitat
Clear water in open areas of moderate and deep reefs.
Typical Adult Size
3 to 5 feet tall.
Sightings
Occasionally seen in Caribbean and Bahamas; seldom in Florida.
Natural History
Preyed upon by a variety of fishes and probably sea turtles. Feeding leaves noticeable bright, golden pits.

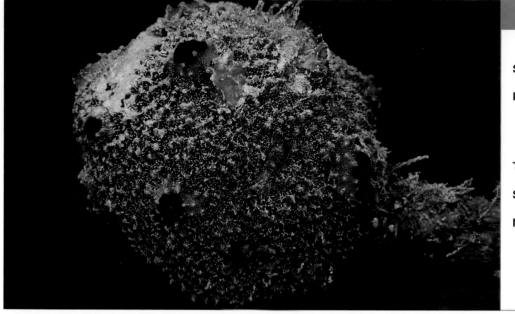

AT A GLANCE

BLACK BALL SPONGE

Scientific Name
Iricinia strobilina
Habitat
Reef, on and between coral heads and on walls. Generally prefers areas with a lot of sunlight.
Typical Adult Size
1.5 feet in diameter.
Sightings
Occasionally seen.
Natural History
Food source for whitespotted filefish. Large oscular openings bunched at top in slight depression in otherwise spherical sponge.

A NOTE OF CAUTION

A few species of sponges are toxic to humans, so avoid touching any sponges. Merely brushing against some species can prove to be a painfully memorable experience that can persist for weeks. Reactions vary, but a burning sensation or a bad rash and itching is common. The most common culprit is the touch-me-not sponge (fire sponge). In most specimens tiny, white parasitic worms can be seen.

AT A GLANCE

FIRE SPONGE, TOUCH-ME-NOT SPONGE

Scientific Name
Neofibularia nolitangere
Habitat
Shallow near shore reefs, in rubble zones, and on walls.
Typical Adult Size
1 to 3 feet long and wide.
Sightings
Too commonly seen!
Natural History
Beware, touching this sponge can result in an irritating rash that persists for one week or longer. Large, irregular openings and irregular, bumpy, dark red-to-orange-to-brown surface. Typically inhabited by large numbers of small, white polychaete worms which are a good identifying characteristic. Small worm snails (1/3 inch diameter tubes) also commonly on surface. Small gobies often associate with this sponge.

7

Phylum: *Cnidaria*

CORALS, SEA ANEMONES, JELLYFISHES, AND PORTUGUESE MEN-OF-WAR, FIRE CORALS AND OTHER HYDROIDS

The phylum Cnidaria includes corals, sea anemones, jellyfishes, Portuguese-men-of-war and hydroids. The cnidarians are considered to be among the most beautiful of all marine invertebrates. Many species appear delicate and are often described as flower-like. But beware! Their delicate appearance conceals a deadly armament of powerful stinging cells. Creatures such as **Portuguese men-of-war** and **sea wasps** are closely related to **sea anemones** and **corals** because they possess virulent stinging cells. In fact, the most significant distinguishing characteristic of the members of the phylum Cnidaria is that all possess stinging cells which are typically concentrated in their tentacles. It is a characteristic with which many divers are more famil-

Like all cnidarians, jellyfishes contain stinging cells called cnidoblasts in their tentacles. These potent cells are used to paralyze their prey. In this jellyfish the trailing tentacles are packed with deadly stinging cells. Note the small fish which carefully hide amongst the deadly tentacles of the jellyfish and thereby escape larger fishes which must avoid contact with the potent tentacles. The smaller fish have chosen the more predictable of two evils, but if they should get careless even for an instant, they will wind up as an hors d'oeuvre for the jellyfish.

iar than they would wish!

Most cnidarians live their adult lives permanently attached to the sea floor, or they drift about in currents, having little control over their speed and direction. In order to protect themselves from potential predators and capture food, cnidarians depend heavily on their stinging cells. They are not capable of pursuing their prey or outdistancing potential predators. Instead, these animals have evolved the ability to immobilize their prey or enemies on contact. Experiments have shown that it takes only three milliseconds for some cnidarians to fire their explosive stinging cells after an animal has come in contact with it. This lightning-fast response time is one of the fastest cellular responses in all of nature!

The stinging cells, called cnidoblasts (also known as nematoblasts), are equipped with structures known as nematocysts. Although nematocysts appear in a variety of basic designs, all look somewhat like a miniature harpoon. The nematocysts are always coiled and ready for action. When stimulated by physical contact, chemical detection, or even a wave of increased water pressure caused by slight movement, the cnidoblasts explode, releasing the coiled nematocysts. Collectively, a number of nematocysts ensnare the intended victim

and may release a deadly poison. The poisons are fast-acting and can rapidly paralyze prey. The enshrouding tentacles are then drawn in toward the cnidarian's mouth where the prey is consumed.

Human skin is too thick for the nematocysts of many corals, some anemones, and even some jellyfishes to penetrate. However, in other species, including a number of delicate corals, anemones, hydroids and jellyfishes, the nematocysts are capable of delivering painful stings. Reactions in humans vary on an individual basis, but severe burning and itching, swelling and painful rashes are common. In some cases stings of sea wasps, some other jellyfishes, and Portuguese men-of-war have proved fatal.

Worldwide, there are approximately 10,000 species of cnidarians. From the point of view of a biologist faced with the task of classifying animals, cnidarians are considered to represent the simplest forms of what can generally be described as complex organisms. Scientists have separated cnidarians into four classes. The class Anthozoa describes the hard corals, the soft corals and the sea anemones. The class Scyphozoa includes all jellyfishes. Hydroids, fire coral and the Portuguese man-of-war are described in the class Hydrozoa, while sea wasps are in the class Cubozoa.

During daylight hours the polyps of most hard corals are retracted (left). They come into full bloom in the evening when they feed. After dark, the polyps extend their tentacles to the currents (above), and use their nematocysts to capture plankton and other nourishing particulate matter.

All cnidarians occur in one of two body forms. One form is the polyp. As divers, we are most familiar with the polyp form in adult corals and sea anemones. In these animals the polyps are attached to the bottom by means of a foot-like disc, a feature which is not always immediately evident to the casual observer. Each tiny polyp is an individual animal. Its mouth is on the surface opposite the attached disc, and the mouth and tentacles face toward the water.

The second body plan in cnidarians is the medusa, a form commonly taken on by jellyfishes. As a medusa, the animal is free-swimming and the mouth and tentacles are usually, though not always, pointed downward toward the sea floor. In many respects, the polyp form and the medusa form are quite similar. Each has a central mouth surrounded by tentacles, but they appear as inverted images of one another.

SEX LIVES OF CNIDARIANS

The story of the polyp and the medusa is not quite as simple as it might first seem. During the life cycle of many cnidarians, the animal experiences both a polyp stage and a medusa stage. In the polyp stage, corals reproduce both sexually and asexually. In some species the corals are separately sexed, meaning some polyps are males and others are females, while in other species the corals are simultaneous hermaphrodites. This means the same coral is both male and female at the same time.

In its asexual form, coral polyps are bottom dwellers that reproduce by budding. In their medusa stage, the animals are free-swimming and reproduce sexually.

Why would nature create an animal that has an asexual and a sexual stage of life? The accepted answer in the scientific community is a fundamental concept in the theory of evolution. This concept centers around the belief that Mother Nature has only one goal for each species—survival. In order for a species to survive, it must be able to successfully reproduce.

One method of successful reproduction is for individual animals to reproduce a genetic replica of themselves by budding. No sexual partner is needed, and this method is referred to as asexual reproduction. The primary advantage of asexual reproduction is that the participation of a partner is not required. As a result, it is possible over time for a single coral polyp to reproduce

through asexual reproduction, or to bud so many times that an entire coral reef can be formed.

The next logical question to ask is "If animals can reproduce asexually, why has sexual reproduction evolved?" The answer is that the genetic diversity provided by sexual reproduction plays a key role in protecting species against potential threats. In animals born from asexual reproduction, any environmental factor that threatens any one animal poses the same threat to every animal in the population. For example, a disease that killed a single coral polyp could eliminate an entire coral reef very quickly.

The process of cross fertilization as a result of sexual reproduction results in a population of animals that are genetically dissimilar. Even though each animal shares many common characteristics, at a genetic level the concept of diversity plays an extremely important role in the ability of the species to survive in a world of ever-changing environmental factors.

Given that some corals do cross-fertilize, the problem of immobility or lack of access to a partner must be overcome. Corals, like many other sessile invertebrates that cross-fertilize, must have a population of willing and capable partners ready to reproduce at the same time. Science is only now learning about reproduction in corals, but in recent years massive coral spawnings have been observed underwater. At a given time, cued by the release of hormones known as pheromones which advertise a state of readiness, corals release enormous quantities of sexual cells into the water.

The intricacies of the exact timing of the event are not completely understood, but scientists have learned to accurately predict coral spawns in some locales. In areas where spawnings have been reasonably well documented, the entire event lasts only a matter of hours. In some instances, spawning occurs on only one night of the year. In other cases, corals spawn for only a few hours on two or three consecutive nights during the year.

TYPES OF CORALS

Few sights in nature are as spectacular as the grandeur we behold when we look through crystal-clear Caribbean waters and gaze over the expanse of a coral reef. In a typical Caribbean reef system, dozens of species of massive hard corals and delicate soft corals catch the eyes of awestruck divers. For many it comes as quite a surprise to learn that corals are actually living animals. Each individual flower-like coral polyp is considered to be an organism, yet with few exceptions they cannot survive outside the colony.

Perhaps even more fascinating is the realization that the great coral reefs found in tropical seas around the world are dynamic, ever-changing ecosystems. The actual foundation of the reef is the collective skeletal remains of trillions upon trillions of once-living coral polyps, most of which were no larger than a dime. Yet over the ages, these polyps have created reef systems that extend for hundreds of square miles. Located on the Caribbean side of Central America, the gorgeous offshore reef system of Belize forms a

AT A GLANCE

STAR CORAL

Scientific Name
Montastrea annularis
Habitat
Reef.
Typical Adult Size
Forms heads 1.5 to 4 feet high.
Sightings
Commonly seen.
Natural History
Several species of corals are commonly called star coral. They are among the most important reef-building corals. Appear in mounds, flattened sheets and hemispheres.

barrier reef that is second in size only to Australia's Great Barrier Reef. So prolific are the corals found throughout this system, and on most other Caribbean reefs, that dozens of species can be spotted within minutes of beginning a dive.

Corals are typically classified in one of two major categories. They are: (1) the stony corals, also called hard corals, and (2) soft corals, ani-

mals which add considerable beauty, but whose skeletons do not significantly contribute to the foundation and growth of the reef in terms of adding limestone. The stony corals include all of the species that are known as reef builders. Soft corals do contribute to reef growth by adding sediment, but it is not as enduring or significant as the limestone left behind by hard corals.

Most divers and snorkelers tend to think of corals in their adult stage, during which they are permanently attached to the bottom in the form of a polyp. As adults, corals occur in a variety of dazzling forms. Some polyps prefer a solitary existence while many other species live in large colonies where the individual animals share a common skeleton or stalk. **Sea whips** are an example of colonial soft corals, while most of the true reef-building corals, such as the species commonly referred to as **star corals** and **brain corals,** are colonial hard corals.

Some corals are vividly colored while others appear brownish, off-white, tan and drab green. When feeding, the individual polyps of many corals take on a flower-like appearance as the tentacles reach out into the water column in an effort to trap their food. Individual polyps range in size from a pinhead to several inches in diameter.

HARD CORALS

All true reef-building hard corals are colonial animals. The living generation of polyps resides atop the limestone skeletons of generations of their ancestors. Because hard corals form the foundation for all of the tropical reefs of the world, they are considered to be the most significant invertebrates in warm shallow seas.

Identifying hard corals is rather easy because the polyps secrete large external skeletons. These skeletons are hard, giving rise to the name hard or stony corals. In tropical seas

CORAL SPAWNING

It was sunset, the beginning of the eighth night after the August full moon. Looking out over the water from the back deck of the boat, nothing really looked any different to me. But the scientists assured me tonight was the night and I was looking forward to our dive, which was scheduled for 9:20 P.M. sharp.

If this year was to be like years in the recent past, for approximately 60 to 90 minutes, somewhere between 9:00 and 11:00 P.M., at least two species of star corals and one species of brain coral would spawn, releasing fly's eye-sized packets containing millions of sperm and eggs. Other corals, as well as a host of invertebrates such as Christmas tree worms and brittle stars, would also procreate.

As we were suiting up, the slick began to hit the surface. It was happening, just as the scientists had assured me it would. There were thousands of tiny white, brown and pink packets floating on the surface. The corals were spawning.

Some coral colonies are all male, some all female, and others are hermaphrodites (both male and female). It depends upon the species involved. Montastrea annularus, the small star coral, is hermaphroditic. Montastrea cavernosa, the large star coral, is either male or female. The brain coral, Diploria, is hermaphroditic. In all species, all of the polyps in a single colony are clones, having been borne from the same parents.

Some corals can self-fertilize, others are thought only to cross-fertilize. Diversity is a key to survival in an environment where predators and competitors are fast learners.

The spawning is a wild sight to see underwater. Some heads of brain corals and small star coral look like popcorn ma-

chines with tiny packets forming on the coral head, and then being released into the water column where they float toward the surface. Most packets hold together for some time before deteriorating, an act which releases sexual cells into the water where they have the best chance to join the cells from other colonies. In some instances the release is slow and steady, and in other cases the release is simultaneous, as if someone flipped a switch releasing hundreds, perhaps thousands of egg packets.

In Diploria, the males release a milky substance into the water which contains sperm. The females release packets of eggs.

A variety of fishes and some invertebrates gather to feed on the nutrient-rich packets. During this spawning I watched a normally reclusive brittle star turn opportunistic by boldly venturing out on top of a coral head to grab several arms full of packets.

Recently it has been learned that there is often some spawning on both the seventh and ninth night after the August full moon, and in some years the spawning occurs over four to five hours instead of in a 60 to 90 minute span. When other corals spawn is still a mystery.

Scientists are excited about the spawning for a variety of reasons, but one that is particularly encouraging to many is the fact that larvae from one area might soon be able to be transplanted to an area that has lost corals due to environmental disasters.

Back on deck after the dive, we noticed a small slick of packets on the water. Then we removed our gear, tucked our cameras away for the night, and looked out over the surface. The slick was gone, and once again I couldn't tell that this night was different from any other.—Marty Snyderman

AT A GLANCE

GIANT BRAIN CORAL

Scientific Name
Colpophyllia natans
Habitat
Reefs.
Typical Adult Size
3-foot-high mounds.
Sightings
Commonly seen.
Natural History
Brain corals are among the most common stony corals on the reef. Polyps are laid out in convoluted rows. Neon gobies and peppermint gobies often reside on the surface of brain coral.

AT A GLANCE

ELKHORN CORAL

Scientific Name
Acropora palmata
Habitat
Usually in water less than 40 feet deep. Especially common in fore reef along windward side of islands and wave-swept shores.
Typical Adult Size
Varies greatly. Some colonies to 12 feet, with individual 4- to 6-inch-wide branches to length of 4 feet.
Sightings
Commonly seen.
Natural History
Fast-growing, shallow water, colonial hard coral is one of most important reef-building corals.

almost everything that you might want to describe as a solid, ornate rock is probably a type of hard coral.

But just because these colonies are hard and appear rugged does not mean that stony corals are not delicate. Many can be severely damaged or even killed by being lightly handled. Severe damage does not require a direct hit with a boat anchor. All it takes is a kick from a fin to harm generations of living polyps. Many species of hard corals secrete a layer of mucus that helps to protect the coral and to ensnare food particles. The layer is often removed when coral is handled, exposing the coral to a wide variety of environmental threats.

The common names of many hard corals are indicative of the general appearance of many species of hard corals. For example, some of the most prominent species of Caribbean corals are commonly called **staghorn, elkhorn, finger, flower, brain, pillar, star, plate** and **lettuce coral.**

Hard corals are not just randomly scattered throughout the reef community. Instead, each species has a preferred niche within the reef structure. For example, elkhorn coral is usually found in shallow water where the surf breaks, or just slightly deeper. During periods of low tide the tips of their branches may even protrude from the water. Several species of corals commonly called star corals and brain corals are found in fairly shallow patch reefs, as well as along and over the reef crest. Star corals often form plates when they are growing in deeper waters, a structural advantage which allows more exposure to sunlight used by symbiotic zooxanthellae, vital algae, on which the coral depends. Pillar coral favors the reef crest and the flat prior to the buttress zone. Staghorn coral typically favors calm water just inside the reef crest. Finger coral typifies the reef crest, while plate coral, lettuce coral, flower coral and green corals are more typical of deeper reef areas.

In their adult stage hard corals use their potent stinging tentacles to ensnare suspended plankton that drift by in currents. Most polyps of hard corals shun the light of day and will feed only during the evening hours. At night when the polyps feed they take on the appearance of a flower bed.

Hard corals require a water temperature in excess of 68°F in order to flourish. In addition, some water movement in the form of currents and upwellings is required, and the surrounding water must be relatively clean. Corals are easily suffocated in dirty water as debris settles onto them and gets trapped in the mucous coating. Reef communities are often severely damaged by commercial development on nearby land as debris from construction projects spills onto reefs. In recent years throughout the Caribbean, Bahamas and Florida, many governmental agencies and construction companies have been working closely with environmental organizations to protect reef communities from this type of damage.

FIRE CORALS

The use of the word coral when referring to animals commonly referred to as fire corals shows how laymen's language often conflicts with scientific language. Many

---

PHOTO TIP

The axiom which suggests that photographers "get down, get close, and shoot up" when shooting wide-angle images often applies. In order to make the corals stand out, try framing coral heads against a contrasting water background instead of shooting down or directly into reef. Also try shooting at minimum focusing distance with a wide-angle lens to capture the interesting textures of the many corals, particularly the brain corals, whose convoluted nature is often captivating on film.

AT A GLANCE

STAGHORN CORAL

Scientific Name
Acropora cervicornis
Habitat
Reef.
Typical Adult Size
2 feet long.
Sightings
Commonly seen.
Natural History
Staghorn coral is commonly found along the approach to the reef buttress in calm water areas. Stands become partially overgrown by filamentous algae and certain damselfishes vehemently protect these areas.

AT A GLANCE

CUP CORAL, FLOWER CORAL, TUBASTREA CORAL

Scientific Name
Tubastrea aurea
Habitat
Reef, walls, wharf pilings, shipwrecks, and almost any other available hard surface.
Typical Adult Size
Clusters to 1 foot across, dime- to quarter-sized polyps.
Sightings
Commonly seen in some areas; seldom in others.
Natural History
Large individual polyps on end of tubes. Polyps open to feed at night, usually retract during the day.

AT A GLANCE

PILLAR CORAL

Scientific Name
Dendrogyra cylindricus
Habitat
Reef flats.
Typical Adult Size
Varies greatly. Some heads 2 to 3 feet high, while many are over 8 feet.
Sightings
Commonly seen in some areas.
Natural History
This is one of the few hard corals whose polyps are commonly seen feeding during the day. Color varies from tan to green.

WHAT ARE ZOOXANTHELLAE, AND WHY WOULD YOU CARE TO KNOW?

Zooxanthellae (pronounced zo-zan-thell-ee) are microscopic, single-celled algae that are the foundation of all food chains in tropical reef communities. They are crucial to the existence of all coral reefs and to all creatures that depend upon coral reef communities!

If you are not aware of the existence of zooxanthellae, don't be surprised. Few non-scientists are. But don't underestimate their importance. Without trillions of zooxanthellae, coral reef communities—from the corals themselves to sharks, barracuda and other apex predators—simply would not exist.

Zooxanthellae are an integral part of a mystery concerning the dynamics of coral reef communities, a mystery that puzzled scientists for years. All major food chains are built on a foundation of plants, not animals. Through the process of photosynthesis, plants convert the sun's energy into simple sugars and other nutrients. In scientific terms plants are, therefore, considered to be primary producers. Animals which gain their energy by preying on the plants are classified as first level consumers. Other animals which feed on the first level consumers are called second level consumers, and so on up the food chain.

However, the transfer of energy from one level to the the next is rather inefficient. In fact, on average only about 10 percent of the energy available on one level is transferred to the next level. This means that it takes about 10 pounds of plants to create 1 pound of animals that prey upon the plants. In turn, 10 pounds of reef fish are required to support 1 pound of barracuda on the next level of the chain.

While this relationship has been well accepted for years with regard to most food chains, it was not until the post-World War II era that scientists really understood how tropical reef communities supported themselves. Although they are present, large plants simply are not abundant in most coral reef ecosystems. The lack of plant life puzzled scientists. It is important to realize that it is not just fishes that are consumers. Even corals and other tiny invertebrates are known to be consumers.

In terms of sheer quantity, or biomass, it appeared as if there were far more consumers than producers in tropical seas. However, logic dictated that if this were the case, coral reef communities simply could not exist.

In temperate and polar seas, enormous quantities of single-celled plants called phytoplankton are known to provide the foundation of most food chains. The sheer numbers of these plants often turn the water green and greatly reduce visibility. Phytoplankton is eaten by small animals known as zooplankton which in turn are consumed by larger invertebrates and vertebrates. But like all other food chains, even in temperate and polar communities only between 6 and 20 percent of the energy is transferred up each rung of the food chain ladder.

By comparison, there is very little phytoplankton in most tropical seas, a characteristic which greatly contributes to the exceptionally clear quality of tropical waters. The question that perplexed scientists was, how was it possible for coral reef communities to function in a setting where there seemed to be more consumers than the producers could support?

In the years immediately after World War II, scientists studying the effects of nuclear testing in the South Pacific atolls discovered significant quantities of algae living in two places. Algae were found to be (1) living in the sand on the reef bottom and on dead coral, and (2) living inside the polyp tissues and skeletons of the corals themselves. Zooxanthellae are the algae living inside the corals. They are so numerous that in some instances the biomass of zooxanthellae comprise as much as 80 percent of the total weight of the coral polyps. With these discoveries scientists finally had proof that the food chains of tropical reef communities operated under the same fundamental laws of nature that govern all other food chains.

Zooxanthellae share a symbiotic relationship with the coral polyps. The algae supply the coral with oxygen and nutrients as by products of photosynthesis, enabling the corals to live, reproduce and build their skeletons. In turn, the algae benefit by receiving a safe place to live and gaining access to the raw materials, such as carbon dioxide and inorganic nitrogen, which are necessary to conduct successful photosynthesis. These raw materials are given off by the metabolic processes of corals. This type of symbiotic relationship in which both organisms gain and neither is harmed is defined as mutualism.

Zooxanthellae also contribute significantly in another way. The algae take calcium ions from the water and transform them into calcium carbonate, which is used by the corals in the creation of their skeletons.

AT A GLANCE

SEA PLUME, GORGONIAN

Scientific Name
Pseudopterogorgia sp.
Habitat
Shallow reef areas.
Typical Adult Size
3 feet tall.
Sightings
Commonly seen.
Natural History
They do not contribute to the long-standing physical nature of the reef, but they provide hiding places and ambush points for many reef fishes during the lifetime of the gorgonian. Sea plumes often have tiny stinging hydroids attached to their tips.

AT A GLANCE

SEA ROD, GORGONIAN

Scientific Name
Pseudoplexaura sp.
Habitat
Shallow reef areas.
Typical Adult Size
4 feet tall.
Sightings
Commonly seen.
Natural History
Although they do not contribute to the long-standing physical nature of the reef, they provide hiding places and ambush points for many reef fishes.

AT A GLANCE

SEA FAN

Scientific Name
Gorgonia ventalina
Habitat
Shallow reef areas.
Typical Adult Size
1.5 to 3 feet tall.
Sightings
Commonly seen.
Natural History
Creates a fan-like filter oriented across the path of the prevailing current putting its polyps in an optimal position to remove plankton and other food particles from the water. They are often preyed upon by the flamingo tongue snail.

divers think of fire corals as corals, but they are actually more closely related to hydroids than to corals.

A description of fire corals can be found in the section on hydroids later in this chapter.

SOFT CORALS

The colonial animals commonly called **sea fans**, **sea plumes**, **sea rods**, **sea fingers**, **sea whips**, **deepwater gorgonians**, **wire corals** and **black coral** are often referred to as soft corals because unlike the reef-building hard corals, they do not incorporate the hard calcium carbonate into their skeletons. The term gorgonian corals is also commonly used to describe these species, and is derived from their order, Gorgonacea. The polyps of black corals are structurally more similar to the polyps of hard corals (hexacorals) than they are to the polyps of gorgonians (octocorals).

Like the hard corals, the various species of soft corals are typically found in characteristic places on the coral reef. Sea fingers, sea whips, sea plumes and sea rods are usually found in relatively shallow water along the reef flat.

Common sea fans are often found on the reef flats as well, but the healthier specimens are more likely to be seen in slightly deeper water near the top of drop-offs and along the walls. Sea fans typically grow in a plane that stretches across, rather than in line with the path of prevailing current. This orientation allows each individual polyp the maximum opportunity to gather food. Several species of sea fans inhabit Caribbean waters, and most are between one and five feet tall. Two of the most common species are the **green sea fan,** which usually has a greenish or brownish tint, and the **purple sea fan.** A variety of animals such as brittle stars, basket stars, hermit crabs, solitary hydroids and flamingo tongue snails (cowries) can often be found on the sea fan or on the skeletal base.

Wire corals are usually found along walls and drop-offs. Though their stiff skeleton is only as thick as a wire coat hanger, these colonial corals may extend out from the wall for six feet or more. Wire corals are well named and look like green twisted wire.

Another species of sea fan, commonly called the deep-water gor-

Like many hard corals, soft corals are colonial organisms with individual polyps sharing the same stalk. In this photograph, you can see a number of extended white polyps which are feeding. Each polyp contributes to the strength of the stalk.

AT A GLANCE

DEEP-WATER GORGONIAN

Scientific Name
Icillogorgia schrammi
Habitat
Along the wall.
Typical Adult Size
4 to 6 feet in diameter.
Sightings
Commonly seen.
Natural History
Form a stinging net which reaches out perpendicular to the prevailing currents. The polyps tend to remain retracted unless the current is flowing.

gonian is often seen along drop-offs at depths below 50 or 60 feet. More often than not, these gorgonians are mistaken for black coral. They appear as broad, black sea fans growing perpendicular to the wall and currents, but actually the skeletal stalks of deep-water gorgonians are an attractive pink and the polyps are translucent or white.

Unfortunately, many people are familiar with black coral because the species is used to make jewelry. The incredibly slow-growing black coral is removed from the water, cleaned and polished. The end product takes on a shiny black appearance. It is sad that the perceived beauty of the jew-

elry has led to the demise of this beautiful coral in many sites. Living black coral does not look black and this confuses many divers. In a natural setting black coral trees appear bright yellow, tan or orange. The branches of the trees have a feather-like appearance and are wonderful to behold.

Not too many years ago, black coral was quite common even in relatively shallow water. However, in many parts of the Caribbean it has been commercially harvested for many years. Black coral grows very slowly, taking a minimum of several decades to reach commercially valuable sizes. As a result of this ex-

PHOTO TIP

Deep-water gorgonians are wonderful backdrops for close-focus wide-angle photos using your Nikonos with either a 15 mm or 20mm lens, or similar lens with a single lens reflex system. Use the sun to backlight these expansive gorgonians and their margins will literally appear to glow when the polyps are out feeding. Compose your photo with a brightly colored foreground subject such as an azure vase sponge, and frame a deep-water gorgonian just behind the sponge. Shoot at an upward angle into blue water, and position the sun behind the gorgonian. The backlit gorgonian seems to add another dimension, giving the photograph a three-dimensional appearance. Be sure that the depth-of-field indicators on your lens indicate the foreground (from the sponge through the gorgonian) is in sharp focus.

ed to live amongst these deadly tentacles. The **giant Caribbean anemone**, the **corkscrew anemone** and the **knobby anemone** are commonly home to Pederson's cleaning shrimp, pistol shrimp, spotted cleaning shrimp and anemone crabs. Diamond blennies are also commonly seen amongst the tentacles of giant Caribbean anemones. These animals gain protection from predators when they are within the anemone's tentacles yet are able to avoid being stung themselves.

The giant Caribbean anemone is one of the more common species of Caribbean anemones. Often reaching a diameter of a foot or more, the animal look like a beautiful undersea flower instead of a marine invertebrate.

Anemones have a body plan that consists of a ring of tentacles connected to a circular disc. The mouth is located in the middle of the disc. Most anemones also have a stalk or base, but the stalk is often blocked from view.

The tentacles of sea anemones are armed with extremely potent stinging cells. Surprisingly there are a number of animals that have adapt-

ploitation and slow growth, trees of most species of black coral are far less common than they were only a few decades ago. Divers who truly appreciate the natural beauty of the reefs should avoid buying black coral in any form.

SEA ANEMONES

Sea anemones are among the most delicate and attractive of all the reef invertebrates. Lacking a hard skeleton, they tend to flow back and forth with the surge. Their long, flowing tentacles often make the

light-green tentacles possess beautiful pink or purple tips which are packed with powerful stinging cells. **Branching anemones** and **sun anemones** are much smaller anemones that grow in very low profile on the reef. The sun anemone enjoys relative obscurity within crevices as does the branching anemone, which is usually partially hidden within the superstructure of the reef.

Corkscrew anemones are also commonly called ringed anemones. This species bears special mention because its stinging tentacles are especially potent. Even the slightest contact with human skin often results in a painful welt. Groups of stinging nematocysts are arranged in lightly colored, corkscrew-shaped rings around the tentacles, giving rise to both of the common names used to describe this anemone. The tentacles of the corkscrew anemone usually are four to six inches in length. They generally appear transparent with the exception of obvious striations. They are also home

AT A GLANCE

CORKSCREW ANEMONE

Scientific Name
Bartholomea annulata
Habitat
Shallow areas at the sand-coral interface or around patch reefs. Projecting from holes in the reef.
Typical Adult Size
6 inches in diameter.
Sightings
Commonly seen.
Natural History
Very powerful stinging cells. Home to cleaner shrimps and pistol shrimp.

PHOTO TIP

Anemones and their inhabitants provide wonderful subject material for macro photography. Not only do the tentacles of anemones make fascinating close-ups, but the fact that they are home to several species of shrimps and diamond blennies makes them a real macro hot spot. Use your extension tube system or a housed camera to explore this community. Be careful not to touch the tips of the anemone as this will cause them to withdraw and spoil the fun!

to Pederson's cleaning shrimp as well as pistol shrimp.

The knobby anemone is often mistaken for the corkscrew anemone because of their similar size and appearance. However, the striations in the tentacles are absent in the knobby anemone. They have small bumps spread uniformly throughout their tentacles, a feature which proves to be a good identifying characteristic. These anemones are also meccas for cleaner shrimps.

Several species of tiny anemone-like **zoanthids** live on sponges. For many years scientists considered zoanthids to be parasites that robbed the sponges of their own feeding surfaces. However, recent studies have rendered this belief to be only partially true. While the zoanthids deprive the host sponges of some feeding surface area, they also help provide vital protection for the sponges against sponge-eating filefishes and angelfishes. Studies have shown that these fishes avoid feeding on sponges that serve as hosts for the zoanthids. Whether it is the foul taste, the potent sting of the zoanthids, or a combination of the two that repels sponge-eating fishes remains a mystery.

Cerianthid anemones, often called **tube-dwelling anemones**, are residents of many sand communities. The banded tentacles of these tube-dwelling anemones are a combination of brown and white. Dur-

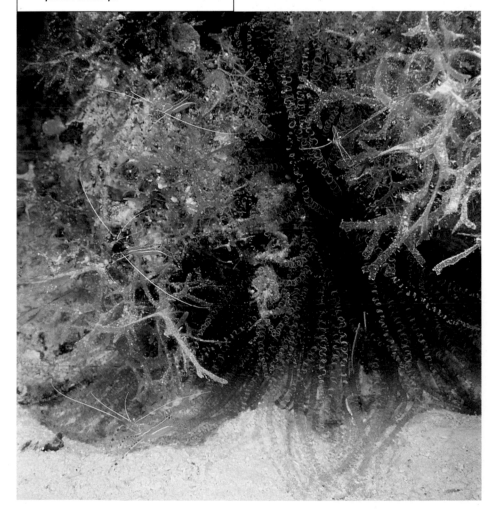

AT A GLANCE

ORANGE BALL ANEMONE, ORANGE BALL CORALLIMORPHARIAN

Scientific Name
Pseudocorynactis caribbeorum
Habitat
Reefs and sand near reef-sand interface.
Typical Adult Size
Disc diameter 1.5 inches.
Sightings
Seldom seen.
Natural History
A corallimorpharian, described in different order than anemones despite common name. Possess radially arranged tentacles as opposed to anemones. Nocturnal feeders that often retract quickly when disturbed or illuminated by a dive light.

either very stubby, or tiny and forked. They radiate out from the center of the oral disc of the polyp, forming concentric circles, a characteristic that can be used to help distinguish corallimorpharians from anemones. In addition, the mouth of a corallimorpharian protrudes outward, while the mouth of an anemone appears low-lying and slit-like. Corallimorpharians are common in very shallow limestone areas and may occasionally be found on the reef.

As far as most Caribbean explorers are concerned, the most noteworthy corallimorpharian is probably the animal we know as the **orange ball anemone,** which should more accurately be named the **orange ball corallimorpharian.** Though actually not a true anemone, it is one of the rarest and most beautiful of all Caribbean species that are commonly referred to as such.

The orange ball corallimorpharian shuns light and is only found on night dives well underneath crevices or within caves. The central disk of an orange ball anemone is often emerald green and the transparent tentacles are resplendent with iridescent orange spherical tips. Once your dive light strikes these anemones, they begin to close up immediately, so be careful to light orange ball anemones only with the periphery of your light.

JELLYFISHES

Jellyfishes are relatively poor swimmers. While they are capable of controlling their attitude and direction to some degree through the pulsating rhythm of their bell, jellyfishes tend to end up wherever the combination of currents, wind, wave action and upwellings take them. Many species of jellyfishes are armed with potent tentacles, and while they cannot pursue divers and snorkelers, they often occur in concentrated numbers due to the con-

ing the day they bury themselves in their tubes and withdraw into the sand. At night they unfurl their tentacles to feed. When you see them, it is usually best to avoid shining your light directly at the anemone because a bright light will cause them to withdraw into their tubes.

Occasionally, several species of anemone-like cnidarians known as **corallimorpharians** catch the attention of observant divers. These small anemones grow very low to the reef and seldom form a tentacular crown in excess of three inches in diameter. Typically, corallimorpharians look like a mat of small anemones. Others, including some of the more prominent species, are solitary.

The tentacles of corallimorpharians are numerous, and usually

stancy of prevailing conditions. As a result, if they are present at all, jellyfishes often occur in large numbers.

From one perspective, the best advice is to beware! If you see one jellyfish, you may well encounter a large number of the same species in the water on that same day. On the other hand, many jellyfishes are gorgeous animals. The combination of the rhythmic pulsations of their bell and their long trail of tentacles provides a sight that tends to mesmerize divers. Some jellyfishes are vividly colored, but many are transparent to off-white. In many natural lighting situations they blend in remarkably well with the light colors of the surrounding waters.

Like other animals, jellyfishes must be able to capture their food, but their lack of control over their own mobility severely limits their ability to pursue prey. Like other members of the phylum Cnidaria, nature has enabled them to solve

AT A GLANCE

MOON JELLY

Scientific Name
Aurelia aurita
Habitat
Open sea, may be carried over reef areas.
Typical Adult Size
6 to 14 inches in diameter.
Sightings
Commonly seen in blooms, often absent at other times.
Natural History
Short, peripheral tentacles are less virulent than many other species. Four prominent gonadal rings in center of bell.

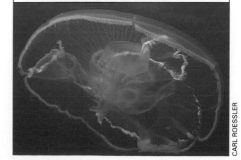

CARL ROESSLER

their problem through the use of potent stinging cells. The potency of a sting on humans varies from very weak in a few species, to extremely painful in many species, to fatal in a few isolated cases. Reaction in humans from jellyfish encounters varies not only from species to species but from person to person.

Not all jellyfish stings prove harmful to humans all the time. The jellyfish commonly called the **moon jelly** have very short tentacles and most people feel only a slight prickly sensation if they touch one. Some people insist they feel nothing at all. However, others have reported intense pain and severe welts caused by contact with moon jellies. The bottom line is, if you touch what you believe to be a moon jelly, you are taking a risk. If you misidentify the species or you are one of the unfortunate people who do suffer a reaction, you can pay heavily for your mistake. And even if touching the jellyfish does not hurt you, handling such a delicate animal can be very harmful to the jellyfish.

It is important to remember that jellyfish do not consciously decide to fire their stinging cells. The process which causes the cnidoblasts to fire is mechanical or chemical, and occurs within fractions of a second. In some cases, even after a jellyfish is dead and has washed up on the beach, the cnidoblasts are still capable of inflicting a potent sting.

Because jellyfishes are such poor swimmers, they must rely on clumsy, unsuspecting or curious prey to blunder into their tentacles. In the majority of jellyfishes the tentacles are difficult to see. They are nearly transparent, much like monofilament fishing line. In some species, though fortunately not in those commonly encountered in the Caribbean, Bahamas and Florida, the tentacles trail out as far as 40 feet behind the bell.

The prey of most jellyfishes consists of small fishes and a variety of planktonic tablefare. Some fishes actually hide amongst the deadly

tentacles. For years it was commonly believed that these fishes were immune to the stinging tentacles, but studies have shown that this is not the case. These fishes are extremely wary and they use the tentacles as a means of protection. But if they accidentally bump into a tentacle, they too will become an ensnared victim.

Sometimes observant divers will see crabs riding on the bell of a jellyfish. Their hard, thick shell protects these crustaceans from the stinging tentacles. The crabs drift along plucking plankton out of the water and at times robbing small bits of food captured by the jellyfish.

Once a jellyfish stings and entangles its prey, it draws in its tentacles and brings the victim under the bell where the mouth is located.

The species of jellyfishes that tend to cause the most problems for divers and swimmers in Caribbean

AT A GLANCE

UPSIDE DOWN JELLYFISH, MANGROVE JELLY

Scientific Name
Cassiopeia xamachana

Habitat
Shallow sand flats in protected back reefs.

Typical Adult Size
Bell, 5 to 8 inches in diameter.

Sightings
Commonly seen in many mangroves, back bays and lagoons with mud or sand bottom.

Natural History
Commonly rest on bottom, on bell with tentacles facing up toward sun to assist growth of symbiotic algae (zooxanthellae) that live within tissues. Jellyfish receive part of their nutrition from algae. Moderately painful, toxic sting that results in rash.

waters are commonly called **sea wasps** (see page 262). Fortunately, these species prefer to inhabit deeper waters during the day when most diving is done. At night, however, sea wasps tend to ascend toward the surface where they feed on plankton. On very calm nights in particular, these jellyfish may amass around the areas where bright lights shine into the water. Be very careful to check the water before making night dive entries and exits, and wear a suit to protect you. Using your secondary regulator to purge the area above you before your ascent on nights when sea wasps have been spotted will help clear the area above you and prevent stings.

Sea wasps are typically less than 10 inches long and many are even smaller, but even the small ones pack a painful punch. The bodies of sea wasps are transluscent, and the animals are difficult to see.

Sea wasps, sometimes called box jellies, derive their name from the

fact that their bell is shaped like a box. Four tentacles are attached to the bell, one on each corner. In some box jellies the tentacles are branched so that it appears that there are far more than four main tentacles, but a close examination reveals otherwise. As a general rule, any jellyfish that has four main tentacles attached to the bell should be avoided.

FIRE CORALS, PORTUGUESE MEN-OF-WAR AND OTHER HYDROIDS

Most hydroids tend to go unnoticed even by well-seasoned divers. But whether conspicuous or not, any diver who has ever come in contact with the potent stinging tentacles of a hydroid is unlikely to ever forget

hydroids are colonial species which look like delicate, white feathers. The branching hydroid is the largest of the Caribbean hydroids and may reach up to 10 inches in length. Feather hydroids form feather-like colonies that grow to about six inches in length. Both of these species are commonly found under overhangs or in caves and will cause pain, itching, and in some cases nasty welts if they touch bare skin. Another colonial species, the **slender hydroid**, looks like a small, budding twig. New divers often mistake colonial hydroids for a type of plant.

Solitary hydroids are typically about the size of a dime, and are found on the very ends of the branches of purple sea plumes. From this perch the hydroids can reach out into the water column and snare their prey of plankton which floats along in the current. While this vantage point is apparently beneficial to the hydroid, its presence appears harmful to the sea plume. The branch of the sea plume near the hydroid often dies and the sea plume will not bear polyps close to the hydroid.

Many divers have never seen a solitary hydroid despite years of Caribbean diving because of the hydroid's small size and light coloration. However, once you discover one in a location, you can probably find them on almost any dive. Solitary hydroids are quite common in the waters of the Cayman Islands and Belize, but they are uncommon on reefs from the U.S. Virgin Islands

AT A GLANCE

CHRISTMAS TREE HYDROIDS

Scientific Name
Halocordyle disticha
Habitat
Reef.
Typical Adult Size
1.5 inches.
Sightings
Commonly seen.
Natural History
Extremely potent stinging cells are used to capture prey and to deter predators.

their painful experience. Certainly that is the case with the **Portuguese man-of-war** and the **fire corals**, which are actually more closely related to hydroids than they are to any other class of cnidarians.

Some hydroids are colonial and others are solitary. **Christmas tree hydroids** form tiny colonies whose stinging polyps appear like ornaments hanging from a miniature Christmas tree.

Branching hydroids and **feather**

Divers and boaters most commonly sight the Portuguese man-of-war by noting the purple float bobbing along on the surface. Underneath the float trail tentacles packed with extremely potent stinging cells. The tentacles may trail back for twenty feet or more in some cases. The virulent stinging cells in the tentacles will readily paralyze small pelagic fishes, and they will inflict an extremely painful sting on humans. Depending upon the sever-

AT A GLANCE

PORTUGUESE MAN-OF-WAR

Scientific Name
Physalia physalis
Habitat
Surface waters, usually in open sea, but occasionally drift over reefs.
Typical Adult Size
Float, 6 inches; tentacles trail from several feet to several yards.
Sightings
Occasionally seen as a rule, but sometimes commonly seen.
Natural History
Potent stinging cells in tentacles prove deadly to variety of small fishes, and can be very serious for humans.

AT A GLANCE

SOLITARY HYDROID

Scientific Name
Not possible to distinguish exact species from photograph.
Habitat
Reef, atop sea plumes.
Typical Adult Size
.75 inch diameter.
Sightings
Commonly seen.
Natural History
Very powerful stinging cells used to secure prey and protect hydroid. Live on the ends of sea plume branches.

south to Bonaire.

Despite its appearance, the Portuguese man-of-war is not a type of jellyfish, but actually a hydroid.

AT A GLANCE

BRANCHING FIRE CORAL

Scientific Name
Millepora alcicornis

Habitat
Reef, often overgrows various gorgonians.

Typical Adult Size
Branch-like clumps vary considerably from a few inches high to more than 2 feet.

Sightings
Commonly seen.

Natural History
Extremely virulent stinging nematocysts capture prey, provide defense, and allow them to invade and overtake other corals.

ity of the encounter and the reaction that occurs, medical attention may be required.

A number of small or juvenile fishes often use the tentacles as a place to hide in as they seek safety from potential predators. Juvenile triggerfishes are commonly seen swimming only fractions of an inch from the deadly tentacles. But hiding in the tentacles can prove to be

a dangerous game for the triggerfish, and occasionally one inadvertently becomes a meal for the Portuguese man-of-war.

Fish commonly known as man-of-war fishes can also be found swimming amongst the tentacles of the Portuguese man-of-war. Their relationship with the man-of-war is described as mutualism, a type of relationship in which both members benefit and neither is harmed. These fish do not appear to be at risk, however, some specialists question this conclusion.

Despite their hard or stony appearance, the structures commonly called **fire corals** are not really corals. Fire corals are actually more closely related to hydroids, Portuguese men-of-war and other animals known as siphonophores than they are to true reef-building corals.

While the use of the word "coral" might be incorrect according to a purely scientific definition, the term "fire" is most appropriate. Contact with fire coral can cause an immediate, intense, burning pain. The sting will often develop into an angry red welt or rash that will itch

for days, and in some cases for several weeks.

Fire corals occur in several different forms, all of which should be put into the category of "look, but don't touch." If you look closely at any fire coral, you are likely to see a number of fine, hair-like structures. These structures contain the stinging cells and should be vigorously avoided.

PHOTO TIP

Fire corals make wonderful photographic subjects. Backlighting and sidelighting techniques often work well with fire corals, as these highlight the fine, hair-like tentacles. A nice progression for dissolve slide shows or for side by side prints is to first show a macro shot of fire coral which is lit from the front, and then show the same macro setup, but with extreme side or backlighting. In the first shot the translucent stinging tentacles are often invisible, while in the second shot they stand out around the silhouetted branches of the fire coral.

8

Phyla: *Platyhelminthes* and *Annelida*

MARINE WORMS

When compared to other animals, worms appear to be rather simple creatures, yet they have so many fundamental differences that scientists describe these creatures in a number of different phyla. Two of these include marine worms, and representatives of both are found in Caribbean waters. These are the flatworms of the phylum Platyhelminthes, and the segmented worms described in the phylum Annelida. A discussion of both groups follows.

FLATWORMS
(Phylum: *Platyhelminthes*)

Somewhere in the neighborhood of 30,000 species of worms are described in the phylum Platyhelminthes. The vast majority of these worms (approximately 25,000 species) are parasitic creatures such as tapeworms. Needless to say, most are rather unattractive species. However, many of their marine relatives—the approximately 4,000 species commonly called flatworms—are especially beautiful.

Polyclad flatworms are free-living, non-parasitic worms that are

Feather duster worms are a classic example of how Mother Nature has bestowed great beauty on the marine worms. The lovely crown of a feather duster is actually a vital organ called the areole, which is used by the worm to strip dissolved oxygen and food particles from seawater. Feather duster worms are segmented worms and are described in the phylum Annelida.

often mistaken for nudibranchs. The extremely flattened bodies of flatworms make it easy to differentiate them from thicker-bodied nudibranchs and sea slugs with only a little practice. The forward end of polyclad flatworms has two small sensory flaps that look almost like cat ears.

Flatworms display obvious bilateral symmetry, meaning that their bodies have a distinct head and rear, top and bottom, and their right and left sides are identical mirror images of each other. Bilateral symmetry is an important evolutionary development. As opposed to the radial symmetry found in cnidarians such as corals and anemones, bilateral symmetry is the basic body plan in all

advanced animals that have specialized body parts and organ systems. Bilaterally symmetrical animals are

AT A GLANCE

POLYCLAD FLATWORM, FLATWORM

Scientific Name
Pseudoceros pardalis
Habitat
Reef; under coral rubble and other debris.
Typical Adult Size
2 to 4 inches.
Sightings
Seldom seen.
Natural History
Crawl about the reef feeding on small invertebrates. Very sensitive to light.

more efficient in moving from place to place, a trait which enables them to pursue their food, escape predation, seek mates, and change locations. Animals which display radial symmetry, such as coral polyps, sea anemones and jellyfishes, tend to live their lives either in a more sedentary fashion, or drifting in currents with comparatively little control over their own mobility.

Several other flatworm characteristics are noteworthy. Flatworms are very sensitive to light, and many species try to avoid brightly lit areas. While they lack other sophisti-cated organ systems, flatworms do possess bundles of light-sensitive nerves that can be described as primitive eyes.

Free-living flatworms are both carnivores and scavengers, and most species are highly cannibalistic. Some species take advantage of a mutually beneficial relationship with algae living in their tissues. The algae produce food for the flatworm as a by-product of their own photosynthesis. Many smaller flatworms pursue their prey and generally move about by crawling on specialized cilia-laden cells. Some cells on their underside secrete mucus which also helps the animals glide across the sea floor. In some larger species the cilia are used to push food particles and water along the underside of the animal, and they are not used in locomotion.

Flatworms are hermaphroditic, meaning the same individual possesses both male and female reproductive capabilities at the same time. However, self-fertilization is not the rule. When they mate, each partner deposits sperm in the copulatory sac of its mate. Cross-fertilization presents an interesting dilemma for a species that is also cannibalistic. Exactly how flatworms distinguish between a reproductive encounter and an attack is not well understood. Fertilized eggs are released in the water and develop into planktonic larvae before settling down to live a benthic existence as adults.

Interestingly, some flatworms also reproduce by asexual means. In these species an animal that loses a part not only displays remarkable regenerative properties by recreating the lost part, but that body part often regenerates an entirely new flatworm! Marine flatworms are often found in relatively shallow rubble zones as they crawl on and under the rubble. This debris is often moved around in rough seas and can pin and tear the bodies of flatworms. For many species such an event would be life-threatening, but the amazing regenerative abilities of some flatworms enable them to use rough sea conditions to their advantage.

Divers usually spot flatworms on the bottom, but at times some species swim by using an undulating motion of their body. Most species are between three and six inches long, but despite their relatively small stature, flatworms are always fun to discover!

AT A GLANCE

SPOTTED FEATHER DUSTER

Scientific Name
Branchioma nigromaculata
Habitat
Reef.
Typical Adult Size
Gill whorl approximately 3.5 inches in diameter.
Sightings
Commonly seen.
Natural History
Very sensitive gill whorl that will snap into their parchment-like tube when variations in light or water pressure caused by movement disturb them.

SEGMENTED WORMS
(Phylum: *Annelida*)

TUBEWORMS, FEATHER DUSTERS, CHRISTMAS TREE WORMS AND BRISTLE WORMS

Mother Nature was extremely lavish in the beauty she bestowed upon the marine worms. Some species, such as **Christmas tree worms** and **feather duster worms**, live in permanent or semipermanent tubes of their own construction. Divers often see their exposed gill plumes (technically referred to as radioles) which look like a whorl of colorful feathers extending from the tube. In many species the feathers are both

PHOTO TIP

The colorful whorls that are the gills of Christmas tree and various feather duster worms have long been sought after as subjects by underwater photographers. Frustration, rather than the dream image, is often the end-result of a first attempt when we try to photograph their ornate whorls, because the worms are extremely sensitive to movements and changes in light. Approach them very slowly with your Nikonos and 1:2 framer, and don't be surprised or too disappointed if they quickly seek cover in the protection of their tubes. While they are withdrawn set your framer in place and be very still, for soon (usually within 10 minutes) they will open up like a bouquet between the wands of your framer. Each time the strobe fires they will again withdraw, but will soon reemerge. One tip to remember is that Christmas tree worms found in very shallow areas—where water movement is likely and light shifts are common—are far less sensitive to your presence. Often these worms will not withdraw as you place them inside your framer, and on many occasions they won't even retract between shots!

beautifully colored and quite delicate. Obviously, these lovely animals are a far cry from their terrestrial counterparts. Other species of segmented worms such as **bristle worms** do not live in tubes and are called free-living, meaning they crawl across the bottom.

Worldwide, there are approximately 8,000 species of segmented marine worms described in the class Polychaeta. The term segmented means that the bodies of these worms are divided into distinct sections. These worms have complete digestive, excretory, respiratory, circulatory and nervous systems as well as a number of sensory organs.

In polychaete worms the sexes are typically separate. Fertilization is usually external, and sperm are dispersed over egg masses that are attached to the bottom or floating in the water column. Interestingly,

many male polychaetes do not have permanent gonads. Sperm is produced in cells that line the body cavity. This trait is not typical of other classes within the phylum.

Fertilization produces larval animals called trochophores which look and move like tiny, hairy missiles. They are similar in appearance to the larvae of mollusks. The trochophores dart about through the plankton where they grow, adding segments to their bodies. Some settle and live out their adult lives as bottom dwellers, while other species are pelagic (meaning they live in the water column, not on the bottom) as adults.

Numerous species of segmented worms known as **tube worms** depend upon currents to bring them their food, which consists primarily of a mixture of tiny plankton and organic matter that is filtered from moving water via an intricate sieve/gill mechanism. These sedentary species use feather-like gill plumes to sieve their food and extract oxygen from the water. The tube-dwelling marine worm called a **terrebellid** has white, sticky tentacles which reach out several feet from the tube and stick to the seabed. The tentacles serve as the capture mechanism for food, while cilia on the tentacles sweep the food particles to the mouth in a conveyor-belt fashion.

In sharp contrast to the tube-dwelling worms, free-living species such as bristle worms are able to actively pursue their prey. These worms are mobile predators equipped with formidable muscular jaws, and they have well-developed sense organs that enable them to find their prey.

Divers usually notice the sedentary polychaetes when they see the colorful, feather-like gill plumes. The gill plumes represent only a small portion of the body, and the rest of the animal lives in a self-constructed tube that is either attached to the bottom or burrowed into hard corals and sponges. These worms play an important part in many ma-

AT A GLANCE

CHRISTMAS TREE WORM

Scientific Name
Spirobranchus grandis
Habitat
Reef.
Typical Adult Size
1-inch diameter.
Sightings
Commonly seen.
Natural History
Christmas tree-shaped double gill whorl strips oxygen and food from the seawater. Gills snap in and close a calcified trap door behind them to protect the worm from predators.

rine food chains, being heavily preyed upon by a variety of animals, especially fishes.

Since sedentary worms are attached and cannot flee, their best means of defense is to quickly withdraw into their tubes at the first sign of danger. Often the slightest movement by a diver or a shadow cast will cause these tube dwellers to retract. If you are patient, the gill plumes will probably reemerge before too long, but they will quickly withdraw again if the animal senses any sign of potential danger.

When Christmas tree worms

withdraw their gill plumes, they close their tube with a hard trap door called an operculum. In many species, the operculum is equipped with one or more spines to further deter predators.

AT A GLANCE

RED FAN WORM

Scientific Name
Pomastegus stellatus
Habitat
Atop lettuce, star and finger corals.
Typical Adult Size
1 to 3 inches.
Sightings
Commonly seen.
Natural History
Tube of red fan worm lengthens as animal grows in order to keep pace with growing coral preventing tentacular crown, which plays vital role in respiration, from being overgrown.

Some types of sedentary polychaete worms live in parchment-like tubes which they build. The tubes are made from sand and other inorganic debris combined with secretions from these worms.

Many species of sedentary polychaete worms inhabit the waters of the Caribbean, Bahamas and Florida. These species include **Christmas tree worms**, **spotted feather duster worms**, **giant feather duster worms**, **colonial feather duster worms (Sabellid worms)**, **yellow fan worms**, **red fan worms** and **colonial serpulid worms**. Several of these are pictured in this chapter.

Free-living bristle worms are also extremely colorful creatures. Their typically orange to red to green bodies are bordered with snow-white tufts of fine, bristle-like fibers. While bristle worms appear to be delicate creatures, a bit of advice is

in order. The calciferous tufts, called setae, are somewhat like thin, sharp glass needles and provide a formidable defense around the bodies of these worms. Occasionally, divers will make the mistake of handling bristle worms. Big mistake! The fine, glass-like spines are venomous, and they are quickly embedded into even the thickest of calluses. So while you can't help but admire their beautiful colors, handling them should remain out of the question.

Bristle worms reach a length of about 12 inches, but average size is about 3 to 5 inches long. They are commonly found crawling under coral rubble and other debris in rubble zones. Voracious eaters, bristle worms are often seen crawling on animals upon which they prey. Their favorite prey includes the hydroids, commonly called fire corals; a variety of corals, including

AT A GLANCE

BRISTLE WORM

Scientific Name
Hermodice carunculata

Habitat
Reef, atop gorgonians, on coral heads, on sponges, on sand, and under and on coral rubble.

Typical Adult Size
3 to 10 inches.

Sightings
Common, but not always easy to find.

Natural History
Very fine glass-like bristles covering the body are used to deter predators. These are free-living worms. Typically more active as nocturnal feeders.

PHOTO TIP

Bristle worms make wonderful subjects because of their spectacular color combinations (orange to red and white) and because they are interesting-looking animals. A Nikonos 1:3 extension tube system is the perfect size for many bristle worms. An accessory close-up framer, or a single lens reflex camera with a 50 to 60mm lens, will probably work better with larger specimens. When using an extension tube, notice the worm flare the snowy white bristles that surround its body as soon as you put your framer around it. The reaction may serve as a warning to any predator foolish enough to get close to the glass-sharp spines, or it may be the worm's way of readying its arsenal. Have your camera ready as you place your framer around the worm and shoot as soon as the animal flares its bristles. The flared bristles add eye-catching impact. But be careful, you are playing with fire!

AT A GLANCE

SEA FROST

Scientific Name
Filograna sp.

Habitat
Colonies tend to be in deep, quiet waters, often in caves, and often attached to black coral.

Typical Adult Size
10 inches.

Sightings
Occasionally seen.

Natural History
Colonial worms live in a mass of intertwined calciferous tubes cemented together in clumps which sometimes lack order. Worms feed on particulate matter that drift past in the almost imperceptible currents.

some gorgonians and hard corals; and even large sea anemones. Bristle worms are also known to scavenge on dead animals.

Several other species of free-living polychaete worms also inhabit Caribbean reefs. These species include the **red-tipped fireworm**, the **rough scaleworm**, the **zebra worm** and the **Atlantic palolo worm**. One of the more unusual species is the tiny, white **sponge worm** which is often found on the toxic sponge known as the dread red or touch-me-not sponge.

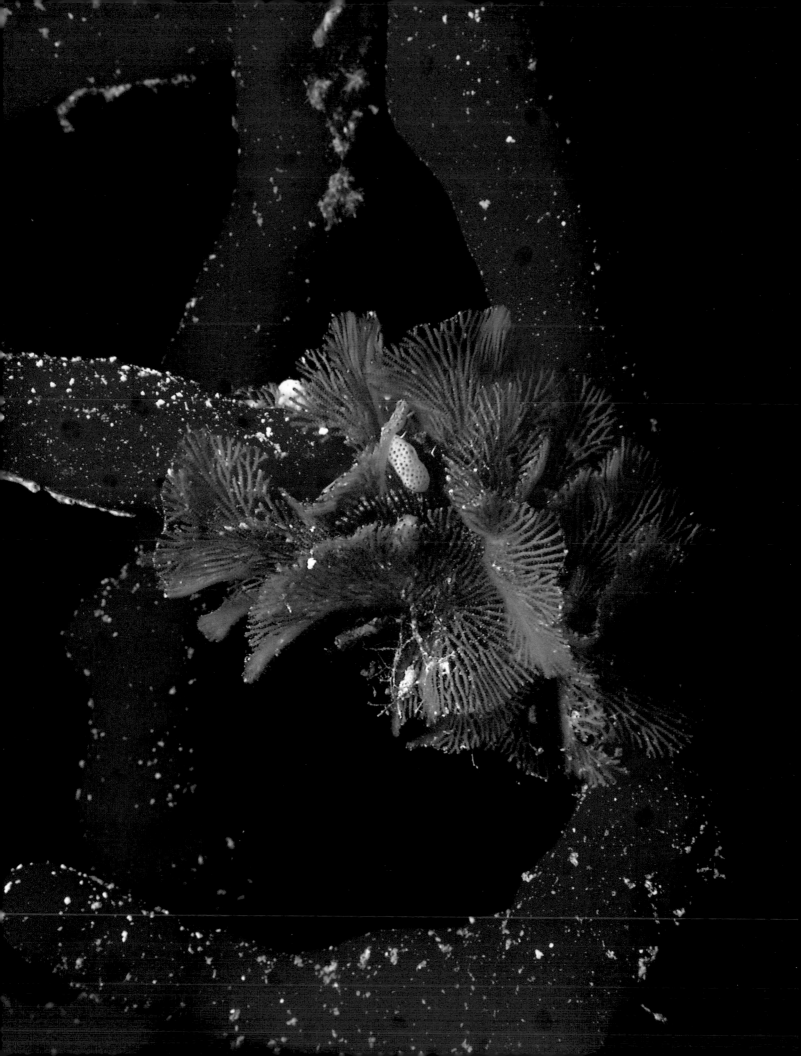

9

PHYLUM: *Bryozoa (Ectoprocta)*

BRYOZOANS

*B*ryozoans are obscure and seldom noticed by most divers, and yet one species, *Schizoporella floridana*, literally built much of south Florida with their calcite skeletons.

If you have never heard of a bryozoan, you are certainly not alone, despite the fact that there are somewhere between 4,000 and 5,000 species worldwide. The small colonial animals are often found on sargassum weed, or in reef communities attached to the substrate or other organisms.

Some species bear a resemblance to moss, and in fact the name bryozoan is derived from the Greek words for "moss" and "animals." Most bryozoans are lightly colored in hues of pink, tan, brown, beige, orange or white. Colonies range in size from only a few inches to several feet across, but even the larger colonies tend to have rather low profiles. Many species look similar to very fine lace-like corals, and even experienced divers commonly mistake the two. Others are occasionally confused with a family of marine worms known as serpulid worms, animals which live inside of white, interwoven calciferous tubes.

An individual colony of bryozoans is often composed of thousands of individual animals all contained

---

AT A GLANCE

BROWN FAN BRYOZOAN

Scientific Name
  Canda simplex
Habitat
  Protected areas of reef communities attached to substrate.
Typical Adult Size
  Colonies 1 to 4 inches.
Sightings
  Commonly seen.
Natural History
  Lives in fan-shaped colonies often around base of coral heads, in crevices, and under ledges in protected areas with little surge or current.

AT A GLANCE

WHITE TANGLED BRYOZOAN

Scientific Name
  Bracebridgia subsulcata
Habitat
  Walls, under ledges and in protected areas.
Typical Adult Size
  Colony 2 to 5 inches.
Sightings
  Occasionally seen.
Natural History
  Often attach to rope sponges and trees of black coral.

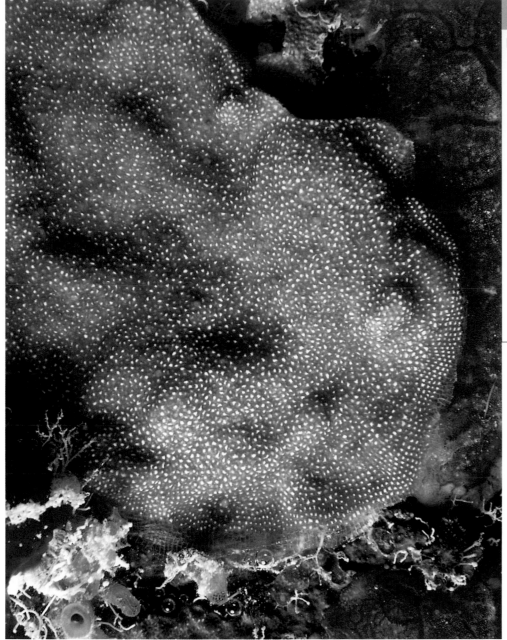

BLEEDING TEETH BRYOZOAN, ORANGE ENCRUSTING BRYOZOAN, BRYOZOAN

Scientific Name
Trematooecia aviculifera

Habitat
Protected areas around reefs with little surge or current, often at base of coral heads, under ledges, and in crevices.

Typical Adult Size
1 to 4 inches in diameter.

Sightings
Commonly seen.

Natural History
Live in thin, encrusting red, pink, orange and gold colonies. Often appear green without use of dive light. Surface of colony appears beaded.

within a common skeletal network. Each animal within the colony is called a zooid. The zooids are well developed, with each containing several intricate organ systems, including respiratory, circulatory, digestive, excretory, muscular and nervous systems. Individual zooids within the colony are specialized to perform certain functions for the good of the whole. Those zooids, whose primary function is to provide defense, are equipped with jaws that enable them to bite intruding organisms.

An anatomical characteristic found in bryozoans is the presence of a small, feather-like organ called a lophophore. This organ helps trap tiny organic particles of food as the animal filters the water.

Bryozoans possess both male and female reproductive organs at the same time. In some species sperm and eggs are produced at the same time, and in other species the cycle of production alternates. Some species of free-swimming larvae are left to fend for themselves, while in others the fertilized eggs are held in a specific brooding area within the colony.

Caribbean bryozoans vary in appearance. Few species have common names, and the animals are usually referred to only in general terms.

Some bryozoans are often confused with serpulid worms, but with a little practice a careful observer can tell them apart.

DISCOVERING THE NIGHT REEF

Nighttime is the best time to discover many of the rarest and most unusual creatures along the reef. However, in order to find these animals, many of which are cryptically camouflaged and tiny, it really pays to slow down. A slower pace during a night dive will often be rewarded with the discovery of interesting nocturnal reef creatures.

A good dive light really helps you focus on the sometimes elusive creatures of the night reef. A head- or camera-mounted system allows the full use of your hands to manipulate dive or camera gear. The advantages such systems offer will become most evident when searching or photographing during a night dive.

There is a completely new cast of characters on the night reef. Many reef fishes which hustle by day, rest at night. They have settled into a state called torpor, which is a kind of nightly hibernation. A "changing of the guard" occurs as the nocturnal animals become active and crawl or swim to the top of the reef structure to feed and reproduce. The large-eyed squirrelfishes and cardinalfishes which are under ledges by day, arc up above the reef by night as they seek out their food. Big eyes discern shapes and movement in the pale wash of the moon and starlight. Octopuses slither amongst the coral crevices, moving with a curious fluidity. As your dive light strikes them, they may freeze like some cat burglar caught out on the prowl. Their colors and skin texture change almost instantly to reflect their emotional state or to match the reef surface as they melt into it. Squids patrol the night water column. Their color cells—chromatophores—sparkle and flare as they hunt. Brittle stars also emerge from the protective lumen of sponges or from reef crevices. Basket stars unfurl their net-like arms once they have crept to the ends of reef outcroppings and onto tall gorgonians. Food-bearing currents deliver plankton to their sticky, forked arms.

Cantankerous crabs and lobsters bear claws and flail spiky antennae as they forage openly on the same reefs which, by day, they take refuge within. These are only a few of the more obvious cast of characters which await you as you explore the night reef.

But there are also tiny jewels whose size is in no way indicative of their great beauty. Colorful nudibranchs leave the cover of crevices to feed on gorgonians, sponges and algae. Decorator crabs reach out into the water column, and the stinging hydroids which adorn their legs catch passing food delivered up by the currents. Orange ball anemones, closed by day, are truly resplendent by night as they unfurl their spherical orange-tipped tentacles.

If you have the chance, don't miss a journey into the ecosystem of the night reef. You'll will be rewarded with some of your most precious underwater sights.—Clay Wiseman

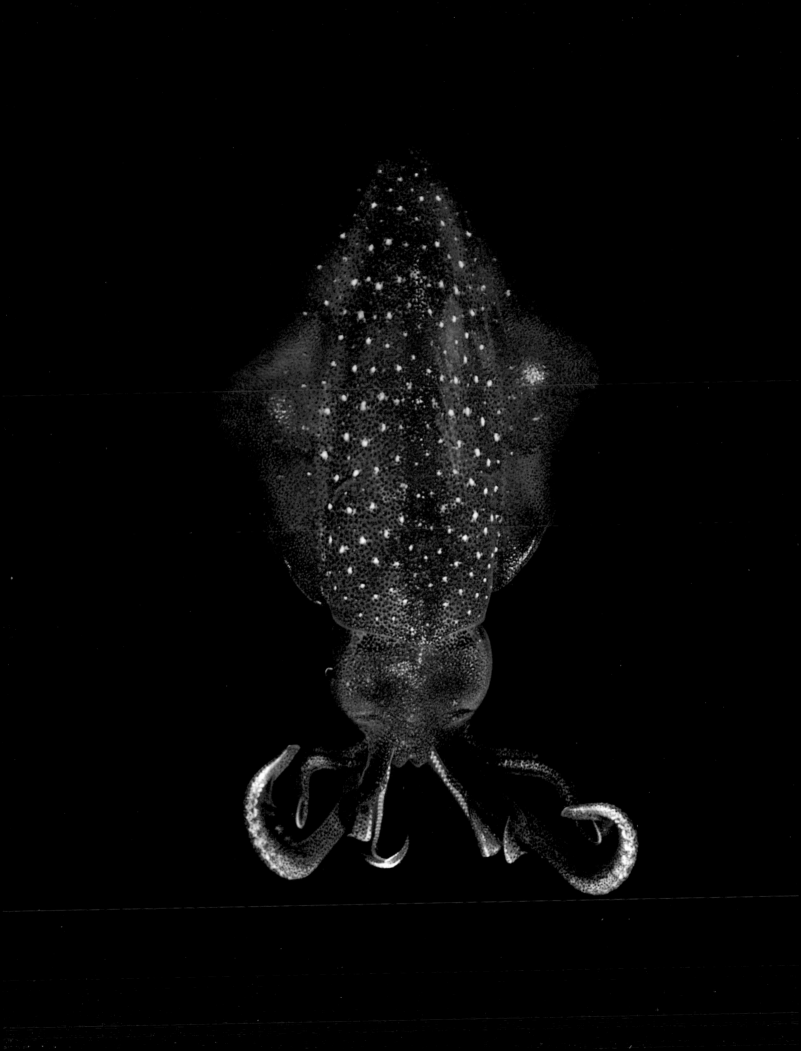

10

Phylum: *Mollusca*

Nudibranchs, Sea Slugs, Snails, Sea Hares, Clams, Scallops, Oysters, Mussels, Octopuses and Squids

Inhabiting marine, freshwater and terrestrial ecosystems, present-day mollusks are a very successful group of animals. The only phylum with more species is that of the arthropods and perhaps the nematodes, a group of worms which are not discussed in this text. To date, scientists have classified more than 110,000 species of mollusks, and new discoveries are being made on a regular basis. Of the known species, approximately 75,000 live in either fresh or salt water.

Compared to members of many other phyla, mollusks are highly developed animals. They have distinct organ systems and sophisticated sensory capabilities. In fact, many specialists consider octopuses and squids to be the most intelligent of all the marine invertebrates.

Certain characteristics are com-

The marine mollusks include snails, nudibranchs, sea hares, sea slugs, chitons, clams, scallops, oysters, octopuses (either the word octopi or octopuses is a correct plural of the word octopus), cuttlefishes and squids. Obviously, mollusks are an incredibly diverse group. Pictured here is an Atlantic oval squid, also called a Caribbean reef squid.

mon to all mollusks. All are bilaterally symmetrical (they are organized fore and aft), all have a brain, or concentrated bundles of nerves, and all possess a specialized organ called the mantle, which surrounds the body and is capable in many species of secreting a hard shell. The bodies of mollusks are separated into three parts: the visceral mass, the head and the foot. The organs of their digestive, excretory and reproductive systems are contained inside the visceral mass. At one end of the body in many mollusks, there is a distinctly recognizable head which contains the brain or concentrated nerve ganglia. In its most obvious form, the foot is like a muscular hook which is used to pull these animals along the bottom, but in other mollusks such as octopuses and squids, the foot is highly modified.

The mantle is a thin flap of flesh that often covers the body. In many species the mantle can be withdrawn and folded into overlapping flaps next to the visceral mass. In those species that have a shell, the mantle secretes and maintains the shell. In some species, such as the flamingo tongue snail, the mantle secretes flaps that are quite hand-

some. In octopuses and squids the mantle has been greatly modified to assist in swimming. While the mantles of these animals are very flexible, they are also thick, strong and muscular.

In some mollusks the mantle controls the flow of water over the gills through an alternating cycle of contraction and expansion. When the animal is stressed, a squid or an octopus can forcibly contract the mantle which simultaneously forces a powerful stream of water through the opening of a highly directable tube called a siphon. Operating like a natural jet engine, the stream of water pushes the animal in the opposite direction.

The gills of mollusks are located in the mantle cavity, a chamber under the mantle. In most species the gills contain numerous blood vessels which allow for a very efficient exchange of gases. Many mollusks are able to extract more than 50 percent of the dissolved oxygen from the water that passes over their gills.

Almost all mollusks have a muscular foot that is used for locomotion, digging and attachment, and in some species the highly modified foot assists in swimming. Snails utilize their foot to crawl across the bottom. These mollusks actually glide across the bottom on a slippery material they create to help them crawl. Clams use their modified foot to help them dig and burrow, while octopuses walk or crawl with a foot that has been highly modified into eight tentacles.

Many mollusks have an external shell which is readily apparent in snails, scallops and oysters, but at first glance appears to be missing in squids, nudibranchs and octopuses. Squids have an internalized shell which has been greatly reduced, while adult nudibranchs and octopuses have done away with a shell altogether.

The shells of mollusks occur in one of three general forms. Some species have a single shell which is often shaped in a spiral configuration. Other species have two shells that are hinged together. These species are referred to as the bivalve (two-shelled) mollusks. The third group, such as chitons, have eight overlapping shells that are arranged in a row. The shell of a mollusk thickens and enlarges throughout the course of the animal's life as the mantle continuously adds to the mass of the protective shell.

Another commonly shared anatomical characteristic of most mollusks, with the exception of the bivalves, is the presence of a rasping, tongue-like organ called a radula. Although the radula varies from species to species depending primarily on the preferred diet, some generalizations can be made. As a rule, the radula is hard and has a number of rows of backward curving teeth. It can be moved at will and is used by grazing mollusks to scrape algae and other food off of sponges, corals and seagrasses. Predatory mollusks, such as octopuses and squids, use their radula to puncture their victims and extract food from their prey, which consists largely of crabs. Some species inject a paralyzing toxin as part of their attack strategy.

Bivalve mollusks, such as scallops and clams, are filter feeders and have no use for a radula. It is believed that these animals have lost their radula through the course of evolution.

In most mollusks, the sexes are separate. However, in some bivalves, snails and sea slugs, a single animal possesses both male and female reproductive organs at the same time. These animals are called hermaphrodites. But even in these species, cross-fertilization rather than self-fertilization is the norm. In some oysters a single animal frequently changes its sex several times during a single spawning season. Those snails described in the genus *Crepidula* form a pile, and amazingly, the one on the bottom becomes a female. And we think human sexuality is difficult to deal with!

The larvae of most marine mollusks are tiny, free-swimming animals called trochophores. They are propelled through the water by a row of hair-like cilia that forms a circle around the middle of their body. In bivalves and most snails a second free-swimming stage follows. In the second stage the animal is called a veliger and the beginnings of the foot, mantle and shell become apparent. Both trochophores and veligers drift in open sea currents, a fact which helps account for the wide range of many species of mollusks.

Most mollusks are relatively small animals, measuring only an inch to a couple of inches in diameter. Many species are considerably smaller. There are also some notable exceptions on the opposite end of the spectrum. Although little is known about the natural history of the giant squid, these cephalopod mollusks have been documented to reach a size of 65 feet long and weigh as much as 550 pounds. Giant squid are the largest mollusk, but not necessarily the heaviest. That honor goes to the giant clams of the Indo-Pacific whose shells alone can weigh as much as 600 pounds.

Depending on their school of thought, evolutionary specialists divide mollusks into either six or seven classes. Of these, only three play a major role in Caribbean reef communities. One class (Gastropoda) includes snails, nudibranchs and sea slugs. Another class (Bivalvia) includes clams, scallops, oysters and mussels. The third class (Cephalopoda) includes squids, cuttlefishes and octopuses.

NUDIBRANCHS, SEA SLUGS AND SNAILS

With more than 80,000 described species of snails, sea slugs, nudibranchs and limpets, the gastropods are the largest class of mollusks. Many gastropods move across the bottom by creeping along on a muscular foot. In some species the foot has been modified to assist in swimming. Gastropods have a single shell, which has been lost during evolution in groups such as the nudibranchs and sea slugs, at least in their adult stage. However, there is clear evidence that both nudibranchs and sea slugs descend from ancestors that possessed a shell, as members of both groups possess larval shells.

When feeling threatened, many gastropods can protect themselves by fully withdrawing into their protective shells. In addition, the opening to the shells can be closed by these animals when they shut a hatch-like plate called an operculum.

The head of snails, nudibranchs, sea slugs and other gastropods is readily discernible from the rest of the body. A pair of tentacles on which the eyes are located can be found on the head of most gastropods. However, in some species the tentacles have been lost. The opening to the mouth is quite simple in some, while in others the mouth has been modified into a long, beak-like proboscis. The radula is located in the mouth.

PHOTO TIP

Both the lettuce leaf and the banana nudibranchs are great macro subjects. While the banana nudibranch is most likely to be found in the evening, it is possible to find lettuce leaf nudibranchs, or saccoglossans, day or night as long as you are searching in fairly shallow reef areas, particularly where there is a healthy growth of filamentous algae. During night dives look for banana nudibranchs feeding on purple-colored bushy sea whips. A Nikonos camera with a 1:1 framer is a good choice for your photographic system, as is a housed single lens reflex system with a 100mm macro lens and a flat port.

Gastropods feed on a wide variety of foods. Some species are grazers, and scrape algae and other food off the sea floor. Some other species are scavengers, and still others are active predators. The radula of many predatory snails is used to bore holes into their prey, a group of animals which includes other species of shelled mollusks. Once the hole is bored the tissues are rasped out by the radula.

Most gastropods have a single spiral-shaped shell. The protective shell is created by secretions from the mantle which include calcium carbonate extracted from the surrounding sea water. The shells of many gastropods are beautifully designed and each species produces a shell that is unique.

Interestingly, nudibranchs and sea slugs have lost their protective shells. However, these animals have developed a very effective alternative means of self-defense. Nudibranchs often create chemical-laden secretions that are noxious to potential predators. In other words, many nudibranchs rely on the fact that they taste bad. In other species of nudibranchs, the animals are able to utilize the stinging cells of certain corals, hydroids and other cnidarians that they feed on by transferring the unfired nematocysts to the cerata (sack-like projections) on their backs. These cerata then hold a powerful cache of arms that provide a formidable defense.

Also seen is the **banana nudibranch**, a cream-colored mollusk whose back is covered with countless cerata resembling miniature bunches of bananas. These slugs are typically seen during night dives as they are very active nocturnal feeders that are partial to the tissues of purple-colored bushy sea whips.

The animal commonly referred to as the **lettuce leaf nudibranch** is also known as the **saccoglossan**. Located within the bodies of these 1.5-

AT A GLANCE

BANANA NUDIBRANCH, WHITE-SPECKLED NUDIBRANCH

Scientific Name
Phyllodesmimum sp.
Habitat
On coral debris, and on and around some sponges and gorgonians.
Typical Adult Size
3 inches.
Sightings
Occasionally seen.
Natural History
Active nocturnal feeders that are partial to the tissues of purple-colored bushy sea whips.

to 2-inch-long sea slugs is a natural greenhouse. These industrious slugs browse the reef areas for their meal of algae, but they digest only part of their take, the cytoplasm which they suck out of the algal cells. The undigested portion includes the intact chloroplasts which are stored in the lettuce-like frills on their backs, and continue to photosynthesize and provide nutrition for the saccoglossan. These slugs can be seen crawling over algae-covered areas of many Caribbean reefs.

Several larger sea slugs inhabit beds of seagrasses in many parts of the Caribbean. These species include the **spotted sea hare**, the **black-rimmed sea hare**, the **black sea hare**, the **ragged sea hare** and the **warty sea cat**. These sea slugs have thicker bodies and prominent rhinophores (a second pair of tentacles found in some mollusks) which extend from their heads. These slugs often hide under coral rubble and rocks during the day, but will move about to feed at night. They emit purple clouds of an ink-like substance when they are harassed or threatened, a defensive ploy which is believed to confuse or somehow deter potential predators.

In Caribbean waters, many gastropods are found in beds of seagrass rather than in the reef community. Perhaps the most prominent reef community representatives are the snails that are commonly referred to as flamingo tongue cowries, actually **flamingo tongue snails**. In the case of these beautiful gastropods, we once again find a conflict between accurate scientific classification and laymen's language. These animals are actually snails, but they are sometimes called cowries. The same is true of their near relative, the rare **fingerprint snail**, referred to by some divers as the **fingerprint cowrie**.

AT A GLANCE

LETTUCE LEAF NUDIBRANCH, SACCOGLOSSAN

Scientific Name
Tridachia crispata

Habitat
Reef, especially in algae-covered areas.

Typical Adult Size
3 inches.

Sightings
Commonly seen where algae growth is heavy.

Natural History
This sea slug feeds on algae and stores the undigested, intact chloroplasts from the algae in frilly gills on its back. Remarkably, the chloroplasts continue to photosynthesize and provide food for the slug.

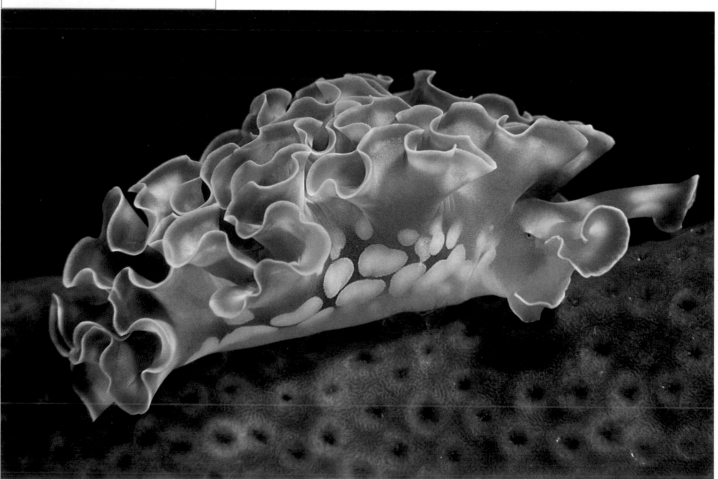

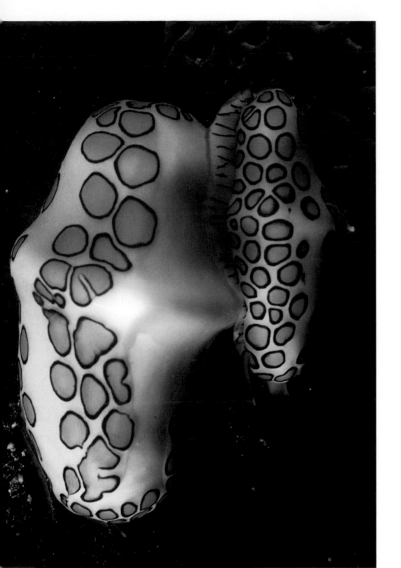

AT A GLANCE

FLAMINGO TONGUE SNAIL

Scientific Name
Cyphoma gibbosum
Habitat
Reef, shallows.
Typical Adult Size
1.5 inches.
Sightings
Commonly seen.
Natural History
Beautiful leopard-skin pattern of mantle tissue often covers shell. Mantle secretes and maintains shell.

AT A GLANCE

FINGERPRINT SNAIL

Scientific Name
Cyphoma signatum
Habitat
Reef, shallows.
Typical Adult Size
1.5 inches.
Sightings
Seldom seen.
Natural History
Beautiful fingerprint pattern is actually the mantle tissue which covers the shell. Mantle secretes and maintains the shell.

Flamingo tongue snails have a beautiful mantle that looks somewhat like the skin of a leopard. If disturbed, the animal will quickly withdraw its mantle, revealing a white to orange-colored shell. Most specimens are less than two inches long, and they are often found on purple sea fans and other gorgonians upon which these snails feed. As a rule, flamingo tongues feed most actively at night, and during the day they are often found near the base of the sea fans.

Fingerprint snails are less commonly seen than flamingo tongue snails, but the two species are very closely related and appear quite similar. The design on the mantle of the fingerprint snail is the main identifying characteristic, and the pattern closely resembles a human fingerprint.

Queen conchs (pronounced conks) are the snails that often end up in *ceviche* and other gourmet treats so characteristic of Caribbean cuisine. Unfortunately, their value as a food source has led to serious over-fishing in many parts of the Caribbean, Bahamas and Florida. A large species of snail, queen conchs commonly exceed 10 inches in length. They inhabit shallow sand patches adjacent to reef structures, sand lagoons and turtle grass beds where they graze on algae and a variety of seagrasses. The shell of the queen conch is typically encrusted with algae and closely resembles the surrounding sand and rubble, however, the inner shell is a lovely shade of orangy-pink.

The eyes of queen conchs are mounted on the end of long black and white stalks that project outward from the shell as the conch draws itself slowly along sandy bottoms. If disturbed, the animal will retract the eye stalks, but if you are patient, you will often be able to wait long enough to see the conch slowly reextend its eye stalks to check for impending danger before beginning to feed again.

To locate a conch, look for the trails they make as they drag their shells over the sand. Don't be surprised if you see a small cardinalfish hanging very close to some conchs.

The fish are commonly called a conchfish because they actually hide inside the live conch's shell given any sign of danger.

Commonly exceeding a length of 15 inches, the snail known as the **trumpet triton** is one of the largest of all Caribbean snails. Residents of the reef community, trumpet tritons have a spiral-shaped, pointed shell designed in checkerboard fashion with alternating patches of beige, dark brown and white. Striking yellow- and black-banded tentacles stand out prominently on the animal's head. Trumpet tritons are primarily nocturnal feeders, preying on a variety of echinoderms especially sea cucumbers. Unfortunately, the story of trumpet tritons is all too familiar. Due to their handsome appearance, they have become a favorite item of collectors, and in many areas human greed has led to their demise or disappearance.

Another interesting large species of snail is the **emperor helmet snail**. Attaining a length of up to 10 inches, these snails are actually capable of crushing long-spined sea urchins with their muscular foot. Once the urchin has been crushed, the emperor helmet snail drills through the urchin's test (skeleton) with its radula in order to extract the internal tissues.

AT A GLANCE

CONCH, QUEEN CONCH

Scientific Name
Strombus gigas
Habitat
Sand, eelgrass beds.
Typical Adult Size
10 inches.
Sightings
Commonly seen.
Natural History
Use their muscular foot to pull themselves over the sand. Eyes on long stalks are retracted when danger threatens.

PHOTO TIP

Flamingo tongue snails are favorites of underwater photographers, and for good reason. Their colorful mantles look like miniature leopard skins which are stretched out to cover their otherwise plain-looking shells. A Nikonos camera with a 1:2 framer works nicely for photographing a single individual, while two flamingo tongues next to one another, a common sight, are best captured with a 1:3 framer. Be extremely careful not to touch the snail when you are photographing it for it will withdraw its beautiful mantle, leaving you with only a plain-looking shell for a subject.

AT A GLANCE

HELMET SNAIL

Scientific Name
  Cassis sp.
Habitat
  Sand, turtle grass beds.
Typical Adult Size
  10 inches.
Sightings
  Occasionally seen.
Natural History
  Use their muscular foot to crush long-spined urchins.

CARL ROESSLER

AT A GLANCE

TRUMPET TRITON

Scientific Name
  Charonia variegata
Habitat
  Reef and sand.
Typical Adult Size
  12 inches.
Sightings
  Occasionally seen.
Natural History
  Tends to hide by day and feed at night. One of the larger Caribbean snails. Preys on sea cucumbers and urchins. Endangered in many areas due to collectors.

Several species of snails are referred to as coral snails. While identification in the field is often possible by specialists who are familiar with the intricacies of shell design, it is difficult for most sport divers to make these detailed distinctions. However, it is worthwhile to note that many of these snails prey directly on coral polyps. They use their proboscis to suck on the living tissues of the corals.

CLAMS, SCALLOPS, OYSTERS AND MUSSELS

Clams, oysters, scallops and mussels are mollusks that are referred to as bivalves. These animals possess two shells that are hinged together by a very strong ligament. One or two strong abductor muscles can be flexed to draw the shells together for protection. It is the adductor muscle of certain shellfish that taste so wonderful when steamed and eaten with a drop of lemon or a touch of butter. In bivalves the mantle secretes both the shells and the ligament, and also covers the vital internal organs.

In addition, the mantle encloses two tubes called siphons which are used to channel water. Tiny beating hairs, called cilia, line the walls of the siphons and are used to create water currents within the animal's body. The water circulates over elaborate folds of blood-rich gills in the process of respiration. These gills also act as a very fine sieve which is capable of removing phy-

AT A GLANCE

FLAME SCALLOP

Scientific Name
Lima scabra

Habitat
Reef, under ledges.

Typical Adult Size
3 to 5 inches.

Sightings
Common, but often go unnoticed. Once you find one, you are likely to be able to find them easily.

Natural History
The hemoglobin in their blood makes the gills glow bright red.

toplankton and other food particles from the water.

Bivalves differ from other mollusks in that they lack a distinct head and radula. However, bivalves do possess a large, muscular foot that is used for digging and for anchoring the animal to the bottom. Some clams are capable of rapidly burying themselves in the sand or mud by digging into the sediment with their foot.

With the primary exception of some scallops which as adults are capable of swimming, rapid crawling and burrowing, most bivalves are immobile. They cement themselves to the bottom or burrow into one place in the reef. They are dispersed from one locale to the next mostly in their larval stage. These bivalves are prodigious spawners, often releasing millions of eggs in a

PHOTO TIP

The white tentacles and the fantastic shade of cherry red found in flame scallops can be a real crowd-pleaser. The animals virtually glow. If you are both patient and skillful, these spectacularly colored bivalves can make wonderful subjects for a Nikonos camera with a 1:3 framer. However, you will probably find that flame scallops are easier to shoot when using a reflex camera since they tend to be perched deep in holes that are often too small for your framer. If you have difficulty placing your extension tube framer exactly as you like, try removing the side posts. In some brands the posts unscrew.

single spawning. Fertilization is external, with group spawning being triggered by pheromones released as

each individual broadcasts its eggs or sperm. Pheromones are specialized hormones which serve as sexual stimulants and attractants. Fertilized eggs and larvae are carried by the currents to their point of settlement.

In addition to their value as sources of food, some bivalve mollusks produce pearls as a result of

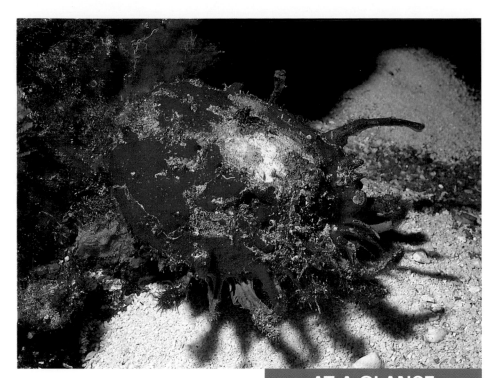

AT A GLANCE

AMBER PEN SHELL, PEN SHELL

Scientific Name
Pinna carnea
Habitat
Many places: mud, sand, on coral heads in crevices.
Typical Adult Size
4 to 8 inches tall.
Sightings
Commonly seen in Caribbean, occasionally seen in Bahamas, and seldom seen in Florida.
Natural History
Like other bivalves, will close shell when disturbed. Often see only barely exposed ends of shells (valves).

AT A GLANCE

THORNY OYSTER

Scientific Name
Spondylus americanus
Habitat
Reef, vertical surfaces.
Typical Adult Size
5 inches.
Sightings
Commonly seen.
Natural History
Has long projections growing from heavily encrusted shells. Grows attached to vertical walls.

accumulated secretions over foreign objects that lodge in the tissues of their bodies.

Caribbean reef communities are often rich in bivalves, but these animals tend to be reclusive as well as heavily encrusted, and therefore are often overlooked. The **flame scallop**, also called the **fire clam** or **rough lima**, is one of the most stunning of all bivalves. Usually found deep in holes and under ledges of the reef, flame scallops are easily recognized with the help of a flashlight as their cherry-red mantle virtually glows between its two shells. The mantle projects outward from the edge of the shells and is lined by many long, white tentacle-like projections which flow back and forth in the currents caused by the flame scallop. If disturbed, a flame scallop will quickly close its shells and draw backward into the cover of the reef by using its muscular foot. At the base of the foot is a gland which secretes threads (known as byssal threads because they are secreted from the byssal gland) that attach the scallop to the reef.

Pen shells are another commonly seen bivalve of the reef. Some speci-

mens partially bury themselves in the sand while others reside in depressions in coral heads. Pen shells are distinguished by their brown to amber parchment-like shells with rippled edges. Pen shells may reach a length of approximately eight inches.

Several species of oysters are often seen by divers although they are commonly unrecognized or misidentified. Among these are the **winged pearl oyster**, the **spiny oyster** which is sometimes called the **thorny oyster**, and the **frons oyster**. Winged pearl oysters can be identified by the distinct, long, nar-

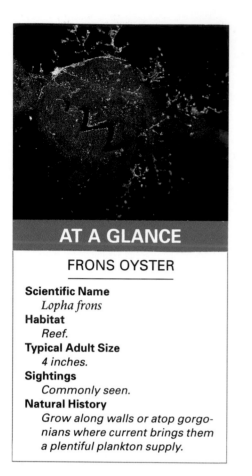

AT A GLANCE

FRONS OYSTER

Scientific Name
Lopha frons
Habitat
Reef.
Typical Adult Size
4 inches.
Sightings
Commonly seen.
Natural History
Grow along walls or atop gorgonians where current brings them a plentiful plankton supply.

row, arrow-like extension of their fan-shaped shell. The typically encrusted shells of winged pearl oysters are usually brownish. These mollusks are normally seen attached to the branches of sea plumes or other gorgonians. From a perch that is usually fairly high up on the sea plume, the oyster can capture its food by filtering the water for planktonic organisms.

Thorny oysters are characterized by their numerous thorn-like projections which extend from the edges of their shells. Many individuals are four to five inches across, but despite their size, they are often difficult to detect because the shells are often encrusted with a combination of algae, sponges and hydroids. Their mantle often gives them away as it ripples with splendid patterns of scarlet, orange and white. You'll need to approach this oyster carefully to see the lovely coloration. Disturbing the animal will cause it

to close its shell in defensive response.

Frons oysters can be identified by the zigzag pattern of their shells. They, too, are often encrusted by a mix of algae, sponges and hydroids, and can commonly be seen growing on various gorgonians and black coral.

OCTOPUSES AND SQUIDS

In the group of mollusks called cephalopods—the squids, cuttlefishes and octopuses—the shell is greatly reduced or even missing. In squids and cuttlefishes the shell is small and internal. Octopuses have given up the shell altogether and exchanged it for various other lines of defense. Worldwide, there are more than 600 species of cephalopod mollusks, and as a group they are considered to be the most intelligent of all invertebrates.

The term cephalopod is derived from the Greek words for "head" and "foot." As you might suspect, the heads of these mollusks are prominent. The foot has been highly modified into sucker-bearing arms which assist in snaring and holding their prey. Squids and cuttlefishes tend to live up in the water column where they feed mostly on fishes. Most octopuses are bottom dwellers that feed primarily on worms, crustaceans and other mollusks.

The tentacles of squids and octopuses are equipped with one or more rows of sucker-like discs, hooks and other adhesive structures which aid in the process of snaring and holding prey. Squids possess 10 tentacles, octopuses have 8, and nautiluses often have as many as 90 tentacles. Once the tentacles grab the prey, the cephalopod bites its victim with its strong parrot-like beak. In many instances, the beak delivers an immobilizing toxin that subdues the prey before it is consumed.

The nervous systems of cephalo-

pods, especially the senses of vision, smell and touch, are highly developed. As a result, these animals are capable of very fast responses to a variety of stimuli. The eyes of these mollusks are elaborate mechanisms that are similar in many respects to the eyes of vertebrates. Cephalopod eyes are capable of sharp focus and of creating an acute image, but the method used is slightly different than that of higher vertebrates. The eyes of squid have been used for years in eye research because of several characteristics which bear strong

Octopuses, like many other mollusks, have rather sophisticated eyes and excellent vision. In this picture you can also see the opening to the tube known as the siphon. An octopus forces water from its mantle through the highly directable tube to gain thrust when swimming.

resemblance to human eyes.

Octopuses have sophisticated chemoreceptors on the end of each tentacle, which help them avoid potential danger, and detect and direct prey toward their mouths. In fact, scientists often say that octopuses possess eight noses. Concentrating their energies on crabs and mollusks, octopuses are very active

AT A GLANCE

CARIBBEAN REEF OCTOPUS

Scientific Name
Octopus briareus

Habitat
Reef.

Typical Adult Size
24 inches.

Sightings
Commonly seen.

Natural History
Large, specialized cells in skin called chromatophores allow instant color changes. Beak located at base of arms is used to bite and sometimes inject a toxin which paralyzes prey.

predators at night.

Octopuses are often quick to seek cover when they detect the presence of a diver. Occasionally, if caught unaware, they freeze, spread out on the reef, and change color and texture immediately as they attempt to disappear into the background. Slinking and sauntering, they seem to melt into the reef, evaporating into any hole big enough for them to squeeze their head into. In fact, one of their most remarkable adaptations is their ability to crawl through tiny holes. Remember, octopuses are invertebrates and their bodies lack a spine. In addition, their bodies lack a hard shell so they can easily change their shape, allowing even large specimens to crawl through tiny holes.

Octopuses have a strong sense of curiosity and often peer back at you from the protection of their lairs. If you attempt to reach into their holes, which are often marked by discarded shells of their prey, octopuses will often squirt a jet of water at you with their excurrent siphons. As a rule, once they feel threatened, they will remain hidden within the safety of their den. If, however, they feel so threatened that they flee the den, it is likely that they will build a new home and will not return to their abandoned domicile.

Vision plays a key role in the ability of octopuses to camouflage themselves. Though there are times when they stand out prominently against the background, as a rule they alter the color of their skin to match that of their surroundings. If an octopus changes its location, it is usually quick to change the hue and tone of its skin to match the brightness and color of its new surroundings. Specialized pigment cells called chromatophores, which are controlled by the animal's muscular and vascular systems, enable octopuses to rapidly

PHOTO TIP

PHOTO TIP

Nighttime is the right time to catch octopuses out on the reef. By swimming just above the reef and aiming your light well ahead of you, you will maximize your opportunity to catch one out before it sees you and quickly jets away. Often they will stand high atop their lair with arms outstretched as they see you coming. You can spot them in this posture if you look 20 feet or so ahead. As soon as you spot one, swim directly toward it and have your Nikonos and close-up kit preset in case the animal flattens its body, flashes colors and freezes. Be quick! You will only get one or two chances to get a shot. A 15mm lens set at minimum distance also works well, especially for larger animals. If you are using a single lens reflex camera system, it is often best not to shine your focusing light directly at an octopus. Try to focus in the periphery of the beam, or focus on another subject the same distance away. Then frame the octopus using the periphery of the beam and take your shot.

change color. This ability to change allows these animals to move about the reef almost as if they were invisible.

At times the bodies of octopuses will ripple in a spectacular display of repeated color changes. The rippling is considered to be a form of communication with other octopuses, and the behavior is especially common during elaborate courtship rituals.

Like squids, octopuses create thrust by forcing a powerful stream of water through their excurrent siphons. This natural jet engine operates by first expanding the mantle, causing it to fill with water. Then powerful muscles quickly contract the mantle, forcing the water out under high pressure through the excurrent siphon. Octopuses may form their bodies into wing shapes when they glide through water. This shape is extremely efficient in water just as it is in air. The wing-shaped body provides lift and allows the animal to glide effectively.

When they swim as opposed to glide, they become quickly exhausted. Even at rest, octopuses metabolize a very high percentage of the oxygen they extract from the water. As a result, they are incapable of creating much in the way of an energy reserve.

Masters of escape, octopuses (like squids) have evolved a veritable cloak to disappear behind. They have the ability to emit clouds of ink from specialized glands as they flee. The ink serves as a smoke screen used to confuse predators. Because of its chemical make-up, it is also used to dull or anesthetize the olfactory receptor used in the sense of smell by potential predators, such as moray eels and other fishes.

Like most mollusks, the sexes of octopuses are separate. Males have a specialized tentacle called a hectocotyle arm which transfers packets of sperm to females. The females lay their fertilized eggs in grape-like strands within the den site. The females constantly guard and clean the eggs for several months before they hatch. They are extremely diligent in their duty, and during this time they neither feed nor leave their den. In many species the females will lose more than 50 percent of their body weight before the young hatch and often the females will die shortly afterwards.

Several species of octopuses inhabit the waters of the Caribbean, Bahamas and Florida. Most of those encountered by sport divers are relatively small. However, the common **Atlantic octopus** has been documented to have a tentacle tip-to-tentacle tip span of up to seven feet. One arm is nearly four times as long as the body. Atlantic octopuses, typically colored whitish to mottled blue-green, inhabit shallow waters, but they are rarely seen. The **white-spotted octopus** attains a tentacle tip-to-tentacle tip span of between three and four feet. Their bodies vary in color from blue-green to orange to brown or gray, and they almost always exhibit a number of large white spots.

Probably the most commonly seen species of Caribbean octopus is the **reef octopus**. Their bodies range in coloration from a mottled off-white to iridescent blue-green to reddish orange. Attaining a tentacle-tip span of between one and two feet, reef octopus are commonly encountered in reef communities, especially during night dives. They have comparatively small bodies and their longest arm may be five times as long as the width of their body.

Several species of **squids** are quite common in Caribbean waters. Although they are occasionally seen during the day, it is far more common to encounter squid during night dives. They are often attracted to divers' lights and to the deck lights of boats. Most species of Caribbean reef squid are rather small, being less than six inches long, but they are exceptionally colorful creatures. Their bodies often pulsate in a fantastic display of ever-changing colors as they hover in mid-water around divers. Yet, too close of an approach by the divers will cause the squids to jet away as they disappear behind clouds of ink.

PHOTO TIP

Atlantic oval squid are commonly seen during night dives. They radiate color when your dive light illuminates them, and they are often curious and reluctant to flee. The closer you get to these animals with your light, the better your chances of enjoying a prolonged encounter. The light seems to disorient Atlantic oval squid, and often they will swim right up to it. This is the time to have your Nikonos and close-up kit ready to capture these wonderful animals on film!

Squids are a very important food source not only for humans but also for many marine creatures. A wide variety of fishes, including sharks, jacks, tunas and many reef species, as well as dolphins, whales and many other animals rely heavily on squids as a primary source of food. In order to survive the constant onslaught, squids reproduce in enormous numbers. They often spawn in large groups and in many species the adults die soon after they mate. Female **Atlantic oval squid** lay whitish egg packets which can occasionally be found around areas of the reef.

Likely the most common species of reef squid, Atlantic oval squid swim in small groups. They possess transparent tentacles that come together in a narrow point when the animal swims. The tentacles are about the same length as the rest of the body. Body color varies immensely. Sometimes Atlantic oval squid appear rather bland, but other times their chromatophores flare to produce vivid hues and iridescent spots.

Squid are believed to use their chromatophores as a means of intraspecies (one squid to another of the same species) communication.

AT A GLANCE

ATLANTIC OVAL SQUID, CARIBBEAN REEF SQUID

Scientific Name
Sepioteuthis sepioidea
Habitat
Water column over reef, sand and along walls.
Typical Adult Size
5 to 10 inches.
Sightings
Commonly seen.
Natural History
Very important food source for many fishes. Specialized cells in skin allow for near instantaneous color changes thought to be used in communication with other members of their species.

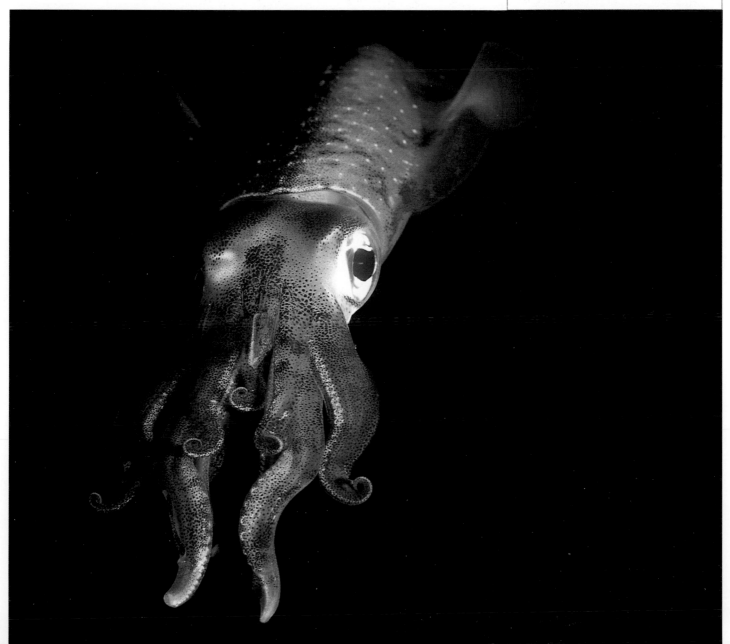

11

Phylum: *Arthropoda*

LOBSTERS, CRABS, SHRIMPS, BARNACLES, COPEPODS, ISOPODS AND AMPHIPODS

Scientists have described more than one million species of living arthropods, a number which indicates that there are more arthropods on earth today than all the members of other phyla added together. In fact, more than 75 percent of all living organisms are arthropods. Of the aquatic arthropods, the class Crustacea includes the most species, being represented by approximately 35,000 different kinds of animals.

Crustaceans include lobsters, crabs, shrimps, barnacles, copepods, isopods and a selection of other animals, namely amphipods and stomatopods, whose rather long scientific names end with the syllable "pod" from the Latin for "foot." Many of these creatures are extremely abundant. Collectively, they serve as a food source for a variety of larger animals which range from tiny reef creatures to the great whales. Crustaceans come in an incredible variety of sizes, ranging from microscopic zooplankton to the giant Japanese spider crab which

All divers, whether photographers, game takers or sightseers, are attracted to spiny lobsters. These crustaceans are active by night and reclusive by day. Occasionally, in the early morning you will find them still out in the open as they are preparing to turn in for the day.

reportedly reaches a full 12 feet from the tip of one pincer claw to the other.

Crustaceans display bilateral symmetry, jointed appendages and a hard exoskeleton. Some possess claws, which are used for defense, or for gathering and capturing food.

The hard shell in most crustaceans is laced with calcium carbonate which adds strength and rigidity. This exoskeleton is a protective shield which also promotes the animal's dexterity by the strategic attachment of muscles to the individual body plates. In evolution, this system of muscular attachment and mobility is a significant development.

Living inside a hard shell does, however, present certain logistical problems. Growth is difficult and it can be dangerous. For crustaceans to increase their size, they must molt or crawl out of their restrictive shells. Like a knight without his armor, these animals are extremely vulnerable during the early stages of molting before the new outer shell begins to harden.

Molting is governed by hormones secreted from glands located in the eye stalks of crustaceans. Prior to molting, crustaceans undergo a period when they feed heavily and store fat. Soon thereafter, they begin to form the foundation of a new shell underneath the old shell. Hor-

monal changes cause the old shell to begin fracturing along strategic lines. The animals then climb out of their old shells. In some cases they will eat part or all of the old shell to help restore the calcium necessary to harden the new shell, and in other cases they will cast their old shell aside.

When molting, the vulnerable animal quickly looks for a hiding place where it can safely wait for the new shell to finish forming and hardening. In many species, it is only during this soft-shell period that females can be mated, though there are exceptions, such as in the case of the spiny lobster. While the body is soft, important hormonal processes come into play, preventing the loss of body fluids and allowing body tissues to swell. Soon the animal's newly formed shell hardens over the bloated body. Given time, another hormonal change allows the excess fluid to be expelled and the animal shrinks within the new shell, allowing ample room for growth. Larval crustaceans may molt a dozen or more times before settling out of the water column onto the reefs. Once settled, they molt several times annually, but this process slows with age.

While some species of crustaceans spend their entire lives drifting in the open sea as plankton, the ones that divers are most familiar with are

AT A GLANCE

SPINY LOBSTER

Scientific Name
Panulirus argus

Habitat
Reef, in caves, holes and under ledges.

Typical Adult Size
12 to 18 inches, not including antennae which nearly double the length of average specimen; many considerably larger.

Sightings
Commonly seen.

Natural History
Primarily nocturnal feeders, but will take advantage of daytime opportunities. Seek refuge during the day, emerge and feed on variety of foods at night.

the lobsters, crabs and shrimps which live on the sea floor. Many of these bottom-dwellers have a very keen sense of touch, taste and vision. Antennae and stiff body hairs are adaptations that contribute to the well-developed sense of touch.

In most crustaceans the sexes are separate, but there are some interesting exceptions. Some shrimps begin their lives as males, but after one mating period they undergo a transformation into females. The courtship rituals of many crustaceans are intricate and elaborate, and mating is typically seasonal.

While less advanced invertebrates simply cast their eggs into the current, crustaceans demonstrate the more advanced trait of providing some parental care. Usually the female provides protection for her eggs by carrying them attached to her swimmerets until the eggs hatch. Females usually produce broods of eggs that number in the hundreds. Newly hatched larvae are often seen during night dives as they are attracted to the bright lights of dive boats. The larvae range far and wide, and are often caught in sampling nets hundreds of miles from the nearest reef by scientists studying life in the open sea. The larvae are preyed upon by a wide variety of fishes and other open ocean predators.

LOBSTERS

Lobsters are probably the most conspicuous of Caribbean crustaceans. They are often seen at night out in the open, foraging for food. During the day, on the other hand, it is more common to see them lurking in the back of caves. Often you will first spot their antennae projecting out from a hole or from under some ledge. Lobsters occasionally make croaking sounds by rubbing the base of their antennae against a ridge.

Two species of lobsters commonly seen at night are the **spiny lobster** and the **rock lobster**. Neither species has claws like their New England cousins, but both species have many sharp spines at the base of their antennae and on their shells. While the rock lobster has a very ornate black, orange and white shell, the spiny lobster is a more plainly colored tan and white.

As a rule, adult spiny lobster are slightly larger than rock lobster. Spiny lobster range from North Carolina to Brazil. As with many marine animals, overexploitation by commercial fishing has led to a serious decline in populations of spiny lobster in many parts of the Caribbean.

Both spiny lobster and rock lobster forage along the bottom looking for snails, worms, mollusks, crustaceans and a variety of other food sources that they can crush with their powerful mandibles.

Another species of lobster sometimes seen during night dives is the odd-shaped **Spanish lobster** (also

CRABS

Crabs appear in a number of forms. Some, like the **arrow crab**, have thin bodies and long, spindly legs. Others, such as the **porcelain crab** and **swimming crab**, have bodies that are flattened from top to bottom. **Decorator crab** cover themselves with sponges, anemones, barnacles and other debris in order to make themselves inconspicuous, while the bright colors of other species serve to boldly advertise their presence. **Hermit crabs** actually carry around the vacated shells of snails

commonly called the **slipper lobster**). Spanish lobster are typically even more reclusive than spiny lobster and rock lobster, and as most people would likely agree, they are less attractive. Slipper lobster do not possess the long antennae found in spiny lobster and rock lobster. Slipper lobster look somewhat like a flattened marine armadillo, and their bodies are more compressed and more heavily armored than those of spiny lobster. The mottled coloration of slipper lobster varies from drab brown to yellow, orange and purple.

AT A GLANCE

SPANISH LOBSTER SLIPPER LOBSTER, RIDGED SLIPPER LOBSTER

Scientific Name
Scyllarides nodifer
Habitat
Reef.
Typical Adult Size
10 inches.
Sightings
Occasionally seen.
Natural History
Prefers underside of ledges even at night. Lacks the antennae of spiny lobster.

AT A GLANCE

RED HERMIT CRAB, RED REEF HERMIT

Scientific Name
Paguristes cadenati
Habitat
Reef.
Typical Adult Size
.75 inch.
Sightings
Commonly seen.
Natural History
Prowl the reefs by night, but stay under cover during the day. Live tucked inside a shell which they exchange for a larger one as they grow.

PHOTO TIP

Giant hermit crabs often prove to be less wary than their smaller cousins. If you want to photograph a giant hermit crab while the animal is reaching far out of its shell, you might try this technique. Swim up to the crab very slowly, preferably from behind. Very gently, hold the pointed end of the shell between your thumb and forefinger, and slowly rotate the shell and animal back toward you until the shell opening is facing upward. The crab may snap into its shell, but soon it will be stretching out of its shell in an attempt to right itself. This provides a good opportunity to get its portrait with a Nikonos extension tube system or with a close-up kit. Always put the crab back.

on their backs. These "clever" crabs carry their shells with them wherever they go and use them as a safe place to retreat into with any sign of danger.

Scientists separate the animals we call crabs into two groups: the hermit crabs and the true crabs. Hermit crabs differ from true crabs in that the posterior, or abdominal section of their body is not protected by a hard exoskeleton. Only the anterior portion is covered by a hard shell. Not only is the abdomen of hermit crabs unprotected, but it is rather soft. Hermit crabs cope with their vulnerability problem by using the shells of deceased snails. As soon as they have completed their first molt, juvenile hermit crabs are quick to look for an empty shell to call home. Once it finds a shell to crawl into, the hermit crab will reside there, taking the shell everywhere it goes until it outgrows the shell. At that time the hermit crab will either find another vacated shell, or it will trade shells with another hermit crab. Scientists who have studied the process report that there are not that many empty snail shells lying around, so shell trading is quite common.

Hermit crabs are well represented in Caribbean waters. The largest species is the **giant hermit crab**, which often inhabits the shells of deceased queen conchs. Giant hermit crab are brown to maroon, and are not as cherry red as their smaller cousins, the **red hermit crab**. The carapace of giant hermit crab is commonly between three and four inches wide, while red hermit crab attain a maximum size of about one inch.

Found in reef communities, lagoons and on sand patches from Brazil to North Carolina, giant hermit crab have a right pincer that is larger than the left, bluish eyes and banded antennae which are colored red and white. Like other crabs, the eyes of giant hermit crab are on stalks. This allows a hermit crab to retreat inside its shell when it senses danger,

and then to slowly creep out, eyes first, to see if it is safe to reemerge. Swift movements by divers or handling the shell will usually cause the crab to quickly withdraw.

Other species of hermit crabs include the **smooth-clawed hermit crab**, the **flat-clawed hermit crab**, the **star-eyed hermit crab**, the **bar-eyed hermit crab** and a species which is simply called the **hermit crab**. A telltale characteristic of smooth-clawed hermit crab is that these animals, as their name suggests, lack hair and their claws are quite smooth. In addition, the left claw is larger than the right. The flat-clawed hermit crab is characterized by its small size (about half an inch across) and its comparatively large, white claw which is almost as wide as the length of the crab's body.

The star-eyed hermit crab and bar-eyed hermit crab look similar and occur together throughout the Caribbean, but it is possible to distinguish between the two species by looking at their eyes. In the cornea of each eye of the star-eyed hermit crab, there is a star pattern, while there is a horizontal black bar in the corneas of bar-eyed hermits.

The species that is simply called the hermit crab is often observed carrying the tricolor anemone on its shell. When these fascinating hermit crab change shells, they also pick off their anemone and place it on their new shell. The stinging cells of the anemone help protect the crab from octopuses and other potential predators. The hermit crab is quite colorful, having red and white-banded legs, blue eyes and yellow antennae.

Although they are easy to find during the day near the base of sponges and gorgonians, it is usually easier to find hermit crab at night when they are out feeding. Most species are scavengers.

TRUE CRABS

The bodies of true crabs are com-

pletely covered by a hard shell, a feature which distinguishes them from hermit crabs. In addition, the bodies of true crabs are considerably flattened, they possess five pairs of legs, and their reduced tails are tucked underneath their abdomens. The vast majority of true crabs live on the sea floor, and most are rather poor swimmers.

Crabs are described in the order Decopoda (ten-footed). All true crabs have ten appendages, with the forward two being modified into pincers or claws in most species. The remaining eight legs are used for walking, or in a few cases for walking and/or swimming.

The pincers and claws vary considerably from species to species. An examination of these appendages provides valuable insight into the lifestyles of the various species of crabs. Those species that have tiny, almost delicate-looking claws are far more likely to graze on a variety of algae. Crabs with large, heavily armored, powerful claws are more likely to be carnivorous and feed on snails, clams and a variety of other animals that must be crushed before they can be eaten.

One of the largest of the Caribbean species of true crabs is the **Car-**

PHOTO TIP

King crabs (spider crabs) are far too large to photograph with an extension tube system. A typical specimen is two feet wide, meaning they are right in the size range where they can be filmed well with a number of lenses. A Nikonos RS with either the 50mm or the 28mm lens, or a housed single lens reflex camera with a similar lens would be an excellent choice. A standard Nikonos 35mm or 28mm lens will also work well from two to three feet away, and you can also get good results by using a 20mm or even a 15mm lens set at minimum focus. Be careful with your lighting to avoid harsh shadows, as these crabs are often seen resting back under ledges and in depressions.

ibbean king crab. King crab weigh up to eight pounds. Their carapace alone can be up to six inches wide, and their leg span may reach an impressive two and a half feet or more! The bodies of king crab are usually a mottled brownish color, though some specimens are much lighter than others. Their thin, yet formidable, claws are a bluish gray. Although king crab are occasionally seen resting in a depression in the reef during the day, it is far more common to encounter them at night when they are foraging for algae.

The **green reef crab** is one of the

more common species of Caribbean crabs. Its carapace is only about one inch long and it is a dark green color. In some reef communities almost every stand of branching coral seems to harbor a handful of these small crabs. Taking a quick glance over the branching coral, you probably won't

see a single crab. However, if you stop and peer down between the branches, you just might see a handful of crabs scurrying about as they try to hide.

Sponge spider crab are one of the more colorful species. These crabs are rather small, attaining a maximum length of only 1-1/2 inches. Because of their size, they are easy to overlook, but if you do see one,

AT A GLANCE

OCELLATE SWIMMING CRAB

Scientific Name
Portunus sebae
Habitat
Turtle grass beds, sand and back reefs to moderate depth.
Typical Adult Size
Carapace 2 to 4 inches.
Sightings
Occasionally seen.
Natural History
Rear legs adapted for swimming. As pictured, male on top grasps the female until she molts, at which time the pair will mate.

AT A GLANCE

TEARDROP CRYPTIC CRAB

Scientific Name
Pelia mutica
Habitat
Reefs.
Typical Adult Size
Carapace .25 to .75 inch in diameter.
Sightings
Commonly present, but very easy to overlook.
Natural History
A type of decorator crab that disguises itself by attaching bits of living sponges to its carapace, head and legs.

you can't help but admire nature's handiwork. The carapace and rostrum are covered with stiff, hooked hairs which adhere to pieces of sponges that are strategically placed by the crab. Algae, hydroids and other encrusting organisms also grow on the crab's body.

Stone crab, a favorite cuisine of many, and the abundant **blue crab** are important food sources in many parts of the Caribbean. Other commonly seen species include the **rough-clawed porcelain crab**, the **spotted porcelain crab**, and a variety of species known as **box** or

shame-faced crab. The shame-faced crab are named for the way they appear to hide their faces with their oversized claws. These claws are used like shovels so that the shame-faced crab can quickly bury themselves in the sand and avoid potential predators. One of their claws also bears a hook-shaped projection that looks somewhat like a bottle opener and is used to pry open mollusk shells.

Flat crab are often found hiding under the protective spines of long-spined sea urchins. As the name suggests, their body is greatly flattened. The carapaces of flat crab are brown and the legs have a series of yellow bands.

Swimming crab are the exception to the rule that crabs crawl and cannot swim. Their rear legs have been modified into small paddles which push these crabs sideways through the water with surprising rapidity. Swimming crab are usually encountered in beds of turtle grass, on sandy bottoms, and in shallow back reef areas.

The thin, small-bodied, delicate-looking **arrow crab** bears some resemblence to the terrestrial daddy longlegs spiders. Arrow crab have medium-brown to gold-banded bodies with long, thin legs, and a

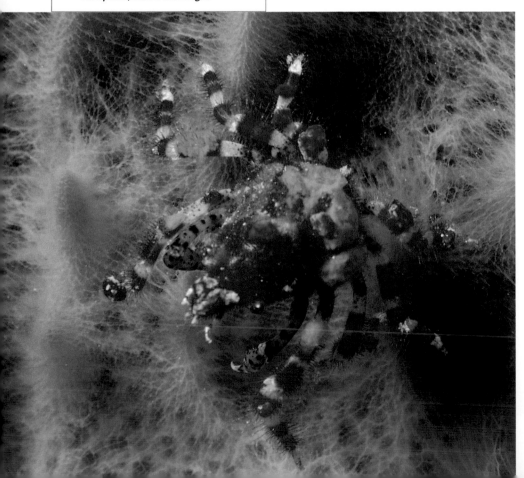

PHOTO TIP

Despite their rather strange appearance, arrow crabs are one of those macro subjects that photographers can't turn down no matter how many pictures they already have. Try several different formats. When you are using 1:2 or 1:3 framers, keep in mind that these spindly crab can't all be in focus, but what really is critical is the eye(s) and rostrum. They must be sharp as a tack for your image to be a real knockout.

Try a side profile too and you can get from the tip of the rostrum to the end of the carapace in sharp focus. Interesting photos can be shot using close focus with the Nikonos 15mm lens, with large arrow crabs held very close to a diver's face mask.

No matter what lens or camera system you use, be sure you have some color contrast between the golden-brown crab and its background. Many an arrow crab photograph has proved disappointing because the crab got lost in the background.

pronounced rostrum or snout. Often a clump of algae is found growing on the rostrum. Their tiny pincers are bright purple. Arrow crab are quite common, and on any night dive it is almost impossible not to encounter several if you look under ledges, on sea fans, or on sponges. These crabs are a favorite subject of macro photographers.

SHRIMPS

Shrimps are major contributors to almost every niche in the marine environment. Worldwide, there are more than 2,000 species and they are well represented in Caribbean waters. With so many species living in a variety of habitats, it should not be surprising that shrimps are a rather diverse group of animals. Most species are scavengers, but others play important roles as cleaners, and many species serve as vital sources of food for a wide variety of predatory fishes.

Shrimps have long bodies that are usually divided into two major sections. One section is comprised of the head and thorax, which are fused together into the cephalothorax. The second section is a segmented abdomen.

Most species are excellent swimmers, but shrimps are usually seen walking about on the reef unless they need to make a hasty retreat. During the day many shrimps are reclusive, seeking shelter under coral heads, in and under sponges, in anemones, and in dark crevices of the reef. At night, many species emerge to scavenge for food.

You can usually spot shrimps at night by noting their bright-red eyes reflecting the light from dive lights, even from a considerable distance. Sometimes, shrimps are easy to approach once they have been spotted, but other times, they will instantly disappear by swimming away or by burying themselves in the bottom.

The abdomen and tail of shrimps are proportionately longer than those of crabs and even lobsters. Shrimps use their tail and abdomen when they swim. By rapidly flexing their abdomen and tail muscles, shrimps can propel themselves backwards surprisingly fast. The burst of speed gives them a good chance of avoiding predation. The underside of a shrimp's tail has several broad, well-developed appendages called pleopods, which enable most of them to swim slowly forward while maintaining fine maneuvering capabilities and body control.

Shrimps are highly mobile creatures. As such, they rely heavily on their well-developed senses of touch and sight to maneuver around the potential hazards of the reef. One of the most noticeable characteristics of

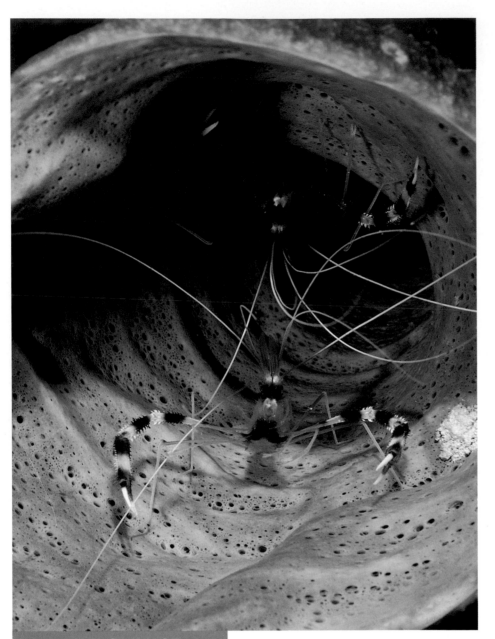

AT A GLANCE

BANDED CORAL SHRIMP, BARBERPOLE SHRIMP

Scientific Name
Stenopus hispidus
Habitat
Reef.
Typical Adult Size
2 inches.
Abundance
Common.
Natural History
Participates in some fish-cleaning activity, removing para-sites, bacteria, fungi and dead tissue. Cleaning considered vital to health of reef communities.

cies is the **banded coral shrimp** (also known as the **barberpole shrimp**).

Banded coral shrimp are charac-terized by the alternating red and white bands that cover their entire body, their large claws, and their long, white antennae. These shrimp are usually two to four inches long, and they are commonly seen under-neath ledges by day or roaming about the reef at night. Look for their antennae projecting out from under ledges and you can easily find these colorful reef inhabitants. Banded coral shrimp are part-time cleaners, and you may see them preening the skin of eels and various fishes, but they are just as likely to be seen picking bits of food from the bot-tom.

The **Pederson's cleaning shrimp** is a gorgeous species that is com-monly seen living on or around a variety of anemones. The bodies of Pederson's cleaning shrimp are an eye-catching combination of blue, purple and white. They are very ac-tive cleaners that play a vital role in many reef communities by ridding various fishes of parasites, dead tis-sue, bacteria and fungi. These shrimp advertise their intent by sit-ting on or near their host anemones and vigorously waving their long, white antennae in an effort to attract nearby fishes over to their cleaning station. Moray eels and a variety of groupers are among the fishes that are most often seen utilizing the ser-

shrimps is their elongated, wispy antennae which are used to feel their surroundings. They are extremely quick to dart away when they de-tect danger, and the length of their antennae provides the body and vi-tal organs with a margin of safety when danger is detected. In some cases, the antennae are torn free by a predator, but the body is saved. The eyes of shrimps are located on moveable stalks, another feature which helps them remain aware of their surroundings.

One of the most conspicuous spe-

AT A GLANCE

PEDERSON'S CLEANING SHRIMP

Scientific Name
Periclimenes pedersoni

Habitat
Reef, sandy rubble, and especially nestled amongst the tentacles of many anemones.

Typical Adult Size
1 inch.

Sightings
Commonly seen, especially around a variety of species of anemones.

Natural History
Very important cleaning shrimp. Removes parasites, bacteria and fungi from reef fishes.

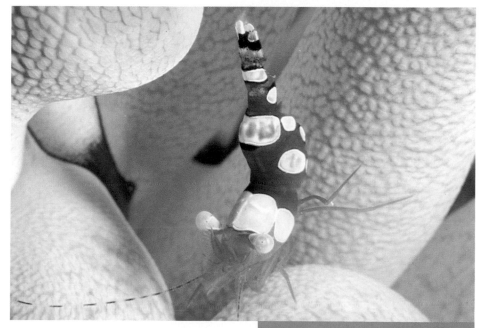

vices of Pederson's shrimp.

Two other species of shrimp are also commonly found on anemones. One species is very close in size and appearance to Pederson's shrimp, although it appears less delicate and may not participate significantly in cleaning services. This species is the **Yucatan anemone shrimp**.

The numerous, very small shrimp which are white and purple or brown, and which are often found around the base of the giant Caribbean anemone are known as **Thor anemone shrimp**.

As is the case with Pederson's cleaning shrimp, these other anemone shrimps are immune or somehow manage to avoid the potent stinging cells of the anemones with which they associate. These shrimp are not cleaners, and scientists point out it is likely that they gain protection by mimicking Pederson's cleaning shrimp since many reef fishes

avoid preying on that species.

One species of cleaner shrimp looks nothing like the Pederson's shrimp. This is the **scarlet lady cleaning shrimp**. These shrimp are commonly found in pairs deep in holes within the reef. They are scarlet red with white longitudinal racing stripes.

Nocturnal creatures, **red night shrimp** are commonly seen roaming the reef at night. Their bodies are fire-engine red with some white spots and vertical whitish stripes.

AT A GLANCE

THOR ANEMONE SHRIMP

Scientific Name
Thor ambionensis

Habitat
Reef; at base of tentacles of giant Caribbean anemone.

Typical Adult Size
.5 inch.

Sightings
Commonly seen.

Natural History
Remains hidden within giant Caribbean anemone and feeds on scraps missed by anemone.

Their large eyes sit high on their head and glow brilliant orange when reflecting a dive light.

Sponge shrimp have clear whitish bodies with deep red stripes running horizontally down the body. During the day, they retreat into tube sponges and can be seen bobbing back and forth as they await night-fall. Even at night, sponge shrimp often appear hesitant to emerge from the protection of their tube sponges, leaving only their antennae protruding past the top rim.

A number of species are commonly grouped together and are referred to as **pistol**, **snapping** or **popping shrimps**. They are found in a variety of different habitats. Some live in sponges, sharing a commensal relationship, while others live in burrows. Still another species of pistol shrimp is found nestled within the tentacles of the ringed anemone. This species has one small pincer and one that is considerably larger. The large pincer is used to produce a snapping sound which can be loud enough to startle unsuspecting divers. The sound is created when the pincer is rapidly closed. First the pincer is locked into an open position, then muscles in the claw start to contract and create tension in an attempt to close the pincer. The increased tension causes the pincer to suddenly release, creating a loud snap.

It is believed the shrimp uses the sound to warn other shrimp to stay clear of its territory, and to stun its prey, which usually consists of a variety of small fishes. Pistol shrimp are red to orange, and sometimes purple with mottled markings. They can easily be discovered by looking for their long, banded antennae projecting from the base of ringed anemones. If you place your fingers just out of reach of their antennae, they will often emerge cautiously and snap a powerful claw at you.

Mantis shrimps are best known for their razor-sharp, lightning-fast claws which are used in defense and to capture prey. With their oversized claws, they resemble their terrestrial cousins, the praying mantis. Their claws are incredibly sharp and powerful. There are reports of fisherman who have lost a finger to a mantis shrimp while trying to untangle it from a net.

The numerous species of mantis shrimps range in size from less than one inch long to over one foot. Collectively, these shrimps are often re-

AT A GLANCE

ANEMONE SHRIMP

Scientific Name
Periclimenes yucatanicus
Habitat
On and around several species of anemones, commonly the giant Caribbean anemone, the corkscrew anemone and the branching anemone.
Typical Adult Size
1 inch.
Sightings
Commonly seen in some areas.
Natural History
This species of shrimp is apparently immune to stinging tentacles of anemones. Masquerades as a cleaner and probably gains protection from potentially predatory fishes through its disguise and antics.

AT A GLANCE

SCARLET LADY SHRIMP

Scientific Name
Lysmata grabhami
Habitat
Reef, back in recesses.
Typical Adult Size
1.5 inches.
Sightings
Occasionally seen.
Natural History
Active cleaner of reef fishes.

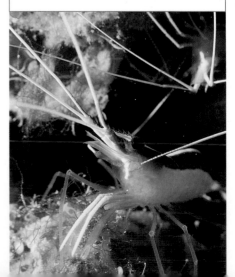

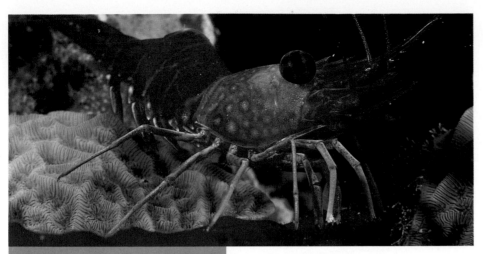

AT A GLANCE

RED NIGHT SHRIMP

Scientific Name
Rhynchocinetes ringens
Habitat
Reef.
Typical Adult Size
1.5 inches.
Sightings
Commonly seen.
Natural History
Prowls the reef by night and seldom seen during the day.

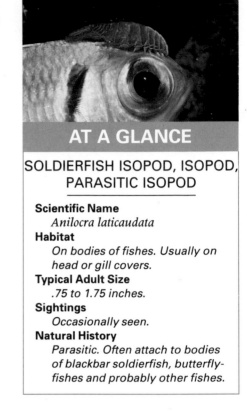

AT A GLANCE

SOLDIERFISH ISOPOD, ISOPOD, PARASITIC ISOPOD

Scientific Name
Anilocra laticaudata
Habitat
On bodies of fishes. Usually on head or gill covers.
Typical Adult Size
.75 to 1.75 inches.
Sightings
Occasionally seen.
Natural History
Parasitic. Often attach to bodies of blackbar soldierfish, butterfly-fishes and probably other fishes.

ferred to as stomatopods by the scientific set. Many species are quite colorful.

Divers often see mantis shrimps resting at the top of their sandy burrows or near holes in the reef. They are quick to retreat to safety when they feel threatened. Pay heed to the warning and do not try to pry a mantis shrimp out of its hole with your finger or anything else that you want left in one piece.

Usually the claws of mantis shrimps are folded up like the blades of a pocket knife. The claws of the various species differ according to their natural diet, and are believed to be species specific. Those that prefer to feed on animals with hard shells, like snails, have strong, jackhammer-like claws that can deliver quick and repeated blows in order to smash the shell. Other mantis shrimps feed primarily on soft-bodied creatures such as a variety of

worms and small fishes. These mantis shrimps have razor-sharp claws lined with small spines that help them grasp their victims.

ISOPODS, COPEPODS AND AMPHIPODS

Isopods, copepods and **amphipods** are the common names given to a variety of comparatively small, unattractive and often overlooked arthropods. It is worthwhile, however, to note several facts. Copepods feed on single-celled phytoplankton, and in turn are a major component in the plankton supply.

Some copepods and isopods live their lives attached to the bodies of larger animals including bony fishes, sharks, rays, dolphins, turtles and whales. Copepods burrow into the skin of their host, while isopods hold on by clinging. Many copepods and isopods gain nutrition, surprisingly, not by eating away on the bodies of their hosts, but by taking food from the water flowing by them. Most copepods and isopods are much smaller than their host, so their presence is more of a nuisance than it is life threatening. However, if present in significant numbers, parasitic copepods and isopods can kill their host.

Isopods look like the terrestrial crustaceans commonly called pill

bugs. Isopods are often seen on rocky shorelines and around boat docks as they hide in the cracks and crevices on shore. Most species are scavengers that feed on a variety of algae and organic debris, but some isopods parasitize fishes.

The term amphipod refers to a wide variety of crustaceans that are commonly called sand fleas, beach hoppers and water fleas. Amphipods are relatively small creatures that are often present in huge numbers, and collectively they serve as a valuable food source for many larger animals.

Amphipods are commonly found from the shoreline to the deep ocean. Those that inhabit sandy beach areas are often thought to be terrestrial insects. The confusion arises because they do live on land, and unfortunately, they do bite people. The bites are irritating and can often itch for several days. Usually these beach-dwelling amphipods will bury themselves in the sand by day and emerge as the sun begins to set.

12

Phylum: *Echinodermata*

Sea Stars, Crinoids, Brittle Stars, Basket Stars, Sea Cucumbers, Sea Urchins and Sand Dollars

Just about everybody is familiar with at least some of the animals called echinoderms. Sea urchins and sand dollars are universally recognized because their dried skeletons are prized collectibles. Sea stars have become symbols of the marine environment. Sea cucumbers are the black sheep of this phylum in that divers find many species to be rather unattractive. These four are among the most familiar creatures seen during a walk along many seashores. All of these animals are scientifically classified as echinoderms, and collectively they are an interesting lot for a variety of reasons.

Echinoderms are an ancient group of animals that are well known from fossil records. Today there are approximately 6,000 species of echinoderms and all are bottom-dwelling organisms that live exclusively in the marine environment. Most species are found in temperate seas, but the phylum is also well represented in tropical and polar bodies of water, including the Caribbean and associated waters.

The term echinoderm is derived from the Greek "echinos," meaning

Brittle stars commonly take refuge in or among sponges by day, emerging at night to feed. Like many echinoderms, brittle stars can regenerate lost arms and may give one up to a predator in order to escape.

spiny, and "derma," meaning skin. The skin of almost all echinoderms is covered with spines or wart-like projections. But despite its appearance, the skin of most is surprisingly delicate and easily damaged. Filled with thousands of nerves, the sensitive skin protects the animal and surrounds an internal skeleton which, in some cases, is made up of calcium-impregnated plates. As the animal grows, the plates expand to supply structure and support. The spines of echinoderms are attached to these plates.

Other prominent characteristics found in echinoderms are a five-part radial symmetry; distinct organ systems, including tube feet; and the lack of a true brain. Considering the fact that the nervous system of echinoderms is made of a number of simple nerve rings with no central command headquarters, they are capable of surprisingly complex response patterns. The bodies of some echinoderms are covered with small pincer-like organs called pedicellariae, which are used in defense. Echinoderms crawl about the sea floor on thousands of tiny tube feet, which are part of a water vascular system that operates in a coordinated fashion to allow slow but purposeful movement.

When echinoderms walk or crawl, they pump seawater through a series of internal body canals. The

water is used to inflate some of the tube feet, which causes them to extend. In many species, the ends of the tube feet are equipped with suckers which attach to the sea floor and hold tight as specialized muscles in the walls of the tube feet contract to pull the animal forward. The cycle is repeated over and over as the animal slowly but surely traverses the bottom.

The five-part symmetry is immediately obvious in most sea stars and brittle stars, as five arms typically radiate out from a centrally located body disc. However, the pentamerous symmetry is not as readily apparent in basket stars, crinoids, sea cucumbers, sea urchins and sand dollars, but a close investigation will reveal its presence.

In most echinoderms the sexes are separate, but both sexes appear similar. Spawning is usually achieved by releasing sperm and eggs into the water. The resulting larvae spend from a few days to several weeks as plankton before settling down to live their adult lives as bottom-dwellers.

One of the most remarkable traits of all echinoderms is their ability to regenerate lost body parts. For example, some sea stars and brittle stars that lose an arm will grow a nearly perfect replacement. In some species if the lost arm carries with it a portion of the central disc, it will generate a whole new individual and the old individual will also generate a new arm! This ability is an important part of the survival strategy of many echinoderms, as they willingly sacrifice body parts to escape predation.

Modern echinoderms are described in five classes. They are the sea stars, the crinoids, the brittle stars, the sea urchins and sand dollars, and the sea cucumbers.

SEA STARS

Most of the world's approximately 1,500 species of sea stars inhabit the sea floor of temperate and tropical seas where they serve important roles as marine predators. Of the sea stars found in tropical oceans, most live in the Indo-Pacific, but several species do inhabit the waters of the Caribbean, Bahamas and Florida.

The arms of sea stars are thick and prominent, a feature which sets them apart from brittle stars. Most sea stars have five arms, but members of some families possess many more. The mouth of a sea star is located on the underside of the central disc. Neatly arranged rows of tube feet are located on the underside of each arm or ray. In some echinoderms, crinoids for example, the mouth is positioned on the upward-facing surface of the body. But sea stars find their food on the sea floor, not up in the water column, and having the mouth on the underside has its obvious advantages.

Some sea stars have developed the ability to feed on bivalve mollusks. These sea stars are able to grasp the shells of bivalves with the suckers on their tube feet and force them partially open. While holding the shells open, the sea stars extrude their own stomachs through their mouths and in between the shells of the mollusk, and begin to digest their prey externally. Most sea stars do not feed in this manner, but those that do are capable of pushing their

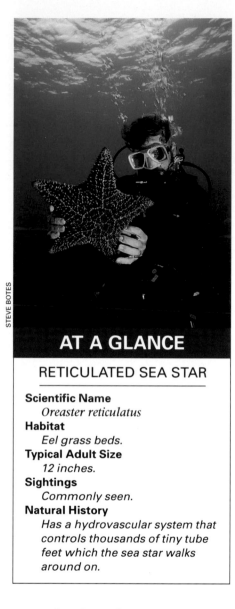

STEVE BOTES

AT A GLANCE

RETICULATED SEA STAR

Scientific Name
Oreaster reticulatus
Habitat
Eel grass beds.
Typical Adult Size
12 inches.
Sightings
Commonly seen.
Natural History
Has a hydrovascular system that controls thousands of tiny tube feet which the sea star walks around on.

stomachs through an opening that is a small as .04 inches wide. Some scientists believe that when the sea star grabs the mollusk, it uses leverage to pull the shells apart. Others support the theory that the sea star forces the mollusk close to the point that it begins to run out of oxygen and is forced to open itself up. Still other scientists maintain that the shells of most mollusks do not seal perfectly and that the sea star does not need to force the shells apart at all. Those who adhere to this theory point out that sea stars can push their stomachs through very small gaps between the shells of mollusks.

As a general rule, sea stars are not prominent members of Caribbean

reef communities. Most Caribbean sea stars are found on sandy bottoms or in eel grass beds, but several species bury themselves in the sand as they dig through soft bottoms in search of food. These species include the **nine-armed sea star** and the **margined sea star**, both of which lack suckers on their tube feet. These sea stars utilize a number of microscopic hairs on their arms to trap their prey and force it into their mouths. They swallow their prey whole, and later discard the shells and other undigestible parts through their mouths.

In contrast, the large sea star known as the **cushion**, or **reticulated sea star**, possesses plenty of large tube feet on the underside of its arms. They have an intricate pattern of bumps on the upper side of their stiff bodies, which are often orange, but the bodies may also be colored yellow or beige. These sea stars do not burrow for their food, but instead find their prey on the surface of the sandy sea floor or in eel grass beds. Cushion stars have deep, thick bodies and thick, wide arms. One of the more prominent Caribbean species because of their large size, cushion stars may attain a length of 20 inches from arm tip-to-arm tip.

Beaded sea stars, **spiny beaded sea stars**, **red spiny sea stars**, and **brown spiny sea stars** are also common on soft bottoms in Florida, and all but the brown spiny sea star are also found in parts of the Caribbean. **Limp sea stars** acquired their common name from the fact that their arms are extremely limp and sag readily if you pick the animal up. **Comet stars** often have one long ray and four shorter rays of equal length.

CRINOIDS (FEATHER STARS)

Occurring in an array of brilliant colors, including gold, orange, red, blue, green, brown, white, black

AT A GLANCE

GOLDEN CRINOID

Scientific Name
Nemaster rubiginosa

Habitat
Reef.

Typical Adult Size
14 inches.

Sightings
Commonly seen.

Natural History
At night commonly perch high atop coral heads and sea fans. Generally hide their central disk and grasping cirripedia within recesses of the reef. Filter feeders using "sticky" arms to trap food.

crinoids are often called, will perch themselves high atop sea fans and coral heads where their arms are best exposed to food-bearing currents. Crinoids are suspension feeders, capturing small planktonic organisms with their tiny tube feet. The arms of crinoids are branched into small structures called pinnules, and each pinnule contains a number of small tube feet. The entire pinnule is covered with secretions which trap food that is then grabbed by the tube feet as the crinoid's arm is curled inward toward the mouth.

Different species of crinoids have anywhere from 5 to 200 arms. When first developing, crinoids have only a few arms, but some of these spe-cies develop additional arms as they grow. The feathery arms will stick to nearly anything that touches them and they are extremely delicate. Be very careful not to touch their arms as they are quick to fall off if even gently tugged on. Crinoids have very simple excretory and reproductive systems, but they possess a complex water vascular system used to

and various combinations, **feather stars** or **crinoids**, can be found in waters around the world. Feather-like in appearance, the arms of these delicate stars project outward from the reef like the feathered plumes of a peacock. The most spectacular Caribbean species, the **golden crinoid**, looks somewhat like a basket made of long yellow branches.

During the day, divers often see only the delicate, feathery arms reaching out of a crevice, but at night many species of feather stars, as

Crinoids are believed to be among the oldest of all sea creatures. When they first appeared in the waters of planet Earth, crinoids were attached to the sea floor by large stalks, and they simply reached up into plankton-rich waters to capture their prey. It is speculated that as time passed, crinoids were forced to become more mobile in order to catch their prey and escape predators. As a result, most lost their stalks. This photograph of a stalked crinoid was taken in Grand Cayman from a submarine at a depth of about 600 feet. Throughout the Caribbean these crinoids are found only in waters far beyond sport diving depths.

AT A GLANCE

BLACK & WHITE CRINOID

Scientific Name
Nemaster grandis

Habitat
Reef.

Typical Adult Size
Arms up to 10 inches long.

Sightings
Occasionally seen.

Natural History
Unlike golden crinoid, this species is often completely exposed during the day, sitting atop coral heads and on gorgonians. Short, stiff feet called cirri grasp substrate.

operate and coordinate the thousands of tube feet on their feathery arms.

Claw-like legs called cirri or cirripedia grip the sea floor and enable feather stars to anchor themselves. They can also change location by crawling slowly along the bottom, and some species can swim for short distances by undulating their bodies. Some are commonly seen only a few feet from the surface, while other species live deeper than 1,500 feet.

Several species of crinoids are commonly seen around the reefs of the Caribbean. Among them are the beautiful **golden crinoid**, the **white crinoid, black-and-white crinoid, green crinoid, red crinoid** and the small **swimming crinoid**. One of the more common crinoids in many parts of the Caribbean is the golden crinoid, a reef resident that commonly catches the attention of divers because of its rich golden color. Golden crinoids have twenty arms, all of which can be as long as 10 inches. The more subtly colored white crinoids are smaller than golden crinoids. Quite often only a few of the arms of white crinoids extend out of crevices at any one time. The 40 arms of black-and-white crinoids can be close to 10 inches in length. The arms and the branched segments or pinnules on each ray are black, and the pinnules have white tips. When compared to other Caribbean feather stars, one of the most unusual characteristics of black-and-white crinoids is that the entire animal is often completely exposed on top of a coral head during the day.

Not seen as often as other species, green crinoids are secretive animals that often hide in crevices even at night. They anchor themselves to the bottom with as many as 90 cirri. The rays of red crinoids often appear brownish underwater because the species is normally found deeper than 50 feet, where red light from the sun has been filtered out by the water. Another of the more reclusive species, red crinoids are usually seen only at night.

Swimming crinoids are the smallest of all the Caribbean feather stars. Each of the ten thin rays of these delicate animals are only two to three inches long. The rays boast red and white alternating bands. Swimming crinoids may be seen during the day, but more typically they are seen at night perched high up on sea fans and sea plumes. These nimble crinoids are capable of crawling across the substrate, but they also swim by moving their arms in rhythmic undulations.

AT A GLANCE

BRITTLE STAR

Scientific Name
Unidentified species

Habitat
Hidden in coral rubble, under ledges, and in and under sponges during the day; on sponges and coral at night.

Typical Adult Size
8 inches.

Sightings
Commonly seen.

Natural History
Brittle stars are extremely sensitive to light. Most hide during the day and emerge at night to feed. They are quick to flee and may readily sacrifice an arm to save the rest of the body when threatened by predators. Can regenerate lost arms.

BRITTLE STARS AND BASKET STARS

At first glance it might not be obvious that **brittle stars** and **basket** **stars** are closely related animals. In fact, the basic design of brittle stars and basket stars is very similar. Their bodies are composed of a central disc that is distinctly separate from the animal's slender arms, but the brittle stars have many more arms.

On many reefs, brittle stars seem to occupy almost every conceivable place. Some species bury themselves in the sand; others hide in crevices in the reef, but most of the species which we commonly encounter live in or on sponges. Brittle stars tend to shy away from light, so they are mostly seen at night. During the day they usually seek shelter in dimly-lit crevices, under the sand, and deep in the base or on the underside of sponges. Their arms are lined with a number of spines arranged in rows. Brittle stars also possess very

AT A GLANCE

BASKET STAR

Scientific Name
 Astrophyton muricatum
Habitat
 Reef, atop gorgonians.
Typical Adult Size
 2 feet.
Sightings
 Commonly seen.
Natural History
 Hide within recesses of the reef by day, but emerge at night and spread out their basket-like arms to filter plankton from the water column.

PHOTO TIP

Capture these impressive animals on film at night by using a wide-angle lens such as a 15mm, and focusing and framing from about 18 inches away from the basket star. At this close distance you will have some parallax problems, so be sure to correct by placing your lens in the position your viewfinder was in when you composed the shot.

If you are using a TTL system, be sure to set your film speed, and you will probably want to bracket, especially in those situations where the basket star and its perch do not occupy 75 percent of the frame. Bracket by fooling your TTL system by dialing in faster and slower film speeds than the one you are actually using.

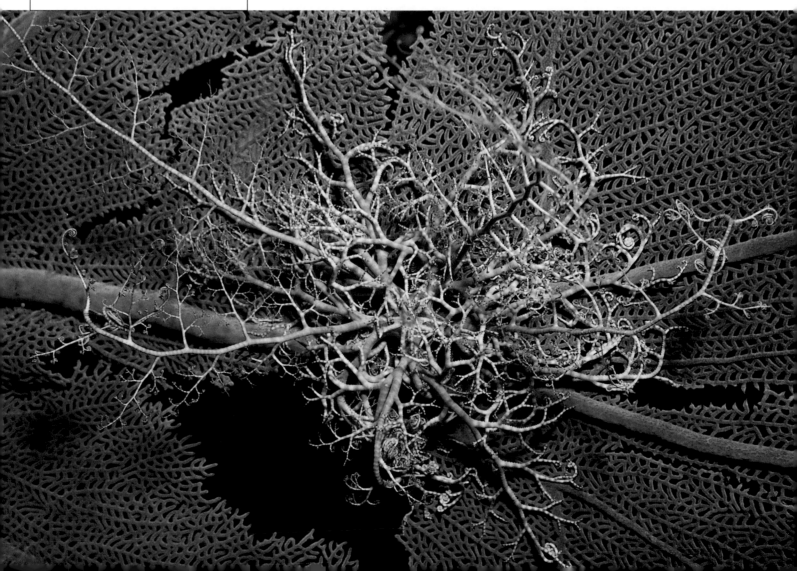

AT A GLANCE

BASKET STAR, SEA ROD BASKET STAR

Scientific Name
Schizostella bifurcata

Habitat
Sloping fore reefs and in groups on gorgonians.

Typical Adult Size
Disc diameter to 1 inch.

Sightings
Occasionally seen.

Natural History
Usually noticed when gathered together in dense groups on gorgonians, typically sea rods. During day, wrap arms tightly around gorgonian and look like a miniature brain. During night, unfurl to feed. Arms branch once or twice, making it possible to distinguish them from small crinoids.

fine tube feet distributed along these rows. In some species, the spines are quite dense and give the arms a thick, fuzzy appearance. During the day, observant divers often see only the exposed tips of the fuzzy arms.

At night brittle stars emerge to feed. Often a single sponge serves as the feeding ground for several dozen brittle stars. Some brittle stars are suspension feeders, capturing plankton out of the water column. Other species sift through sand, searching for organic debris and small invertebrates that are on the sea floor, while still others are active predators that pursue a variety of small invertebrates and vertebrates. Once the food has been captured, the tube feet are used to help guide the food from the arms into the central mouth.

More than 20 species of brittle stars inhabit the waters of the Carribean, Bahamas and Florida. Among the most common are the **red brittle star, Swenson's brittle star, ruby brittle star, Oersted's brittle star** and the **long-armed nocturnal brittle star.**

Basket stars have five arms as do brittle stars, but the arms of basket stars are branched at the base. The branches are also branched, and the repeated branching eventually creates a mass of arms that looks much like a large tangled ball of yarn. With the cover of darkness and encouraged by a little current, this tangled ball often moves high atop promontories of the reef and unfurls its arms. The now untangled arms form a tightly woven basket-like filtering mechanism which sweeps the waters for plankton and other organic matter. Tube feet are arranged in regular patterns along each of the arms to help the animal secure itself and pass along food particles to its central mouth.

As their common name suggests, brittle stars are somewhat fragile. They are quick to sacrifice an arm or two in order to escape from predators and will often shed an arm if touched, so avoid contact with these delicate animals. Most brittle stars are surprisingly agile and quite mobile. Their speed helps them avoid predators and capture prey. Even during the day, brittle stars will often come to food, traveling considerable distances.

SEA CUCUMBERS

Sea cucumbers are the vacuum cleaners of the reefs. Using their brush-like mouths, they ingest and process organic material from sediment and sand found around reefs. Sea cucumbers often leave neat rows of deposits of excreted inorganic materials behind them.

Some sea cucumbers possess the

ability to eviscerate or expel their sticky stomachs when threatened. Predators get distracted or repelled by the expelled stomach and the sea cucumber chugs on. Amazingly, sea cucumbers can regenerate a new stomach in only a few days.

When relaxed, the bodies of sea cucumbers are flexible and elongated, but when disturbed they have the ability to shorten and harden their bodies. If handled, most species are quick to protect themselves in this manner.

Sea cucumbers differ from the other classes of echinoderms in that they are soft bodied, slug-like animals whose bodies lack spines. Outwardly they bear little resemblance to their ancestors and this becomes obvious when you view a cross-section of the animal. They have five elongated radial muscles, demonstrating the characteristic body plan (pentamerous or five-sided symmetry) found in all echinoderms. The skin of many sea cucumbers is leathery, and in most species is covered by many wart-like projections. Most sea cucumbers spend their lives lying on the sea floor, though a few of

the approximately 1,500 species can swim.

The mouth of a sea cucumber is located on one end of its sausage-shaped body, with the animal's anus on the opposite end. The mouth lacks teeth, but it is surrounded by anywhere from 8 to 30 mop-like tentacles that are used for feeding. The tentacles are actually modified tube feet. In some species, the tentacles secrete a mucous net that is used to trap small planktonic organisms that the sea cucumbers prey upon. When a sea cucumber feeds, each tentacle is wiped off periodically inside the animal's esophagus to remove the food and replace the coating of mucus.

When feeding, some species of sea cucumbers ingest sediment off the sea floor. Organic nutrients are extracted from the sediment and tube-shaped castings of processed waste material are left behind. In many parts of the world especially the Far East, sea cucumbers are highly valued as food.

On close inspection of sea cucumbers, you will likely see a number of tube feet on the body in addition

to the modified tentacles that surround the mouth. The tube feet may be scattered about the body, or distributed only in five lateral grooves. The tube feet help the animals crawl across the bottom, and in many instances the animals use a combination of wriggling and pulling with their tube feet to move along the sea floor. Some species have one surface that is slightly flattened, and they orient themselves with the flattened side down. In these species the tube feet are located on the flattened side.

In other species the tube feet are scattered evenly over the body and there is no flattened body segment as all sides look the same.

Most sea cucumbers are comparatively sluggish animals, especially those that live within sport diving depths. Several deep-water species are surprisingly active swimmers.

Sea cucumbers possess an intricate internal system of branched respiratory trees. Seawater is pulled in and then expelled in a series of contractions as oxygen is extracted from the water and carbon dioxide is removed from the sea cucumber's system.

The sexes of sea cucumbers are separate in most species, though some are hermaphrodites, meaning that a single animal possesses both male and female reproductive organs. Eggs and sperm are released into the water. Fertilization produces free-swimming larvae which undergo several stages of metamorphosis before developing into small adults.

Caribbean species of sea cucumbers are found on the reef, on sandy bottoms, and in eel grass beds. However, the elongated **tiger's tail** sea cucumber is almost always seen projecting outward over the sand from the protective recesses of the reef.

Although several species of Caribbean sea cucumbers can often be seen on sand patches at all hours of the day, the animals feed mostly at night. Approximately 20 species of sea cucumbers are found in the waters of the Caribbean, Bahamas and Florida. Among the most common species are the tiger's tail and the **donkey dung sea cucumber.** Commonly exceeding six feet in length, tiger's tail sea cucumbers are large yet reclusive. Their brownish to gray bodies are usually seen at night on sand bottoms where they feed. The body is covered with spine-like warts. The tiger's tail grabs the reef with the hind section of its body and then sweeps its head and mouth across the sand in search of food.

The donkey dung sea cucumber

is a stout species which reaches about 20 inches when fully grown. The upper side of the body is covered with small bumps while the underside is quite flattened. Donkey dung sea cucumbers are often seen in the middle of sand holes where they process sediment and leave behind neat packets of residue.

SEA URCHINS AND SAND DOLLARS

The bodies of both **sea urchins** and **sand dollars** display five-part symmetry as do all echinoderms, but both of these groups lack arms. In sea urchins and sand dollars, five rows of neatly arranged tube feet protrude through the hard calcified plates. The fused plates and pores can easily be seen when you look at the shells, or the tests as they are called.

Sea urchins look like pin cushions with the pointed ends sticking out. Few marine creatures inflict the amount of pain and suffering on divers and snorkelers as do sea ur-

chins. Their long, needle-like spines have managed to find their way into the skin of many divers, snorkelers and even beachgoers wading along the shoreline. In the vast majority of cases the spines are not overly toxic, but they are painful and difficult to remove.

Examining the spines under a microscope will reveal a shape like a multi-barbed fish hook. They are

AT A GLANCE

LONG-SPINED URCHIN

Scientific Name
Diadema antillarum

Habitat
Reef, in holes during the day, but on top at night.

Typical Adult Size
10 inches in diameter.

Sightings
Commonly seen in many areas, though almost eliminated from many reef communities in Florida by blight.

Natural History
Very long spines help protect them from predators. Their defenses are not formidable against triggerfishes, however, which flip the urchins over and attack their undersides.

AT A GLANCE

CLUB URCHIN, SLATE PENCIL URCHIN

Scientific Name
Eucidaris tribuloides

Habitat
Reef, in holes during the day, but on top at night.

Typical Adult Size
1.5 inches in diameter.

Sightings
Commonly seen.

Natural History
Come out of their recesses in the reef at night to graze on algae.

designed to penetrate easily and difficult to remove. In addition, the spines are brittle and often break if you try to remove them with a pair of tweezers.

Soaking in hot water can help lessen the pain. Use a topical ointment to prevent infection and a drawing salve to help bring the pieces of spine to the surface of your skin. Often the fragments won't be expelled for several weeks, so be extremely careful not to touch or settle on urchins.

The worst offender is the **long-spined urchin**, whose long, needle-like spines project outward for as much as 12 inches from their central disc. These urchins are blackish and neon blue, and should be given ample leeway, especially at night when they leave the recesses of the reef to graze on algae.

The bodies and spines of the **reef urchin** and **club urchin** are very colorful and far less hazardous than the long-spined urchin. The reef urchin has a scarlet disc with cream-colored spines, while the club urchin has a finely detailed red and cream-colored disc, and blunt, often encrusted spines.

The **jewel urchin** flaunts a similar color scheme on its disc as well as emerald-green spines and purple-tipped pedicellariae, small pincer-like organs found on the surface of many echinoderms which help keep the body clean.

Given the fortress of spines carried by the long-spined urchin, one would think that these urchins would be avoided on the reef. How-

ever, this is not always the case. Queen triggerfish commonly take hold of a spine of these urchins and flip them over so that they can get to the unprotected underside.

Boring urchins have dull red to black bodies with dark spines and are seen in very shallow reef areas where they actually bore holes into coral heads with their sharp teeth. Boring urchins reside in their holes during the day and leave them at night when they graze for food. A

AT A GLANCE

JEWEL URCHIN

Scientific Name
Lytechinus williamsi

Habitat
Reef, in holes during the day, but on top at night.

Typical Adult Size
1.5 inches in diameter.

Sightings
Commonly seen.

Natural History
Come out of their recesses in the reef at night to graze on algae.

stand how these animals are so closely related. Sea urchins and sand dollars walk across the bottom by using their tube feet, and some urchins gain additional thrust by manipulating their spines.

The sexes of sea urchins and sand dollars are separate as they are in most echinoderms. Many species simply release eggs and sperm into the water. Other species brood their offspring before releasing them.

AT A GLANCE

REEF URCHIN

Scientific Name
Echinometra viridis
Habitat
Shallow reefs.
Typical Adult Size
2-inch diameter body, spines 2 to 4 inches.
Sightings
Occasionally to seldom seen.
Natural History
Hides during day, emerges to feed on algae at night.

often cover their bodies with algae and other debris.

In contrast to the other echinoderms, **sand dollars** have flat, disc-like bodies that are shaped like large silver dollars. Once you compare the tests of sand dollars to sea urchins, it becomes much easier to under-

AT A GLANCE

SEA BISCUIT, HEART URCHIN

Scientific Name
Meoma ventricosa
Habitat
Sand; often in sandy areas within turtle grass beds.
Typical Adult Size
3 to 8 inches in diameter.
Sightings
Occasionally seen, but generally in places that are not often dived.
Natural History
Burrow into sand; preyed upon by helmet snails.

small, colorful fish, known as the greenbanded goby, often associates with boring urchins. This goby takes refuge amongst the urchin's protective spines.

Two other species, the **red heart urchin** and the **edible urchin** have circular bodies with very short spines. Their bodies are three to seven inches across and two to three inches thick. Red heart urchins, like other heart urchins, are usually buried under the sand and are only seen on rare occasions. The upper surface of red heart urchins displays a large five-rayed star pattern.

Edible urchins have dark bodies with short whitish spines. These urchins do not bury themselves, but

13

Phylum: *Chordata* Subphylum: *Urochordata*

TUNICATES (SEA SQUIRTS AND SALPS)

Most animals described in the phylum Chordata (the chordates) possess a backbone, and as a result, are referred to as vertebrates. However, this is not the case with tunicates, a group of animals that includes sea squirts and salps. Lacking a backbone, these invertebrates are described in the subphylum Urochordata. They are chordates, but they are not vertebrates.

Chordates share four common characteristics: (1) a single, hollow nerve cord that lies just beneath the dorsal surface of the animal; (2) a flexible supportive rod made of cartilage called a notochord; (3) pharyngeal slits; and (4) at some point in their lives they have a tail.

In their larval stage, tunicates possess a notochord which is considered to be the forerunner of the backbone in vertebrates, and it is interesting to note that in the human embryonic stage, we have a notochord which eventually develops into a portion of our spine. Tunicates

also have other well-developed internal organs including a stomach, intestines and a heart.

Tunicates are described in two classes: the ascidians (class Ascidiacae), commonly referred to as sea squirts, and the thaliaceans (class Thaliacea), typically called salps.

SEA SQUIRTS

Sea squirts are surprisingly common animals. Worldwide, there are approximately 1,500 species. As adults, most are bottom dwellers which live in shallow water. Some tunicates live in highly interdependent, geometrically shaped colonies, while other species are solitary.

Sea squirts are relatively simple animals. They vary in size from a kernel of corn to the whole cob. Their bodies have no particular shape. Some species are tube-like, others barrel-shaped, and some look like a blown-up plastic bag on a stalk. One end of the body in both colonial and solitary species is attached to the sea floor, while the other end has two openings. A sea squirt obtains food and oxygen by drawing water into the opening called the oral opening, and then passing it through a mucus gill net where the food and oxygen are extracted. The water is then passed out through the second opening called the excurrent, or atrial, opening.

Some tunicates secrete a tough, cellulose-based sac called a tunic, which surrounds the animal and gives meaning to the common name tunicates. In some colonial species,

there may be one common tunic and one common opening to the surrounding water.

Tunicates are often mistaken for sponges, but with only a little practice it becomes fairly easy to tell the two groups apart. The outer surface of tunicates is shiny, slimy and gelatinous-looking, while the surface of sponges appears dull and cloth-like. The pores or openings on the surface of sponges vary in size in the same specimen, and they tend to be irregularly spaced. The holes in the surface of tunicates are similarly sized, paired and often regularly spaced. If you peer down the openings of sponges, you may see a number of channels, but you will not see internal organs because sponges lack organs and specialized tissues. Tunicates, on the other hand, have internal organs that are clearly visible in many cases. However, the tunic of some sea squirts occludes the internal organs.

Among the most common species of Caribbean ascidians are the **giant tunicate**, **yellow tube tunicate**, **lightbulb tunicate**, **strawberry tunicate** and the **purple tunicate**. Standing three to four inches tall and one to two inches in diameter, yellow tube tunicates are large solitary animals that are quite common and very easy to recognize. As their common name suggests, lightbulb tunicates bear a strong resemblance to a lightbulb. Clusters of these tunicates are often found on vertical walls and beneath ledges. Distinctive identifying characteristics include a translucent outer surface and a white, or purple and white, ring around the incurrent opening.

AT A GLANCE

PAINTED TUNICATE

Scientific Name
Clavelina picta
Habitat
Reef.
Typical Adult Size
3 inches.
Sightings
Commonly seen.
Natural History
Larval tunicate has primitive notochord making these animals very advanced invertebrates.

AT A GLANCE

GIANT TUNICATE

Scientific Name
 Polycarpa spongiabilis
Habitat
 Reef.
Typical Adult Size
 3 inches.
Sightings
 Commonly seen.
Natural History
 Body often covered with algae.

The dull-red strawberry tunicates are only about an inch or so in diameter. Their nearly spherical colonies typically contain many individuals. Purple tunicates appear similar to lightbulb tunicates in terms of their shape and size. However, purple tunicates are quite striking due to their deep-blue to purple coloration. Individuals possess a translucent tunic. Each animal stands about one inch high, and clusters may be as large as one foot in diameter. Colonies of purple tunicates are commonly found attached to gorgonians and dead coral.

SALPS

Salps are free-swimming tunicates, also called pelagic tunicates. At first glance, individual salps look a lot like small jellyfish. Salps are capable of self-propulsion, but for the most part, these translucent, gelatinous-looking animals float in mid-water going wherever the prevailing currents take them. Salps have an incurrent opening on one end of their body and an excurrent opening on the other. Muscular contractions draw water in through the incurrent opening and push the water through the body, providing thrust for locomotion in a rudimentary form of jet propulsion. Food and oxygen are extracted from the water which is then expelled through the excurrent opening.

Salps reproduce by asexual budding. At times a number of buds are attached to one another in linked chains commonly called salp chains. The chains are often spiral-shaped or curled in a captivating circular pattern. Some species of salps are colonial, always occuring in linked chains, while the adults of other species live a solitary existence.

Salps are sometimes confused with jellyfishes and comb jellies because many species are semi-transparent and tend to drift in mid-water currents. Like many species of jellyfishes and comb jellies, many salp species are one to six inches long and two to four inches in diameter.

Distinguishing salp chains, like the one pictured here, from jellyfishes and comb jellies is not difficult. The internal organs of salps are apparent upon close inspection, as you will often see a pea-sized, orangy mass located near one end of the body. Salps do not have the potent trailing tentacles found in jellyfishes, and they lack the ciliated strands found in the bodies of comb jellies. Jellyfishes are cnidarians, while comb jellies are members of the phylum of invertebrates known as ctenophores.

SECTION
IV

Marine Life: The Vertebrates
Phylum by Phylum

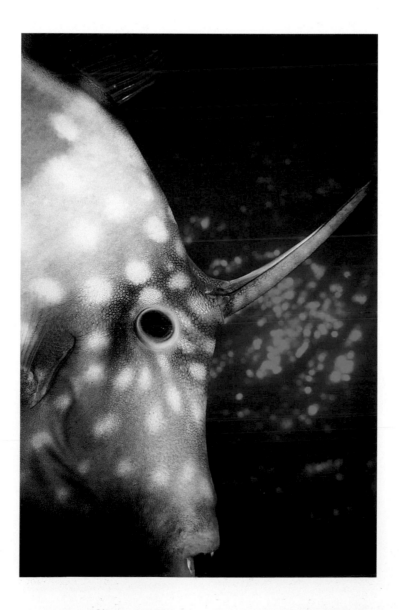

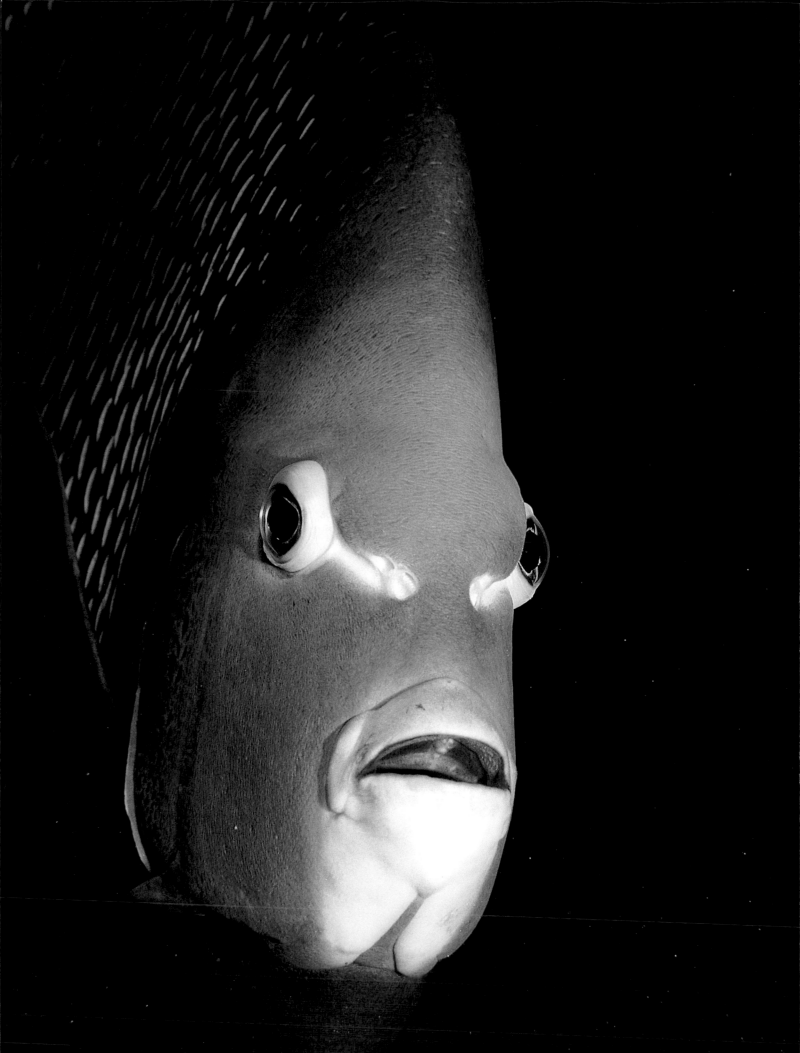

14

Phylum: *Chordata* Subphylum: *Vertebrata*

THE WORLD OF FISHES: AN OVERVIEW

Ichthyologists estimate that there are approximately 28,000 species of fishes living in the waters of planet Earth. Of these, close to 12,000 live in the marine environment, and most marine species inhabit tropical seas. In terms of evolutionary time, however, the Caribbean is a comparatively young sea. As a result, less than 1,000 species of fishes live in the Caribbean. Obviously that is a lot of species for snorkelers and scuba divers to enjoy, but by comparison to the waters of the Indo-Pacific, the Caribbean is species-poor.

There are three major classes of fishes. They are (1) the bony fishes, class Osteichthyes; (2) the cartilaginous fishes, class Chondrichthyes; and (3) the roundmouth fishes such as lampreys, class Cyclostomata. Sport divers are typically interested in only two of these classes, and those are the ones covered in this book. These classes are the bony fishes: species such as angelfishes, butterflyfishes, groupers, squirrelfishes, puffers, gobies, blennies, etc; and the cartilaginous fishes: the sharks, rays and skates.

The vast majority of fishes are

Opposite page: French angelfish, symbolic of marine wildlife in the Caribbean, Bahamas, and Florida, are always a welcome sight for divers and a special challenge to underwater photographers.

Section opener: Marine vertebrates are well represented in all the Caribbean and associated waters. This group includes sharks, rays, bony fishes, sea turtles, manatees, dolphins and whales.

bony fishes. The major difference between bony fishes and cartilaginous fishes is that the skeletons of bony fishes are made from bone, while the skeletons of all sharks, rays and skates are made of cartilage. This means that the world's largest fish—the whale shark, an animal that reaches proportions of close to 50 feet and 50,000 pounds—does not have a single bone in its entire body!

For many years, it was believed that cartilaginous fishes first appeared on earth approximately 450 million years ago while bony fishes were only 120 to 150 million years old. However, recent evidence from fossil discoveries suggest that bony fishes are perhaps as old as 350 million years.

Bony fishes and cartilaginous fishes differ in a number of other ways as well. Most bony fishes possess an internal organ called a swim bladder which helps them ascend, descend and achieve neutral buoyancy. The swim bladder adds or subtracts gases from the bloodstream, and thereby, expands or contracts as it helps the fish alter its buoyancy. The use of a swim bladder is a great energy saver, as those fishes that have swim bladders do not have to expend as much energy swimming in order to control their buoyancy.

Sharks, rays and skates lack a swim bladder, and if these animals stop swimming they will quickly sink. A lighter weight skeleton made of cartilage is one adaptation that helps cartilaginous fishes combat the potential problem caused by the lack of a swim bladder. However, many cartilaginous fishes, es-

pecially those that live in the open sea, must swim all day, every day of their lives, to avoid sinking.

The gills of most bony fishes are covered by a bone-like flap called an operculum, which is moved back and forth to pump oxygen-rich water over the gills. Sharks, rays and skates have five to seven gill slits on either side of their head, but they lack an operculum. As a result, many cartilaginous fishes must swim constantly to wash oxygen-filled water over the tissues in their gills.

The skin of bony fishes is covered by protective scales. The size of individual scales varies considerably from species to species, but in many species the scales can easily be seen with the naked eye. In sharks, rays and skates, the scales are absent. The skin of cartilaginous fishes is comprised of small, tooth-like structures called dermal denticles (skin teeth), and in their developmental process, the skin of sharks, rays and skates grows from the mouth back. When viewed under a microscope the skin looks like thousands of miniature teeth that are aligned in the same direction. This is why the skin of a shark feels very rough if you rub it in one direction, but smooth as velvet if you rub it in the opposite direction.

Another difference between bony and cartilaginous fishes is the positioning of the mouth. In most species of cartilaginous fishes the mouth is said to be underslung, meaning positioned below the snout. The whale shark is one of several obvious exceptions, having its mouth in the very front of its face. The mouths of bony fishes are typically located at the front of the body, in a position known as the terminal position.

Bony fishes reproduce through external fertilization by a variety of methods of spawning. Cartilaginous fishes reproduce by internal fertilization. Sexing sharks, rays and skates in the water is relatively easy if you get a chance to look at their underside. The males of all species possess a pair of claspers which are located about three-fourths of the way down the body, on the underside on sharks, and near the base of the tail in rays and skates. The tube-like claspers are part of the male reproductive system, each being somewhat analogous to a penis. In females, a slit in the underbelly can usually be seen in the same general area where the claspers are positioned in the males of the same species.

FISH SENSES

Fishes rely on a combination of the senses of sight, feel, taste, hearing and smell in their daily lives. Sight is extremely important to many species, especially those living in relatively clear, shallow water, while sight is surprisingly unimportant to others. The eyes of fishes are similar to human eyes in many respects and are considered to be well developed. Fishes are, however, able to move each eye independently, and each eye can be rotated to enable the fish to see over a very wide field of view—hence the term fish-eye lens.

The ability to see a wide field is extremely valuable in a world where predators strike in near total silence. As a general rule, color vision in bony fishes is believed to be much more refined than that of sharks, rays and skates. Bony fishes that live in shallow reef communities often demonstrate good color vision, while deep-water species lack color receptors.

WHEN TO SAY *FISH* AND WHEN TO SAY *FISHES*

Exactly when to use the word *fish*, and when to use *fishes*, is often misunderstood. The use of the word *fishes* sometimes seems a little "high brow," but actually the two words have different meanings. The term *fishes* is the correct plural when collectively referring to more than one species. The word *fish* is the correct singular and plural when only one species is involved.

For example, it is correct to say that a great barracuda and a French angelfish represent two different species of *fishes*. And it is also proper to say that there are 20 or more *fish* in a school of barracuda, as long as all the *fish* in the school are the same species of barracuda. If more than one species of barracuda are in the school, they should be referred to as barracudas. The same is true with other groups of animals, such as lobster/lobsters, shrimp/shrimps, and squid/squids.

All fishes have a system of nerves and specialized organs, called the lateral line system, that runs down the outside of their bodies. The lateral line system enables fishes to feel pressure waves created by the motion of other animals and objects in the water. The system is very sensitive and is believed to play an important role in helping fishes avoid predators. It also enables schooling fishes to swim in close proximity to one another while making instantaneous turns without having collisions. The lateral line systems of bony fishes is thought to be more highly developed than those of cartilaginous fishes.

Sharks partially compensate for their underdeveloped lateral line system by using special organs in their snouts called the ampullae of

In their daily lives, fishes rely on a variety of senses including sight, hearing, smell, feel and taste. Which senses are most important varies from species to species. Vision is especially important in many reef species which live in relatively clear, shallow water.

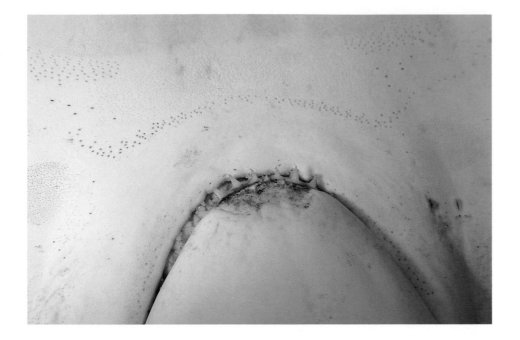

The clusters of dark dots above the mouth of this hammerhead shark are the highly specialized organs known as ampullae of Lorenzini. They help sharks detect the electrical fields emitted by their prey.

Lorenzini. The ampullae look like tiny gel-filled pits and are extremely sensitive to pressure and to electrical fields. In fact, sharks have the ability to detect electrical fields that are 10,000 times more faint than fields that can be detected by any other known group of animals. Biological functions, such as a beating heart, create an electrical field which surrounds all living animals. The detection of an electrical field translates into the detection of potential prey, and this ability helps make sharks superb hunters.

The keen ability to detect electrical fields also helps explain why sharks eat aluminum cans and occasionally bite the metallic swim steps of boats. For millions of years an electrical field has meant food to sharks. However, it is only in recent years that our species has been confusing the issue by placing man-made metal objects in salt water. The metal objects combine with salt water to create an electrical current which sometimes fools sharks into thinking these objects are a natural food source.

Sound also plays an important role in the lives of many fishes. Squirrelfishes, groupers, triggerfishes and other fishes produce grunting sounds that are believed to be important methods of communication. For example, when alarmed the grunting noise produced by a squirrelfish is thought to serve as a warning to other members of its species that danger is present. Seasoned fishermen are well aware that noise created in a boat by clumsy peers means cheeseburgers, not fish, for dinner. The noise from divers' bubbles can have the same effect.

Many fishes rely heavily on their sense of smell. Species such as moray eels employ their sense of smell to locate prey. Some parrotfishes spin a cocoon of mucus around their bodies when they sleep at night in order to mask their odor. Along the same lines, octopuses emit ink when threatened, not so much as a smoke screen to obscure vision, but because chemicals in the ink are known to dull the olfactory senses of eels. In addition, when threatened, some fishes are known to emit chemicals which have a detectable odor intended to warn other members of their species of impending danger.

Studies have shown that taste is not relied on as heavily as are the other senses. By contrast, fishes are often extremely sensitive to touch, and many are quick to flee upon contact with a foreign object, such as a fish hook.

DIVERSITY IN FISHES

Fishes are a highly diversified group of animals. They vary widely in terms of their size, shape, what part of the marine environment they inhabit, what they like to eat, how they protect themselves, how they reproduce, and in general, how and where they fit into nature's overall plan. Each species has carved out its own niche and is therefore slightly different than every other. Some fishes, such as angelfishes, coneys and squirrelfishes, are brilliantly colored and stand out prominently in their natural settings. Others, like scorpionfishes and flatfishes, are drab and well camouflaged. Some species, such as barracudas, sharks, jacks, marlin and tunas, are true speed merchants, while still others such as frogfishes, batfishes and balloonfishes are very poor swimmers. The slow swimmers have learned to rely on adaptations other than speed to ensure their survival.

Fishes vary in size from tiny gobies, whose length is measured in fractions of an inch, to 50-foot-long, 50,000-pound whale sharks. Obviously these species fit into different niches; whale sharks live in the open sea, while gobies are usually found inhabiting the reefs. Surprisingly, whale sharks, like many small gobies, feed primarily on plankton.

Not only do fishes that live in different parts of the ocean vary significantly from one another, but species that live in that same habitat vary. It is a well-accepted theory among scientists that two species cannot

HOW FISHES USE COLOR

While the rich colors of this queen angelfish are certain to capture our attention, scientists do not completely understand how fishes use their coloration. Some fishes are thought to be brightly colored to advertise their presence. In some cases, the bright coloration is intended to serve as a warning that says "I am here, leave me alone." In some species, males and females are different colors, a feature which helps in attracting or selecting a potential mate. The same is true in species in which adults and juveniles are colored differently.

Scientists believe that the bright colors and intricate patterns of many fishes actually make it more difficult for potential predators to see an entire fish all at once. In effect, the bright color patterns are so distracting that they break up the look of the fish.

Many species of reef fishes flash or change colors as part of a communication process when they are requesting cleaning services. Once satisfied that the cleaning is complete, they again change colors.

The color changes are governed by specialized cells in the skin called chromatophores, which are directly connected to a fish's nervous system. As a result, fishes are able to contract or expand each cell, bringing about a nearly instantaneous color change. Many fishes such as flounders and scorpionfishes commonly change their color to match their surroundings. This ability indicates that the eyes of these fishes are somehow connected with the nerves that control the color cells.

---

compete for the same food source during the same time of day in the same manner. Eventually, one species will out-compete the other, and the loser will be forced to move on or perish. In many tropical seas hundreds of species can be found in the same reef system, but a close study will show that each species feeds in a slightly different way.

A different daily feeding cycle often allows two species to share a common food source. For example, goatfishes feed on small crustaceans during the day. At night the goatfishes retire, but squirrelfishes emerge from their daytime shelters to feed on the same species of crustaceans. The large eyes of the squirrelfishes are a valuable adaptation that enables them to gather enough light to see their prey at night. With the daylight, the squirrelfishes are quick to seek cover and the goatfishes begin their hunt.

A number of other adaptations also help enable fish to capture their food. For example, some bottom fishes, such as triggerfishes, hog-fishes and trunkfishes, blow jets of water into the sand in an effort to uncover their prey. Goatfishes, on the other hand, utilize their keenly sensitized barbels to help them detect prey that might be hiding under the sand. Still other fishes steal their food by being quick to capture the uncovered, but still uneaten, victims of those species that dig into the sea floor. The bar jacks that follow stingrays across the sand provide a classic case in point.

Puffers and parrotfishes possess large buckteeth and powerful jaws which enable them to crunch up corals. In most cases, these fishes are primarily interested in ingesting various algae that grow on the corals and not the corals themselves. Schooling tangs and surgeonfishes also prey primarily on algae that grows on the coral, but these species pluck the algae off the coral rather than ingest the coral.

The pursed lips and slightly elongated mouths of tangs and damselfishes are well adapted to help them pick at algae which is attached to the bottom. The mouths of many other bottom feeders are positioned slightly toward the lower portion of their head, and in many cases, the mouth is angled slightly downward as well. This subtle, yet important, positioning provides easier access to their food. By contrast, the mouths of many mid-water fishes such as silversides are turned slightly upwards to help them pluck their prey out of bright surface waters.

The use of territory, or the lack of territory, is another way in which fishes demonstrate their diversity. Some species roam the great expanse of the open sea throughout their lives. These species do not defend a territory in which they feed or breed. Some of these species, such as a variety of jacks, tunas and mackerels, live in huge schools, while marlins, sailfishes and sharks typically prefer a more solitary existence. Like their open ocean counterparts, schooling reef fishes, such as snappers, grunts, tangs and surgeonfishes, do not defend a territory. But many solitary reef species do. At times some damselfishes, triggerfishes, blennies and other reef residents stake out territories which they staunchly defend.

Some territorial fishes are only territorial during their breeding season. Others only defend a territory during a certain stage of their lives. For example, surgeonfishes are territorial as juveniles but not as adults.

In still other species, such as many blennies, only one sex is territorial. Male sailfin blennies and bluethroat pikeblennies display demonstratively in order to ward off intruders. In many cases, these displays are directed toward other males of their own species. Studies have shown these displays to be highly successful in avoiding actual physical confrontations. In the vast majority of cases, the intruder chooses to leave the defended territory rather than risk an injury which could prove fatal in the wild.

WHY SOME FISHES SCHOOL

Schooling is an adaptation found in approximately 80 percent of all species of fishes as juveniles, and 20 percent of all species during their adult stages. Exactly why fishes school, like the crevalle jacks seen here, is a question that has intrigued scientists for years. The following theories are thought to be some of the major reasons that various fishes school.

The idea of safety-in-numbers is believed to play a fundamental role in schooling behavior. The old adage that "big fish eat little fish" is generally true. To overcome the problem caused by their diminutive size, many small fishes gather together in schools. It is believed that the schools appear to be a large shape, and potential predators tend to leave large things alone.

Another part of the safety-in-numbers concept is the fact that even if a predator does attack the school, the odds are small that any given fish will be the one the predator chooses to pursue. Each fish operates under the premise that it is safer hiding amongst the school than it is roaming the waters alone.

And when a predator attacks, the movement of all the fish within the school sometimes confuses the predator. This momentary confusion is often long enough to allow all the potential prey to escape. In nature, it simply doesn't work for a predator to swim through a school of fish with mouth agape, while hoping to get lucky. The predator must select a single victim and be able to pursue it with all its energy and cunning.

To combat this confusion, some predators, such as a variety of jacks and tunas, work together by hunting in schools. They frighten their prey into smaller groups, making it easier to target a single victim.

Another advantage of schooling is to be close to one another for breeding purposes. Close proximity makes it easier for the species to reproduce more offspring than potential predators can consume, thus ensuring the survival of their species.

Schooling also can help overcome the defenses of territorial fishes. For example, some damselfishes are highly territorial. The damsel will bite or ram into any fish that invades the algae patches it cultivates within its domain. By invading the damsel's realm in large schools, surgeonfishes can overcome its defenses. It is impossible for a single damsel to ward off a school of voracious surgeonfishes, and the surgeons are able to consume considerable quantities of algae despite the damsel's spirited efforts.

Schooling is also believed to make swimming easier by reducing the resistance of the water. Just as race car drivers "draft" the car in front of them by staying close behind in order to reduce wind resistance while getting sucked or pulled along by the car in front, schooling fishes position themselves in a similar manner.

While some fishes certainly benefit from schooling behavior, there is a cost as well. Certainly it takes a lot more food to feed a school of fishes than it does to feed a single fish. And any diver who has watched fishes feed is well aware that graciously sharing the available food is not a concept that fish abide by. Even schooling fishes are competitive feeders, but this cost does not outweigh the advantages of schooling for many species.

15

Phylum: *Chordata* Subphylum: *Vertebrata* Class: *Chrondricthyes*

RAYS AND SHARKS

The chance to swim alongside rays and sharks is alluring, but can also be a little intimidating. Often misrepresented and certainly misunderstood, these magnificent creatures are shrouded in mystery. Rest assured, almost everyone fortunate enough to encounter rays and sharks in the wild cherishes the experience.

MANTA RAYS

Often they first appear only as a shadow in the distance. Something inside you says that this shadow is not just a figment of your imagination, and you stop and stare into the blue hoping to get a closer look at the distant creature. Sometimes you never get as much as a fleeting glance, and on those days you never really know if the shadow was a cloud passing overhead or a large animal passing along the edge of visibility.

But on many other days you get lucky! Within only a few moments the shadow reappears out of the distance. Majestic and full of grace, it evolves into a magnificent **manta ray.**

Occasionally, mantas demonstrate considerable curiosity and will readily approach divers. The rays may circle repeatedly or simply

Rays and sharks are very closely related. Encountering either, even if at a distance, is often enough to make a dive memorable. Pictured here is a Caribbean reef shark.

cruise back and forth in an effort to examine you as closely as you would like to examine them. These are dives that are treasured forever. During these magic encounters, divers marvel at one of the sea's most graceful residents. Remarkably efficient and perfectly designed, manta rays move with an ease that sets them apart.

Manta rays are incredibly powerful animals with greatly enlarged pectoral fins that resemble wings. These "wings" provide both lift and propulsion so efficiently that with a single beat of their mighty fins, mantas are capable of a burst of power and speed that allows them to disappear into the distance in a matter of seconds.

More typically, these majestic animals are seen gliding effortlessly

AT A GLANCE

MANTA RAY

Scientific name
Manta hamiltoni
Habitat
Mid-water.
Typical Adult Size
10 feet.
Sightings
Occasionally seen.
Natural History
Enlarged pectoral fins work like wings and allow mantas to "fly" through the water. Use highly modified gill apparatus to filter plankton from the water.

through the water with almost imperceptible movement of their wings. Their lazy appearance can be most deceiving. Often divers decide to pursue large mantas as they swim

The lobes are actually used to help direct plankton-bearing water into the ray's mouth.

Little study has been done on the natural history of mantas. It is known that they are migratory creatures and believed to cover long distances over huge expanses of ocean. They are seen along drop-offs and over shallow reefs in tropical waters around the world. For many years, the Caribbean manta was thought to be a separate species from the large Pacific manta ray, but recent studies have shown them to be different populations of the same species.

Manta rays attain dimensions of 20 feet across from wingtip to wingtip and weigh as much as 4,000 pounds. Like many large creatures, manta rays are filter feeders. They prey primarily on planktonic crustaceans and small fishes. Especially in areas rich in plankton, it is common to see mantas doing backflips underwater as they use their cephalic lobes to direct water and plankton into their mouths. When not in use, the lobes are often retracted and curled up next to the head.

Mantas provide a classic example

PHOTO TIP

Chasing a manta ray often scares the animal. Try hanging almost motionless in the water and let the ray approach you. This technique doesn't always work, but is very efficient when it does, and it allows you to enjoy the magic of the moment as you watch the manta approach. Often the rays swim directly overhead. Try not to hit them with your exhalation bubbles as they are likely to frighten the rays.

Mantas make wonderful subjects for silhouettes. Try framing the rays directly against the sun with a wide-angle lens, such as a Nikonos 15mm or 20mm lens. Shoot natural light at 125th of a second or faster to freeze the individual rays of sunlight in the "sunburst," and the manta's action.

were believed by many to be dangerous monsters of the deep. Manta rays were often called devilfish in the sea lore of ancient mariners because of their supposed evil or dangerous nature, and because of the horn-like appendages called cephalic lobes found in front of the head.

past. While the divers are kicking as hard as they can, the mantas appear to be merely gliding, almost motionless, but can easily widen the gap between themselves and the pursuing diver. It's a comical scene to observe, but it is usually a frustrating and humbling experience, as well as highly educational, for the eager diver.

When humans first took to the sea several thousand years ago, mantas

MOMENTS WITH MANTAS

Often they appear only as mere shadows along the edge of visibility. Sometimes you never see anything else. But there are times when they swim right up to you, gliding gracefully, turning slightly, obviously in complete control of every movement. If there is a marine animal that is more graceful and more compelling than a manta ray, I have not yet seen it.

Their hydrodynamic design, fluid movements and power capture the hearts of almost any diver who swims side by side with a manta ray. In my experience the best encounters, those that lasted the longest and where I got my best look in the most relaxed setting, occurred when I was disci-

plined enough not to chase the ray. When I make myself hang in midwater and allow the ray to come to me, the encounters are usually the best. Of course, the mantas don't always come in, and on occasions I have enjoyed a great dive by swimming after them. But as is the case with most big animals, if the manta doesn't want to be around a diver, pursuit is laughable.

Though I have ridden mantas in the past, I like to think I have grown to a point where I realize that there is so much to appreciate and learn about mantas that trying to ride one somehow cheapens my experience.—Marty Snyderman

of camouflage through countershading, a characteristic found in many open-sea animals. The upper portion of their body is predominantly black, while the underbellies vary from all white to splotchy white and black. This coloration helps mantas blend in with the surrounding water, something they do amazingly well despite their large size. A potential predator viewing a manta from above looks down on a dark ray against a background of dark water, while an upward view reveals a light belly against light surface waters.

Some large sharks are believed to prey on mantas. The rays use their countershading, speed and size to ward off the sharks when they can. Although mantas have little commercial value, probably the biggest threat to the species are nonselective fishing nets. The long time it takes them to reach sexual maturity, and the fact that they do not reproduce in large numbers, casts a serious shadow of doubt as to whether these wonderful animals will be able to survive mankind's all too common use of nonselective fishing gear.

Mantas lack the barbs of stingrays and are not at all dangerous to divers, except due to their size. When swimming with mantas, it is important to realize that they cannot swim backwards. A head-on with a two-ton manta will flood your mask to say the least! Be gentle. And while there is no question that riding a manta ray can be a lot of fun, there is something inherently wrong with the concept of a half-dozen divers trying to pile on en masse in order to observe and enjoy the natural beauty of a wild ray. These kinds of actions can cause severe stress for the animals.

Remoras, fishes which attach themselves to mantas and many other species, often accompany manta rays. The remoras commonly affix themselves atop the heads of the host rays by using a sucker-like disc located on the top of their heads. As a result, they spend a great deal

---

MIDNIGHT MUNCHIES

Manta rays, like so many of the oceans' larger creatures, feed on plankton. I have on occasion seen them feeding during the day, swallowing mouthful after mouthful of green, nutrient-rich water, but usually when I have seen mantas feed, it happened at night. Concentrations of plankton often gather in the lights under an anchored dive boat. Few things seem to be as inviting from a manta's perspective.

I wouldn't really call them voracious feeders, but they are very persistent and appear rather oblivious to divers and anything else in the water. The rays will swim toward the swarms of plankton, mouth agape so wide that you feel like you can see right into the animal's stomach. The

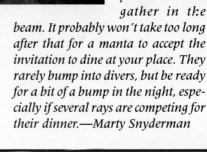

rays unfurl the cephalic lobes along the side of their head, and use them to funnel the plankton into their mouths. Often they gather the plankton by doing backflip after backflip after backflip as they swim between pockets of tiny crustaceans and other planktonic creatures.

If you have a chance to witness the phenomenon, don't hesitate to give it a try. Just shine your light out in front of you and soon a swarm of plankton will gather in the beam. It probably won't take too long after that for a manta to accept the invitation to dine at your place. They rarely bump into divers, but be ready for a bit of a bump in the night, especially if several rays are competing for their dinner.—Marty Snyderman

---

of their lives resting upside down. Remoras can let go and reposition themselves at will. The relationship between remoras and manta rays is not completely understood. Certainly, the remoras benefit by being able to hitchhike from meal to meal by riding on the rays, and they gain some degree of protection simply by being so close to such a large host animal. Some specialists believe that the mantas benefit by having the remoras rid them of parasites, but other scientists question this belief.

Manta rays are often seen on or near the surface of calm waters from the deck of a boat. Sometimes a watchful eye will see the dark upper body as the ray cruises just beneath the surface, but often the giveaway is the appearance of the tip of one, or both of the pectoral fins

knifing through the surface water. It is common for new sailors to mistake the fin tips for the dorsal fin of sharks, but with only a little experience it becomes easy to distinguish between them.

At times, mantas will leap completely out of the water, flipping over before crashing back to the surface. Some scientists speculate that the mantas do so in order to shed parasites, but whatever the reason, it is a spectacular sight. Other species of smaller rays, which look like mantas, are also known to hurtle themselves out of the water. Often observers believe they have seen baby mantas, but it is more likely that they are actually seeing other species of rays.

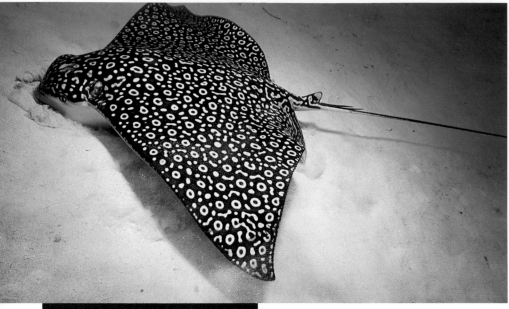

AT A GLANCE

SPOTTED EAGLE RAY, SPOTTED RAY

Scientific Name
Aetobatus narinari
Habitat
Cruises mid-water along the wall, feeds in sand.
Typical Adult Size
5 feet.
Sightings
Occasionally seen.
Natural History
Grubs through sand using powerful jaw muscles and mortar-like teeth to crush small mollusks and crustaceans.

SPOTTED EAGLE RAYS

Few scenes in the underwater world are as captivating as that of a squadron of **spotted eagle rays** cruising over the edge of a drop-off in the crystal clear waters of the Caribbean. Countershaded, like so many animals that live in the upper water column, spotted eagle rays are especially handsome creatures. Their backs are dark black to bluish with dozens of white to gold spots. The distinct spots may be solid or donut-shaped. By contrast, the underbellies of these rays are completely white. A spotted eagle ray is a type of stingray, and most specimens have a long, thin tail equipped with two to five barbed spines that can be used for defensive purposes. At birth, spotted eagle rays are close to 20 inches long, and when fully grown they attain a wingtip to wingtip span of five feet or more.

Despite the fact that divers commonly see spotted eagle rays swimming along walls or over reef flats, these rays do spend a considerable amount of time on the sea floor where they rest and feed. Spotted eagle rays dig through bottom sediment in search of small fishes, shrimps, oysters, clams and other mollusks, especially conchs. They have large powerful jaws which are capable of crushing their prey.

These rays are sometimes seen in large schools or squadrons, and on other occasions they are solitary. In some populations of rays the animals tend to school only when mating, but this is not always the case. Exactly why spotted eagle rays school remains unclear.

SOUTHERN STINGRAYS

Southern stingrays are the large, commonly seen, bottom-dwelling rays that inhabit sand flats in waters ranging from New Jersey to Brazil. They reach a maximum size of about five feet across, though most specimens are considerably smaller. They have dark gray to black upper bodies, whitish underbellies, numerous low spines extending down the back, and a long, thin tail that is equipped with one or more long, sheathed barbs. While southern stingrays are not at all aggressive toward divers, the venomous barbs should not be ignored. They are intended to discourage other animals

AT A GLANCE

SOUTHERN STINGRAY, STINGRAY

Scientific name
Dasyatis americana
Habitat
Sandy areas.
Typical Adult Size
2.5 to 4 feet.
Sightings
Commonly seen.
Natural History
Enlarged pectoral fins work like wings, enabling stingrays to "fly" through the water. Powerful jaws and crushing teeth allow them to feed on small crustaceans and mollusks which they uncover in the sand.

PHOTO TIP

Southern stingrays are easy to approach, especially if you keep a low profile and move slowly. The most difficult problem to overcome is exposure setting because their dark bodies are contrasted against light-colored sand. Keep your strobe high and out to the side so that you do not light the foreground sand, and even at that, try turning down the power of your strobe. If you use a TTL exposure system, bracket the exposure or "lie to your system" by dialing in a faster film speed than you are actually using. The 20mm or 28mm lens with the Nikonos system are good for shooting rays. You should be able to get close enough with these lenses to nearly fill the frame. If you are shooting where the rays are not easily spooked, you might try using a 15mm lens and exaggerate the upward angle as the rays swim right over you. In either case, look out for backscatter caused by suspended sand particles. You will most likely be well served by holding your strobes out to the side to minimize backscatter.

from settling on top of the rays when they are at rest, and are used as a means of defense if the animals are threatened by sharks or other potential predators. Well-developed barbs are from four to eight inches long and can inflict a painful wound. The barbs contain a toxin which can cause pain, and any wound should be thoroughly cleaned because the spines are typically overgrown with bacteria.

When at rest, southern stingrays bury themselves in the sand in order to become less conspicuous. Often, all you will see is a large mound in the sand with an opening for an eyeball. Stingrays utilize an interesting adaptation that enables them to breathe when almost completely covered with sand. The openings to their gills, like those of other rays, are located on their underside. This positioning could present a problem because the gill openings are often pressed flat against the sand in an area where water flow is restricted, and where sand and other debris are present. Southern stingrays have large openings called spiracles, which are located high atop their head immediately behind the eyes. Water is taken in through the spiracles and passed over the gills where oxygen can be removed. Then the water flows out of the body along the sea floor. This respiratory

adaptation enables the rays to use water located higher up in the water column where there is far less sand and other debris.

The positioning of the eyes high atop the head of the southern stingray is a useful adaptation. This allows them to bury the rest of their body and still be able to use their vision to keep on the lookout for potential predators.

Southern stingrays feed on a variety of fishes, worms, clams and crustaceans that are found in the sand and in seagrass beds. They actively dig through the sand to find their prey, which they crush with

PHOTO TIP

AT A GLANCE

YELLOW STINGRAY

Scientific Name
Urolophus jamaicensis
Habitat
Reef or rubble areas.
Typical Adult Size
1.5 feet.
Sightings
Uncommonly seen.
Natural History
Stout spine on tail used to deter predators. Like other rays, their pectoral fins are greatly enlarged into "wings."

their large, powerful jaws. The mouths of southern stingrays are underslung, being located on the underside of their head toward the front of the body. Serving to aid them in locating food, their nostrils are also located on the underside of the head.

One of the feature attractions of Grand Cayman is diving with a dozen or more southern stingrays at two sites known as Stingray City and Amazing Rays. These world-renowned sites are located inside the reef along the North Wall in about 15 feet of water. The rays that live there are quite comfortable around divers and appear to enjoy being hand-fed. However, one should always keep in mind that these rays are wild animals, and they do not like being grabbed, handled or stepped on. Not only is handling and grabbing potentially dangerous, but it will remove the protective mucous coating from a ray's skin, making it vulnerable to infection.

Southern stingrays are often accompanied by **bar jacks**, and occasionally they are also followed by **goatfishes**. The relationship between the species is not completely understood. It is generally believed

that the jacks and goatfishes readily feed on prey that is uncovered, yet overlooked or unwanted by the rays.

Reproduction in southern stingrays is ovoviviparous, meaning that the female produces shelled eggs with yolk which are held in her body. The young develop inside the eggs but do not receive any placental nourishment from their mother.

YELLOW STINGRAYS

Yellow stingrays are small, bottom-dwelling rays that inhabit reef communities, bays, lagoons and harbors from North Carolina to Trinidad, and are found throughout the Caribbean. They are also common in the Gulf of Mexico. These rays often go unnoticed because of their relatively small size and their splotchy pattern which allows them to blend in with the bottom. The upper bodies of yellow stingrays are typically a dark, reticulated pattern with numerous yellow spots on a light-colored background. Yellow stingrays do not have a dorsal fin. The bodies of the adults are usually about one and a half feet long, and their tails are generally shorter than the body.

As a general rule, when encountered by divers, yellow stingrays tend to give ground rather quickly, but at times they will staunchly defend their realm. This does not mean that yellow stingrays aggressively pursue divers. They do not. But neither do they always swim away when divers approach. Yellow stingrays are armed with a venomous spine that can inflict a painful wound, so admiring them from a distance is a wise philosophy.

Yellow stingrays feed on a variety of shrimp, and are believed to also readily prey on small fishes and clams.

ELECTRIC RAYS

One other species of ray that should be mentioned is the **lesser electric** ray. They range from North Carolina to northern Argentina, including the Gulf of Mexico. Lesser electric rays are small bottom-dwelling rays that attain a maximum size of only 18 inches or so. They are easily identified by their small size, their fan-shaped tail fin, and plainly colored upper bodies. In some individuals dark markings are present on the upper body.

Lesser electric rays are most commonly found along sandy shorelines and are occasionally encountered on the reef. Sometimes the rays lay on top of the sand, but often they bury themselves in order to become as inconspicuous as possible.

Like most other electric rays, lesser electric rays are poor swimmers since they lack certain muscles found in other rays which assist in swimming. Instead, electric rays possess highly developed electrical organs that are composed of muscle tissue in which the normal electrical generating capacity is greatly increased. These specialized organs are built with stacks of cells that function in a manner similar to the cells in batteries. A series of large nerve trunks enable the rays to have voluntary control over these organs, allowing the animals to discharge an electrical current at will. The output of current lasts for only a short time.

Electric rays typically use their current-producing ability to ward off predators and stun their prey. Lesser electric rays feed primarily on a variety of annelid worms, animals which do not need to be stunned to prevent them from escaping. So it is likely that they use their ability to create an electrical shock primarily as a means of defense. Since electric rays are poor swimmers, they are somewhat defenseless immediately after they release a jolt of electricity. Apparently it tires the rays to release one jolt and create a new follow-up jolt, so they cannot afford to use their ability frivolously. From a diver's point of view, this is good news because it means that unless they are harassed, electric rays are unlikely to be aggressive. They have too much to lose and little, if anything, to gain.

While the shock created by some electric rays is intensely painful, studies have shown that lesser electric rays create a maximum voltage of only 37 volts. This can create an unpleasant jolt, but it is unlikely to be dangerous.

SHARKS

Of all the groups of marine animals, none captivate and fascinate people more than sharks. Perhaps the most misunderstood of all the creatures in the animal kingdom, sharks evoke intense emotions in humans. We admire their beauty and grace, respect their predatory capabilities, but most of all, we fear them. If we introduce logic and facts into our considerations, our fears truly seem unfounded. On the other hand, when you consider all of the mythology about sharks that has been part of human history for eons, and the exploitation and misrepresentation by both the print and visual media, it becomes easy to see why so many people have unwarranted misconceptions about the true nature of sharks.

Real life sharks are radically different from the mythical man-eating monsters of sea lore and Hollywood films, but trying to convince the media-inundated public how badly misunderstood sharks are can prove to be a demanding task. Contrary to the public misconception that all sharks are super predators of great size, more than 80 percent of all shark species are smaller than six feet long when fully grown.

According to fossil records, sharks have existed on planet Earth in one form or another for close to 450 million years. Put another way, the fossil record of sharks is three times older than that of dinosaurs, and more than 100 times older than the first human fossils. Of course, sharks have undergone extensive evolutionary processes over that time. The sharks that live today are similar in some respects, yet considerably different in others, to the creatures that roamed the oceans long ago. According to paleontologists, the most ancient fossil credited to a still-living group of sharks dates back approximately 180 million years, and most of the species that are now considered modern sharks are believed to be about 100 million years old.

Worldwide, there are more than 350 species of sharks divided into eight major orders. Sharks differ greatly in terms of where they live, what they eat, who eats them, how they give birth, and how they fit into Mother Nature's overall plan. Consider the following example of size difference: When fully grown, the **pygmy shark** found in the waters of the Philippines is only slightly more than six inches long, while the **whale shark** can attain proportions of up to 50 feet and 50,000 pounds.

Sharks like **mako sharks** roam the open sea feeding primarily on schooling fishes and squid, while **nurse sharks** are bottom-dwelling animals that live in the comparatively shallow water of reef communities, where they feed on crustaceans, mollusks, worms and small fishes. **Tiger sharks** prey on fishes, turtles and even birds, while **bonnethead sharks** prey primarily on a variety of small crustaceans.

As far as shape is concerned, it is immediately obvious that the eight species of **hammerhead sharks** are quite different from **silky sharks**, **Caribbean reef sharks**, **bull sharks**, **lemon sharks**, **tiger sharks** and other species.

Many scientists believe hammerheads are only 120 to 150 million years old—relatively young in terms of evolutionary time. Their relative youth leads some scientists to believe that their head shape is somewhat of an experiment in nature.

One way in which the various species of sharks differ considerably is in their method of giving birth.

Many species, such as all hammerheads and lemon sharks, bear live young. Other sharks lay eggs which settle to the bottom, allowing the embryo to develop over a period of time that can exceed one year. Still other species, such as the **great white shark** and **mako shark**, are described as intrauterine cannibals. In these species, shelled eggs develop inside the female. The young develop by receiving nutrition from a yolk sac inside the egg. They hatch while still inside the female, but they are not released into the wild at that time. Instead, they devour their siblings and any unhatched eggs while still inside the female. When there is no more food remaining, the young emerge. Talk about being born with well-developed instincts! Although scientists are not positive, it is believed that in the case of great whites two young are eventually released into the wild, one being developed in each uterine canal.

WHALE SHARKS

Approaching proportions of 50 feet and 50,000 pounds, **whale sharks** are the world's largest fish. While numbers like these make impressive statistics, an actual underwater encounter makes these numbers take on a whole new meaning. In more ways than one, a full-grown whale shark appears to be more like a living reef than a single fish. Schools of jacks and other fishes often swarm in front of the shark's face, while literally dozens of remoras commonly attach themselves to the shark's body.

The first time you see a whale shark, you might fail to notice the remoras and many other details because you are simply overwhelmed by the shark's massive size. But if you get lucky and the encounter is prolonged, you are likely to see a number of creatures that accompany the shark.

Like most of the oceans' larger creatures, whale sharks are filter feeders. Despite what Hollywood film producers might like us to think about an almost 50-foot-long shark, whale sharks are only equipped to feed on small planktonic crustaceans and small schooling fishes. The mouth of a whale shark is lined with

---

AT A GLANCE

WHALE SHARK

Scientific Name
Rhincodon typus
Habitat
Open sea.
Typical Adult Size
30 feet.
Sightings
Uncommonly seen.
Natural History
Whale sharks are the largest of all fishes. They are plankton feeders, using specialized gill rakers to sieve plankton and some small fishes from the water.

between 3,000 and 5,000 teeth, the largest of which is only about a tenth of an inch long. When feeding, the shark searches for dense concentrations of plankton. Once it finds such a concentration, the shark opens its mouth as wide as it can, taking in as much water and plankton as possible. The plankton gets hung up on the shark's teeth and gill rakers, while the excess water flows out through its massive gills. The shark then closes its mouth, swallowing the plankton before starting the process all over again.

Commercial tuna fishermen in a variety of locations have reported seeing whale sharks feeding on schools of small tuna that were near the surface. When alarmed, the tuna sometimes gather into tight schools, and the whale sharks take advantage of this reaction by swimming straight up into the school, mouth agape, in an attempt to consume as

The massive mouths of whale sharks contain several thousand tiny teeth which help trap food as the sharks filter vast amounts of plankton and small schooling fishes.

PHOTO TIP

To photograph a whale shark is one of the greatest dreams of all underwater photographers. Encounters are rare and always exciting. Very few photographers, even professionals, have good shots of whale sharks, so any shot is highly coveted. These fish are so big that in most cases, you will need a wide-angle lens such as a Nikonos 15mm or 20mm lens. For full-body shots, forget your strobe(s), since you have to be ten feet or more away from the shark to fit the whole animal into your frame. Choose an angle with as much ambient light hitting the shark as possible, and use a fast shutter speed if you have the luxury of a lot of ambient light to freeze the motion (1/125th or 1/250th will give sharp results). Bracket like crazy because you may only get one good chance for such a valuable portrait! Be careful not hit the whale shark with your bubbles—this often disturbs them and will cause them to quickly flee. Your strobe should prove useful for a full-face portrait if you are fortunate enough to get that close.

many tuna as possible.

Like many creatures that roam the open sea, whale sharks are distinctly countershaded, being dark on their upper body and lightly colored on their underside. Whale sharks are characterized by their blue to greenish gray to black upper bodies that are covered with hundreds of yellow to white spots, and a wide mouth located in the front of their head in the terminal position. The mouth of an adult can be more than 10 feet wide. A series of pronounced lateral ridges run lengthwise down the side of a whale shark's body. In addition, they have a very large dorsal fin that rises almost five feet off the back, and a very large tail fin. Despite the large eyes that appear in so many native drawings, whale sharks actually have surprisingly small eyes—so small, in fact, that they can be hard to locate.

Whale sharks typically cruise just slightly faster than divers can comfortably swim. Often you can catch up with one, but it usually takes as much kicking effort as your legs

have to give. One of the most fascinating parts of a whale shark encounter is when after you expend all that effort and are able to get directly in front of the shark, literally only a few feet away, you will be pushed along by a wall of water without having to exert any effort of your own. A large whale shark pushes a huge wall of water, which in turn pushes you along out in front of the shark. However, you do need to be careful because at times some characteristics of the flow can change, and the shark can bump into you. Needless to say, a bump from a 50,000 pound animal cannot be taken lightly. Whale sharks are not aggressive toward divers, but do keep in mind that they are very large, wild animals.

Whale sharks typically inhabit the open ocean in tropical seas around the world, and while they are not common in reef communities, sightings do occur. However, because they are not commercially valuable, funding for study has been lacking. As a result, much remains

AT A GLANCE

GREAT WHITE SHARK

Scientific Name
Carcharodon carcharias
Habitat
Open sea.
Typical Adult Size
15 feet.
Sightings
Seldom seen.
Natural History
Apex predators. One of the few species of sharks that may attack humans.

to be learned about their natural history. For example, their migration patterns, if any, are unknown.

GREAT WHITE SHARKS

Great white sharks are generally thought to prefer the shallow wa-

ters of continental shelves in temperate seas, and they are rare in the waters of the Caribbean, Bahamas and Florida. However, sightings do occur in these areas, and one of the largest great white sharks ever documented was caught off the coast of Cuba. Though there is some question regarding the accuracy of the measurements, this monster was said to be 21 feet long, tipping the scales at a whopping 7,100 pounds. By comparison, Hollywood's version of the great white shark in the movie *Jaws* was 25 feet long. Of course, the sharks got even larger in the sequels—larger and far more vicious than in real life.

Despite all the highly publicized research that has been conducted with great white sharks in recent years, scientists still do not know a lot about the species. It is likely that our fear of great white sharks is

more directly linked to a combination of media exploitation, their enormous size, and our own natural fear of the unknown, than it is to the true nature of these magnificent creatures.

Great whites are usually described as having heavy, spindle-shaped bodies with a moderately long, conical snout. In other words, they look like an enormous football that has been overpressurized. White sharks possess long, flat, triangular-shaped teeth with distinctly serrated edges which are used to tear through and cut their prey. Individual teeth can be more than two inches long, but there is apparently no direct correlation between the size of the teeth and the overall size of an individual animal.

White sharks are distinctly countershaded, a color pattern that helps them blend in with the surrounding water. They are slate gray to black above, and white below. Such coloration in a superpredator is indicative of how beneficial countershading must be. Apparently, even great white sharks rely upon stealth, and not just their overall strength and size to take their prey.

Divers who have filmed great white sharks from cages in Australia and Mexico convey astonishment at how even large great white sharks seem to disappear by blending into

DISAPPEARING IN THE LIGHT

Seventeen feet long and 3,000 pounds. That is a lot of fish, especially when the fish is a great white shark. I watched in wonderment and awe. The shark appeared both powerful and graceful at the same time. Shimmering rays of sunlight danced across the shark's back as the animal made a pass in front of me. I remember thinking how, with my photographic eye, I was looking for a shot that depicted "Jaws," but what I really saw was pure beauty.

We were enjoying superb diving conditions, with at least 100-foot visibility in iridescent blue water on a sunny day with just a slight breeze. The water was so clear that I could easily make out details on the shark's body. As it closed the gap between us, I could see the jagged edges of those tall, triangular-shaped teeth in the animal's upper jaw. The shark made a pass, I shot a few frames, and then watched as it turned away.

The shark swam slightly downward, turned to its left as if to circle back toward me, and then I just lost it. I blinked and stared into the distance concentrating my hardest, but I couldn't locate the seventeen-foot, 3,000-pound shark. It was there just a second ago. I was mighty happy to be inside a shark cage.

Suddenly, the shark appeared directly in front of me. It was exactly where I thought it was going to be, but I didn't know how it got there. I couldn't understand how I could

just not see such a huge fish.

Throughout the remainder of that dive and over the course of the next several days, the exact same thing happened on a number of occasions. In just the right, or wrong, lighting situation, depending upon whether I considered the event from the predator's perspective or from the prey's, the shark would all but become invisible right before my eyes. When viewed from above, the animal's dark back blended with the dark water and sea floor, and when seen from below, it's light underbelly blended into the light hues of the surface water. The shark was classically countershaded, dark on the top and light on the bottom. This form of camouflage is thought to help many animals blend with their surroundings, but I suppose I was guilty of thinking of countershading only as a defensive mechanism, something to be used by the hunted, not the hunter.

The great lesson for me was that stealth serves the hunter well, even one that is so large and powerful as to be considered the ruler of its domain. No matter how big and bad and powerful a beast, there is considerable advantage in being able to sneak up on prey undetected.

Great whites are rarely encountered in the Caribbean and associated waters, and the incidents described occurred in South Australia. But the lesson learned taught me a lot about the lives of the hunted and the hunters.—Marty Snyderman

their surroundings in many lighting situations, even in water with excellent visibility.

The tail of a great white shark is described as being almost homocercal or lunate, meaning that the tail is nearly symmetrical, with the upper and lower lobes being close to the same shape and size. Most other species of sharks possess obviously asymmetrical tails with the upper lobe being considerably larger than the lower lobe. However, it is interesting to note that homocercal tails are characteristic of many of the ocean's fastest swimmers, including members of the tuna family. Tail size is a good indication that white sharks are capable of rapid bursts of speed.

While the tail is a key to identification, in the wild it can be rather difficult and impractical to focus your attention on that end of the animal. If you are able to do so, you will notice that the tail appears to be disproportionately large.

The body of great white sharks is equipped with a pair of prominent, strong caudal keels, which stand out as large bulges along the shark's side immediately in front of the tail. The caudal keel provides added strength and increased stability to the tail.

White sharks are capable of maintaining a higher core temperature than that of the surrounding water, a characteristic that is unusual in fishes. Most fishes are cold-blooded, and their core temperature is regulated by their surroundings.

In most temperate seas, adult white sharks are believed to prey primarily upon seals, sea lions and other marine mammals. In tropical waters, it is likely that fishes, including other sharks and rays, make up a significant portion of their diet.

SHORTFIN MAKO SHARKS

Shortfin mako sharks inhabit the open waters of the Caribbean. Makos are members of the same family of sharks as great white sharks, and the species look remarkably similar in many respects. Makos are considerably smaller as adults, and though they reach a reported length of 12 feet, many specimens are less than 6 feet long. They are rarely seen in reef communities, but are occasionally seen cruising over open ocean pinnacles and along deep walls.

Shortfin mako sharks are believed to be among the fastest swimmers in the sea, an especially valuable asset considering their prey. Makos feed primarily on fast-moving fishes such as jacks, tuna, bonito, swordfish and other sharks. Designed to help them snag their prey,

AT A GLANCE

SHORTFIN MAKO SHARK

Scientific Name
Isurus oxyrinchus
Habitat
Open sea.
Typical Adult Size
6 feet.
Sightings
Occasionally seen.
Natural History
Incredibly fast-swimming shark which preys on schooling fishes and squid. Very large gill slits and specialized gill apparatus allow extremely efficient oxygen uptake to help allow rapid, sustained swimming.

the teeth of mako sharks are long and narrow. Makos do not saw through the fish they snare. Instead, they use their teeth to help them pin their prey when they catch it. A close inspection of shark teeth reveals just how different the more than 350 species of sharks really are. Their teeth and diet are species specific, and each species possesses teeth that are designed to help it fit into its own particular niche in nature.

Mako sharks are distinguished by (1) a long, distinctly pointed snout; (2) a thick, fusiform body (meaning that, like great white sharks, their bodies look somewhat like enormous, overpressurized footballs); (3) extremely large gills, which allow for a highly efficient gas exchange; (4) a pronounced caudal keel; and (5) an almost perfectly lunate tail. In the water makos appear rather frightening. They look like a gaggle of teeth attached to the front end of a torpedo. Rows of long, sharp teeth are almost always exposed, giving the impression that they are too large to fit into the shark's mouth.

When excited or nervous, makos move in a jerky fashion, darting back and forth in a rather unnerving manner. This is a sharp contrast to the slow, graceful movements of

many sharks.

Numerous long, thin parasitic copepods are often seen in the mouth, or attached to the dorsal fin of shortfin makos. These sharks often have nasty-looking scars near the corners of their mouths which are caused, at least in part, by the parasites. The combined effect of rows of exposed teeth, the wounds, and the streaming copepods give mako sharks a look that many Hollywood producers would love to put on the face of any sea monster.

Despite their fearsome impression, makos are generally very wary animals. They only rarely approach divers unless spearfishing or baiting is involved.

BULL SHARKS

Bull sharks are impressive, powerful-looking reef sharks that are distinguished by their stocky build, squared off snout and small eyes. Adults are known to reach a length of 11 feet. They have large, triangular dorsal fins that are sharply pointed. There are no distinct markings on the fins except that the trailing edge of the tail fin is sometimes dusky in color.

By temperament, bull sharks are often curious. At times, they will approach divers and unprovoked attacks have been documented, but bull sharks are usually more comfortable keeping some distance between themselves and divers. However, bull sharks readily come to bait. Beware—when baited they are often very aggressive in their effort to get to the bait.

Bull sharks inhabit all tropical and subtropical seas. They are also known for their habit of entering freshwater rivers and lakes. Though it is rare, bull sharks have been caught more than 100 miles up the Mississippi River, and they are also

PHOTO TIP

Try to frame reef sharks against a background of water rather than reef when you can, especially if you are shooting from farther than five feet away. Their countershaded coloration makes them blend in with the reef. A water background will help the shark stand out in your frame. Encounters close enough to warrant the use of a 15mm lens are rare; therefore, a 20mm or 28mm lens with a Nikonos camera may be more appropriate when shooting reef sharks.

the same species of sharks that inhabit Lake Nicaragua in Central America. Bull sharks bear live young.

SILKY SHARKS

Silky sharks typically inhabit the waters of the open sea, but they are occasionally seen in reef communities near drop-offs. Silkies have a classic reef shark look with slightly stocky bodies, and elongated, rounded snouts. Their bodies are typically gray on top and white below, but some specimens have jet-black upper bodies.

Silkies are generally considered

to be fast-swimming, open-ocean sharks. They have a superb sense of hearing, a trait which enables them to detect their favorite prey of mackerel, mullet, tuna and squid from considerable distances.

Silkies are one of the species that are often filmed in the open water off Nassau, in the part of the Bahamas known as Tongue of the Ocean where the Caribbean and Atlantic meet. The water at Tongue of the Ocean is thousands of feet deep, and diving there is a true bluewater ex-

DOUG PERRINE

AT A GLANCE

BULL SHARK

Scientific Name
Carcharhinus leucas
Habitat
Near reefs and coastal areas.
Typical Adult Size
8 feet.
Sightings
Occasionally seen.
Natural History
Broadest of the reef sharks typically encountered in Caribbean. Swim up into fresh water systems.

AT A GLANCE

SILKY SHARK

Scientific Name
Carcharhinus falciformis
Habitat
Mid-water.
Typical Adult Size
4 to 7 feet.
Sightings
Occasionally seen.
Natural History
Shark of the open sea, but may occur in areas of offshore reefs or oceanic islands. As with many sharks, females often bear scars caused by bites of males during courtship and mating (note photo). Skin of females of same species up to 3 times as thick as skin of males, especially around pectoral girdle.

---

perience. In unbaited situations, silky sharks rarely show aggression, but the game can change in the blink of an eye when bait is used. Larger silkies reach a length of 10 feet and should not be taken lightly. They are almost always included on lists of sharks considered to be dangerous to man. Yet it should be noted that to our knowledge, the guided silky shark dives in the Bahamas have an excellent safety record.

Silky sharks, like many sharks,

attached to the shark's lower body, and they turn dark when they attach atop the head or elsewhere on the upper body. Apparently, camouflage plays an important role even in the lives of remoras.

Silky sharks inhabit tropical waters worldwide. They were once thought to be a different species than the silky sharks which inhabit the Pacific, but further studies have shown them to be different populations of the same species. Silky sharks bear live young.

CARIBBEAN REEF SHARKS

Ranging from Florida to Brazil, the **Caribbean reef shark** is one of the most frequently encountered of all reef sharks in the Caribbean and associated waters. Reaching a maximum length of close to 10 feet, Caribbean reef sharks have slightly stocky bodies, bluntly rounded snouts, long and narrow pectoral fins, and dusky markings along the

anal fins and tail fin.

In recent years, several dive operators in Nassau have taken sport divers to see and film Caribbean reef sharks. These trips are a lot of fun. Caribbean reef sharks are powerful-looking animals, and they are easily large enough and dramatic enough to make superb photographic subjects. A number of other species, including nurse sharks and occasional hammerheads, have also been drawn in by the bait.

Caribbean reef sharks prey primarily on a variety of reef fishes. In

are often accompanied by remoras. The remoras commonly make themselves lightly colored when they are

ENCOUNTERS WITH CARIBBEAN REEF SHARKS

I had photographed whale sharks, great white sharks, schools of scalloped hammerheads so thick they blocked out the sun, blue sharks, mako sharks, lemon sharks, gray reefs, silvertips and more, before I ever saw my first Caribbean reef shark. Though I was eager to jump into the waters off Nassau so I could observe a species of shark I had not seen before, I really wasn't expecting the experience to be anything extraordinary. Funny how the ocean works though. High expectations almost always seem to lead to disappointment, but so often when we just go with the flow we get treated to memories that last a lifetime.

My first impression, and one that has persisted, is that Caribbean reef sharks are big, impressive, somewhat imposing animals. Heavy-bodied and muscular, they remind me more of silvertips, which dominate many Indo-Pacific reefs than sleeker species such as blue sharks and whitetip reef sharks. And even though I have been around a lot of sharks over the years, size still gets my attention. No doubt about it, Caribbean reef sharks swim with an air that exudes power and strength, characteristics which somehow translate into dominance. They appear to be the ruler of their domain, and

I do not take them lightly.

Like many sharks, Caribbean reef sharks tend to be sexually segregated. At some sites, Tom Campbell and I saw almost all males, and at others all females. Though the males were smaller, they tended to be a bit more aggressive when bait was in the water, but it was immediately obvious that females are also quite capable of fending for themselves.

Years ago, when the Bahamian dive operators first began to run shark dives, the feature attraction was a full-on feeding frenzy. The word through the grapevine was, the wilder the action, the better the dive. In recent years, however, some operators have cut back on the bait supply in order to lessen the intensity of the frenzies. I really enjoyed the slowed down dives. There were still plenty of sharks around, and I got some great photo opportunities, but things seemed to be much more "under control." Just as important was the feeling that I was seeing the sharks as they naturally are, not in an artificially created setting.

The bottom line for me is that, if given a chance to join another Caribbean reef shark dive, I'd go in a heartbeat. I had a blast.—Marty Snyderman

AT A GLANCE

LEMON SHARK

Scientific Name
Negaprion brevirostris
Habitat
Mid-water, reefs and sand flats.
Typical Adult Size
8 feet.
Sightings
Uncommonly seen.
Natural History
Acute sense of smell enables them to detect minor salinity variations which helps females locate areas to give birth. Also helps lemon sharks locate food.

AT A GLANCE

CARIBBEAN REEF SHARK, REEF SHARK

Scientific Name
Carcharhinus perezi
Habitat
Reefs and shallows, especially in exposed areas.
Typical Adult Size
7 feet.
Sightings
Occasionally seen.
Natural History
Wary, but often quick to come to bait.

a natural setting, there is little to fear from this species or any other shark. However, they are known to be aggressive around bait, including speared fish. Pay heed.

They are viviparous, meaning they bear live young.

LEMON SHARKS

Lemon sharks are one of the most well-studied of all shark species. Ranging from New Jersey to southern Brazil, lemons are well documented throughout the Caribbean, Bahamas and Florida. Although they are often caught by long liners that fish in several hundred feet of water out in the open sea, lemon sharks are common residents of many reef communities. Lemon sharks also

inhabit lagoons, estuaries and the shallows of the sand flats where they feed upon a variety of bony fishes, crustaceans, and other sharks and rays.

Aerial photography and population studies have allowed scientists to learn a lot about the lemon shark population in Bimini. Lemon sharks attain a maximum length of just over 11 feet. Surprisingly, large specimens are commonly seen in water that is as shallow as three feet or less in the tidal flats of Bimini in the Bahamas. Lemons have a very keen sense of smell which they use to locate prey and to detect different percentages of salinity in the water, a feat which is thought to help the females locate their pupping grounds. Hearing and the ability to detect slight variations in the earth's magnetic field may also play vital roles in helping lemon sharks orient themselves.

Like other cold-blooded fishes, lemon sharks tire easily. When they pursue their prey, they must capture it within a short time or they will exhaust themselves. Studies have shown that in natural conditions, lemon sharks can live to be at least 75 years old, and they might live as long as 125 years or more.

Lemon sharks are heavy-bodied animals characterized by their short snout, equal-sized dorsal fins, and pale yellow-brown bodies. Lemon sharks bear live young. Litter sizes vary from as few as four young to as many as seventeen.

NURSE SHARKS

Nurse sharks are among the more commonly observed shark species in Caribbean reef communities. Like many sharks, they are primarily nocturnal animals, meaning that they are most active at night. During the day, they can often be seen resting on the bottom under low-lying ledges and in caves. Nurse sharks are extremely docile creatures, and as a rule are easy to approach. However, their teeth are sharp and their jaws are powerful enough to crush the hard shells of crustaceans and mollusks that they prey upon. The bottom line is that nurse sharks are sharks. They should not be taken for granted, so please don't fall into the trap of trying to handle them because they have a reputation for being so docile.

While many specimens are only 3 to 5 feet long, Caribbean nurse

---

AT A GLANCE

NURSE SHARK

Scientific Name
Ginglymostoma cirratum

Habitat
Reef, under ledges and in sand.

Typical Adult Size
5 feet, but documented to over 14 feet.

Sightings
Uncommonly seen.

Natural History
During the day they are normally inactive and tend to rest on the bottom under ledges or between reef fingers. They become more active in the evening.

sharks have been documented to reach a length of just over 14 feet long. The bodies of the adults are tan to brown, while the juveniles have a number of small black spots on their similarly colored bodies. In some respects, the pug face of a nurse shark looks more like that of a typical catfish than the face of a classic shark. They have broad mouths located near the front of the head. The long, whisker-like barbels located under the mouth are another excellent identifying characteristic. The barbels are chemosensory organs that help these sharks locate potential prey which might be buried in the sand or under coral rubble. Nurse sharks prey primarily on bottom-dwelling invertebrates, especially lobsters, crabs and sea urchins, and they also eat a variety of small bony fishes.

Throughout the world, several species of sharks are commonly called nurse sharks. The Caribbean species inhabits the waters of the Western Atlantic ranging from Rhode Island to Brazil. Female nurse sharks produce shelled eggs, which develop inside them, without the young receiving any placental nourishment directly from the mother.

BLACKTIP SHARKS

Blacktip sharks are named for the prominent black tips of their pectoral, second dorsal and lower tail fins. In some individuals the tips of the first dorsal, upper tail, pelvic fins, and anal fins might also be black. Blacktips are typically smaller and more slender than other species, such as bull sharks, lemon sharks and tiger sharks. Though blacktips do attain a maximum length of eight and a half feet, most specimens are considerably smaller. They have long, pointed snouts, and their first dorsal fin is distinctly pointed.

Blacktips are often seen in shallow reef areas along coastlines where they are active swimmers.

Occasionally they are seen jumping entirely out of the water, a behavior that is also observed in thresher sharks and mako sharks, but not in many other species. Blacktip reef sharks prey primarily on a variety of small bony fishes, but they also readily prey on crustaceans and squids. They inhabit tropical and subtropical seas around the world.

AT A GLANCE

BLACKTIP SHARK

Scientific Name
Carcharhinus limbatus
Habitat
Worldwide in tropical seas.
Typical Adult size
4 to 6 feet long.
Sightings
Seldom seen.
Natural History
One of 48 requiem sharks. Far ranging, active swimmers following seasonal water currents. Often dominated by large competing sharks. Not well studied.
Note
This shark is different from the blacktip reef shark (Carcharhinus melanopterus).

TIGER SHARKS

Attaining a maximum documented length of just over 16 feet, **tiger sharks** are the largest of reef sharks seen in the Caribbean. Even immature individuals are impressive-looking animals. Tiger sharks usually roam the deep water off the seaward side of reef flats, but they also frequent deep channels and passes where strong currents are common.

Tiger sharks are so named because of the numerous broad vertical stripes which stand out on the backs of the adults, giving them a look that vaguely resembles a tiger. They have a broad, squared-off snout, a large mouth, and rows and rows of flat, serrated teeth that are triangular in shape. The teeth are short, broad and distinctly notched, creating a perfect design that greatly assists in cutting and crushing the shells of turtles, and in tearing flesh from the bodies of marine mammals and large fishes, such as marlin, that cannot be swallowed whole. From a diver's point of view, the vertical stripes on the back serve as a better identifying feature than does the

DOUG PERRINE

DOUG PERRINE

AT A GLANCE

TIGER SHARK

Scientific Name
Galeocerdo cuvier

Habitat
Tropical and temperate seas from shallow reef communities to open sea.

Typical Adult Size
10 to 15 feet long.

Sightings
Seldom seen.

Natural History
One of 48 species of requiem sharks. Like many larger sharks, tigers are far-ranging, active swimmers following seasonal water currents. Extremely diverse diet including billfish, other sharks, dolphins, crustaceans, squids, turtles and birds. Big size and distinct vertical stripes are key identifying features.

shape of the teeth!

Tiger sharks have extremely varied diets. They are known to enter shallow waters near reef flats in order to prey on sea birds that rest on the surface. Tiger sharks also feed on turtles, large game fishes, small bony fishes, other sharks, a variety of bottom-dwelling crustaceans, squids, octopuses and large stingrays. In addition, they are opportunistic feeders commonly found in areas where garbage is dumped on a regular basis.

At times, tiger sharks appear to be slow, lethargic swimmers, but do not be deceived. They are capable of quick acceleration. Tagged specimens have been documented to travel as far as 50 miles in a single day.

Reproduction in tiger sharks is classified as a modified form of viviparity. The female produces shelled eggs which develop inside her body. Nutrients from the female are received by being absorbed through the thin shell of the egg, but there is no direct placental connection. Tiger sharks produce litters of between 10 and 80 young.

HAMMERHEAD SHARKS

Worldwide, there are at least eight species of sharks that are commonly called hammerheads, though scientists continue to research and debate the exact number. Exactly why hammerheads are so strangely shaped is a matter of scientific speculation. Some specialists believe that the greatly flattened and elongated head of hammerheads serves like the wing of an airplane, giving the animal added lift at the front end of its body. The extra lift is believed to make them more efficient swimmers.

Scientists also point out that hammerheads have sensory organs located at the extremities of the head. Spreading their sensory receptors enables them to be more accurate in their effort to pinpoint the direction of incoming stimuli. In effect, hammerheads are believed to be better able to quickly locate potential prey and potential problems.

The eyes of hammerhead sharks are positioned on the outside ends or edges of their wing-like head, providing them with a very wide field of view. Highly developed olfactory organs and electroreceptive organs are also located in the head.

The largest of the eight species of hammerheads is the **great hammerhead**, a species that occurs mostly in tropical seas around the world. Documented to reach a length of 20 feet, they can be distinguished from other hammerheads by their large size, tall dorsal fin, and the fact that the leading edge of the head is relatively straight and smooth, not scalloped or ridged, with the exception of one noticeable indentation in the center. Great hammerheads are usually seen by divers when cruising

along drop-offs. On occasion, they show some curiosity toward divers, but they are rarely, if ever, aggressive in unbaited situations. Great hammerheads feed on a variety of bony fishes, other sharks, rays and bottom-dwelling crustaceans. Like all hammerheads, they are viviparous and bear live young.

Scalloped hammerheads are thought to be the most abundant species of hammerhead in tropical areas. In recent years, they have become well known for their schooling behavior, a phenomenon that is commonly witnessed in some areas. Exactly why several dozen to several hundred mature scalloped hammerhead sharks would gather in a school remains a mystery to scientists. Perhaps mating, or perhaps migration are keys to the answer.

Solitary scalloped hammerheads are also commonly observed. Whether solitary or schooling, seeing a scalloped hammerhead will make any dive a memorable one.

These sharks prey chiefly upon a variety of bony fishes, crustaceans, squid and octopuses.

Bonnethead sharks are small members of the hammerhead family. Most of them are only three to four feet long, and the largest on

AT A GLANCE

SCALLOPED HAMMERHEAD

Scientific Name
Sphyrna lewini
Habitat
Open sea, sometimes near reefs.
Typical Adult Size
7 to 10 feet.
Abundance
Uncommon.
Natural History
Sometimes seen schooling in groups numbering in the hundreds. Eyes far out on stalks of head may allow better lateral vision.

record is only five feet long. Bonnetheads range from North Carolina to Brazil, most commonly inhabiting shallow bays, estuaries and sounds in the Florida Keys, Cuba and the western Bahamas where they prey primarily on bottom-dwelling crustaceans. They are not found in other parts of the Caribbean.

Bonnetheads can be distinguished by their gray to brown bodies with pale underbellies, and the smooth, shovel-like shape of their heads. They are considered harmless to man, and they are only rarely seen by divers and snorkelers.

PHOTO TIP

Try shooting at a slightly upward or even a slightly downward angle as opposed to level. The heads of hammerhead sharks are surprisingly thin, and in a level shot from both a head-on angle and from the side, the head often "disappears" because it blends in with the shark's body. Shooting down is going against the proverbial book of underwater photography, but with hammerheads this angle often works well.

16

Phylum: *Chordata* Subphylum: *Vertebrata* Class: *Osteichthyes*

BONY FISHES

The sheer diversity of bony fishes in the Caribbean and associated waters is truly astonishing. On almost every dive, everywhere you look, you will be awed by nature's handiwork. Resplendent colors, an array of shapes and other adaptations which enable different species to fit into their particular niche, and fascinating behaviors can be observed on a daily basis. For many of us, the dazzling array of bony fishes is diving's feature attraction.

TARPON

Having a very distinctive, somewhat prehistoric-looking appearance, **Atlantic tarpon** are among the most dramatic and unusual of all Caribbean fishes. As is the case with all members of their family, Atlantic tarpon are the direct descendants of primitive fishes. Like many primitive fishes, Atlantic tarpon are noted for their large individual scales which can measure more than three inches in diameter. In addition, a distinctive physical characteristic of tarpon is that they have very large eyes. The name of their genus, *Megalops*, is derived from the combination of two Greek words that

Like the black grouper pictured here, the vast majority of fishes are bony fishes, such as angelfishes, squirrelfishes, eels and gobies, not cartilaginous fishes, as are sharks and rays. Scientists distinguish between cartilaginous fishes and bony fishes by placing the two groups in separate classes.

means "large eye."

Atlantic tarpon are known to reach a size of 8 feet and 350 pounds. Even the much smaller specimens are spectacular for scuba divers and snorkelers to encounter. This is especially true on bright sunny days as shimmering rays of sunlight dance over their silver backs.

Though Atlantic tarpon are occasionally encountered as solitary creatures, they usually gather in schools ranging from 20 to 200 fish. The schools often hover or patrol slowly back and forth in caves and crevices where they feed. When found in schools during the day, tarpon are usually easy for divers to approach. They are widely distributed on both sides of the Atlantic. In the western Atlantic, tarpon range from Cape Cod, Massachusetts to Brazil, and they are found in many

parts of the Caribbean. Tarpon are capable of surviving in both fresh and salt water, a feat most fishes are not capable of. As a result, tarpon are commonly found in mangroves, estuaries, rivers and other backwater areas, as well as in open sea reef communities.

When feeding, tarpon prefer to

AT A GLANCE

ATLANTIC TARPON

Scientific name
  Megalops atlanticus
Habitat
  Reef and estuaries, mid water.
Typical Adult Size
  4 feet.
Sightings
  Occasionally seen.
Natural History
  Usually schooling, prowls for baitfish.

PHOTO TIP

Tarpon make dramatic photographic subjects, but they are difficult to expose properly because their silver skin is highly reflective. Placing a diffuser over your strobe will soften strobe light, and in some instances this technique will help eliminate the glare from their bodies.

prey on small baitfish especially silversides and some small crustaceans. If you approach the feeding action slowly, you can often get close enough to watch the tarpon "herd" baitfish into a tight ball before suddenly rushing through the ball of bait. The several species of small fishes generally known as silversides commonly gather in large caves and shipwrecks. When silversides are discovered by hungry tarpon, the feeding activity is often very intense as the tarpon continually pursue the baitfish for hours on end. For divers this is good news because once you find the tarpon feeding, you are likely to be able to stay with the action for a long time since the baitfish rarely flee the scene. Instead, they tend to scatter and regroup in tight schools in the same area. Adult tarpon tend to feed primarily at night, but during periods of heavy feeding they readily eat in the daytime when an opportunity presents itself.

Atlantic tarpon are open-ocean broadcast spawners. An average size female produces as many as 12 million eggs in a single spawning. The eggs drift as far as 100 miles offshore before hatching. The hatchlings look like tiny transparent ribbons, and as is the case with so many fishes, the hatchlings do not bear much resemblance to the adults. Some of the larval fishes eventually find their way into shallow water where an astonishing metamorphosis occurs. When they reach a length of approximately one inch they then shrink to about half that size and take on the appearance of adult tarpon. Remarkably,

this phenomenal transformation occurs within only a day or a little longer.

LIZARDFISHES

Lizardfishes are among the most unique of all Caribbean fishes. In a fashion similar to their terrestrial namesakes, lizardfishes often rest motionless on the bottom, propped up on the tips of their fins. Of all the Caribbean lizardfishes the **sand diver** is the most common. Sand divers are cigar-shaped fishes that generally inhabit rubble zones and sand. The species acquired their common name from their tendency to bury themselves in the sand when threatened, and when laying-in-wait for unsuspecting prey. At times, observant divers will see sand divers hiding in the sand with only their head and eyes protruding. Most individuals are a mottled combination of red and white to brown and white, and they are quick to change color to match their surroundings. Sand divers attain a maximum size of about 18 inches, but most specimens are considerably shorter.

Using their tail for added thrust, sand divers are capable of very quick forward bursts. When hunting, they lie well camouflaged on the bottom and wait for unwary prey to venture

PHOTO TIP

Being ambush predators, sand divers remain very still and use their quick color changes to camouflage themselves so that their prey will venture within range. As a lay-in-wait predator, they are very reluctant to move and give away their whereabouts. This tendency can work to your advantage because even when seen, sand divers are slow to move. To photograph them you should settle to the sandy bottom at least a few yards away before making a very slow approach. Keep your body close to the bottom as you near the lizardfish. If possible move toward the sand diver on a line which is interrupted by a gorgonian or coral head. This technique will help you appear nonthreatening and should allow you to get within three feet for a great portrait using your housed camera or Nikonos with a 28mm lens.

AT A GLANCE

SAND DIVER

Scientific Name
Synodus intermedius
Habitat
Sandy areas.
Typical Adult Size
7 to 14 inches.
Sightings
Occasionally seen.
Natural History
Well camouflaged, ambush predator.

within striking range before quickly darting forward to snare their victims. Sand divers have powerful jaws and numerous long, thin, razor-sharp teeth that help them grab and hold their prey. Voracious eaters, sand divers feed on squids, shrimps and a variety of reef fishes including basslets, grunts and sardines.

EELS

Worldwide, there are 22 families of eels, and believe it or not, all eels are fishes! Of course, several significant differences between most bony fishes and the infamous moray eels are readily apparent. Eels lack the large gill covers found in true fishes. True fishes use their gill covers to pump oxygenated water over their gills in the process of extracting oxygen from the water. The absence of gill covers requires eels to use their mouth as a bellows-type pump to constantly circulate a fresh supply of oxygen-filled water over their gills. Hence, eels are continuously opening and closing their mouths as they breathe.

Three families of eels are prominent in Caribbean waters—the moray eels, the garden eels and the snake eels.

PHOTO TIP

Few subjects are as dramatic as moray eels. The look created by their breathing is mistaken by many as a warning sign that the eels are about to bite anything that gets within biting range—divers included. Those divers familiar with typical eel behavior realize that this look belies the true nature of morays. In natural settings they are generally quite shy and pose no threat to divers who keep their hands to themselves. Don't crowd morays or make sudden movements, and they will often cooperate for 36 exposures taken with your housed camera or Nikonos and 28mm lens.

MORAY EELS

There are approximately 100 species of moray eels, and none have a more dramatic appearance than that of the Caribbean **green moray**. The largest of the Caribbean species, green morays commonly reach a length of six feet. As their name suggests, green morays are usually green, but they do have a distinct brown phase. They have large, powerful jaws, and

often their long, narrow, fang-like teeth are exposed as they respire. Feeding primarily on a wide variety of crustaceans, small fishes and mollusks (especially octopuses), green morays are active nocturnal predators in reef communities.

The olfactory region in the brains of moray eels is well developed, and they rely heavily upon their sense of smell when hunting. In addition, their lack of gill covers and the absence of paired fins enables morays to back up without getting hung up on outcroppings as they skillfully maneuver in the tight quarters of a reef community. Many fishes cannot go backwards quickly, but instead are forced to make a U-turn when they want to back up. Not so with morays. Their ability to back up helps them be successful reef predators.

There are two additional adaptations which help all morays in their role as predators. First, their scales are very small when compared to those of most other fishes; second, their skin is covered by a lubricating layer of mucus. Both adaptations help morays maneuver through small openings in the reef system without getting hung up.

During the day, morays tend to hide in crevices. Often only their head is visible as it extends past the opening. If you spot a moray, look closely and you might notice a variety of cleaner shrimp, gobies and other fishes cleaning the moray by ridding it of parasites, bacteria and dead skin. In a classic case of a symbiotic relationship that is further defined as mutualism, both the eel and the cleaners benefit, and neither party is harmed. While a variety of fishes serve as cleaners, the light purple-colored and magnificently nimble Pederson's shrimp are the primary shrimp involved. It is not uncommon to see one eel being simultaneously cleaned by more than a half-dozen gobies, a Spanish hogfish, and several shrimps.

During those cleaning sessions, you might actually see a cleaner dart inside the mouth of the eel to carry out its task. This behavior is quite common and the morays obviously have some instinctive understanding of the long-term importance of being cleaned, and do not eat the cleaners. In some cases a moray will open its mouth almost as wide as it possibly can in order to signal the cleaners that the eel would like its mouth to be cleaned. And when the moray wants the cleaners to exit, the eel will rapidly open and then partially close its mouth several times in quick succession.

A variety of morays, in addition to green morays, inhabit the crevices of Caribbean reef communities. These include the **goldentail moray**, the **viper moray**, the beautiful **chain moray**, the **purplemouth moray**, and the **spotted moray**. Reaching a maximum length of about two feet, goldentail morays are among the smaller and more reclusive species of moray eels. Goldentail morays are gorgeous animals possessing hundreds of gold spots on their dark bodies.

Viper morays are most easily identified by noting the shape of their distinctly arched jaws and fang-like teeth. Chain morays are usually between one and two-and-a-half feet long, and are wonderful-looking animals. They have bright yellow chain link-like markings which loop around their dark bodies. Found in shallow reefs throughout the Caribbean in areas where especially clear water is the rule, chain morays are most common in the eastern Caribbean. They are, however, occasionally seen in the waters of the western Caribbean, Bahamas and Florida.

Usually encountered in shallow coral and rocky regions, spotted morays are the most common species of moray found in the reefs of the Western Atlantic. They have yellowish backs and white underbellies, and their bodies are covered with numerous dark brown and black spots. Spotted morays are medium-sized, attaining a maxi-

AT A GLANCE

GOLDENTAIL MORAY

Scientific Name
Muraena miliaris
Habitat
Reef, in crevices.
Typical Adult Size
2 feet.
Sightings
Occasionally seen.
Natural History
Reclusive by day, active by night.

AT A GLANCE

SPOTTED MORAY

Scientific Name
Gymnothorax moringa
Habitat
Reef, within crevices.
Typical Adult Size
2.5 feet.
Sightings
Commonly seen.
Natural History
Reclusive by day, active by night.

mum length of approximately four feet.

Garden Eels

No presentation on Caribbean eels would be complete without including **garden eels.** Members of the family of eels known as conger eels, garden eels are those shy "now you see them, now you don't" sand dwellers that can make you and your diving buddy think you have lost your minds. Garden eels usually live in colonies. When undisturbed, they rise up out of their burrows and face into the current so they can pick particles of food out of the water column. From a distance, garden eels often appear to be gracefully sway-

AT A GLANCE

GARDEN EEL

Scientific Name
Nystactichthys halis
Habitat
Powdery sand.
Typical Adult Size
10 inches.
Sightings
Commonly seen in deeper sand areas.
Natural History
Sway over sand burrows as they feed on plankton.

ing back and forth to some mystical undersea music that you cannot hear. Their motion is reminiscent of cobras that move in response to the motions of snake charmers. But as you approach, garden eels are quick to slither back into their burrows, and if you get too close or move too fast, they will rapidly withdraw completely out of sight. If you look away, it often appears as if the entire colony has suddenly vanished, and due to their shy nature, garden eels are unlikely to reappear unless you back off a considerable distance.

Snake Eels

Snake eels are generally spotted and have highly prominent nostrils protruding from their heads. They are usually seen swimming over sand or rubble, and occasionally in reef communities. The long, slender

AT A GLANCE

BLACK SPOTTED SNAKE EEL

Scientific name
Quassiremus productus
Habitat
Rubble areas.
Typical Adult Size
2 feet.
Sightings
Occasionally seen.
Natural History
Reclusive by day, active by night.

bodies of most species of snake eels have strong, sharply defined tails which enable them to wriggle backwards and rapidly bury themselves in the sand. These eels tend to remain buried during daylight hours and emerge at night to forage along the bottom for food.

Despite the fact that snake eels are commonly mistaken as some type of sea snake, they are not dangerous. Presently there are no sea snakes found in Caribbean waters. However, many specialists warn that it is only a matter of time before some Pacific sea snakes are likely to arrive in the Caribbean via the Panama Canal.

SILVERSIDES

Approximately 10 species of fishes, including a variety of anchovies, sardines and herrings, are commonly called silversides. All are silver, minnow-sized baitfish. In natural settings it is impossible even for most specialists to distinguish these species from one another. Silversides are schooling fishes, and it is not at all unusual for a single school to be comprised of several species of these baitfish and number in the thousands.

The dense schools are often found over shallow reefs, in caves, in the cuts and canyons between towering coral heads, and swarming in and around shipwrecks. The shimmering schools are a beautiful sight as the bright silver-colored fishes move in perfect synchronization with one another, providing divers with a long-lasting source of entertainment. Flashes of silver from rays of

AT A GLANCE

SILVERSIDES

Scientific Name
Various species. Includes at least 10 species of silver, minnow-sized baitfish.

Habitat
In caves or wrecks seasonally.

Typical Adult Size
1 to 2 inches.

Sightings
Occasionally seen.

Natural History
Form huge flowing schools; food for many larger fishes.

sunlight reflecting off their bodies as they swim can attract attention from a considerable distance.

The reflections attract predators as silversides are heavily preyed upon by many reef fishes including groupers, jacks, barracuda and tarpon. When they rush the silversides, the schools scatter and then regroup with fluid grace. The flowing movement with which the school breaks apart and forms again is a captivating scene. The schools of silversides never seem to flee the area, but instead just part and regroup after the predators attack. As a general rule, if you find a school, you can return for a second or third dive and relocate the fish.

Flyingfishes, Balao, Ballyhoo and Halfbeaks

Atlantic flyingfish, **balao**, **ballyhoo** and **halfbeaks** are all species that live near the surface. These fishes are colored in a manner that helps them blend in extremely well with the lighter hues of surface waters. Despite the fact that they are quite common, these fishes are normally overlooked by divers.

Flyingfish acquired their names from their rather unique ability to leave the water and glide through air near the surface to escape predation from dolphins, sailfish, marlin, sharks and a variety of other species of open-sea hunters. Boats often scare these fish into "flight." While they do not actually fly, flyingfish do glide on highly modified pectoral fins. The glides of some species can last for up to 13 seconds and easily cover 150 yards or more. Some species have been clocked in the air at speeds of up to 35 miles per hour. Before flyingfish leave the water, they rapidly beat the lower lobe of their tail back and forth to gain speed. Rarely seen near shore, Atlantic flyingfish are commonly

seen by boaters in the open sea.

Balao, ballyhoo and halfbeaks tend to live in the top few feet of water. They are fast swimmers and often leap clear of the water when frightened or excited. Being darkly colored on the top and lightly colored on the bottom to blend in with surface waters, these species are classically countershaded, a feature which combined with their small size, often enables them to hide from predators and go unnoticed by divers. They are a favorite bait of many sportfishermen, and are also heavily preyed upon by a variety of jacks, groupers, billfish and other larger fishes.

Balao, ballyhoo and halfbeaks are sometimes confused with the the **redfin needlefish**, **keeltail needlefish**, **houndfish** and **cornetfish**.

Houndfish, Cornetfish and Needlefishes

Described in the family Belonidae, houndfish are the largest of the needlefishes. Cornetfish are members of the family Fistulariidae. Sometimes called the bluespotted cornetfish, they grow to six feet long and are slightly larger than houndfish. Cornetfish can be recognized by their darkish brown to green bodies with blue spots and the long tail filament that trails behind the tail. This filament is not included in the body length measurement. Cornetfish are often found hovering over reef bottom and in beds of seagrass, as well as swimming near the surface with needlefishes and houndfish.

Trumpetfish

Reaching a length of up to three feet, **trumpetfish** have thin, extremely elongated bodies and a long snout equipped with a large and unusually shaped mouth that has a dis-

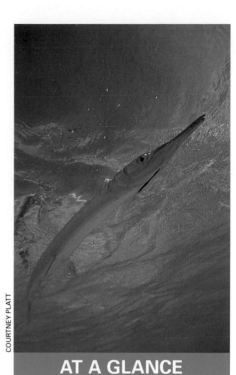

COURTNEY PLATT

AT A GLANCE

HOUNDFISH

Scientific Name
Tylosurus crocodilus
Habitat
Top several feet of water, often within inches of surface.
Typical Adult Size
2 to 4 feet.
Sightings
Occasionally seen, but often go unnoticed.
Natural History
Blend in extremely well with various hues of water near surface. Largest of the needlefishes. Tend to be wary of divers.

tinctly puckered look. Trumpetfish often orient themselves vertically or at odd angles in order to blend in with sea fans and sea whips.

The lower jaw of a trumpetfish is equipped with barbels which are sometimes used to take advantage of the curious nature of unsuspecting prey. Trumpetfish use the barbels as a lure by hanging in a head-down vertical position with barbels extended. The barbels lure prey, preferably blennies, small grunts, squirrelfishes, damselfishes and shrimps, which the trumpetfish

As is the case with many fishes, the coloration of the juvenile trumpetfish pictured here is considerably different than that of the adult. Naturally occuring color differences within the same species is a factor that makes identifying fishes a tricky pursuit.

AT A GLANCE

TRUMPETFISH

Scientific Name
Aulostomus maculatus
Habitat
Reef, hides amongst gorgonians.
Typical Adult Size
2 to 3 feet.
Sightings
Commonly seen.
Natural History
Ambush predator; often seen shadowing groupers or hiding head down amongst branches of gorgonians, sea rods and others.

PHOTO TIP

When hanging head down in a near vertical orientation, trumpetfish are often involved in ambush predation and they are very reluctant to blow their cover by rushing away. If you slowly approach them for a portrait, they will often continue to maintain a vertical position amongst the gorgonians until you get within shooting range. Concentrate on shooting vertical formats.

sucks into its long, narrow snout. Although the mouth of a trumpetfish looks small, it is capable of opening wide enough to ingest fish with bodies that are three to four inches deep.

Trumpetfish appear in a wide variety of colors from brown to reddish brown, with pale silver lines and small black dots, to brilliant yellow, and they are capable of quickly changing from one color pattern to another. The colors do not indicate sexual differences and the purpose of being one color or another remains unknown.

SEAHORSES AND PIPEFISHES

There are two species of **seahorses** and several species of **pipefishes** that occur in Caribbean waters. The bodies of these unusual fishes are encased in a hard plated shell of armor that has an almost bone-like quality. Both seahorses and pipefishes have long tubular snouts with very small mouths that are used to suck in their tiny planktonic prey.

Seahorses are among the most ornate and delicate-looking of all fishes. Most individuals are less than six inches long. The genus name of seahorses, *Hippocampus*, is derived from the Greek "bent horse," and refers to the way in which their faces resemble those of horses. Seahorses are often discovered drifting in sargassum and floating over beds of seagrass, but as a rule they are most commonly seen in shallow waters near shore where they anchor themselves to coral branches, blades of seagrass, mangrove roots and other solid objects with their long, flexible tails. Seahorses are rather poor swimmers. Lacking the powerful tail fin found in many fishes, they swim with their bodies in a vertical position and propel themselves by rapidly beating their small dorsal and anal fins.

One of the more fascinating aspects of the lives of seahorses involves their reproductive behavior. Female seahorses deposit up to several hundred eggs inside a pouch in the belly of the male. The eggs incubate in the pouch for approximately six weeks. Males appear to encourage the hatching process by rubbing their bellies against other objects. The juveniles are about half an inch long at birth, and soon swim away from the adult male to begin life on their own.

The **longsnout seahorse** and the **lined seahorse**, the two most com-

throughout their range, but they are often common in localized areas.

The approximately 20 species of Caribbean pipefishes can be distinguished from seahorses by their long, thin and flat bodies, and the fact that pipefishes are much faster swimmers when they want to be. Telling one pipefish from another, however, can be rather challenging.

BIGEYES

Two species of commonly seen Caribbean fishes, the **glasseye snapper** and the **bigeye**, are described in the family known as bigeyes. These hand-sized fishes are one of many species of bright red fishes that have large eyes. The members of the bigeye family are primarily nocturnal creatures. Their large eyes are designed to help them seek out their prey at night. Bigeyes can be distinguished from other red fishes by their sharply upturned mouths and unforked tails.

Normally a solitary species,

AT A GLANCE

GLASSEYE SNAPPER

Scientific Name
Priacanthus cruentatus
Habitat
Caves by day, reef by night.
Average Adult Size
8 inches.
Sightings
Commonly seen.
Natural History
Oversized eyes make night hunting possible.

AT A GLANCE

LONGSNOUT SEAHORSE

Scientific Name
Hippocampus reidi
Habitat
Reef, especially around mangroves.
Typical Adult Size
3 to 5 inches.
Sightings
Seldom seen.
Natural History
Long snout creates suction for feeding on plankton; prehensile tail for grasping; male gestates eggs until birth.

mon species found in the Caribbean, have a number of color phases, and positive identification underwater can prove difficult for most non-specialists. Both species are rather rare

current and surge. When approached by divers, squirrelfishes will often erect their spines as they show their concern, but typically these fishes will not flee from the protection of their overhang.

When feeling threatened and hiding in a hole, several species in the squirrelfish family are quick to produce loud grunting sounds with their swim bladders in an effort to ward off predators. It is also believed that the sounds are used to claim territory. Both the squirrelfish and the **longjaw squirrelfish** are highly territorial.

As darkness settles in, the activity level of squirrelfishes and soldierfishes increases, and they soon begin to roam the reef in search of a

---

AT A GLANCE

SQUIRRELFISH

Scientific Name
Holocentrus ascensionis
Habitat
Caves by day, reef by night.
Typical Adult Size
8 inches.
Sightings
Commonly seen.
Natural History
Oversized eyes make night hunting possible.

---

and tendency to frequent the underside of reef ledges. The bodies of squirrelfishes are short and stocky, and they have distinctly forked tails. Dorsal spines and fins are usually white or yellow. Being derived from the Greek word meaning "spiny all over," the name of their genus, *Holocentrus*, reflects their design.

As a rule, during the day squirrelfishes tend to hang almost motionless under or close to overhangs as they drift back and forth with

---

AT A GLANCE

LONGSPINE SQUIRRELFISH

Scientific Name
Holocentrus rufus
Habitat
Caves by day, reef by night.
Average Adult Size
8 inches.
Sightings
Commonly seen.
Natural History
Oversized eyes make night hunting possible.

---

glasseye snappers occur worldwide in tropical seas. Bigeyes often gather in small schools, and members of any given school are typically uniform in color, although the color varies from solid red to vertically banded silver and red. Some bands are usually evident, but that is not always the case.

SQUIRRELFISHES AND SOLDIERFISHES

Squirrelfishes and **soldierfishes** are among the most conspicuous of Caribbean reef fishes because of their bright red coloration, prominent spiny fins, oversized dark eyes,

variety of crustaceans. While the **blackbar** soldierfish is most likely to be found up in the water column, feeding on a variety of mid-water invertebrates, other squirrelfishes tend to orient themselves near the bottom where they feed on various bottom-dwelling crustaceans and mollusks.

Reef squirrelfish and **dusky squirrelfish** are other members of the squirrelfish family which are very close in size and appearance to longjaw squirrelfish. To differentiate between the species, look for the dark patch far forward on the flared dorsal fin of the reef squirrelfish, and note the overall darker red hues of the dusky squirrelfish.

During the day, look for blackbar soldierfish in caves and don't be surprised if you see a parasitic isopod dug in on the forehead of these often-plagued fish. These isopods feed on the blood and body fluids of soldierfish and other fishes.

AT A GLANCE

LONGJAW SQUIRRELFISH

Scientific Name
 Holocentrus marianus
Habitat
 Caves by day, reef by night.
Typical Adult Size
 8 inches.
Abundance
 Common.
Natural History
 Oversized eyes make night hunting possible.

AT A GLANCE

BLACKBAR SOLDIERFISH

Scientific Name
 Myripristis jacobus
Habitat
 Caves by day, reef by night.
Typical Adult Size
 8 inches.
Sightings
 Commonly seen.
Natural History
 Oversized eyes make night hunting possible.

PHOTO TIP

Their daytime inactivity, coupled with their reluctance to leave the protection of their overhangs, makes squirrelfishes veritable sitting ducks for fish portraits. Add to this their wonderful shades of red and orange, and you have a great opportunity to shoot portraits that will jump off the screen or the printed page. Use either a Nikonos with a 28mm lens or a macro lens such as a 50mm, 55mm or 60mm depending on your camera system. Since squirrelfishes tend to hang under ledges, be extra careful to place your strobes low enough so that overhangs don't block out the beam of strobe light. Approach slowly and breathe quietly. When you get close, they usually flare their dorsal spines warning you that you are threatening your successful encounter.

SEA BASSES AND GROUPERS

The extraordinarily diversified family of sea basses and groupers that are commonly found in the Caribbean and associated waters includes a variety of species that range in size from the tiny **tobaccofish**, which attains a length of about five inches, to the giant **jewfish**, which can reach lengths of eight feet. Even though variety is the rule, there is a thread of common characteristics that flows through this group known as sea basses, or by their family name, the serranids. Most species have a lower jaw which projects well forward, and all have rather large mouths compared to their overall body size. The mouths are equipped with rows of slender yet very sharp teeth, which in most species include several prominent canines. They feed primarily on crustaceans and other fishes, and many species are a highly valued food source for humans.

Many sea basses and groupers, especially the larger individuals, hover close to the bottom or lie on the bottom near caves, crevices and ledges, places that offer a safe refuge should they need it. When on the prowl, these fishes creep along the bottom, creating the deception that they are incapable of quick bursts of speed. Studies have shown that some groupers can go from a resting stop to full speed within one fortieth of a second. In fact, the movement of their tail is so fast that it creates a small explosion in the water. The loud boom that can easily be heard by divers who are out of visual range is the result of water rushing to fill the instantaneous vacuum created by the rapid movement of the tail.

Many sea basses are quick color-change artists. In some cases, color alteration is intended to help these fishes camouflage themselves as they stalk their prey. Groupers often flash one color when they are at a cleaning station requesting service, and then change color when they are satisfied that the job has been completed. Some species also change color when they feed. In addition to these color changes, the commonly seen coney is one of a number of species in this family that are believed to change their coloration according to the different stages of their lives. All of these color changes combine to make positive identification challenging, and the world of sea basses a very colorful world.

Most sea basses and groupers also display some intriguing sexual traits. Groupers, for example, begin their lives as females. Once they reach sexual maturity, they produce ripened eggs. Later these exact same fish undergo a remarkable transformation when they change into males, fully capable of producing sperm. Some sea basses can simultaneously produce sperm and ripened eggs. However, in order to prevent the genetic problems caused by inbreeding, these species reduce the odds by spawning in large groups in areas where they gather in incredible numbers during specific times of the year.

Adult Caribbean groupers can, at least to some degree, be classified according to their size. **Coneys, graysbys, red hinds** and **rock hinds** are among the smaller species. All are less than 18 inches long. Medium-sized species include the **tiger grouper, Nassau grouper, red grouper, yellowmouth grouper** and **comb grouper. Black groupers, yellowfin groupers, snowy groupers** and **marbled groupers** can get quite large, but jewfish are by far the largest species of Caribbean grouper.

Truly a spectacle of Caribbean

AT A GLANCE

NASSAU GROUPER

Scientific Name
Epinephelus striatus
Habitat
Reef.
Typical Adult Size
1.5 to 3 feet.
Sightings
Commonly seen.
Natural History
Ambush predator, gather in huge numbers to breed.

PHOTO TIP

Many sea basses and groupers are easily approached by divers. Full body and full face shots of these fishes are quite dramatic. Slow, deliberate movements will often enable you to work at close range and obtain the exact shooting angles you desire. Use a Nikonos with a 28mm lens or a reflex system for a great portrait of these powerful and often colorful fishes.

waters, Nassau groupers attain a maximum size of 4 feet and 55 pounds. They often display a strong sense of curiosity about divers, approaching and following them throughout their dive. For photographers, they are ideal subjects since they pose as if schooled in the art.

Nassau groupers typically inhabit cave-filled reef areas in waters between 40 and 100 feet deep. During the day they tend to remain near the openings of caves, crevices and ledges, or behind the cover of sponges and sea fans as they await the approach of their unsuspecting prey, which consists of various fishes.

Nassau groupers are probably the easiest of the large species of Caribbean groupers to identify. They typically appear to have a white body covered with irregularly spaced vertical bands that vary from brown to dark green. However, their coloration sometimes varies significantly depending on their activity. But no matter what color phase they are experiencing, Nassau groupers always have a black "saddle spot" on their caudal peduncle, a thickened stalk which supports the tail.

Nassau groupers are quite common throughout the tropical western Atlantic, and range from Bermuda and North Carolina to the Gulf of Mexico to Brazil. Juveniles are usually found in the shallower waters of seagrass beds.

Jewfish are the largest of all of the bony fishes that inhabit Caribbean reefs. Members of the grouper family, these behemoths may attain a size of 8 feet long and 700 pounds. Needless to say, it is a thrill to find yourself staring eyeball-to-eyeball with a fish that is as much as five times your own size. Their size appears to give these monsters confidence around divers, and though they are not all that common, when encountered they are frequently easy to approach. Other fishes, known as remoras, are often seen accompanying, or even attached to, jewfish. Some jewfish lack remoras,

AT A GLANCE

JEWFISH
(ACCOMPANIED BY REMORA)

Scientific Name
Epinephelus itijara
Habitat
Reef.
Typical Adult Size
Around 5 feet.
Sightings
Occasionally seen.
Natural History
Ambush predator, largest of the groupers.

AT A GLANCE

TIGER GROUPER

Scientific name
Mycteroperca tigris
Habitat
Reefs and walls.
Typical Adult Size
2 to 3.5 feet.
Sightings
Commonly seen.
Natural History
Often resting near bottom in secluded areas, and frequently seen at cleaning stations.

AT A GLANCE

CONEY, GOLDEN CONEY, BICOLOR CONEY

Scientific name
   Epinephelus fulvus
Habitat
   Reef and rubble areas.
Typical Adult Size
   10 to 14 inches long.
Sightings
   Commonly seen.
Natural History
   Three distinct color phases for the same species: blue spots over reddish brown upper body with white below; blue spots over gold to yellow body; and blue spots over red to brown body.

others have only one, and still others have what might be described as an entourage. The remoras are thought to feed on scraps dropped by the jewfish, and perhaps help clean these huge fish of various ectoparasites, dead tissue and bacteria.

Jewfish like to reside in cave systems, in shipwrecks and around harbor pilings. Preferring to remain close to the bottom, they are rather sedentary fish, but they are capable of astonishing bursts of speed. Jewfish are apex or top level predators that possess a large mouth filled with plenty of very sharp teeth. They feed primarily on crabs, lobsters and a variety of fishes.

Growing to a maximum length of about 12 inches, **coneys** are the most common and most attractive species of small groupers found in Caribbean waters. They prefer comparatively clear water and are usually more abundant at small offshore islands near reefs, where they cruise close to the sea floor. Coneys prefer

AT A GLANCE

BARRED HAMLET

Scientific Name
Hypoplectrus puella
Habitat
Reef areas.
Typical Adult Size
5 inches.
Sightings
Most commonly seen hamlet in Caribbean; occasionally seen in the Bahamas and Florida.
Natural History
Stays close to bottom.

AT A GLANCE

SHY HAMLET

Scientific Name
Hypoplectrus guttavarius
Habitat
Reef areas.
Average Adult Size
5 inches.
Sightings
Occasionally seen.
Natural History
Stays near bottom. Like other hamlets, simultaneously possesses male and female reproductive organs. Born female, later becomes male.

hamlets are typically found at depths of 75 feet or less, while other species prefer deeper waters.

Among the more beautiful hamlets are the **indigo hamlet**, the **shy hamlet** and the **golden hamlet**. Golden hamlets are considered rare and are generally found only at depths in excess of 120 feet. Like other hamlets, these species prey primarily on small crustaceans and other fishes.

Hamlets are hermaphrodites, meaning that they simultaneously possess both male and female sex organs. However, like other serranids they are born females and later transform into males. At any given time, hamlets produce only sperm or eggs.

Typically only three to seven inches long, **tobaccofish** are among the smallest members of the sea bass family. A common species throughout their range, tobaccofish prefer to

AT A GLANCE

BUTTER HAMLET

Scientific Name
Hypoplectrus unicolor
Habitat
Reef areas.
Typical Adult Size
5 inches.
Sightings
Commonly seen in some areas.
Natural History
Usually seen in pairs.

times continues to be used when referring to the butter hamlet. Some specialists still suspect the one species theory to be valid.

The **butter hamlet** is considered to be the most common hamlet in the Florida Keys, while the **barred hamlet** is believed to be the most common in the Caribbean. Barred

AT A GLANCE

TOBACCOFISH

Scientific Name
Serranus tabacarius
Habitat
Sandy areas.
Typical Adult Size
5 inches.
Sightings
Commonly seen.
Natural History
Very common member of the rubble and sand community.

AT A GLANCE

HARLEQUIN BASS

Scientific Name
Serranus tigrinus
Habitat
Sandy areas.
Typical Adult Size
5 inches.
Sightings
Commonly seen.
Natural History
Very common inhabitant of the sand community.

inhabit the sandy areas adjacent to coral reefs. Like other members of their family they tend to swim close to the sea floor, and although their coloration may vary, tobaccofish usually appear whitish with tan to orange patches, and have a number of black bars along their head and back.

As a rule, tobaccofish tend to show some caution about approaching divers. However, if you are slow, patient and deliberate in your movements, they will often be overcome by their innate sense of curiosity.

The wild color patterns of **harlequin** bass set them apart from many other species of smaller sea basses. Harlequin bass are boldly colored, their light to pale bodies decorated with black vertical stripes and a number of prominent black spots, especially near the head, tail and on the dorsal fin. The mouth and head are often highlighted by swathes of

yellow patches, while their dark eyes are trimmed by a light gold to white border. The pointed head of the harlequin bass also serves as an identification key in helping to distinguish them from other small sea basses.

Harlequin bass prefer to inhabit the shallow waters of rubble zones, reefs and beds of seagrass where they hunt for a variety of small crustaceans. These curious fishes are common in many areas of the Caribbean.

BASSLETS

Despite their small stature, the family of fishes called basslets includes some of the most spectacularly colored fish species found anywhere in the world. Members of the basslet family reach a maximum length of about three inches. These fishes are usually found below ledges and overhangs, near the openings to tunnel-like passageways in the reefs, and along the drop-offs.

Not too many years ago, scientists considered basslets to be members of the sea bass family. However, the basslets do significantly differ from sea basses and groupers in that the lateral line of basslets is either absent or not continuous, while the lateral line system in sea basses and groupers is continuous and com-

plete. The lateral line system is a series of sensitive nerves that run laterally or horizontally down the outside of a fish close to the midbody. These nerves are quite sensitive to the sound waves and pressure waves created by the movement of other animals in the surrounding water.

Those members of the basslet family whose genus is *Gramma* are often referred to as grammas. For example, even in casual conversation, the species *Gramma loreto* is often called a **royal gramma** or **purple gramma**, as well as a **fairy basslet**.

Fairy basslets represent their family well and are among the most colorful of all Caribbean reef fishes. Although their maximum length is

spurts, starting and stopping abruptly as they dart about the reef. When approached by divers, these colorful fishes often retreat into the protected recesses of a reef, but if divers are patient, fairy basslets often return to the scene.

Fairy basslets are common in the Caribbean and the Bahamas, but are not known in Florida.

Also included in this family of fishes is the **blackcap basslet**, a species which is usually found in somewhat deeper water than fairy basslets generally inhabit. When the two species are evident along a wall, there seems to be an obvious

AT A GLANCE

BLACKCAP BASSLET

Scientific Name
Gramma melecara
Habitat
Wall or drop-off.
Typical Adult Size
2.5 inches.
Sightings
Commonly seen in some areas.
Natural History
Demonstrate a distinct line of zonation starting at approximately 60 feet, just slightly deeper than the zone preferred by fairy basslets.

AT A GLANCE

FAIRY BASSLET, ROYAL GRAMMA, PURPLE GRAMMA

Scientific Name
Gramma loreto
Habitat
Reef and wall, often near underhangs and ledges.
Typical Adult Size
1.5 to 3 inches.
Sightings
Commonly seen except Florida.
Natural History
Often orient to nearest reef or ledge and may appear to be "upside down" from diver's point of view.

when under ledges and overhangs appears quite natural to fairy basslets. However, they do not always orient in this manner.

Fairy basslets often swim in short

about three inches, their vivid purple heads, bright yellow bodies and curious antics make them standout performers in many reef communities. Fairy basslets are often seen swimming in a position that might be described as upside down. But of course, what is upside down to us may be right side up and very natural for a fairy basslet. Swimming belly toward the reef even

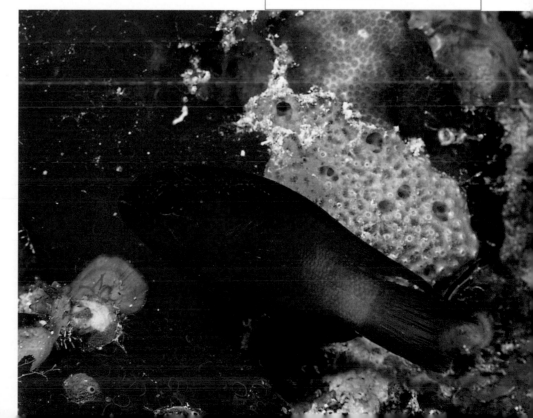

breakpoint of around 60 feet where fairy basslets become less prominent and blackcap basslets more common. Fairy basslets tend to prefer the top 100 feet of water, while blackcap basslets are often found as deep as 200 feet.

Basslets feed primarily on planktonic crustaceans, such as copepods and the larvae of shrimps.

SOAPFISHES

Soapfishes secrete a thick layer of mucus which coats their bodies, detering most predatory fishes from feeding on them. This adaptation is one that greatly improves the species' odds of survival.

Soapfishes tend to be rather reclusive and secretive fishes, but they often allow divers to approach within close range. They often rest on the bottom of mixed sand and coral, but they do not sit upright in the water. They tend to lean over and prop themselves against corals. Many divers mistake their natural posture for that of an injured fish, and it is certainly easy to understand how such a mistake can be made. Their dorsal and anal fins are rather soft. They undulate, and their appearance contributes to the mistaken perception that soapfishes are injured.

Adult soapfishes range from about six inches to just over a foot long. These fishes usually acquire their adult coloration by the time they reach a length of two inches. The largest of the Caribbean soapfishes is the **greater soapfish**, a species which is found throughout the tropical Atlantic. In the western Atlantic, greater soapfish are found in the waters off Bermuda, throughout the Caribbean, and from Florida to Brazil. Greater soapfish vary in color from a drab brown to reddish-brown to gray.

Their bodies are usually covered with pale splotches that give them an overall mottled appearance. Other species have paler bodies covered with dark blotches.

Soapfishes prey on small crustaceans and small fishes, mostly wrasses.

CARDINALFISHES

At least 19 species known as cardinalfishes inhabit Caribbean waters. These small but brightly colored reddish fishes are usually less than four inches long. Their large dark eyes are indicative of their nocturnal feeding habits. While many species are quite common, they are often unnoticed by divers because they tend to inhabit the darker areas of caves and crevices during daylight hours, coming out on the reef only under the cover of darkness. Cardinalfishes emerge as the sun sets to hunt for small fish, some invertebrates and a variety of plankton. Most species forage near the bottom, but some feed near the surface.

AT A GLANCE

GREATER SOAPFISH

Scientific Name
  Rypticus saponaceus
Habitat
  Reef, sand/reef interface.
Typical Adult Size
  6 to 10 inches.
Sightings
  Occasionally seen.
Natural History
  Secrete mucus body coating that deters predators.

AT A GLANCE

WHITESTAR CARDINALFISH

Scientific Name
  Apogon lachneri
Habitat
  In caves, under ledges.
Typical Adult Size
  2 inches .
Sightings
  Occasionally seen.
Natural History
  Nocturnal feeder, hides during day. Can be distinguished from other cardinalfishes by brilliant white "star" located to the rear of the dorsal fin.

One of the more fascinating behaviors of cardinalfishes is that the adults orally incubate their eggs, carrying them in their mouths until they hatch. In most species, the oral incubation is conducted primarily by the male, but in other species the female plays an active role in the process.

Some species of cardinalfishes hide within the stinging tentacles of sea anemones. Others seek cover amongst the spines of sea urchins, and still others hide in tube sponges. **Sponge cardinalfish** are commonly found within the cavity of tube sponges and other sponges. Another species of cardinalfish, known as **conchfish**, is actually known to reside in the mantle cavity of living queen conchs during the day. Fishermen often find several conch-fish inside the shell of conchs when they clean their catch.

A list of the most common and most attractive Caribbean cardinalfishes includes the **twospot cardinalfish**, **dusky cardinalfish**, **barred cardinalfish**, **flamefish**, and the **pale cardinalfish**, which appears very similar in appearance to **rough-lip cardinalfish**, **mimic cardinalfish** and **broadsaddle cardinalfish**. Telling one species of cardinalfish from the next is easy in some cases but very challenging in others. Fortunately, all of the cardinalfishes appear superficially similar to one another, and as a result, are easy to differentiate from other families of fishes.

SAND TILEFISH

Sand tilefish are common in sandy rubble zones, but despite their numbers, many divers remain unaware of the presence of these fish. That is because sand tilefish are extremely wary. They are often seen hovering horizontally over a sand or rubble bottom. From afar, the most distinctive feature of their cigar-shaped bodies is the rippling of their long, continuous pale blue dorsal fin, which undulates as they pause to keep an eye on their surroundings. They have elongated white to whitish-blue bodies with a gold head and a dark spot on the tail.

If you spot a sand tilefish and try to approach, it will usually move toward a two-ended lair of its own construction. They pick up bits of rubble in their mouths and deposit them in a pile. They then proceed to excavate their lair by pulling out one

AT A GLANCE

SAND TILEFISH

Scientific Name
  Malacanthus plumieri
Habitat
  Sand/rubble areas.
Typical Adult Size
  12 inches.
Sightings
  Commonly seen.
Natural History
  Create a home burrow within piles of rubble which they build and vigorously maintain.

piece of rubble at a time until they have a protective shelter complete with both an entrance and an exit. If you or any potential threat approach too aggressively, the fish will disappear into the hole.

Sand tilefish usually remain within 10 yards or so of the safety of their tunnel, which they enter head first if they are sufficiently concerned or startled. At times sand tilefish hover tail down over the opening and it appears that they can back into their tunnel, but at the last instant they make a U-turn and enter the opening head first. Sand tilefish are territorial and will chase other fishes away from their burrows, while at the same time, they are quite willing to steal rocks and debris from the constructed mounds of other sand tilefish. Sometimes, observant divers will see two sand tilefish in or near the same hole. They are likely to be a mated pair.

Sand tilefish attain a maximum length of about two feet. Juveniles do not construct burrows until they reach a length of about seven inches. Sand tilefish prey upon a variety of brittle stars, crustaceans and small fishes that inhabit the sand and rubble zone.

JACKS, SCADS, POMPANOS AND PERMIT

Jacks, **scads**, **pompanos** and **permit** are among the swiftest and most exciting fishes in many reef communities. Most species are not actually considered residents of the reef, but are characterized as members of the nearby open-sea community which visit reefs while hunting. Most species feed on a variety of small schooling fishes and crustaceans. As adults, many jacks, scads and pompanos are schooling fishes. Permit are normally schooling fish that are rarely seen in the Caribbean, Bahamas and Florida.

Most of these silvery fishes are highly excitable, and tight schools often swirl rapidly around divers.

AT A GLANCE

BLACK JACK

Scientific Name
Caranx lugubris
Habitat
Open water.
Typical Adult Size
2 feet.
Sightings
Occasionally seen.
Natural History
Powerful predatory fishes; tend
to be solitary.

broadcast spawners, releasing sperm and eggs in the open sea. While the adults do pair off, spawning often occurs in large groups. Fertilized eggs float with the plankton until they hatch, unless they fall prey to any of a wide variety of open sea predators. Scientists often discover juveniles drifting with jellyfishes, rafts of sargassum weed, and with other debris that offers some protection. As a general rule, juvenile fishes have sleeker bodies than do the adults, but this is not the case with juvenile jacks, scads and pompanos. The juveniles have deeper bodies and a banded pattern, a feature lacking in the adults.

Among the more common species of jacks seen around reef communities are the **crevalle jack, black jack, horse-eye jack, yellow jack** and **bar jack.** Distinguishing one species of jack from all the rest can prove chal-

AT A GLANCE

BAR JACK

Scientific Name
Caranx ruber
Habitat
Open water, over reef or sand.
Typical Adult Size
9 to 14 inches.
Sightings
Commonly seen.
Natural History
Often seen shadowing stingrays, hogfishes and goatfishes. Black body not always evident, but usually blacken when feeding along sea floor.

Active predators, they provide wonderful entertainment by making sudden and often repeated passes through schools of panicked baitfish.

Jacks, scads and pompanos enjoy worldwide distribution with approximately 140 species representing the family in tropical and temperate seas. As a general rule, the adults are found in deeper water that is not too far from shore, yet is seaward of the outside walls.

Although their bodies appear to differ considerably, they do share a number of common physiological characteristics. Perhaps the most noticeable is their deeply forked tail, a feature shared by many of the sea's fastest swimming fishes.

Jacks, scads and pompanos are

AT A GLANCE

CREVALLE JACK

Scientific Name
Caranx hippos
Habitat
Open water, along drop-off.
Typical Adult Size
18 to 30 inches.
Sightings
Commonly seen.
Natural History
Young commonly school, sometimes with horse-eye jacks; older specimens often solitary.

lenging in the field.

Bar jacks are often seen shadowing or closely following stingrays or other fishes, especially hogfishes and goatfishes that feed in the sand community. The behavior is not completely understood, but the jacks are frequently seen sifting through sand that the rays and other fishes have just excavated, probably in an effort to find uncovered crustaceans.

Horse-eye jacks and young crevalle jacks are commonly seen slowly cruising the walls in schools that vary in size from only a handful to several hundred. Often they are seen swirling in circular patterns, each following the tail of the fish in front of it.

The dark eyes of horse-eye jacks are oversized, indicating active nocturnal feeding behavior. Young horse-eye jacks are known to inhabit brackish backwater areas and may even enter fresh water. As adults, they can be distinguished from other jacks by their normally yellow tail.

Greater amberjacks are an impressive species of Caribbean jacks. Attaining a size of almost 6 feet and 150 pounds, these monsters are extremely powerful. Greater amberjacks, usually just called amberjacks, are characterized by their long, sleek body and the amber streak which runs lengthwise down the body. Tending to be slightly smaller than greater amberjacks, **amaco jacks** are a similar-looking species but with slightly higher backs. Both species normally inhabit open waters, but they do visit reef communities where they make lightning-fast strikes on small schooling fishes.

SNAPPERS

A variety of medium-sized fishes called snappers inhabit reefs and mangrove communities throughout the Caribbean. Many species of snappers have rather distinct profiles. Most have pronounced trian-

gular-shaped heads and long, pointed faces. In most snappers, the tails are slightly notched, but not nearly as forked as the tails of jacks. The majority of snappers have yellowish fins, and their mouths are smaller than those of the sea basses. In two species, the **schoolmaster** and **yellowtail snapper**, distinctly yellow fins make a good identifying feature.

Most snappers are primarily nocturnal hunters that feed on a variety of smaller fishes, crabs, shrimp, other crustaceans and a variety of mollusks. The adults of smaller species prefer to feed on shrimps and crabs, while adults of larger species prefer to prey on smaller fishes.

As a rule, juvenile snappers look similar to the adults, much more so than is the case with most other fishes. Juveniles tend to inhabit shallow mangrove areas and estuaries where salt water and fresh water mix. While adults of some species do inhabit these same brackish waters, it is much more common to encounter juveniles.

Many species, especially the **red snapper**, the **blackfin snapper** and the **silk snapper** are highly sought-after food fishes. Beware! They are occasionally responsible for cases of fish poisoning in humans. These species tend to inhabit deeper waters and are only rarely seen by sport divers. However, many snappers do inhabit shallower water and are commonly seen. These species include the **schoolmaster, yellowtail snapper, mutton snapper, lane**

PHOTO TIP

Use the aggressive demeanor of yellowtails to your advantage when you are shooting fish portraits. While most fishes tend to be evasive, now you have a species that won't leave you alone. This allows you plenty of opportunity to compose and shoot portraits of yellowtails with a reflex system or a Nikonos system with a 28mm lens.

AT A GLANCE

SCHOOLMASTER

Scientific Name
Lutjanus apodus
Habitat
Reef.
Typical Adult Size
14 inches.
Sightings
Commonly seen.
Natural History
Nocturnal feeder; hover almost motionless in schools by day.

GRUNTS

Worldwide, the family of grunts contains about 175 species of small, colorful reef fishes that are closely related to snappers. Many species of grunts are quite common throughout the Caribbean, Bahamas and Florida. The name "grunt" aptly fits many species which make audible grunting sounds by grinding the pharyngeal teeth located in their throats. The sound is then greatly amplified by their swim bladder which is positioned adjacent to the throat. Grunts commonly make their sounds when they are caught or cornered, but they also produce these grunts when no danger is present. Exactly why the behavior evolved remains a mystery to ichthyologists.

often swim in mid-water high above the reef while most snappers linger close to the bottom. Yellowtails often boldly approach and follow divers for extended periods of time. In areas where they are commonly fed by divers, yellowtail snappers often swarm divers the instant they enter the water. And even when no food is offered, these fish often follow divers throughout their dives.

AT A GLANCE

YELLOWTAIL SNAPPER

Scientific Name
Lutjanus chrysurus
Habitat
Over reef.
Typical Adult Size
11 inches.
Sightings
Commonly seen.
Natural History
Mid-water feeders, unusual in that most snappers are bottom feeders.

snapper, **gray snapper**, **dog snapper** and **mahogany snapper**. The latter two species tend to be found on reefs below 30 feet, while the rest occasionally venture into extremely shallow areas.

Many snappers lurk in the shadows of branching hard corals and gorgonians, where they drift back and forth with the surge. At times they rest on or inside large sponges. Many species of snappers are rather wary of divers, but there are exceptions, the most noteworthy being the yellowtail snapper.

Common throughout the Caribbean, Bahamas and Florida, yellowtail snappers are unusual in that they

AT A GLANCE

PORKFISH

Scientific Name
Anisotremus virginicus
Habitat
Reef.
Typical Adult Size
12 inches.
Sightings
Commonly seen.
Natural History
Able to make audible sounds with pharyngeal teeth.

Grunts are characterized by their forked tails and horizontal striping. Many species have blue-and-yellow striped bodies, and many have dark margins or spots along their fins. But there are some notable exceptions, namely the **margates** and the **sailor's choice**. These fishes are combinations of silver, white and black.

One of the most gorgeous of all grunts is the **porkfish. Bluestriped grunts** and **French grunts** are two additional species that are especially colorful.

During the day, most grunts tend to drift in relatively inactive schools in sheltered areas and over reefs. School sizes vary from only a few fish to gatherings of several thousand. You can probably creep very close to schools by moving in a slow and deliberate fashion, but if you move too rapidly or too clumsily, the schools will tend to break apart and move away.

After the sun sets, grunts typically move out into the surrounding reef community to search for food. These fishes have well-developed eyes, which help them locate prey at night.

The mouths of grunts vary in size. Those species that possess larger mouths, such as **white grunts** and **Spanish grunts**, most commonly prey on a variety of worms, mollusks, crustaceans and fishes. A selection of copepods and shrimps constitute the main diet of the smaller-mouthed species, such as the **smallmouth grunt.** The mouths of grunts are situated in a comparatively low position on their heads, an adaptation which helps them snare their bottom-dwelling prey. Some grunts are quick to open their mouths when confronted with danger, and many experts theorize that the pink coloration of the inside of the mouth in several species is thought to help these fishes ward off predators.

Divers occasionally see two grunts facing each other with their mouths open wide as if they are kissing. Sometimes the grunts keep a small distance between each other, and at other times they make contact and actually "kiss" or push each other. Scientists speculate that the

gated faces.

Porgies tend to hover, either inching forward or backpedaling with their pectoral fins. Though they are wary of divers, they are very curious. They will often follow divers, maintaining a safe distance by always keeping a sea whip or coral head between themselves and the diver. Their mannerisms remind one of a child playing a game of hide and seek.

Porgies are typically seen along the edges of reefs, and over sand patches and rubble zones that are adjacent to reefs. They tend to hover a few feet off the bottom as they search for food, which consists mostly of a variety of bottom-dwelling mollusks and crabs. Like many bottom feeders, porgies often blow jets of water into the sand to uncover prey.

The **jolthead porgy** is the most silver of all the porgies. However, not all porgies have predominantly silver bodies. The **pluma**, which is found in the eastern Caribbean and the Bahamas but not in Florida, has a distinctly yellow back with blue stripes on the dorsal fin and below the eye. The backs of **saucereye porgies** are crested with yellow, but the bodies are mostly blue and silver. These fish have a noticeable blue ring under each eye which is the root of their common name.

AT A GLANCE

BLUESTRIPED GRUNT

Scientific Name
Haemulon sciurus
Habitat
Reef.
Typical Adult Size
12 inches.
Sightings
Commonly seen.
Natural History
Able to make audible sound with pharyngeal teeth.

behavior is either a display of sexuality and courtship, or of territoriality.

PORGIES

The fishes commonly known as porgies are easily identified by their distinctive features. Most are medium-sized fishes that have tall, thin, silver bodies with greatly elon-

AT A GLANCE

FRENCH GRUNT

Scientific Name
Haemulon flavolineatum
Habitat
Reef.
Typical Adult Size
10 inches.
Sightings
Commonly seen.
Natural History
Able to make audible grunting sound with pharyngeal teeth, which is probably used to communicate with other French grunts.

AT A GLANCE

JOLTHEAD PORGY

Scientific Name
Calamus bajonado
Habitat
Reef and sand, often near interface.
Typical Adult Size
14 inches.
Sightings
Commonly seen.
Natural History
Uses water jets to search for food in the sand.

AT A GLANCE

SAUCEREYE PORGY

Scientific Name
Calamus calamus
Habitat
Reef and sand, often near interface.
Typical Adult Size
8 to 15 inches.
Sightings
Commonly seen.
Natural History
Curious approach toward divers.

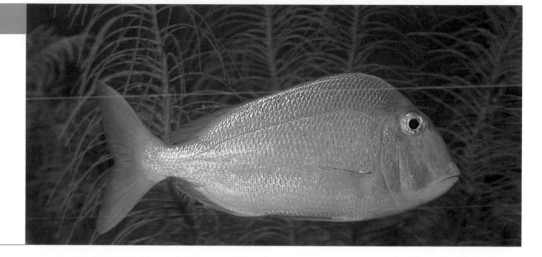

SEA CHUBS

Two species of chubs, **bermuda chubs** and **yellow chubs**, are similar looking fishes that often mix in medium-sized schools. Both species have elliptical bodies that appear to vary in color from gray to silver with white blotches. A close inspection will reveal thin yellow stripes running laterally along the body and a dark bar underneath the eyes. Although yellow chubs may have distinct yellow markings, differentiating between the two species is

AT A GLANCE

BERMUDA CHUB

Scientific Name
Kyphosus sectatrix
Habitat
Reef, along drop-off.
Typical Adult Size
14 inches.
Sightings
Commonly seen.
Natural History
Seen in tight schools along drop-offs.

AT A GLANCE

SPOTTED DRUM
(Adult, Left; Juvenile, Bottom)

Scientific Name
Equetus punctatus
Habitat
Reef, under ledges.
Typical Adult Size
8 inches.
Typical Juvenile Size
Body 3 inches, trailing fin 6 inches.
Sightings
Occasionally seen, but commonly seen in some areas.
Natural History
Profound transformation from juvenile to adult; able to make audible noises thought to be used in communication with other members of their species; often swim in a repeated pattern.

PHOTO TIP

Maximize your opportunity to shoot chubs by trying to appear passive and nonthreatening when you see a school coming down the wall. Hover motionless and slow your breathing. Preset your aperture and distance settings because if you are fumbling about when these fish buzz you, you probably won't get a second chance. If, however, you are ready to go with your eye to the viewfinder, they'll often pass within four or five feet and allow you one or two well-composed frames. The key is to be ready before the school reaches you. Before entering the water for a dive, preset your camera (use a default setting like f/5.6 and 3+ feet with 100 ASA film) for a "grab shot." Check your settings as you swim along—your light meter reading and aperture will likely change as you descend and ascend, and when you face toward or away from the sun.

not always easy. Most adult chubs are between one and two feet long.

Schools of chubs are usually found over reefs and along the top edge of drop-offs. They are often curious about divers, and will make a close pass or two. Just when you think you are going to get a perfect frame, these fishes often lose their curiosity and swim down the wall.

DRUMS AND CROAKERS

Several of the Caribbean species of drums and croakers that are easily approached and seemingly unafraid of divers are boldly colored and rather oddly shaped. These species include the **spotted drum, jackknife fish** and **highhat**. The striking bodies of these fishes are marked with alternating dark and light bands. As juveniles, these species have an elongated dorsal fin that rises high

PHOTO TIP

The juvenile spotted drum makes a prized portrait. Their extremely long dorsal fins lure us like a signal flag, and their habit of flitting about, confining their presence to a small area, allows us to take great shots of a very unusual juvenile fish. If you are going to employ a single lens reflex camera, use a long macro lens so as not to make the spotted drum nervous because of your proximity. If you are using a Nikonos, try using a close-up kit with a 35mm lens, and have your buddy provide gentle prodding so that the little drum swims toward your framer. Hold still! They will swim through a stationary framer, but chasing them with the framer will cause them to become skittish, and skittish fish don't photograph well.

The key is to learn how to work with each species. As is the case with many fishes, don't chase when trying to film spotted drums. They often swim a repeating pattern, and if you set up and wait, they will usually cruise through again and again, making them an easy mark for a patient photographer using a housing.

off their back, and their tail trails far behind the rest of the body. In fact, in their juvenile stage these fins are normally longer than the rest of the body.

As a juvenile develops, the dorsal fin begins to shorten, and by the time the body of these fish attains a length of about three inches, the dorsal fin and body are close to the same length. As adults the dorsal fin is shorter than the body, but it is far longer and more prominent than the dorsal fins of most other fishes.

Drums and croakers often make easily audible drumming and croaking noises in their natural habitat. In some species the sounds are produced by a series of muscles attached to the fish's swim bladder. The gas-filled bladder amplifies the noise so that it can be heard at a considerable distance.

Some species in this family lack the swim bladders found in most bony fishes. Interestingly, these fishes have adapted a method of producing similar grunting sounds by grinding their teeth together.

The fact that all drums and croakers produce sounds has led ichthyologists to conclude that the sounds must serve an important function in their communication. Researchers have determined that the noise activity increases during mating season. Noise patterns also differ between night and day.

Worldwide, there are approximately 160 species that belong to the family of drums and croakers. Their sizes vary from the smaller Caribbean species to fishes that weigh in excess of 200 pounds.

Drums and croakers are carnivorous, feeding on a wide variety of crustaceans, mollusks and worms. The sensitive chin barbels of spotted drums and jackknife fish help them detect food by enabling them to taste chemicals in the sea floor.

Highhats are often found in only a few feet of water where they sometimes gather in small groups. Jackknife fish tend to be found on offshore reefs in water that is more than 50 feet deep.

Though they are often confused with one another, distinguishing between jackknife fish, highhats and spotted drums is not difficult. As adults, spotted drums have a number of prominent white spots along their dorsal fin and tail. The other two species lack the spots. Jackknife fish have a single broad horizontal body stripe that extends from the tip of the tail through the leading edge of the dorsal fin. Several vertical bands run through the face. Adult highhats have a number of horizontal stripes running the length of the body, and they lack vertical stripes.

When the fishes are juveniles, telling them apart is a bit tricky, but it can be done in the water. The stripes of juvenile highhats run horizontally making it easy to separate juvenile highhats from juvenile spotted drums and jackknife fish.

The black stripes of the latter two species are vertical. As a rule, the stripes of juvenile spotted drums are darker, broader and closer together than those of juvenile jackknife fish.

Sand drums, cubbyus and **reef croakers** are much less conspicuous species. During the day, reef croakers and cubbyus are occasionally seen drifting under small overhangs and in crevices while gathered in small groups. Sand drums, as their name suggests, are much more likely to be seen in sand communities where they feed. Sometimes their bodies appear to be whitish, and at other times they display a series of dark vertical bands on a light body. The trailing edge of their tail is squared off compared to other similar-looking fishes.

GOATFISHES

Goatfishes are distinctive due to their whitish barbels which look like long chin whiskers. The barbels are usually apparent, and if you watch a swimming goatfish for any length of time, you will almost always see it lightly touch its barbels against the bottom. The barbels are equipped with sensory organs that help the fish locate food by feel and by detecting the presence of certain chemicals. When goatfishes feed, they push their barbels into the sea floor in an effort to find a variety of bottom-dwelling invertebrates. Quite often, a puff of sand or mud rises as they dig into the bottom with their snout in an attempt to grab their prey.

Sometimes the chin barbels are not apparent. When swimming but not feeding, goatfish can fold the barbels back against the lower jaw.

Four species of goatfishes are found in the Caribbean. They are the **yellow goatfish**, the **spotted goatfish**, the **red goatfish** and the **dwarf goatfish.** The yellow and spotted are the most commonly seen. When they feed, yellow goatfish tend to be soli-

PHOTO TIP

Shimmering schools of glassy sweepers are attractive targets for photographers. But beware—the shimmering is indicative of the reflective nature of these fish, which can lead to overexposure. Use a diffuser to tone down your strobe(s), and/or shoot at half or quarter power. Place your strobe(s) out to either side to minimize reflection. Another approach you might try, if you are shooting a TTL system, is to set your ASA higher than the speed of the film you are actually using. If you are shooting on manual settings, bracket with slightly higher f-stops (more closed down) than your strobe(s) normally requires.

AT A GLANCE

YELLOW GOATFISH

Scientific Name
Mulloidichthys martinicus
Habitat
Sand and rubble areas.
Typical Adult Size
9 inches.
Sightings
Commonly seen.
Natural History
Use sensory chin barbels to "taste their way around" and find prey.

AT A GLANCE

GLASSY SWEEPER

Scientific Name
Pempheris schomburgki
Habitat
Caves.
Typical Adult Size
4 inches.
Sightings
Commonly to occasionally seen, but only in caves and dark tunnels.
Natural History
Cave dwellers.

gate near the opening of caves. At night, sweepers emerge to feed on zooplankton. Tarpon, jacks, sea basses and other predatory fishes prey upon sweepers. When the predators rush them, the schools of sweepers flow back and forth.

Two species of sweepers are

tary or to band together in small groups. However, when not feeding, they often gather in large schools that swim over reefs. In contrast, spotted goatfish are much more solitary. Spotted goatfish have three distinct splotches on each side of their body, while yellow goatfish have yellow fins and a prominent yellow stripe that runs horizontally from eye to tail.

SWEEPERS

Sweepers are small, deep-bellied fishes usually seen in easily approachable schools that hover under deep ledges and in or around caves by day. They have large dark eyes and yellow-brown to copper bodies that shimmer when even a tiny amount of reflected sunlight dances across their bodies as they congre-

found in Caribbean waters. They are the **glassy sweeper** and the **shortfin sweeper**. Glassy sweepers are slightly larger, attaining a maximum length of about six inches, while shortfin sweepers rarely exceed four inches. Shortfin sweepers lack the dark band found at the base of the anal fins of glassy sweepers.

BUTTERFLYFISHES

Butterflyfishes are often seen swimming around reefs in a flitting manner that is somewhat reminiscent of

AT A GLANCE

SPOTFIN BUTTERFLY

Scientific Name
Chaetodon ocellatus
Habitat
Reefs.
Typical Adult Size
6 inches.
Sightings
Commonly seen.
Natural History
Usually in mated pairs, black bar passes through eyes helping in effort to confuse and evade predators.

AT A GLANCE

FOUREYE BUTTERFLY
(ADULT, TOP; JUVENILE, LEFT)

Scientific Name
Chaetodon capistratus
Habitat
Reefs.
Typical Adult Size
4 inches.
Typical Juvenile Size
2 inches.
Sightings
Adults commonly seen, juveniles only occasionally seen.
Natural History
Usually in mated pairs; black bar passes through eyes helping to confuse and evade predators; shy and reclusive as juveniles.

butterflies in a garden. Many butterflyfishes are beautifully colored, and their swimming antics and striking faces make admirers out of most of us.

Most butterflyfishes have roundish, laterally compressed, white to silver-colored bodies with some vertical stripes, but the stripes are not always evident. Their snouts are slightly elongated, which allows them to feed on small invertebrates that could otherwise escape by hiding in reef fissures. The mouths of

butterflyfishes are relatively small, and most species have one or more distinct spots located high on their sides. As a rule, adult butterflyfishes are shorter than six inches, and the longsnout butterflyfish is only about half that length when fully grown.

The approximately 100 species of butterflyfishes are associated with tropical reef communities around the world. Although they are rarely abundant in terms of numbers, at least one of the commonly seen Caribbean species seems to be present on almost every reef. Butterflyfishes are benthic creatures, tending to swim just a few inches off the bottom. Often a male and female swim together; at other times they prefer a solitary existence.

Butterflyfishes are excellent swimmers. Not all reef fishes can swim backwards, but butterflyfishes can. They demonstrate superb body control, and can slither deep into cracks and crevices to escape predators and to capture food. Butterflyfishes feed on a variety of food sources, including some bottom-dwelling algae, some sponges, worms, a variety of crustaceans, and mucus from the tentacles of hard corals, soft corals and zoanthids. They usually forage by day and at night enter a sleep-like state called torpor. In this state they often rest exposed on or against corals and are not easily aroused. Their daytime and nighttime coloration is often significantly different.

Many butterflyfishes have a false eye spot on their tail, and other similar markings on their head and tail, which are believed to mislead or confuse predators. The false eye spot is a large dark spot located high on either side of the back near the tail. The mark is exactly where you would expect the eye to be located if the butterflyfish were facing the opposite direction. Scientists believe that the markings are intended to make potential predators—mostly moray eels and other fishes—mistake the fish's tail for its head. They also believe that predators often lead the butterflyfishes to the rear where the fake eye is, which allows them to escape forward in an unanticipated direction. Many butterflyfishes have a dark vertical stripe running through their real eyes, making the false eye spots appear even more prominent and disguising the location of the actual eyes and head.

Butterflyfishes utilize a reproduction strategy of producing a large quantity of eggs that hatch into larvae and drift in the open sea. Those larvae that survive their pelagic existence eventually settle out of the plankton into the reef community. In the early stages of their benthic existence, small butterflyfishes hide in protected shelters in the reef, but in time they grow large enough to safely roam the reef out in the open.

AT A GLANCE

REEF BUTTERFLYFISH

Scientific Name
Chaetodon sedantarius
Habitat
Reef.
Typical Adult Size
4 inches.
Sightings
Commonly seen in Florida Keys; occasionally to seldom seen in Caribbean.
Natural History
Wary; stops and tries to blend in when approached rather than flee.

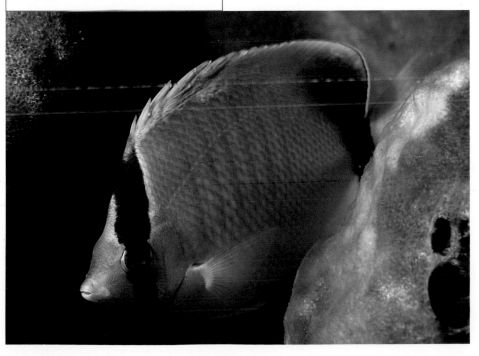

Juveniles tend to prefer shallow water and a solitary lifestyle. The general body shape of the juveniles is similar to that of the adults, but their coloration and markings are considerably different.

Most species of butterflyfishes are quite similar in terms of behavior and shape, though their coloration and markings make field identification of the five commonly seen Caribbean species comparatively easy in most cases.

Longsnout butterflyfish are probably the least commonly seen. However, their striking looks warrant a photograph! A shy species, they mostly inhabit deeper reefs and vertical walls. Furthermore, longsnout butterflyfish tend to prefer a solitary and rather reclusive lifestyle.

Butterflyfishes are sometimes mistaken for angelfishes, but it is easy to tell them apart. Butterflyfishes tend to be much smaller than angelfishes. In addition, butterflyfishes have snouts that are more elongated and pronounced than those of the more blunt-headed angelfishes. Angelfishes have a prominent spine on their gill cover while butterflyfishes do not.

ANGELFISHES

There are approximately 80 species of angelfishes inhabiting the shallow waters of tropical and semitropical reef communities around the world. All are described in one of the seven genera (the plural of genus) in the family Pomacanthidae.

The bodies of angelfishes are disc-shaped. Most adults attain a length of at least one foot, and some reach two feet. Most have blunt yet rounded heads, and all have a large spine along the rear edge of each gill cover, a characteristic which helps distinguish them from butterflyfishes. Until the mid-1970's, butterflyfishes and angelfishes were included in the same family.

But no matter how the scientific community describes them, classifies them and analyzes their behaviors, it is their stunning beauty and grace which captivates so many divers. Without question, angelfishes are among the most gorgeous of all reef fishes. With only a few exceptions, angelfishes are brightly colored, appearing to be Neptune's version of the "coat of many colors."

Angelfishes are benthic species, meaning that they live the vast majority of their lives within a few feet off the sea floor. Most live in reef communities, and although they are seen over sand bottoms and grassy flats, as a rule they tend to hover near coral or rock reefs which provide them with both food and protection.

The home range of angelfishes varies both with the species and the size of the individual fish being considered. Larger individuals tend to roam over a wider expanse of reef during a given day than do smaller fishes. Some species, however, such as the **rock beauty**, rarely venture far from a single coral head.

Adults of many species, such as the **queen angel** and **French angel**, often prefer to travel in pairs. Because they are often seen in pairs, many divers assume the pairs are mated for life. However, studies

AT A GLANCE

FRENCH ANGELFISH
(ADULT, TOP; JUVENILE, RIGHT)

Scientific Name
Pomacanthus paru
Habitat
Shallow reef and lagoons.
Typical Adult Size
16 inches.
Typical Juvenile Size
3 to 8 inches.
Sightings
Adults commonly seen; juveniles occasionally seen.
Natural History
Usually in mated pairs, feed on sponges; juveniles are cleaners.

have shown that while French angelfish are usually monagamous, queen angels are not. Queen angels tend to pair up within the territory of the male, but outside of that realm, females will readily mate with another willing male.

Adult angelfishes rarely appear to have confrontations with other fishes.

They are diurnal—actively swimming over the reef and feeding during the day, and entering a "sleeping" state at night. After sunset, angelfishes take cover in the reef, slithering into holes and crevices where they take refuge until sunrise. Despite covering large territories in a reef system, many angelfishes return to the same hole to sleep in the same position each night. In order to evade potential predators when they sleep, many angelfishes swim as far back into crevices or other cover as they can, aligning their slender bodies with contours in the reef.

Omnivorous feeders, all angelfishes feed primarily on sponges, with various species showing distinct preferences for different types of sponges. Studies have shown that the diet of rock beauties is almost

PHOTO TIP

It is rare to see the juvenile phase of most reef fishes, and even rarer for juveniles to be as stunning as juvenile French or gray angels. Portraits of these youngsters are especially striking, and they are wonderful complements to the shots of adults you may already have. So next time you find yourself in very shallow reef areas or in a lagoon, keep your eyes peeled for these little fishes. The fact that they are involved in cleaning activity can work to your advantage. If you approach them very slowly, they'll often continue to flitter back and forth, inviting all comers to be cleaned, including you and your camera system!

PHOTO TIP

Although many people question whether it is a wise practice to feed fishes on a regular basis, it has been done for years in some places in the Caribbean. So you should not be surprised if French or gray angels swim right up to you in these locations. These "trained fish" will pose for you, and they make wonderfully colorful, close-focus foreground subjects for your Nikonos and 15mm lens. Get a little below the fish and meter the water around them. Shoot at an upward angle. If you are shooting on manual, be sure to set your aperture for the brightest light source, whether it be your strobe or the ambient light reading (if ambient light meter reading is f/8 and your strobe output is f/11 for the distance you are shooting, then set your aperture on f/11 or your strobe will burn out your angelfish). If you are shooting with a TTL exposure system, meter the water around the angelfish until you get simultaneously lit LEDs of 1/60 and 1/125 inside your viewfinder. Let the strobe fill in automatically to provide the proper foreground exposure. In either case make sure that you get close, shoot upward angles, and bracket.

If you are not close enough to the angelfish so that it occupies at least 75 percent of your frame and you are using a TTL system, bracket by "lying to your system," (telling the system that you are using a faster film speed than you are actually using). Tricking the system can help prevent foreground overexposure.

AT A GLANCE

GRAY ANGELFISH

Scientific Name
Pomacanthus arcuatus
Habitat
Reef areas.
Typical Adult Size
16 inches.
Sightings
Commonly seen.
Natural History
Usually in mated pairs, feed on sponges.

100 percent sponges. Other species feed on algae, tunicates, anemones, some gorgonians, zoanthids, some corals, hydroids, bryozoans and some tiny crustaceans.

Some scientists maintain that the bright colors and dazzling patterns of angelfishes are intended to help camouflage them while they feed on bright sponges and zoanthids in colorful reef communities. However, from the point of view of a casual observer, it is difficult to understand how anyone could consider adult angelfishes to be well camouflaged. In many cases, their radiant beauty seems to draw attention. Another commonly adhered-to viewpoint within the scientific community is that many potential vision-dependent reef predators, such as barracudas and jacks, do not see colors very well. They hunt at night, during the hours when brightly colored angelfishes are hiding in the deep recesses of the reef.

AT A GLANCE

QUEEN ANGELFISH
(ADULT, ABOVE; JUVENILE, RIGHT)

Scientific Name
Pomacanthus ciliaris
Habitat
Reef areas.
Typical Adult Size
14 inches.
Typical Juvenile Size
To 6 inches.
Abundance
Adults commonly seen; juveniles occasionally seen.
Natural History
Usually in mated pairs; feed on sponges; juveniles provide fish-cleaning services.

AT A GLANCE

ROCK BEAUTY

Scientific Name
Holacanthus tricolor
Habitat
Reef areas.
Typical Adult Size
10 inches.
Sightings
Commonly seen.
Natural History
Usually in mated pairs, feed on sponges.

However, some scientists believe that if the "break up" theory were correct, you would see a lot of preda-

Still another theory is that the vivid colors and strong markings of some species make it difficult for potential predators to see an entire angelfish all at once. This theory maintains that the bold colors tend to break up the shape of a single fish.

tors strike at, but miss, angelfishes. That does not appear to be the case, as most fishes simply seem to ignore angelfishes.

In most cases, juvenile angelfishes are spectacularly colored, but their colors and color patterns are usually distinctly different from the adults. As the fishes approach sexual maturity, their patterns change to help other adults identify potential mating partners.

In many species, the juveniles serve within the reef community as cleaners, ridding other fish of bothersome ectoparasites. It is commonly accepted among icthyologists that the bright coloring of the juveniles helps them advertise their presence as cleaners.

In addition to their bright coloration, juvenile French angels utilize a fluttering swimming motion to make their presence known to other fishes that might need cleaning.

The juveniles of some species are also thought to feed on the mucous coating of squirrelfishes, soldierfishes, cardinalfishes and other reef species. Juvenile angelfishes are often highly territorial, a trait not common to the adults. Young angelfishes are often seen chasing away fish that intrude into their realm, including members of their own species.

Male angelfishes tend to be slightly larger than females. During actual spawning, eggs and sperm are released during short upward swims into the water column in which the male and female swim with their bodies in close contact. Usually the activity is repeated several times during courtship, which usually occurs in the evening. The transparent eggs are released into the water column, and each contains a single drop of oil which provides buoyancy. Females release between 25,000 and 75,000 eggs each evening, and upwards of 10 million eggs over the course of a spawning cycle.

Blue angelfish are quite common in the reef communities of Florida and the Florida Keys, but they are

STEPHEN FRINK

rare or missing in the Bahamas and the Caribbean. Blue angels lack the bright yellow face and burnt-orange to yellow tail of queen angels, though the trailing edge of the tail is bordered in yellow. Juveniles of the two species are quite similar in appearance.

It is interesting to note that blue and queen angelfishes do interbreed. This produces myriad hybrid species which often have prominent markings from both species.

Cherubfish are the smallest species of angelfishes and are often re

AT A GLANCE

BLUE ANGELFISH

Scientific Name
Holacanthus bermudensis
Habitat
Reef areas.
Typical Adult Size
14 inches.
Sightings
Commonly seen in Florida, seldom seen in Bahamas, seldom seen in Caribbean.
Natural History
Usually in mated pairs; feed on sponges; juveniles seen mostly at night

AT A GLANCE

CHERUBFISH, PYGMY ANGELFISH

Scientific Name
Centropyge argi
Habitat
Deep reef areas.
Typical Adult Size
3 inches.
Sightings
Occasionally seen.
Natural History
Prefers deep areas.

ferred to as **pygmy angelfish**. Because of their small size, many divers mistake cherubfish for damselfishes. But as the name cherub strongly suggests, these fishes are members of the angelfish family. Cherubfish have deep-blue bodies with yellow to orange blotches on the face. They are quite common in Florida, but much less so throughout the rest of their range. Cherubfish are shy yet active, and they dart in and out of crevices in the reef. They are usually wary of intruders including divers. Cherubfish bear a strong resemblance to the flameback angelfish, a species most commonly encountered around the reefs of the southeastern Caribbean.

DAMSELFISHES

Damselfishes are small, feisty fishes which occur in reef communities and grass beds in temperate and tropical seas around the world. Many of the approximately 275 species are strongly territorial and will readily defend their chosen turf against all comers, from the tiniest reef fishes to intruders the size of divers. Their pugnacity is especially evident in nest-guarding males during mating season. In some species, the females also actively defend their nests.

Divers commonly come across the nests of some damselfishes. These nests are built by the males on flat patches of dead coral, on rocks, or on pier pilings. Preparation of the nest in some species is a story in itself. First the nest sites are cleared of any algae or other debris. Then the male gathers and cultivates specific algae and plants them in the nest site. After the male has successfully cultivated the algae, the female lays patches of adhesive eggs. Once the eggs have been laid, the male fertilizes the eggs. Either the male or female guards the site constantly, and often both can be seen swimming over the nest site in an effort to ward off potential predators and to aerate the eggs.

Most damselfishes are shorter

AT A GLANCE

LONGFIN DAMSELFISH
(JUVENILE)

Scientific Name
Stegastes diencaeus
Habitat
Reef.
Size
1.5 inches.
Sightings
Commonly seen.
Natural History
Appears very different from adult; adult is solid dark brown to black, with noticeably long tail; adult male actively guards nest.

AT A GLANCE

THREESPOT DAMSEL

Scientific Name
Stegastes planifrons
Habitat
Reef.
Typical Adult Size
3 inches.
Sightings
Commonly seen.
Natural History
Actively "farms" filamentous algae and vigorously defends nests of cultivated algae.

than six inches long. The bodies of many are characterized as being round to oval, and flattened from side to side. Damselfishes have a single nostril located on each side of the snout, as opposed to the pair of nostrils on each side as do most other fishes

Of the 20 to 30 major genera within the damselfish family, the genus *Stegastes* is the most prominent in the Caribbean. Most of the species in this genus are brilliantly colored as juveniles, but drab as adults. The juveniles are often covered with a number of iridescent stripes and spots. *Stegastes* include a variety of commonly encountered Caribbean damselfishes—the **threespot, cocoa, dusky, beaugregory** and **bicolor.**

Several species of fishes commonly called **chromis** are also members of the damselfish family. Chromis have more elongated bodies than other damselfishes. They are also characterized by their deeply forked tail fins, and they differ from most other damsels in that chromis tend to feed more in mid-water instead of on or near the bottom.

Two species of frequently encountered chromis are the **blue chromis** and the **brown chromis.** In addition, several other species in the genus *Chromis* are also common in many Caribbean reef communities. Among them are the **purple reeffish, yellowtail reeffish,** and **sunshinefish.**

An abundant species, blue chromis are one of the most attractive of all reef fishes. Their bodies are col-

ored a brilliant, iridescent blue. They have black eyes and black trim on the upper back, tail and underbelly. Typical of the chromis, blue chromis have elongated bodies with deeply forked tails. They are quite common in reef communities in Florida, the Bahamas and in the majority of the Caribbean. Blue chromis are commonly seen in large schools alternately swimming and pausing as they hover in mid-water above reefs while feeding on planktonic creatures that drift by. Approximately half of their diet consists of copepods, and they are also known to feed on a variety of shrimps, tunicates, fish eggs and siphonophores, free floating colonial invertebrates described in the phylum Cnidaria. When feeding, blue chromis tend to face into the current and wait for their food to drift toward them.

They are generally quick to seek shelter in the reef when danger is present and when divers approach in a hasty manner. But if divers move slowly and deliberately, blue chromis tend to gather close to the bottom and then go about their business.

Sometimes the brilliant blue fades toward gray when the fishes hide in the reef. It is believed the color change is intended to make

AT A GLANCE

BLUE CHROMIS

Scientific Name
Chromis cyanea
Habitat
Reef.
Typical Adult Size
3 inches.
Sightings
Commonly seen.
Natural History
Mid-water plankton feeder.

them less conspicuous.

Brown chromis occasionally mix with blue chromis. Reaching a maximum length of just over six inches, brown chromis are the slightly larger species. As their name

PHOTO TIP

The extreme territorial nature of damselfishes makes them an easy subject for either a single lens reflex camera system or a Nikonos with a close-up kit. In many cases, damselfishes will actually race out and attack your framer, allowing you the perfect opportunity to get a portrait of these fearless fishes! Be careful not to damage the nest site.

PHOTO TIP

Blue chromis are an eye-catching shade of electric blue that looks great on film. To shoot their portraits, use a single lens reflex system with a long macro lens, and wait for a little current to come up. With the current comes their food of plankton, and their feeding behavior intensifies. When feeding, blue chromis tend to let down some of their defenses, and they will often allow you to get quite close if you move slowly.

AT A GLANCE

SUNSHINEFISH

Scientific Name
Chromis insolata
Habitat
Reef.
Typical Adult Size
2 inches.
Sightings
Commonly seen.
Natural History
Extreme discrepancy in coloration between juvenile and adult.

AT A GLANCE

BROWN CHROMIS

Scientific Name
Chromis multilineata
Habitat
Reef.
Typical Adult Size
3 inches.
Sightings
Commonly seen.
Natural History
Mid-water plankton feeder.

AT A GLANCE

SERGEANT MAJOR

Scientific Name
Abudefduf saxatilis
Habitat
Reef.
Typical Adult Size
7 inches.
Sightings
Commonly seen.
Natural History
Actively guards eggs from all potential predators.

suggests, the bodies of brown chromis appear in various shades of brown, ranging from olive brown to brownish gray. As is the case with blue chromis, brown chromis often hover in loose schools in mid-water above the reef where they look for plankton.

Purple reeffish have small oval-shaped bodies that are a deeper purple than the blue found in most blue chromis. Purple reeffish are found in Florida, but they are not reported in the Caribbean. Yellow-tail reeffish are also found in Florida, and they are rather rare in Caribbean waters. A colorful species, yellow-tail reeffish tend to inhabit reefs in water deeper than 75 feet.

Sunshinefish are common in many reef communities throughout the Caribbean, Florida and the Bahamas. The juveniles are so colorful that they are almost gaudy. Their upper backs are bright yellow, while their head, body and tail are a deep purplish-blue. A short, light iridescent blue stripe runs horizontally just above the eye. As adults, their bodies tend toward drab olive to brown, but many individuals retain the stripe above the eye. The adults and juveniles are often found mixed together in groups near the sea floor. Sunshinefish prefer deeper reefs and walls. It is not uncommon in some areas to see sunshinefish and blue chromis plagued with parasitic iso-

pods which usually attach to the fish's lower jaw.

Sergeant majors are members of the damselfish family and are found in tropical, semitropical and temperate waters around the world. The common name "sergeant major" is actually used to describe several species of fishes, but all look very similar and behave in nearly identical fashion. The Caribbean or western Atlantic species of sergeant major ranges from Rhode Island to the middle of South America. Being found over reefs, in tide pools, over beds of seagrass, around pilings and docks, and in a number of other habitats, this species is extremely common.

Sergeant majors have oval-shaped profiles with bodies that are laterally flattened. Divers often mistakenly believe that there are two common species of sergeant majors found in the Caribbean because there are two distinct color phases which depend chiefly upon the hues of the surrounding reef or bottom. When swimming over sandy bottoms, they are usually light green along the underbelly and yellow on the upper body and back. When swimming in dark caves and crevices, and sometimes at night, sergeant majors turn very dark. Even in its dark phase, the black vertical bars on the body are generally evident.

Sergeant majors are bold fishes that often swim away from the protective confines of reef structures. In many instances they readily approach divers. It is not at all uncommon to hear stories from divers whose ears, hair, ankles and backs of their knees were nipped by sergeant majors. In some cases, human body parts must look like tasty morsels, and on other occasions the divers probably intruded into the realm of a nesting fish. Sergeant majors are not territorial except when they are nesting.

Sergeant majors feed on a wide variety of prey, and are thought to have one of the more diversified diets of all fishes. When swimming in mid-water, sergeant majors feed on plankton. When scouring the sea floor, they feed on a selection of tunicates, fish eggs, shrimp larvae, sea anemones, corals and other cnidarians.

Another similar species sometimes confused with sergeant majors is the **night sergeant**, although sergeant majors are much more common. Reaching a length of 10 inches, night sergeants attain slightly larger sizes than the adult sergeant majors, which are usually 5 to 7 inches long. The vertical stripes of night sergeants are much less conspicuous.

WRASSES

Worldwide, there are approximately 500 species of wrasses. As a family,

they are among the most abundant fishes in the reef communities of both tropical and temperate seas. Being found from the shallowest to the deepest reefs, the wrasses of the Caribbean are no exception.

Perhaps the most fascinating characteristic of the wrasses is that many change sex in the middle of their lives. As a rule, their coloration also changes dramatically with the sex change. Ichthyologists often classify wrasses according to their stage of life. Each phase has its own color pattern, a characteristic that confused specialists for years. At one time scientists listed many more species of wrasses. We now know that about half of those species were different phases of the same species. Many species are yet to be well studied.

The progression of phases goes as follows: the juvenile phase; the intermediate, which is sometimes called the initial phase or the adult phase; and the terminal or dominant phase, during which a fish is often called a supermale. In many species each phase has a distinct color pattern which can be radically different from that of other phases, but not always.

Some wrasses begin their lives as males and remain males in every phase. These specimens are called primary males. Other fish begin their lives as females and later transform into males. They are called secondary males. In many species, males have been documented invading the territory of another male to steal spawnings. Supermales are usually vividly colored fish that are larger than other members of their species. They expend considerable effort chasing smaller males out of their territory, and courting females.

If a supermale dies or is removed from the population, the next largest and most dominant fish in the immediate local population, either a primary male or female, quickly changes into the supermale. Amazingly, the transformation takes only a few days. Equally fascinating are

the results of studies that have shown that in some wrasses, if the original supermale is suddenly reintroduced into the population, the transforming primary will revert back to its primary phase. And we often think our sex lives are complicated!

The key question asked by scientists is not necessarily how, but why wrasses change sex. The answer, though not completely understood, is that the species respond to changes in population in an effort to maintain the balance necessary for successful reproduction, a factor which helps ensure survival of the species.

When breeding, initial phase wrasses spawn in large orgy-like gatherings. However, once a fish becomes a terminal male, this fish establishes a territory and mates with a harem of females, but usually with only one at a time.

Wrasses have prominent canine teeth that angle outward, creating a very noticeable buck-toothed look. These teeth enable them to grab a variety of crustaceans and to gain a grip on mollusks so they can pull them off the bottom. The hard shells of mollusks and the exoskeletons of the crustaceans are then crushed by molar-like pharyngeal teeth located toward the back of the mouth. The juveniles of some wrasses, especially **Spanish hogfish**, rid other fishes of ectoparasites.

According to some specialists, the family of wrasses consists of three groups or subfamilies of fishes: the cigar-shaped wrasses, the **razorfishes** and the **hogfishes**. Other specialists include all wrasses in the same family, insisting only that wrasses and parrotfish belong in separate subfamilies. The cigar-shaped wrasses tend to hover near the bottom and remain close to one site on a reef for the majority of their lives. Caribbean species of cigar-shaped wrasses include the **puddingwife, creole wrasse, yellowhead wrasse, bluehead wrasse, yellowcheek wrasse, slippery**

dick, clown wrasse and **dwarf wrasse**. In their terminal phase, these species tend to be highly territorial. In their juvenile and intermediate phases, many species are seen feeding together, but they become much more solitary in their terminal phase. These wrasses are typically diurnal, feeding during the day and burying themselves in the sand at night. Some species such as the creole wrasse feed mostly on plankton plucked out of mid-water, while others feed on bottom-dwelling invertebrates.

Razorfishes have high foreheads and their bodies are flattened from side to side, or laterally compressed. They are best known for their tendency to dive into the sand and quickly bury themselves in an effort to avoid potential predators.

Hogfishes are believed to be the most primitive wrasse. They are seen during the day foraging in the sand for a variety of invertebrates. Hogfishes have a large, protruding mouth that helps them dig through sand bottoms, and they often blow jets of water into the sand in order to uncover hiding prey.

Reaching a size of 3 feet and 20 pounds, adult hogfish are the largest of all the wrasses found in the tropical western Atlantic, a characteristic which is alluded to by their species name, *maximus*. Their common name, hogfish, seems appropriate as well. The adults have long, hog-like snouts. Hogfish have voracious appetites, feeding mostly on a variety of mollusks in addition to sea urchins, crabs, hermit crabs and barnacles. Hogfish range from the waters of North Carolina to the northern shores of South America. They are usually encountered along the sand/reef interface or over sandy bottoms, but they are occasionally seen roaming over reef structures.

Initial phase and terminal phase hogfish are easily distinguished by the three long spines at the front of their dorsal fin. The spines of the juveniles are present, but they are not as prominent or as long in comparison to their overall body length.

Hogfish are capable of near instantaneous color changes, and they often change color to help them blend in with their surroundings. Specialists claim that they also change according to whether they are at rest or moving because even in the same environment, different colors work best to help the fish blend in, depending on whether they are still or on the move.

Hogfish are commonly called hogsnappers in the Bahamas and some other parts of the Caribbean, but they are wrasses, not snappers. The term snapper has probably gained its popular usage because hogfish, like many snappers, are highly valued as food, and their profiles are somewhat similar.

Creole wrasse are beautiful fishes that are often seen in schools along the top edge of drop-offs. They are an abundant species throughout the Caribbean, Florida and the Bahamas, and can be distinguished by their purple bodies and dark foreheads. Although the younger individuals have bodies that are bluer than those of the purple adults, creole wrasse do not exhibit the radical color changes found in so many other wrasses. Although sometimes confused with blue chromis, with only a little practice, creole wrasse are easy to identify.

Creole wrasse are easy to approach when they are being cleaned. At cleaning stations, they often hover head down in a near-vertical position to request service. They remain in that position until they no longer want to be cleaned.

Creole wrasse are plankton feeders, and you can often sit for extended periods and watch them pick their microscopic-sized prey out of mid-water, especially when currents are running.

Spanish hogfish are vividly colored through all stages of their lives. The adults have a bright purple back and yellow mid-body, underbelly and tail. Their eyes are rimmed in

AT A GLANCE

HOGFISH

Scientific Name
 Lachnolaimus maximus
Habitat
 Reef and sand areas, often near interface.
Typical Adult Size (Terminal Male)
 2 feet.
Sightings
 Commonly seen.
Natural History
 Blow jets of water into sand in search of food items.

AT A GLANCE

SPANISH HOGFISH

Scientific Name
Bodianus rufus
Habitat
Reef.
Typical Sizes
14 inches.
Sightings
Commonly seen.
Natural History
Juvenile Spanish hogfish provides cleaning services for many reef fishes.

scarlet. The juvenile Spanish hogfish has a more pointed snout and is an aggressive cleaner, ridding other fishes of ectoparasites.

One of the more distinctive features of Spanish hogfish is that their basic color pattern is essentially the same throughout their lives, an unusual feature in wrasses. Spanish hogfish are sometimes mistaken with hogfish, probably more because of the similarity in name rather than in color, shape or size. Adult Spanish hogfish are more colorful and are usually only about half the size of adult hogfish.

Spanish hogfish have well-developed, rather pronounced, teeth that

A FISH WORKS FOR ITS DINNER

I am not sure I realized that there was something different about the Spanish hogfish, but something about its behavior was unusual enough to capture my attention. As I tried to move in for a closer look, the fish quickly moved away keeping its tail toward me. After moving several feet, it turned, and I discovered that the Spanish hogfish was holding a small crab in its mouth. I did not see the original capture, but I did get a close enough look to be sure that the crab was definitely alive and trying to do whatever it could to survive.

Even with a potential meal in its mouth, the wrasse faced a dilemma. It did not appear capable of crushing the crab, so it was looking for a perfect place to "plant" the crab—a spot where the crab couldn't hide before the fish could back up a few inches and then charge in to take a bite. The "charge and bite" technique allowed the fish to bite chunks of meat out of its unfortunate victim.

As soon as I figured out what was going on, I backed off so that I wouldn't influence the outcome. I wanted to watch the episode unfurl. The Spanish hogfish carried the crab from place to place. Sometimes the fish would release the crab, back up, and then charge in for a bite. In other instances, the fish would almost let go of the crab, but at the last instant it would decide that the spot didn't work. From the predator's point of view, it appeared as if the rejected areas were too close to potential hiding places and escape routes. Every time the fish did "release and plant," the area was flat and exposed. Several times I watched the wrasse place the crab on a large, flat encrusting sponge.

In addition to an obvious concern about its potential meal escaping, the Spanish hogfish appeared to be doing its best to stay away from larger fish that might try to steal its dinner. Although I am not certain, I think that was the "something unusual about the way the fish was behaving" that caught my attention in the first place. The hunter was trying to stay away from me, a potential threat to steal the catch. Voluntarily sharing its meal was definitely not the idea.

The episode provided an insightful lesson about the value of food and the struggle for survival.—Marty Snyderman

AT A GLANCE

CREOLE WRASSE

Scientific Name
Clepicus parrai
Habitat
Hovering in loosely organized schools along edge of current-swept walls and over outer deep reefs.
Typical Adult Size
7 inches.
Sightings
Commonly seen.
Natural History
Gather in loosely organized schools. Often mix with schools of blue chromis. Pluck plankton out of water column. Generally easy to approach, especially when current is running and fish are feeding.

are designed to be able to chew through sea urchins and crush crabs. They also feed on shrimps, brittle stars, snails and hermit crabs.

Yellowhead wrasse are absolutely voracious eaters. Reaching a maximum length of only eight inches, these small, cigar-shaped carnivores have amazing feeding habits. Their prominent teeth give their head a distinct buck-toothed look, and they are razor sharp, enabling yellowhead wrasse to crunch

through a variety of hard-shell invertebrates—crabs, shrimps, chitons and sea urchins. Yellowhead wrasse also prey on brittle stars, polychaete worms and the remains of other fishes.

Their genus, *Halichoeres*, is a Greek name that sheds light on their eating habits. The translation means "hog of the sea."

Pairs of yellowhead wrasses are occasionally seen facing each other, mouths open, as if they were kiss-

AT A GLANCE

YELLOWHEAD WRASSE

Scientific Name
Halichoeres garnoti
Habitat
Reef and sandy rubble.
Typical Adult Size
6 inches.
Sightings
Common.
Natural History
Often seen facing off in display of territoriality or sexuality.

AT A GLANCE

BLUEHEAD WRASSE
(SUPERMALE)

Scientific Name
Thalassoma bifasciatum
Habitat
Reef.
Typical Adult Size
5 inches.
Sightings
Commonly seen.
Natural History
Juveniles are very active cleaners.

AT A GLANCE

GREENMOUTH RAZORFISH

Scientific Name
Xyrichtys splendens
Habitat
Seagrass beds, rubble zones, and sand.
Typical Adult Size
2 to 5 inches.
Sightings
Occasionally seen, but often overlooked.
Natural History
When frightened, they quickly bury themselves in sand. Often reemerge within a few minutes.

PARROTFISHES

On almost every reef dive in the Caribbean, Florida and the Bahamas, divers will see one or more species of parrotfishes. Parrotfishes graze on algae associated with corals, and many species often travel in loosely organized groups. As a family, parrotfishes are characterized by the following features: large, strong teeth that are fused together to form beak-like jaws; elongated bodies which are slightly flattened from side to side; and large blunt heads.

ing. The display probably has to do with dominance or territoriality, but scientists are not certain. At night these fish bury themselves in the sand.

As juveniles, the **bluehead wrasse** appears and acts very different from the adults. Juveniles are bright yellow and are likely to travel in small groups foraging around various gorgonians, or they can be more solitary and actively involved in fish cleaning services. In this stage they are typically only 1.5 to 2.5 inches long.

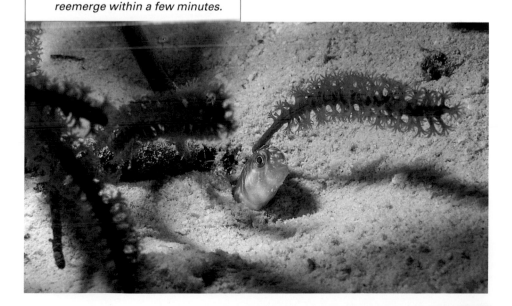

AT A GLANCE

STOPLIGHT PARROTFISH
(SUPERMALE)

Scientific Name
Sparisoma viride
Habitat
Reef.
Typical Adult Size
15 inches.
Sightings
Commonly seen.
Natural History
Graze on algae associated with coral and then excrete sand.

AT A GLANCE

STOPLIGHT PARROTFISH
(ADULT)

Scientific Name
Sparisoma viride
Habitat
Reef.
Typical Adult Size
12 inches.
Sightings
Commonly seen.
Natural History
Graze on algae associated with coral and then excrete sand.

Like the birds we know as parrots, many parrotfishes are quite colorful, with endless hues of blue, green and red. In addition, parrotfishes also have very sharp beaks like their avian counterparts. Parrotfishes use their beaks to scrape algae off rocks and corals.

In their effort to eat algae, it is inevitable that parrotfishes consume considerable amounts of coral. Most specialists agree the coral skeleton is not used by parrotfishes and is excreted. This behavior plays an important part in the cycle of life in coral reef communities. The excreted limestone becomes sand and helps replace the sand which is continually being washed over the wall. If parrotfishes are feeding nearby, you will often hear the loud crunching sounds they make while scraping the corals.

These two photographs illustrate that identifying parrotfishes underwater is difficult because there are so many species and color phases.

Parrotfishes feed in a variety of ways. Some feed individually, others in loosely organized schools, and still other species feed predomi-

PHOTO TIP

Discovering a parrotfish sleeping in its cocoon provides a wonderful opportunity to capture an example of how animals protect themselves in the marine environment. Start your night dive at least two hours after sundown. Try using a Nikonos camera with a close-up kit (you may want to remove the framer if the parrotfish is back in a hole), or a 15mm lens set for minimum distance. A Nikonos RS or a housed camera with a 50mm or 55mm macro lens will also work well.

A second strobe used for backlighting will help make the translucent cocoon stand out in the picture, but when backlighting be sure to avoid pointing the backlighting strobe directly at your lens. Bracketing exposures is especially valuable when backlighting.

nately in tightly packed herds. Ichthyologists maintain that feeding in schools is probably part of an effort to confuse potential predators and to overwhelm territorial fishes such as some damselfishes. Solitary damselfishes will usually try to push other fishes out of their realm, but even the most tenacious damselfish can be overwhelmed by the sheer numbers of schooling species.

Parrotfishes are very closely related to wrasses. In fact, some taxonomists classify them in different subfamilies of the same master family. Many specialists suspect that similar reproductive biology and life phases are found in parrotfishes and wrasses, but others insist that additional studies need to be conducted before drawing this conclusion. Almost all agree that there is a lot left to learn about their reproductive biology.

Like the wrasses, parrotfishes are capable of experiencing three phases of life. They are the juvenile phase, initial phase and terminal phase. The term "terminal phase" is the equivalent of the term "supermale." In some nomenclature systems, when fishes are in the initial phase they are referred to as adults. In each color phase, most parrotfishes exhibit distinctly different colors, but there are noticeable exceptions, such as midnight parrotfish which exhibit the same dark blue coloration in all phases.

AT A GLANCE

QUEEN PARROTFISH
(SUPERMALE)

Scientific Name
Sparisoma vetula
Habitat
Reef.
Typical Adult Size
15 inches.
Sightings
Commonly seen.
Natural History
Graze on algae associated with coral and then excrete sand.

In many parrotfishes and wrasses, juveniles and adults can be either male or female. Some individuals, either males or females, will eventually be transformed into supermales. In other words, some females change sex in mid-life and become males. Distinguishing initial phase (adult) males from initial phase (adult) females in the field is virtually impossible even for specialists, so to be safe the term "non-terminal adult" or "primary adult"

AT A GLANCE

YELLOWTAIL PARROTFISH
(TERMINAL MALE)

Scientific Name
Sparisoma rubripinne
Habitat
Shallow rubble zones, sea grass beds, and occasionally on reefs.
Typical Adult Size
9 to 15 inches.
Sightings
Commonly seen.
Natural History
Graze on algae associated with coral and then excrete sand. Sometimes sit on bottom. Commonly change color to blend with surroundings.

is often used when describing the adults.

In other species of both parrotfishes and wrasses, all hatchlings are born females. All primary adults are also females, but some of these adult females will change sex in mid-life and become supermales.

Experts can use the coloration to determine exactly what phase of life a known species of parrotfish is experiencing. Most sport divers learn over time to identify a variety of species in several phases, but due to sheer numbers, becoming skilled at

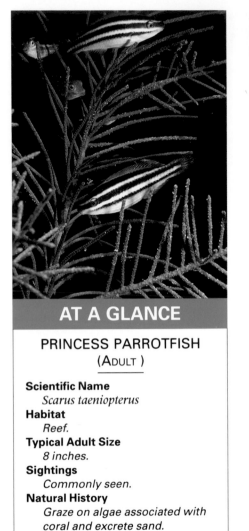

AT A GLANCE

PRINCESS PARROTFISH
(ADULT)

Scientific Name
Scarus taeniopterus
Habitat
Reef.
Typical Adult Size
8 inches.
Sightings
Commonly seen.
Natural History
Graze on algae associated with coral and excrete sand.

AT A GLANCE

REDBAND PARROTFISH
(SUPERMALE)

Scientific Name
Sparisoma aurofrenatum
Habitat
Reef.
Typical Adult Size
10 inches.
Sightings
Commonly seen.
Natural History
Graze on algae associated with coral and excrete sand.

AT A GLANCE

MIDNIGHT PARROTFISH

Scientific Name
Scarus coelestinus
Habitat
Reef.
Typical Adult Size
2 feet.
Sightings
Commonly seen.
Natural History
Graze on algae associated with coral and excrete sand.

identifying parrotfishes requires considerable diving experience. Usually those who can identify the species in the field have some specialized need that requires them to be able to do so.

Some parrotfishes (those described in the genus *Scarus*) are well known for the mucous cocoons they sometimes form at night. These fishes sleep inside their cocoons in a likely effort to mask their odor and go undetected by potential predators such as eels. The cocoons are made of mucus, and take between 30 and 60 minutes to make. (See photograph of princess parrotfish supermale on page 29.)

Many parrotfishes are extremely wary of approaching divers and other fishes during the day, yet they

AT A GLANCE

BARRACUDA

Scientific Name
Sphyraena barracuda
Habitat
Reef and along the wall.
Typical Adult Size
4 feet.
Sightings
Commonly seen.
Natural History
Their long, sharp, canine-like teeth are used to capture small fishes. Barracuda will change color to match the reef as they wait to ambush their prey.

often sleep out in the open on sand bottoms or in areas of reefs where they are only partly protected. The color phases of parrotfishes are often radically different when the fish are resting in the evening.

BARRACUDAS AND SENNETS

Worldwide, there are 20 species of barracudas. As a group they are among the fastest swimming fishes in the sea. The body of a barracuda has a classic fusiform shape, slender and elongated, a shape that is common to many of the ocean's swiftest swimmers. In fact, the **great barracuda**, a species that is so commonly seen throughout the Caribbean, has been clocked at 22 miles per hour. Utilizing the advantages provided by their build, barracudas are quick-striking predators whose speed, stealth and mouthful of long, razor-sharp teeth combine to enable them to capture the smaller fishes that they prey upon.

Although barracudas have a reputation for being dangerous, the tales of sea lore are usually exaggerated far beyond truth. Great barracuda often display a strong sense of curiosity about divers, and will frequently shadow or follow divers. Their fang-like teeth are usually exposed, and considering their appearance and their size, it is no wonder that new divers are often a bit unnerved by their presence. If you avoid hand-feeding, petting or grabbing, barracudas are likely to leave you alone, although it might make you feel a little uneasy the first time or two a "cuda" seems to hang off your shoulder or fins. It should be comforting to know that the behavior is a common practice and certainly not a sign of impending attack.

Great barracuda commonly reach a length of five feet. When swimming through shallow water on sunny days, their highly reflective silver bodies shimmer as rays of sunlight dance across their backs. Most specimens have dark spots below and some have a gray to greenish hue along the top of the back. Sometimes you will see them close to the reef lurking amongst gorgonians as they wait in ambush. When hiding near the bottom, their coloration is often completely different than it is when they cruise in mid-water. Along the sea floor, the silver coloration is broken up by vertical dark banding patterns which help barracudas blend in with their surroundings. The head

PHOTO TIP

Barracuda provide exciting subjects because of their dramatic looks and their unwarranted "bad boy" reputation. People who have not had intimate encounters with barracuda often fail to realize that these fish really aren't dangerous unless they are provoked with bait. As a result, good barracuda photos are bound to be admired and may evoke many a good tall tale. Keep a couple of things in mind when photographing barracuda. They are very reflective, and glare from their body often ruins the picture. Powering down your strobe and diffusing the light with a cloth or beam widener can help reduce the glare. When using a diffuser, be sure to use your exposure system on manual, not TTL or any other kind of automatic exposure as these settings will try to compensate for the diffuser. A low power strobe setting and a diffuser works best.

Also, a curious barracuda when close to you will often face you head-on, making the body disappear. If you shoot from this angle, your pictures often prove to be disappointing. Have patience while you maneuver yourself relative to the barracuda as the fish will often readjust accordingly to continue facing you head-on. After a while you will be able to move to a more pleasing, frame-filling angle. Don't move quickly as this will often spook the big fish.

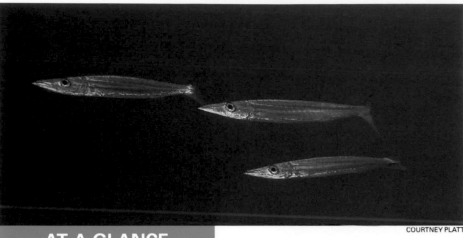

COURTNEY PLATT

Northern barracuda look very similar to southern sennets. Ranging from Cape Cod to Florida, northern barracuda are not found in true Caribbean waters. Members of this species reach a maximum length of approximately 18 inches.

CLINGFISHES

As their name suggests, clingfishes are able to grab hold of the substrate.

AT A GLANCE

SOUTHERN SENNET

Scientific Name
Sphyraena picudilla
Habitat
Reef.
Typical Adult Size
18 inches.
Sightings
Occasionally seen.
Natural History
Form very tight schools; individual fish blend in well with bright surface water.

barracuda are also members of the family *Sphyraenidae*, the same family that includes the great barracuda. From a distance, southern sennets look like schools of miniature barracuda. The schools are often tightly packed with hundreds, and occasionally thousands, of fish. Southern sennets attain a maximum length of only 18 inches. Some schools are easy to approach, while some appear to be frightened by divers' bubbles.

AT A GLANCE

STIPPLED CLINGFISH

Scientific Name
Gobiesox punctulatus
Habitat
Shallow reef areas; sometimes on base of deepwater gorgonians.
Typical Adult Size
1 inch.
Sightings
Occasionally seen.
Natural History
Specialized suction disk allows them to cling to substrate.

has a jutting lower jaw with irregularly spaced, fang-like teeth, and two dorsal fins that are widely separated.

Adult great barracuda are usually solitary, but occasionally they are seen in small schools. Juveniles, on the other hand, are often seen in schools of several dozen individuals. The juveniles commonly inhabit grass flats and shallow sandy plains. When only a few inches long, the recently born great barracuda have a dark stripe running lengthwise down the side of the body.

During night dives, barracuda are often observed in various "states of sleep." Sometimes the slightest noise or movement causes the startled fish to bolt away, but occasionally a diver can swim to within inches and shoot an entire roll of film without disturbing a sleeping barracuda.

Southern sennets and **northern**

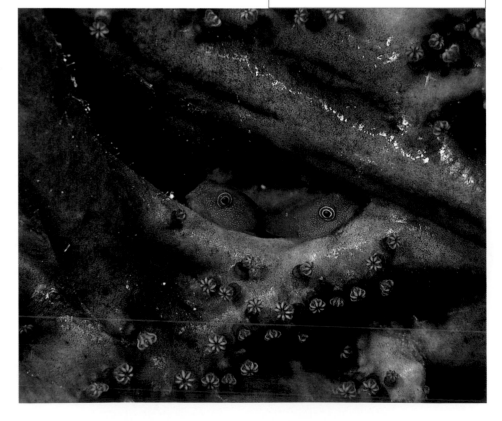

These tiny fishes are equipped with a suction-creating disc formed by modified pelvic fins. The disc is located on the underside of their bodies, and allows them to secure themselves to the bottom where they can hold on even in rough and surgy conditions.

Clingfishes are generally described as being shaped like a teardrop or a tadpole. Most individuals are less than an inch long, and they are not often seen by divers because they tend to inhabit shoreline areas and sea grass beds where they hide under rocks or shells. However, snorkelers and tide pool explorers can learn to find clingfishes if they take the time to search.

JAWFISHES

Jawfishes are relatively small fishes with enormous heads and long, tapering bodies. They are extremely energetic and live in burrows which they constantly excavate and maintain. Immaculate housekeepers, jawfishes always seem to be rearranging the sand and rocks around their homes, making repairs, and constantly tinkering with their domiciles.

Divers usually encounter jawfishes as they hover over their burrows in a heads-up, tails-down vertical attitude. If you stop and watch, you will see their large, dark eyes rotating as they keep a sharp lookout for both food and intruders.

When danger approaches, jawfishes are quick to retreat tail first into their burrows.

Once you learn how to spot their homes, you will also begin to discover that jawfishes sometimes rest in their burrows with only their head and eyes protruding past the opening. The different species often build their burrows in a specific style with shells, coral rubble and other debris arranged in a precise manner. At night most jawfishes cover the opening to their burrow with a shell, stone or chunk of coral.

The home burrows of **yellowhead jawfish** can be over a foot deep. The fish remains close to its burrow, either drifting above it or remaining in the burrow with just its head protruding above the top rim. At the first sign of danger, they are quick to swim close to their burrows, and if the threat increases, they will retreat tail first into them. Yellowhead jawfish spend the majority of their daylight hours either maintaining their burrow or feeding on plankton, usually small crustaceans, which they pluck out of the water as they drift by.

Most jawfishes are strongly territorial. When intruders invade their realm, they are quick to rise up out of their homes and open their mouths in a territorial display that is intended to drive other fishes away. In nature, these displays of-

AT A GLANCE

YELLOWHEAD JAWFISH

Scientific Name
   Opistognathus aurifrons
Habitat
   Sandy rubble areas.
Typical Adult Size
   4 inches.
Sightings
   Commonly seen.
Natural History
   Male broods eggs in mouth.

ten work as intended and they help avoid an actual physical confrontation.

Yellowhead jawfish are one of the more common species found in the Caribbean, the Bahamas and Florida. Small in size, reaching a maximum length of only about six inches, they have a large head and a big mouth as their name suggests. Yellowhead jawfish are highly social and usually reside in the sand flats in colonies of 50 or more. They have a long, tapered body that is mostly yellow to white with blue trim along the edges of their fins.

A male yellowhead jawfish attracts females to his burrow for spawning near dawn and dusk in a display that involves an exaggerated arching of his back and the spreading of fins. Once the female has been persuaded to breed, spawning takes place deep within the male's burrow. Upon conclusion, the male emerges from the burrow with the eggs held in his mouth where he will incubate them until they hatch. Because of this behavior, yellowhead jawfish are referred to as mouth brooders, a trait displayed in most species of jawfishes. (See photograph on page 34.)

BLENNIES

Inhabiting tropical and temperate seas, approximately 600 species worldwide of small, bottom-dwelling fishes that have elongated bodies and bluntly shaped heads are commonly referred to as blennies. The classification and description of blennies is more complicated than in many families of fishes. Most blennies feature strong, well developed pelvic fins. The pelvic fins are located forward of the pectoral fins, and blennies use them as a support to prop up their heads as they lay on the bottom. The image of a perched up head with a curved body behind is the classic portrait of many blennies.

Blennies are commonly confused with gobies because the fishes in both families are small bottom-dwellers that live in similar habitats. Furthermore, members of both families prop themselves up on their pelvic fins when resting. Distinguishing between the two groups is not all that difficult if you keep in mind the fact that blennies tend to curve their bodies when at rest and when swimming, while gobies maintain a much stiffer posture. Blennies have one long, continuous dorsal fin, but gobies have two separate ones.

As a general rule, blennies are rather adept at blending into their backgrounds, even though the different species inhabit a variety of habitats ranging from tide pools to coral reefs to beds of seagrass. Blennies have steep facial profiles and comparatively large eyes which sit high up on their head. Many species have small projections called cirri growing from their head and face. The cirri help these blennies blend with their surroundings, which is often a patch of coral

---

AT A GLANCE

REDLIP BLENNY

Scientific Name
Ophioblennius atlanticus
Habitat
Shallow reef.
Typical Adult Size
4 inches.
Sightings
Commonly seen.
Natural History
Very territorial.

AT A GLANCE

DIAMOND BLENNY

Scientific Name
Malacoctenus boehlkei
Habitat
Reef.
Typical Adult Size
3 inches.
Sightings
Occasionally seen.
Natural History
Lives within tentacles of giant Caribbean anemone without being stung.

AT A GLANCE

ARROW BLENNY

Scientific Name
Lucayablennius zingaro
Habitat
Reef along drop-off.
Typical Adult Size
1.5 inches
Sightings
Occasionally seen.
Natural History
Hang in mid-water with tail cocked, ready to lunge for prey.

to a safe hiding place.

When mating, the male of the species selects a nest site and then undertakes the task of attracting a female. The male displays by doing a series of push-ups on his pelvic fins to attract the female's attention. Sometimes the male will bump the female with his snout. Once wooed, the female enters the nest tail first. The nest is normally a hole or a burrow. She deposits her eggs and the male fertilizes them. The male is left with the task of guarding the eggs, and he is tenacious in the pursuit of his instinctive duty.

Males are highly territorial when they are on their nests. They display demonstratively by rising out of their burrows and flaring their fins. Some also open their mouths. The intent of the displays is to ward off

rubble. Some blennies are spectacularly colored, but others are rather pale and drab. Color is not always a reliable key to identification because many blennies commonly alter their coloration and patterning.

The combination of their small size—most are less than three inches long—and their ability to camouflage themselves makes it easy for divers to overlook many blennies. Once discovered, however, they appear to be both curious and fearless. Even when approached by divers, most blennies hold their ground or swim just a short distance away. Often those that do swim away are quick to return to their original position.

Though tricky to find, **wrasse blennies** are fun to watch. Their appearance bears strong resemblance to juvenile bluehead wrasse, fish which actively clean other fishes, ridding them of parasites, bacteria and dead tissue. Wrasse blennies are anything but cleaners. They are impostors! These deceitful fish often bite chunks of flesh out of tricked victims, and then quickly dart away

AT A GLANCE

BLACKEDGE TRIPLEFIN, TRIPLEFIN

Scientific Name
Enneanectes atrorus
Habitat
Reef.
Typical Adult Size
1.5 inches.
Sightings
Occasionally seen.
Natural History
Sit motionless on sponges and deep-water gorgonians where they blend in.

AT A GLANCE

WRASSE BLENNY

Scientific Name
Hemiemblemaria simulus
Habitat
Reef.
Typical Adult Size
3 inches.
Sightings
Occasionally seen.
Natural History
Mimic juvenile bluehead wrasse and lure fishes into thinking that they are cleaners. Often bites chunks of flesh out of tricked victim.

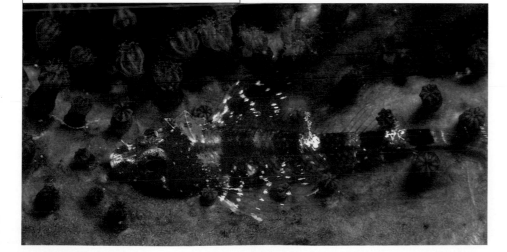

AT A GLANCE

BLUETHROAT PIKEBLENNY

Scientific Name
Chaenopsis ocellata
Habitat
Sandy areas, often in proximity to garden eels or eel grass.
Typical Adult Size
4 inches.
Sightings
Occasionally seen.
Natural History
Males display demonstratively to claim territory and ward off intruders.

AT A GLANCE

SAILFIN BLENNY

Scientific Name
Emblemaria pandionis
Habitat
Rubble zone, sandy areas, holes in limestone bedrock.
Typical Adult Size
2.5 inches.
Sightings
Occasionally seen.
Natural History
Male rapidly and repeatedly unfurls its oversized dorsal fin (sailfin) in display of sexuality to attract mate, or of territoriality to ward off intruders.

erably different from the adults. They look glassy and are nearly transparent. Larval blennies drift in currents before settling into their benthic lifestyle in the shallows.

Blennies feed on a wide variety of food sources. Some are herbivorous while others are ferocious carnivores that rely on their lightning speed and small but sharp teeth to overwhelm their prey.

GOBIES

Despite being both abundant and colorful, gobies are often overlooked by divers because of their small size and their tendency to sit motionless on top of coral heads and sponges. Most gobies are less than three inches long, but once you start to see them, it seems like there is one kind

intruders, especially other males of their species. Interestingly, studies have shown the displays to be highly successful in that confrontations with other males of their species, even larger males, are almost always avoided.

Larval hatchlings appear consid-

of goby or another almost everywhere you look. Ichthyologists suspect that there are as many as 2,000 species of gobies worldwide, a number which would make this family the largest family in tropical seas.

In Search of the Bluethroat Pikeblenny

For every thousand garden eels you see in the powdery sand, you may find one bluethroat pikeblenny, and only if you know what to look for.

To begin your search find a sandy area where there is a garden eel colony. Settle to the bottom and project your vision out beyond ten feet or so, and parallel to the bottom. Any pikeblennies closer to you than ten feet will already have settled deeply within their sand burrows after seeing you approach. These blennies are half the size of garden eels and the exact color of the surrounding sand. They remain dead still, halfway out of their burrows, occasionally rotating 180 degrees to check the area around them. As you near them they will undoubtedly crouch lower in their burrows, and this movement often gives away their presence. Keep in mind that an explosive release of exhaust bubbles or a clumsy move will ensure that you will never get any closer than about ten feet to these blennies. Once spotted, however, a very slow, cautious approach can take you to within inches of the blennies.

Like their cousins the sailfin blenny and the secretary blenny, the pikeblennies are very territorial and hesitate to give up ground to would-be invaders. On several occasions I have approached their lairs cautiously and held a small mirror in front of spunky little bluethroat pikeblennies. The mirror elicited an amazing reaction from the otherwise reticent little fish. Upon seeing their image and apparently mistaking it for a rival blenny, the pikeblennies repeatedly attacked the mirror. They flared their gills revealing the bright blue coloration between the rays of the gill cavity from which this blenny gets its name. The pikeblennies also stretched their jaws filled with a mouthful of teeth that, although invisible to me, are at the pikeblenny scale of things, undoubtedly quite threatening.

After all the hubbub of this display it is easy to see why there are only one or two pikeblennies for every thousand garden eels. They are just too darn mean to tolerate other blennies in close proximity.—Clay Wiseman

AT A GLANCE

SHARKNOSE GOBY
(Yellowphase)

Scientific Name
Gobisoma evelynae
Habitat
Reefs.
Typical Adult Size
1 to 1-1/4 inches.
Sightings
Commonly seen.
Natural History
Active fish cleaner.

AT A GLANCE

NEON GOBY

Scientific name
Gobisoma oceanops
Habitat
Reefs.
Typical Adult Size
1 to 1-1/4 inches.
Sightings
Commonly seen.
Natural History
Active fish cleaner.

Gobies lack gas bladders, internal organs found in many bony fishes which assist in achieving neutral buoyancy. As a result, gobies tend to spend the vast majority of

215

trap air in their gill chambers allows them to accomplish this unusual feat.

Gobies often demonstrate intricate mating rituals. In many species the male first selects a nest site. Then he spreads his fins in a sexual display to attract a mate. The wooed female lays her eggs at the nest site and the male quickly fertilizes them. Then the male displays again in an effort to attract another female. The entire cycle is repeated again and again until the male is comfortable with the number of eggs in the nest. But don't get the wrong impression. The male is not an irresponsible playboy. He staunchly guards the eggs until they hatch.

Different species of gobies tend to be associated with specific organ-

AT A GLANCE

ORANGESIDED GOBY

Scientific Name
Gobisoma dilepsis
Habitat
Reef.
Typical Adult Size
1 inch.
Sightings
Occasionally seen.
Natural History
Sits atop various corals and sponges.

their lives resting on the bottom near a protective shelter, which is often a crevice in the reef or a sponge. The strong pelvic fins of gobies have been modified into a disk that creates suction, allowing them to grasp onto the substrate. This characteristic enables them to live in shallow water where surge is common.

Gobies are often confused with blennies, but with just a little practice it is relatively easy to tell them apart. The most obvious distinguishing characteristic is that gobies

possess two distinct dorsal fins, while blennies have one long, continuous dorsal fin. In addition, gobies tend to hold their bodies in a straight, or nearly straight line, both when they rest and when they swim. In contrast, blennies tend to curve their bodies both at rest and in motion, and swim with a more exaggerated wriggling motion.

Like many other bottom-dwelling fishes, gobies perch themselves up on their pelvic fins while resting on the bottom. And despite the attractive color patterns exhibited by many species, some gobies are often difficult to locate because they blend in so well with their surroundings. Other gobies are active cleaners and they often swim in animated fashion to advertise their presence.

One of the most fascinating adaptations in gobies is the ability of some species to survive out of water for several weeks in succession, as long as they can keep their bodies and gills moist. The ability to

PHOTO TIP

Cleaning stations are favorite locations for underwater photographers. There is no better place to find any number of normally hard-to-approach fishes dropping their guard. Furthermore, any wildlife portrait that shows two animals interacting is inherently valuable and more impressive than a portrait of one animal doing nothing special.

Timing is important, as is subtle presence. Make sure that the fish being cleaned is in the thick of the process. Often they will have their jaws fully distended when the action is most intense. Try to settle close to the reef 10 or 15 feet away from the action, and preferably where you are hidden by some reef growth. Move toward the cleaning station very slowly, remain relaxed and breathe slowly.

Use the reef to try to stay hidden, and shoot from behind any obstacles that might provide cover, rather than just plopping down in the middle of the scene. Do not move your camera between frames or you will spook the fish being cleaned into throwing off the cleaners and fleeing. If your subject spooks, don't move! Often a fish will return shortly as the need to rid itself of external parasites can override the sense of caution.

between yourself and the cleaning activity. If you approach too quickly or too closely, you are likely to interrupt the behavior.

The **greenbanded goby**, **tiger goby** and **shortstripe goby** also tend to associate with specific organisms. Greenbanded gobies are commonly found hiding under the spines of sea urchins. Tiger gobies tend to inhabit algae-covered rocks or live in sponges found in shallow reef communities. Shortstripe gobies are often found perched inside tube sponges.

Many of the species of gobies commonly seen in the sand or rubble zone—the **goldspot goby**, **colon goby**, **bridled goby** and **blue goby**—are lightly colored in order to match their surroundings. **Mask-**

AT A GLANCE

GREENBANDED GOBY

Scientific Name
Gobisoma multifasciatum
Habitat
Shallow limestone areas.
Typical Adult Size
1.5 inches.
Sightings
Occasionally seen.
Natural History
Lives under boring urchin spines.

---

and eels to pick debris from between their teeth and to clean infections. The predators obviously appreciate the service, and they must have some sense of its value, instinctively realizing that it is better to be cleaned again tomorrow than to take advantage of an unsuspecting cleaner by capturing a "free lunch" today.

If you see a cleaning station with gobies at work, it is usually best to slow down and keep some distance

---

AT A GLANCE

PALLID GOBY

Scientific Name
Coryphopterus eidolon
Habitat
Sandy or rubble areas.
Typical Adult Size
2 inches.
Sightings
Commonly seen.
Natural History
Body has evolved to a pale color to match surrounding environment.

---

isms. For example, the Caribbean species that are considered to be active cleaners—the **neon**, **sharknose**, **cleaning**, **yellownose**, **barsnout** and **broadstripe gobies**—are almost always found sitting on top of coral heads. They are occasionally encountered on the upper rim or on the outside edge of sponges, but they are almost never seen inside sponges unless they have been frightened. These gobies feed on a variety of ectoparasites that live on the skin of fishes visiting their cleaning stations. Cleaner gobies are often seen scurrying about on the bodies of the fishes they clean, and at times actually enter the mouths of groupers

GLASS GOBY

Scientific Name
Coryphopterus hylainus
Habitat
Below 90 feet in water column above corals.
Typical Adult Size
2 to 3 inches.
Sightings
Commonly seen.
Natural History
Small aggregations drift together. Dart about in short bursts. Virtually indistinguishable from the masked goby (Coryphopterus persaonatus). Masked goby prefers top100 feet of water. This picture was taken in 140 feet of water.

PEPPERMINT GOBY

Scientific Name
Coryphopterus lipernes
Habitat
Reef.
Typical Adult Size
1.5 inches.
Sightings
Commonly seen.
Natural History
Sits on corals.

ed gobies often gather in groups along the wall and will often be seen in close proximity to arrow blennies. **Glass gobies** are also commonly found along walls, and they are very similar in appearance to masked gobies.

Some species of gobies appear to be generally unafraid of divers and will allow you to get close enough to admire their handsome colors. However, most macro photographers have learned that catching a goby in a perfect pose inside the framer of an extension tube is an entirely different matter. Still other species tend to be wary, rarely giving photographers much of a chance as they are quick to retreat into sponges or crevices in the reef.

TOADFISHES

Like frogfishes and batfishes, toadfishes are often described as being bizarre-looking. Perhaps the best way to describe toadfishes is to say that few other fishes resemble them. The heads of toadfishes are greatly flattened and their wide mouths appear to be far too large for the length of their bodies. Most toadfishes are less than a foot long. A "beard" full of chin barbels, suspected to serve as chemosensory organs, are often prominent and sometimes their teeth are exposed even when the fish is at rest on the bottom.

During the day toadfishes often hide in recesses in the reef, and at night they lay in wait near the openings of crevices and depressions under coral ledges. Toadfishes prefer to feed on a variety of crustaceans and mollusks.

The **splendid toadfish** is commonly seen in Cozumel and some locals affectionately refer to the species as the "Cozumel kitty." Splendid toadfish are distinguished by the distinct pattern of stripes on their head, yellow pelvic fins, and the bright yellow margin of other fins.

Several other species of toadfishes inhabit the Caribbean, but they are rarely seen by divers because they tend to inhabit shallow, muddy areas. The species known as sapo is a favorite food in many areas of the southern Caribbean.

FROGFISHES

One of the more remarkable characteristics of frogfishes is their ability to blend in with their surroundings. Even members of the same species commonly occur in a variety of different color phases ranging from bright orange and yellow to dark brown.

Masters of camouflage, frogfishes are also among the more bizarre-looking fishes. Like batfishes, frogfishes are awkward swimmers at best. The pectoral and pelvic fins of frogfishes have evolved into ap-

AT A GLANCE

LARGE EYE TOADFISH

Scientific Name
Batrachoides gilberti
Habitat
Recesses in reef.
Typical Adult Size
10 inches.
Sightings
Occasionally seen.
Natural History
Has a "beard" of sensory chin barbels. Capable of making loud grunts.

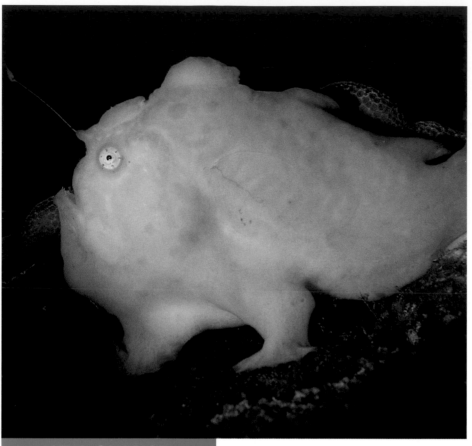

As a rule, frogfishes sit motionless in an effort to blend in with their surroundings rather than flee from impending danger. Once they are certain they have been discovered, they often turn and face away from intruding divers instead of swimming away. Although the tail fin is occasionally used for their best burst of speed, these fishes are more likely to use jets of water forced through their reduced gill openings to move them about. The process is not particularly speedy, but it is rather astounding to watch them move through the water with no apparent movement of their fins.

Finding a frogfish is often a difficult task. Many individuals rest on sponges or coral heads, and their coloration and shape allow them to blend in perfectly. Once discovered, frogfishes can often be found for days and even months on end, resting in almost the exact same spot

AT A GLANCE

LONGLURE FROGFISH

Scientific Name
Antennarius multiocellatus
Habitat
Reef.
Typical Adult Size
4 inches.
Sightings
Occasionally seen.
Natural History
Foremost dorsal spine has migrated forward and developed a lure which is wiggled to attract small fishes as prey.

flage themselves and rest on the sea floor while they wait for unwary prey to venture within striking distance. Frogfishes are equipped with a lure-like appendage on the top of their head which they wiggle intermittently in an attempt to attract unsuspecting prey. While frogfishes are not fast swimmers by any stretch of the imagination, they are capable of making quick lunges that are fast enough to capture their desired prey of small fishes.

According to specialists, frogfishes are capable of opening their mouths faster than almost any other animal, and they have split-second control over the timing. The speed actually causes a near-vacuum and creates a pressure differential which sucks prey into their mouths. Their gill covers are used to help create the suction. Mother Nature truly has some clever tricks up her sleeve!

If a frogfish loses its lure to its prey, it is capable of growing a new one, but it is not a quick process.

PHOTO TIP

With a face that only a mother could love, frogfishes are a real photographic find! Because they are so rare, their portrait is highly sought after by serious underwater photographers. Once found, frogfishes are relatively easy to shoot since they don't like to move. Use a Nikonos with a close-up kit or a single lens reflex camera, but be careful not to prod these fishes as this will cause them to leave the area. Occasionally, you will see a frogfish "yawn" as they work their jaw muscles which must constantly be loose and at the ready to suck in prey with lightning speed. Be ready; an open or partially open mouth makes an interesting shot. Even better, sometimes you will see them wiggling their lure. This is the really challenging picture to capture. The lure and spine to which it is attached are nearly translucent. If you frame the lure against the reef it might all but disappear from your photograph. Use a second strobe to backlight the lure and shoot it against a blue or black background if possible.

pendages that are used mostly to help them walk rather than swim along the sea floor. Furthermore, in frogfishes these fins are fully capable of grasping, an adaptation that helps them hold still as they attempt to ambush their prey.

Frogfishes are part of a group commonly called anglerfishes. These fishes are described as ambush predators because they camou-

A Case of Mistaken Identity: Finding the Longlure Frogfish

Certainly the most curious fishes I have encountered, and spent hours observing and photographing, are the frogfishes. They are also called anglerfishes because of the fleshy appendage they use to lure unwary prey within striking distance of their oversized mouth which is filled with small, though very sharp teeth.

Several species of frogfishes (Antennarius sp.) exist in the Caribbean and associated waters, but you wouldn't know it if you weren't aware of the fact before entering the water. With their excellent camouflage of ocellations (spots) that look just like sponge pores, and with encrusting algae that looks just like any other area of the reef, they are practically invisible, especially for the small fishes unfortunate enough to pass close to them.

For the diver, only the twitching of their "lure" gives away their presence. The small lure is actually the foreward-most dorsal spine which has, in the course of evolution, migrated further forward. In the marine environment, filled with the cornucopia of activity which is its trademark, seeing a frogfish angling is really a feat.

On a dive in the Turks and Caicos I was slithering along, passing my face plate within inches of the reef when I noticed a small black ball sponge which was being watched curiously by a blue chromis. Usually the chromis flitters about, seldom hesitating for more than a minute or two, but this one was actually mesmerized as it watched that sponge. I stared at the ugly sponge as well and all of a sudden a blob on a stick switchbladed out from the sponge. The chromis went for it and disappeared! The sponge ate the blue chromis! Only the "sponge" had amongst its otherwise amorphous form a small circular eye. It was a frogfish and the discovery shocked me. Not just because it was a frogfish, but because it was one that was so well camouflaged that it fooled me and I have seen dozens of the species in the Pacific. The feeling of discovery sent me flying for my camera and my brain subconsciously marked every feature on the reef so I could get back to the exact same spot.

On my return I found the giant barrel sponge and the brain coral, but where was the exact spot? I knew I was looking directly at it! And then it happened...the little lure moved, this time on a dry run. Down part way, down all the way, hold for a second, and then halfway and then back into the groove along that black ball sponge that really wasn't a sponge at all.—Clay Wiseman

and position. If you discover a frogfish and return a few days later but do not find it where it was, be patient. Stop and look around, and often you will find the fish within a few feet of where it was previously. As long as you don't touch or move these fishes, they are not likely to move from the spot where you originally found them.

The bizarre shape and unusual texture of the skin of frogfishes can make it difficult to see the entire fish or individual body parts even when you are aware that the fish is sitting

AT A GLANCE

SPLITLURE FROGFISH

Scientific Name
Antennarius scaber

Habitat
Reefs, often resting in, on, or near sponges.

Typical Adult Size
3 to 7 inches.

Sightings
Seldom seen due to superb ability as camouflage artist.

Natural History
Foremost dorsal spine has migrated forward and developed a lure which is wiggled to attract prey of small fishes. End lure is split. Uses a wide variety of color phases to blend in with surroundings, especially sponges.

AT A GLANCE

SARGASSUMFISH

Scientific Name
Histrio histrio
Habitat
Mats of floating sargassum weed.
Typical Adult Size
4 inches.
Sightings
Occasionally seen.
Natural History
Adapted to hide within mats of sargassum weed.

BATFISHES

Batfishes are also among the most bizarre fishes. In many respects, they neither look nor behave like other fishes. Instead of swimming, batfishes tend to use their pelvic fins to help them walk around on the bottom. In a panic, batfishes will try to swim, but the end result of their efforts is some awkward wriggling that is kindly described as somewhere between humorous and just plain slow. Of course, slow for a fish is often much faster than we can swim in full scuba gear.

In their effort to capture their food, and for protection, batfishes tend to rely on their ability to camouflage themselves. In order to appear inconspicuous, they often lie

which makes the task difficult.

One very unusual species of frogfish, the **sargassumfish**, has adapted beautifully to living amongst floating masses of sargassum weed. Sargassumfish are the exact same color as the weed in which they live, and they have developed skin appendages which resemble the fronds of sargassum weed. They are one of several species that are well adapted for living within clumps of sargassum weed.

AT A GLANCE

SHORTNOSE BATFISH

Scientific Name
Ogocephalus nasutus
Habitat
Sandy rubble areas.
Typical Adult Size
10 inches.
Sightings
Occasionally seen.
Natural History
Walks on fins; swims poorly.

in front of you. Furthermore, many species which live on sponges have body markings that look exactly like sponge oscula, making them nearly invisible. Some frogfishes even cultivate a crop of algae on their skin, a characteristic which helps them be inconspicuous. Many fishes blend in with their surroundings, but frogfishes may be the most remarkable in this respect.

Several species of frogfishes are quite common throughout the Caribbean, but they are only rarely seen because they are such superb masters of disguise. Most individuals are less than eight inches long. Field identification is possible in some instances, but frogfishes demonstrate a wide variety of color phases

HOWARD HALL

AT A GLANCE

FLYING GURNARD

Scientific Name
Dactylopterus volitans
Habitat
Sandy areas.
Typical Adult Size
12 inches.
Sightings
Occasionally seen.
Natural History
Enlarged pectoral fins make gurnard appear to fly when frightened.

flat on sand or rubble bottoms, but when curious or aroused they will prop themselves up on their pectoral fins.

Like frogfishes and other anglerfishes, batfishes use a lure-like appendage on their head to attract unwary prey. Batfishes take advantage of their well-camouflaged bodies while manipulating their lure to gain the attention of a variety of small, curious fishes. Once the unsuspecting prey gets within striking range, batfishes are quick to attack. But if the prey escapes the first strike, it has nothing more to fear from the slow-moving batfishes. Batfishes also feed on a variety of worms, crustaceans and mollusks.

None of the batfishes found in the Caribbean, Bahamas or Florida are considered to be common. They are usually found on sand or mud bottoms where they often bury or partially bury their body, and they are only rarely seen in reef communities.

Three species of odd-looking batfishes inhabit these waters. They are the **shortnose batfish**, **polka-dot batfish** and **pancake batfish**. Commonly between 6 and 12 inches long, the shortnose batfish and the polka-dot batfish are considerably larger than the pancake batfish which is usually between 2 and 4 inches in length. The forward part of the body of a pancake batfish is much more rounded than the bodies of the other two species. Polka-dot batfish have distinct spots on the fins, head and body, while shortnose batfish are generally more mottled. The polka-dot batfish is not found in the true Caribbean, but has been documented in the associated waters of Florida and in the Bahamas.

FLYING GURNARD

Flying gurnards look like a peacock that got lost somewhere along the evolutionary line and ended up as a fish. They have overdeveloped pectoral fins that look much like pea-

AT A GLANCE

SPOTTED SCORPIONFISH

Scientific Name
Scorpaena plumieri
Habitat
Reef.
Typical Adult Size
12 inches.
Sightings
Commonly seen.
Natural History
Dorsal spines are poisonous; masters of camouflage.

cock feathers when the fins are spread.

Their enlarged pectorals are usually the key to confirming a sighting. The pectorals are most evident when the fins are spread, as is usually the case when the fish are frightened. In other circumstances, the pectorals are tucked in against the sides of the body. The forward part of these fins are used to sift through the sand in search of food. The pectoral fins are laced with iridescent blue stripes and dots which are usually most obvious along the outside edges of the fins. Adult flying gurnards are usually about 12 to 14

inches long, but some are reported to reach 18 inches.

Flying gurnards are considered uncommon throughout the Caribbean. When seen, they are usually in shallow areas with sand, rubble or grassy bottoms. Their bodies are tan with dark circular spots. Flying gurnards have bony, squared-off heads that are armor-plated, similar to the heads of scorpionfishes. Two long dorsal rays that stick up from the back of the head are sometimes evident.

Flying gurnards prey on a variety of benthic organisms, including a selection of clams, crustaceans and some small fishes.

SCORPIONFISHES

Scorpionfishes are aptly named. Their potent dorsal, pelvic and anal fins can cause a painful wound if the sharp spines penetrate the flesh of a diver or swimmer. That is not to say that scorpionfishes readily attack humans. They do not. But they are masters of camouflage that are easily overlooked, and they are usually

quite hesitant to swim away or move when approached. It is likely that these fishes know that movement will give away their location, so they tend to stay put. If a diver fails to notice one and settles down on top of it, there can be a painful price to pay. Fortunately for divers, the spines of Caribbean scorpion-fishes are not as toxic as some Indo-Pacific species, such as the well- known lionfishes.

Scorpionfishes have large, somewhat bulbous heads and comparatively stout bodies. Despite the fact that several species have colorful fins and some have reddish bodies, they often go unnoticed because their mottled color patterns blend in so well with the algae, coral and rubble found on the sea floor. Furthermore, some species grow a crop of algae on their skin which helps camouflage them.

If you do see a scorpionfish, there is absolutely no reason to become alarmed as long as you do not touch, grab or hassle it. Scorpionfishes are often inclined to stay put and allow divers to get very close. And if they swim away, they usually travel only a few feet.

Bottom dwellers, scorpionfishes survive as ambush predators that rely on camouflage to help them snare unsuspecting prey with their large mouths. Scorpionfishes lack gas bladders. They are not among the fastest of swimmers, but scorpionfishes are capable of quickly rising off the bottom and sucking in small fishes that are caught off-guard.

Despite the fact that scorpionfishes look similar at first glance, distinguishing between the species is not all that difficult. **Spotted scorpionfish** are believed to be the most common species inhabiting coral reef communities in the Caribbean. They are usually mottled in a wide range of tans and browns. Spotted scorpionfish lack the plume-like appendages above the eyes which are found on many other species, but they commonly have a number of skin flaps on their head and chin. And if they flare their pectoral fins, you are likely to quickly notice that these fins are colored a handsome shade of deep red. A black semicircle with a number of white spots is located at the forward edge of the base of the pectoral fin's top side. Spotted scorpionfish are usually between 6 and 18 inches long.

Reef scorpionfish bear a strong resemblance to spotted scorpionfish. Despite what the common names seem to suggest, reef scorpionfish have more spots on their tail than do spotted scorpionfish. Reef scorpionfish also have a prominent dark spot toward the back of the dorsal fin.

Attaining a maximum size of about seven inches, **plumed scorpionfish** are much smaller than both spotted and reef scorpionfish. Plumed scorpionfish are colored in shades of mottled brown. They have a prominent feather-like plume above each eye and are fairly common in Florida, but far less common in the Bahamas and the Caribbean.

The dark band along the outer margin of the fins of **mushroom scorpionfish** provide a good identifying character, while **spinycheek scorpionfish** can be identified by the three dark patches on their sides. The bodies of spinycheek scorpionfish are often a colorful mottled combination of yellow and brown, or red and brown. Spinycheek scorpionfish are reported only in the waters of Florida and Cuba.

Barbfish are the most common scorpionfish found in the inshore waters of Florida. They look similar to plumed scorpionfish, which are also common in Florida. The large dark spot above the pectoral fins of barbfish can help distinguish them from plumed scorpionfish.

LEFT-EYE FLOUNDERS

Flounders, along with **halibut**, tur-

PHOTO TIP

The ability of peacock flounders to camouflage and/or partially bury themselves makes them reluctant to move away unless they feel threatened and are absolutely sure that they have been seen. That being the case, it makes sense to use a indirect approach along the sandy bottom to try to get close enough to photograph them with a housed camera, Nikonos RS or a Nikonos with a 28mm lens. Be careful not to overexpose! The combination of a reflective sandy background and a white fish will tend to reflect a lot of light. When shooting on manual, bracket several stops on the closed down side using smaller than normal apertures (larger f/ numbers). If you are using TTL, consider setting your ASA higher than the speed of the film you are actually using.

AT A GLANCE

PEACOCK FLOUNDER

Scientific Name
Bothus lunatus
Habitat
Sandy areas.
Typical Adult Size
10 inches.
Sightings
Commonly seen.
Natural History
In transforming from pelagic larvae to bottom-dwelling juvenile, one eye migrates to opposite side of head allowing fish to settle and swim on its side.

bot, **sole** and **sanddabs**, are members of a group of fishes commonly called flatfishes. This name is derived from the fact that the adults commonly lay flat in the sand. As adults, flatfishes have both eyes on one side of their head, and they rest on the bottom on their opposite side. The eyes move independently of each other and can rotate nearly 360 degrees, giving these fishes excellent peripheral vision. The side with the eyes is usually colored like the substrate in an effort to help the fish camouflage itself, while the side that faces the sea floor is usually colored off-white. Adult flatfishes swim in a horizontal position on their sides, rather than in a back up-belly down vertical orientation like other fishes. When flatfish swim, they glide only an inch or so off the bottom closely following the contour.

Perhaps the most fascinating aspect of this characteristic of having both eyes on one side of the head as adults is the fact that in their larval stage, flatfishes have one eye on either side of the head as do most other fishes. Amazingly, as flatfishes start to mature one eye migrates over the top of the head to the other side. The mouth also begins to turn in order to orient to the new positioning of the eyes. This astonishing adaptation is common to all flatfishes.

As adults, flounders are generally found in the sand. The unusual positioning of the eyes enables flatfishes to lay flat or partially bury themselves in sand bottoms with only their eyes protruding.

Another physiological trait that helps flatfishes camouflage themselves is that they are capable of rapidly changing the color of their skin to match that of their surroundings. A number of studies have been conducted to try to quantify their ability to change their color patterns to match their surroundings. Defining that skill in scientific terms can prove tricky, but to the casual observer there is no doubt that flatfishes have an astonishing ability to alter their skin color and pattern. Amazingly, when prodded to settle on top of a checkerboard these fishes can actually take on a checkerboard pattern! Obviously, the combination of camouflage and their ability to bury themselves in the sand causes divers to often overlook flatfishes until they move.

TRIGGERFISHES

Triggerfishes get their name from their unique trigger-like dorsal fin which is used to help them lodge into crevices when they feel threatened. The dorsal fin contains three spines. The most forward spine is the largest and when it is erect dur-

AT A GLANCE

QUEEN TRIGGERFISH

Scientific Name
Balistes vetula
Habitat
Reef.
Typical Adult Size
16 inches.
Sightings
Commonly seen.
Natural History
Dorsal spine locks erect to offer protection from predators.

AT A GLANCE

OCEAN TRIGGERFISH

Scientific Name
Canthidemis sufflamen
Habitat
Along drop-off; nests on reef.
Typical Adult Size
18 inches.
Sightings
Commonly seen.
Natural History
Dorsal spine locks erect to offer protection from predators.

ing a moment of fear, the second spine is moved forward to lock or pin the first spine into an upright position. The fish positions itself in such a way that the erect dorsal spines prevent potential predators from pulling it out of the hole. The forward spine remains locked in an erect position until the fish relaxes. Triggerfishes are usually seen swimming about the reef or over sand rather than hiding within the protective confines of the reef, but they are quick to take cover at the slightest hint of danger.

Triggerfishes have deep, thin bodies with their eyes positioned high on their head. They have pointed snouts and comparatively small mouths, considering their size. Triggerfishes are capable of moving their eyes independently of one another.

Several species of triggerfishes

are commonly seen in many reef communities throughout the Caribbean. Among the more prominent are the spectacularly-colored **queen triggerfish**, the rather plain-looking **ocean triggerfish**, and the **black durgon**.

Queen triggerfish tend to hover close to the bottom where they feed on a variety of echinoderms, mollusks and crustaceans. They have strong jaws and long teeth which enable them to easily bite through the hard body parts of many invertebrates. In fact, queen triggerfish commonly feed on long-spined sea urchins, spines and all!

Relatively little is known about their natural history. The females lay eggs which adhere to coral, rocks or algae. The eggs are well camouflaged. In some species the adults do not care for or guard the eggs, while in other species, one or both adults

AT A GLANCE

BLACK DURGON

Scientific Name
Balistes niger
Habitat
Reef.
Typical Adult Size
10 inches.
Sightings
Commonly seen.
Natural History
Dorsal spine locks erect to prevent fish from being removed from reef's protection by predators.

guard the eggs.

The body of ocean triggerfish is much more drably colored than that of queen triggerfish. Ocean triggerfish are grey to brown and have a distinct black spot at the base of each pectoral fin. They are often seen by divers during nesting season when they spend the majority of their time near a sandy bottom. Nest sites look like small, three to four feet wide depressions in the sand. Ocean triggerfish appear to guard the nests staunchly, almost defiantly. But if you approach, they soon appear nervous and are usually quick to give ground. However, if they do choose to defend, you will want to beware of their long, sharp teeth and strong jaws.

These fish feed primarily on plankton and the blades of a variety of sea grasses. Little is known about their biology, but ocean triggerfish are believed to be polygamous, with males and females mating randomly without any apparent long-term bonding.

Black durgons tend to gather in schools in mid-water. Their bodies definitely share the profile of other triggerfishes, but because of their schooling behavior they are sometimes mistaken for surgeon-fishes. Despite their common name, their body color varies from black to light blue with a yellow patch on the head.

SURGEONFISHES

Many of the approximately 65 species of **surgeonfishes** are among the most common fishes in tropical reef communities around the world. Surgeonfishes obtain their name from the scalpel-sharp spines located on either side of the muscular base of their tail, an area known as the caudal peduncle. The genus name of the surgeonfishes, *Acanthurus*, was born of two Greek words meaning "tail spine." Surgeonfishes are commonly called **doctorfishes** and **tangs**, the latter name being derived from the tang or prong of a fork or other instrument.

Most species of surgeonfishes have one spine on each side of the body which can be folded back into a groove. The spine can be erected at will, and is used for defensive measures. Some species possess several spines. When the tail section of

PHOTO TIP

One of the best approaches for photographing surgeonfishes is to move in when they are in a tight school grazing on algae. The large size of their schools and their focus on feeding seems to make surgeons less skittish and unafraid. You can get good schooling shots using a Nikonos with either a 15mm or a 20mm lens.

the body is moved rapidly back and forth, the razor-sharp spine can inflict serious injury to any fish threatening the surgeonfish or its territory.

The spines are usually a contrasting color to the body, a feature which helps advertise their presence. Nature often provides animals a way to avoid actual physical confrontations by supplying a method of warning potential predators about their capable means of defense. In the case of surgeonfishes, the warning coloration of the spine seems to work well. Ichthyologists commonly report seeing other fishes rapidly give ground when a surgeonfish waves its tail.

The bodies of surgeonfishes, blue tangs and doctorfish are oval-shaped and laterally compressed or flattened from side to side. They have large, prominent eyes and small mouths located on the end of the face in a location ichthyologists refer to as the terminal position.

During the day, divers from Bermuda to Brazil commonly encounter schools of blue tangs grazing on algae on the tops of shallow reefs. Surgeonfish and doctorfish are often mixed in with the blue tangs and readily join in the feeding fray. On some occasions, parrotfishes and wrasses also mix in.

At night, blue tangs can often be spotted resting in a sleep-like state against the base of small coral heads in relatively exposed cracks, and in crevices. Blue tangs vary their color from deep gray or brown to bright blue and even hues of purple. At night their bodies may be covered with several dark bands, but that is not always the case.

The stomach of a blue tang has thin walls, and as such is considerably different from those of ocean surgeonfish and doctorfish. Blue tangs eat algae and some organic debris.

Ocean surgeonfish and doctorfish often ingest sand and coral rubble which they grind up with a gizzard-like organ in their intestines. The sand and coral debris contain sur-

TOP LEFT: KEN LOYST

AT A GLANCE

BLUE TANG
(DAY, LEFT; NIGHT, RIGHT;
JUVENILE, BOTTOM LEFT)

Scientific Name
Acanthurus coeruleus
Habitat
Reef.
Typical Adult Size
7 inches; juvenile 2 inches.
Sightings
Commonly seen.
Natural History
*Plant eaters; often graze on
algae in large schools; enter a
sleep-like state at night; color
varies from blue to gray. Juvenile goes through yellow phase
before turning blue in intermediate and adult stage. As intermediate has yellow tail. All blue as
adult.*

PHOTO TIP

*Nighttime, when tangs are sleeping,
is the best time to get a full-frame
photograph of an individual blue tang
since they can easily be placed within
the framer of a close-up kit. You can
get your image by using a Nikonos
and close-up kit, or with a single lens
reflex system and a 50mm to 60mm
lens. Be gentle and try not to wake
them. If you have difficulty getting
your framer into position, remove the
framer from its mount, being careful
not to drop it onto the coral. You can
get good shots with just a little practice by using the wand as a reference
for your framer.*

prising quantities of organic particles. When consumed by humans,
ocean surgeonfish and doctorfish
will occasionally cause ciguatera
food poisoning from toxins which
do not break down quickly even
when cooked.

The somewhat similar bodies of
doctorfish and ocean surgeonfish are
more streamlined that those of blue
tangs. Doctorfish always have a
number of vertical bars, but in some
color phases the bars are not as
prominent. Ocean surgeonfish lack
the vertical bars, and they have cres-
cent-shaped tails.

Spawning surgeonfishes are often seen in mid-water during late afternoon and early morning. Males
attempt to woo the females by swirling about them. Eggs and sperm are
released into mid-water where fertilization occurs. The eggs contain a
drop of oil, a marvelous adaptation
which makes the eggs float. The fertilized eggs drift with the plankton
and get dispersed over a wide range,
which helps explain the wide distribution of the species. The eggs
quickly develop into two-inch-long
juveniles within only a week, and
sexual maturity is attained in nine
months to a year.

During their pelagic stage, blue
tangs do not have scales and are
transparent except for a silver-col-

place. The scales of filefishes are equipped with tiny spines called spinules which make their skin feel rough, similar to the skin of sharks. Filefishes have elongated snouts with small mouths, protruding lips, beak-like jaws, and teeth which can often be seen projecting outward from the lips. Their paired dorsal and anal fins are identical. Many adult filefishes are able to quickly and dramatically alter their color.

Filefishes tend to be both shy and curious about divers. Although there are notable exceptions, as a rule filefishes do not readily approach divers. However, they will often follow or shadow divers for extended periods of time. Like triggerfishes,

AT A GLANCE

DOCTORFISH

Scientific Name
Acanthurus chirurgus
Habitat
Reef.
Typical Adult Size
10 inches.
Sightings
Commonly seen.
Natural History
Plant eaters, graze on algae.

ichthyologists consider the differences between filefishes and triggerfishes to be significant enough to place them in two separate families. They describe filefishes in the family Monacanthidae, and triggerfishes in the family Balistidae.

Unlike triggerfishes, filefishes do not have a locking second dorsal spine. Filefishes possess a long dorsal spine which is known as their file, but this spine does not lock into

AT A GLANCE

SCRAWLED FILEFISH

Scientific Name
Aluterus scriptus
Habitat
Reef.
Typical Adult Size
2.5 feet.
Sightings
Seldom seen.
Natural History
Usually use their dorsal and anal fins for locomotion.

ored abdomen. Currents eventually bring some fish into shallow reef communities where they settle out of the water column. It is not uncommon to see tangs during this stage of their life when you are on night dives, as these fish are often attracted to the bright lights of dive boats.

FILEFISHES

Filefishes and triggerfishes are so closely related that some specialists group them into the same family, Balistidae. These fishes appear quite similar and tend to swim by synchronizing the undulating motion of their dorsal and anal fins rather than using their tail fin. However, most

filefishes often appear to try to hide by placing a sea fan, sea whip or a branch of coral between themselves and a diver. In their efforts to remain hidden from potential predators and divers, filefishes sometimes hang motionless in the water in a head down, near-vertical attitude. Once detected, however, they tend to move away slowly since they are poor swimmers. Filefishes depend mostly on their rippling dorsal and anal fins for locomotion, but these don't provide the speed found in other fishes that rely more heavily on the strength of their tails.

Some species of juvenile filefishes drift with clumps of sargassum weed and other debris, and scientists commonly capture the juveniles in sampling nets hundreds of miles out to sea. These species en-joy wide distribution as open ocean currents scatter the juveniles across an expanse of reef systems.

Female filefishes are the larger and more colorful sex. During courtship, the female circles the male while he hangs head down. Courtship and displays of territoriality are commonly seen.

Commonly reaching a length of three feet, the **scrawled filefish** is the largest of the Caribbean species. The combination of irregular blue etchings on their lighter bodies, their large size, and their rippling fins tend to catch the eyes of divers. Scrawled filefish are often observed swimming in a head-down position. Ichthyologists speculate that this position evolved as a result of the fact that they feed on a variety of bottom-dwelling organisms, including attached algae, seagrasses, hydroids, corals and other cnidarians.

Whitespotted filefish reach a length of about 18 inches. The body color of whitespotted filefish ranges from a dull coppery color to pale orange. At times you will see a number of dime-sized white spots covering their bodies from head to tail. The spots appear and disappear almost instantly and seem to be controlled by the fish's emotional or behavioral state. A rapid twitching of a filefish's sharp dorsal spine of-ten accompanies the spotted phase, especially when they are first approached. A shallow-water species that is typically found above 70 feet, whitespotted filefish are common in Florida, Grand Cayman and Belize, but they are considered to be uncommon throughout the rest of their range.

Whitespotted filefish often swim in pairs. It is suspected that the pairs are usually a male and a female. Whitespotted filefish, along with various angelfishes, belong to a very exclusive group of fishes that feed primarily on sponges. To a lesser extent these fishes also consume hydroids, gorgonian corals and algae.

Considered common in the Caribbean but uncommon to occasional in the waters of the Bahamas and Florida, **orangespotted filefish** are small, shy fishes that tend to hang near the bottom where they can take cover in branched corals, gorgonians and other structures along the reef. Like other filefishes, orangespotted filefish vary their coloration. In their

AT A GLANCE

WHITESPOTTED FILEFISH

Scientific Name
   Cantherhines macroceros
Habitat
   Reef.
Typical Adult Size
   14 inches.
Sightings
   Commonly seen.
Natural History
   Will show white spots on body intermittently.

most common color phase they have several wide, horizontal brown stripes that are separated by dull yellow stripes. The yellow stripes often lack complete continuity and look like a series of almost connected dashes. A prominent white spot is located at the top of the tail's base, and when startled their conspicuous dorsal spine stands fully erect. Adult orangespotted filefish reach a maximum length of just over eight inches.

Like **fringed filefish** and **pygmy filefish**, **slender filefish** are comparatively small. Distinguishing between these species in the field is difficult. Most specimens are less than four inches long, and they are often mistaken for the juveniles of other species of filefishes and triggerfishes. Their solid or checkered brown to gray on white bodies blend in well with many sea fans, and these filefishes often take advantage of that coloration by hiding amongst the branches of gorgonian corals. Night divers occasionally discover these species hovering next to,

or resting on, a sea fan. Once discovered, these filefishes are often hesitant to leave their cover and as a result they often become very cooperative subjects for macro photographers.

Little is known about the natural history of **orange filefish**. These medium-sized filefish commonly vary their color from pale to dark in order to try to blend in with their surroundings, but their bodies always show a number of small orange spots. Orange filefish normally inhabit grass, mud or sand bottoms. Adults are usually between 10 and 20 inches long. This species should not be confused with the orange-spotted filefish. Though common in Florida and the Bahamas, orange filefish are considered rare in the Caribbean.

BOXFISHES (COWFISHES AND TRUNKFISHES)

Cowfishes and trunkfishes, which are commonly grouped under the heading boxfishes, are especially noteworthy because of their unusual shapes and their comparatively poor ability as swimmers. The scientific name of their family, Ostraciidea, was born of the Greek word for "shell," and alludes to the bodies of

these fishes which are encased in a hard, shell-like carapace. The carapace has holes that allow for the attachment of fins, and the protuberance of the mouth, eyes and tail. As juveniles, the body profile of boxfishes are generally described as rounded to oval, but as adults they are more triangular in shape.

Cowfishes have a sharp, prominent, horn-like spine above each eye, while trunkfishes do not. Members of both groups often appear stiff and encumbered when swimming. Usually they hover or swim slowly by propelling themselves with the undulating movement of their dorsal, pectoral and anal fins. However, when threatened, they gain additional speed by beating their tail.

When swimming, boxfishes rock back and forth as if they are having difficulty maintaining their orientation. Ichthyologists believe they swim in this manner intentionally in order to help them keep an eye on potential predators that might be

AT A GLANCE

SMOOTH TRUNKFISH

Scientific Name
   Lactophrys triqueter
Habitat
   Reef.
Typical Adult Size
   7 inches.
Sightings
   Commonly seen.
Natural History
   Bony plating protects body.

AT A GLANCE

SCRAWLED COWFISH

Scientific Name
   Lactophrys quadricornis
Habitat
   Reef.
Typical Adult Size
   14 inches.
Sightings
   Occasionally seen.
Natural History
   Body protected by bony plate. In different phases, often resembles honeycomb cowfish. Spine above each eye.

behind them. Some boxfishes are capable of emitting strong secretions to ward off potential predators.

The smallest of the Caribbean species of trunkfishes, **smooth trunkfish** attain a maximum length of approximately 12 inches, but most specimens are much smaller. Smooth trunkfish are usually solitary, but are occasionally seen in small gatherings. Despite their poor swimming ability, smooth trunkfish don't seem to mind being observed from close range by curious divers. You will probably notice that from a distance these fish appear to be black with white spots. However, upon closer examination you can see

AT A GLANCE

SPOTTED TRUNKFISH

Scientific Name
Lactophrys bilcaudalis
Habitat
In water column above shallow reefs, near openings to small crevices, and under ledges.
Typical Adult Size
5 to 12 inches.
Sightings
Occasionally seen.
Natural History
Wary, yet curious. Tend to hide when approached. Stiff bodies and stubby fins combine to make them relativley slow swimmers.

hexagonal patterns located at mid-body. Their movements appear downright clumsy at first, but when you try to approach them, you will likely be surprised at how fast they can swim when they use their tails.

Spotted trunkfish are wary but often curious. They are quick to seek shelter, and when safe they often turn around and peer out at divers. Spotted trunkfish are distinguished by their white mouths and white

AT A GLANCE

HONEYCOMB COWFISH

Scientific Name
Lactophrys polygonia
Habitat
Reef.
Typical Adult Size
14 inches.
Sightings
Occasionally seen.
Natural History
Body encased in bony plate. In various phases often resembles scrawled cowfish. Spine above each eye.

bodies which are covered with a number of dark circular spots.

Honeycomb cowfish tend to be very shy and wary of divers. Though their coloration may vary, they typically appear bluish. This species can be further identified by the horn-like spines above their eyes and the honeycomb pattern which covers the body. Adults reach a length of 18 inches. Honeycomb cowfish are often genuinely curious about divers. But if you pursue or approach them too quickly, they will turn away and try to maintain a more comfortable distance.

PUFFERFISHES

Pufferfishes are among the more amusing of all fishes due to their ability to "puff" up like a balloon in order to protect themselves from potential predators. When threatened, they often quickly suck a lot of water into their stomachs, expanding their bodies nearly three times their normal size.

Puffers are divided into two families: the smooth-skinned puffers (family Tetraodontidae) and the spiny-skinned puffers (family Diodotidae). Smooth-skinned puffers include the **bandtail puffer** and the **sharpnose puffer**, and the spiny-skinned puffers include **porcupine-fishes** and **burrfishes**. As a rule, both groups are relatively slow swimmers, and their ability to inflate is a vital survival adaptation. But puffers also have other means of protecting themselves. Some are camouflage artists who manage to blend in well with their surroundings, while other species often bury themselves in the sand or mud to hide from predators. Some species of puffers inhabit reefs, while others prefer to inhabit the sand flats, mangroves and grass beds adjacent to the reef structure.

The bodies of spiny-skinned puffers (**balloonfish**, **web burrfish**, **bridled burrfish**) and porcupinefish are covered with dozens of sharp spines. When the puffers are relaxed, the spines lay flat next to the body. But when feeling threatened, the act of "puffing up" rigidly erects

AT A GLANCE

BALLOONFISH, PUFFERFISH

Scientific Name
Diodon holocanthus
Habitat
Reef, on sand and mid-water.
Typical Adult Size
19 inches.
Abundance
Occasionally seen.
Natural History
Inflates body to erect numerous, sharp spines by swallowing water when threatened in order to ward off potential predators. Usually solitary, but occasionally seen in schools.

PHOTO TIP

The "hide-and-seek" behavior common to sharpnose puffers can be used to your advantage when trying to photograph them with a single lens reflex camera and a longer macro lens. Once the puffer disappears, have your camera focused on the spot where the puffer hid. Often, curiosity overcomes these inquisitive fish and they soon return, allowing you to get a great portrait. There's little chance that sharpnose puffers will let you put a framer around them during the day. However, if you go night diving with a Nikonos and 1:3 extension tube, you can often gently get your framer around a sleepy sharpnose puffer. You might find them by looking up toward the top of overhanging ledges where these fish often rest by clinging to the reef.

Sharpnose puffers are the most common and the smallest of the Caribbean puffers. They are delightful in the way they scurry away as you approach, and then, overcome with curiosity, swim back to watch you.

They prefer to inhabit reef areas, so they are the species that divers encounter the most. Though they are usually solitary, sharpnose puffers are believed to band together when threatened. When approached by divers, these puffers often play a game of hide-and-seek by swimming in and out of the branches of a gorgonian coral. If you go on one side of the coral, the fish goes to the other, and if you change sides, so does the fish. If you move carefully and do not approach too closely, this game can last for an entire dive.

Sharpnose puffers are found on both sides of the Atlantic. On the western side they range from Bermuda to the north coast of South America including the Gulf of Mexico and Florida. Like other smooth-skinned puffers, sharpnose puffers have strong jaws and beak-like teeth. They feed on a variety of plants and animals, including algae, seagrasses, sponges, crustaceans, worms and hydroids.

AT A GLANCE

SHARPNOSE PUFFER

Scientific Name
Canthigaster rostrata
Habitat
Reef.
Typical Adult Size
3 inches.
Sightings
Commonly seen.
Natural History
Ability to swallow water and "puff up" helps them escape predators.

these protective spines. The spines of many species are long and certainly sharp enough to create a lot of discomfort for a diver who grabs too hard, or to the mouth of a potential predator.

In some parts of the world, most notably Japan, puffers are a highly regarded delicacy called fugu. However, unless the fugu is properly prepared, eating it can lead to a lethal type of food poisoning caused by the tetrodotoxin found within certain parts of the puffer's flesh.

CIGUATERA FISH POISONING

Ciguatera is the most common type of fish poisoning in humans, and it is thought to cause more cases of fish poisoning than all other types combined. Ciguatera is believed to originate with microorganisms called dinoflagellates. Small fishes ingest the dinoflagellates, and the small fish are in turn eaten by larger fishes. The dinoflagellates accumulate as they are passed up the food chain, and in many instances by the time humans catch and eat a fish, the dinoflagellates are present in a concentration high enough to cause food poisoning. The toxins are heat-resistant, and cooking does not break them down or eliminate them.

At onset, the symptoms are usually a tingling feeling around the mouth, tongue, lips and throat. In some cases, the symptoms occur within only a few minutes after consuming the affected fish, and in other cases, symptoms have been reported to occur as late as 30 hours after ingesting a meal. Sometimes, extreme nausea, muscular weakness and aching, general discomfort, and/or diarrhea soon develop. The symptoms are often confused with *tourista*. However, these symptoms should not be taken lightly and medical authorities should be consulted because in extreme cases, ciguatera can be fatal.

More than 300 species of fishes have been implicated in ciguatera poisoning. The list includes barracudas, a variety of groupers and sea basses, jacks, snappers, pompanos, triggerfishes, eels, filefishes, parrotfishes and surgeonfishes. This does not mean that these species are never safe to eat. However, it is good advice to keep abreast with the local news for advisories, and inquire from local authorities if you are spearfishing and plan to eat your catch. In many instances, larger specimens of the same species prove to be toxic while smaller specimens do not. Obviously, the toxins have had a longer period of time to accumulate in a larger fish that has eaten more food. To further confuse the issue, ciguatera is much more common in certain seasons in some places, and completely lacking in other seasons or in the same species at the same time in other locations. Exactly when and where ciguatera will occur remains a mystery.

Ciguatera should be distinguished from both (1) scombroid poisoning which occurs when bacteria accumulate in fish that has spoiled from being left on the shelf for too long, and (2) tetrodon poisoning which can result from eating too much of certain kinds of pufferfishes, ocean sunfish, triggerfishes, porcupinefishes and boxfishes.

PORCUPINEFISHES

Porcupinefishes and **burrfishes** are members of a family called the spiny-skinned puffers. These fishes receive significant protection from the stout spines that cover their bodies. Members of this family are often referred to as boxfish because of their squared-off build. However, this box-like shape is found only in their adult stage. Juveniles only vaguely resemble the adults. The young drift in the open sea until they are ready to develop into adults at which time they move into shallow reef communities. Porcupinefishes and burrfishes use their strong jaws and fused teeth (similar to parrotfishes) to crush their prey, which often consists of hard-shelled crustaceans and mollusks.

Burrfish have short, stubby spines which are always erect, while

AT A GLANCE

PORCUPINEFISH

Scientific Name
Diodon hystrix
Habitat
Reef.
Typical Adult Size
18 inches.
Sightings
Commonly seen.
Natural History
When they "puff up" sharp spines erect to deter predators.

porcupinefish have needle-sharp spines which stand erect only when the puffer inflates. If they feel intimidated, the spiny-skinned puffers, like the smooth-skinned puffers, will grossly inflate their bodies by swallowing water into their expandable guts. When the threat dissipates, puffers can rapidly expel the water and return to their normal size.

For years, divers have been handling puffers until they puff up, and it seemed harmless enough. Almost every underwater photographer has an image of an inflated puffer. Over time, some divers have begun to question the practice. We don't always see the harm we cause as the

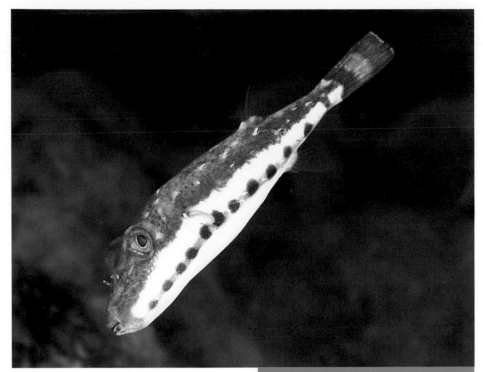

AT A GLANCE

BRIDLED BURRFISH

Scientific Name
Chilomycterus antennatus
Habitat
Reef.
Typical Adult Size
10 inches.
Sightings
Commonly seen.
Natural History
They puff up giving rigidity to their permanently erect spines and making them more ominous.

damage is not immediately obvious. But injury can, and sometimes does, occur. Handling fishes often removes protective coatings from their skin which can lead to serious infections and other problems. And you should also beware—these fishes have very strong jaws equipped with fused teeth which can inflict serious damage to any diver that gets bitten. More than one diver has suffered a

AT A GLANCE

BANDTAIL PUFFER

Scientific Name
Sphoeroides spengleri
Habitat
Reef, rubble zone and seagrass beds.
Typical Adult Size
5 to 8 inches.
Sightings
Commonly seen in some areas.
Natural History
Hover near bottom.

broken finger due to a bite from a frightened pufferfish.

Several species of porcupinefishes and burrfishes are commonly encountered in Caribbean waters. By far the largest of these is the porcupinefish, which reaches a length of three feet as an adult. Porcupinefish are usually found peering out from the openings of caves and crevices, or under ledges where they hide. In addition to their size, porcupinefish can be distinguished by the spots on their fins as well as their bodies.

Balloonfish and burrfishes tend to be considerably smaller than porcupinefish.

JAMES SPOTILA

patterns differ from species to species, but they differ significantly from one population of the same species to the next. In green turtles, for example, some well-studied local populations are known to nest and feed in the same region, while other groups annually migrate 1,500 miles between their nesting and feeding grounds.

Excellent swimmers, sea turtles are well-adapted for long-distance migrations and for sudden bursts of speed when needed. Their flippers have been modified over time to aid in swimming rather than walking. Their powerful fore flippers are long and paddlelike and provide thrust, while the rear flippers are used to enhance stability and provide directional control by serving in a rudder-like capacity. Unlike their terrestrial counterparts, sea turtles are not capable of retracting their head or limbs inside their shell.

Sea turtles usually appear somewhat lethargic and cruise at a rate only slightly faster than divers can comfortably swim. However, they are capable of rapid bursts of speed. In fact, several species have been clocked in excess of 20 miles per hour.

In addition to their ability as swimmers, sea turtles are excellent divers. Leatherbacks are known to repeatedly dive to 1,000 feet, and scientists believe they dive as deep as 3,900 feet at times. As with all cold-blooded animals, sea turtles have comparatively slow metabolic rates. This trait helps them routinely make active dives lasting as long as 45 minutes. When at rest on the bottom, sea turtles have been documented to stay submerged for as long as five hours. This resting period should not be confused with the extended periods of hibernation found in green turtles and logger-

AT A GLANCE

LEATHERBACK TURTLE

Scientific Name
Dermochelys coriacea
Habitat
Usually found in open sea except during nesting season.
Typical Adult Size
Carapace, 4 to 6 feet long; 250 to 1,300 pounds.
Sightings
Seldom seen (endangered).
Natural History
Seven easily noticed, prominent ridges run the length of the shell-like carapace; carapace lacks numerous overlapping plates (scutes) found in other species. Highly migratory, with adults traveling 3,000 miles roundtrip between feeding and nesting grounds. Delicate jaws designed to cut jellyfishes, pelagic tunicates and other food sources in scissor-like fashion. Repeatedly dive to 1,000 feet, maybe as deep as 3,900 feet.

HAWKSBILL TURTLE

Scientific Name
Eretmochelys imbricata

Habitat
Shallow, coastal waters, lagoons, back bays and estuaries, as well as open sea on some occasions.

Typical Adult Size
Carapace, 2.5 to 3 feet; 100 to 200 pounds.

Sightings
Seldom seen (endangered).

Natural History
Hooked, narrow beak which forms tip of upper jaw, and jagged scutes near tail serve as good identifying characteristics. Prey on tunicates, sponges, shrimp and small squid. Non-migratory. Age of sexual maturity ranges from 3 to 13 years.

AT A GLANCE

GREEN SEA TURTLE

Scientific Name
Chelonia mydas

Habitat
Shallow, coastal waters, lagoons, back bays and estuaries as well as open sea on some occasions.

Typical Adult Size
Carapace, 40 inches; 300 to 350 pounds, documented to 649 pounds.

Sightings
Seldom seen (endangered), but probably the most commonly encountered Caribbean species.

Natural History
Color of meat, not shell, responsible for name. Reddish-brown to gray carapace is oval-shaped. Jaws of adults finely serrated to help crop algae and seagrasses. During early stages of life, feed primarily on range of crustaceans, mollusks, echinoderms, some cnidarians and some fishes. Age of sexual maturity ranges from 3 to 13 years.

heads. These species are known to spend several months on end buried in mud on the sea floor.

The diet of sea turtles varies tre-

JAMES SPOTILA

Nesting takes place at night during the warmest times of the year. Here a leatherback lays a clutch of eggs in a "body pit" she has dug.

mendously from species to species. Within the same species, diet varies according to age. Some sea turtles are herbivorous (plant eaters), some carnivorous (prey on other animals), and some are omnivorous (eat both plants and animals). Not surprisingly, sea turtle jaws are designed to help them acquire their favorite food. For example, the jaws of adult green sea turtles are finely serrated, helping them crop algae and seagrasses. During the first year or so of their lives, green sea turtles feed mostly on a range of crustaceans, mollusks, echinoderms, some cnidarians and some fishes.

Hawksbill turtles have a narrow head with pointed jaws, a design that helps them prey on a variety of animals that commonly live or seek refuge in reef crevices. Their food sources include tunicates, sponges, shrimp and small squid.

Loggerheads and Kemp's ridleys have jaws that have been designed for crushing and grinding. In fact the big head of the loggerhead, as well as its barnacle-covered carapace, serve as excellent identifying characteristics. These species feed on a variety of crustaceans, mollusks and jellyfishes, in addition to seagrasses and algae. Leatherback turtles have very delicate jaws that are designed to cut in scissor-like fashion. They feed primarily on jellyfishes, pelagic tunicates and other soft-bodied animals. To help them swallow their prey, the mouths of leatherbacks are lined with small spines that angle back toward the stomach.

Reproduction in sea turtles is a fascinating, though not a completely understood, phenomenon. The age of sexual maturity varies not only from species to species, but also varies dramatically within a given species. For example, in green turtles and hawksbills, studies have shown the age of sexual maturity to range from 3 to 13 years old. However, some studies indicate that sexual maturity may be reached much later.

Distinguishing between the sexes on a dive is rather tricky, but in all species, the tail of the male is longer than that of the female. So when a male and female are together and you can see their tails, it is possible to tell which is which.

When sea turtles mate, two or more males generally pursue the favors of a single female. Fertilization is internal and copulation takes place in the water. At some point, anywhere from a few days to a few weeks after mating, females head ashore to nest.

Nesting behavior tends to follow a set pattern in all sea turtles. Females typically come ashore near high tide at night during the warmest times of the year to lay their eggs. They crawl well beyond the high tide line and dig a "body pit," or hole in the sand that is slightly larger and deeper than their body.

Toward the back of the body pit, the female excavates a small depression called the egg cavity. She de-

AT A GLANCE

KEMP'S RIDLEY TURTLE

Scientific Name
Lepidochelys kempi

Habitat
Shallow, coastal waters, lagoons, back bays and estuaries, as well as open sea on some occasions.

Typical Adult Size
Carapace, just over 2 feet; 80 to 100 pounds.

Sightings
Seldom seen (gravely endangered). In 1995, 800 nesting females were reported in Nuevo Rancho, Mexico.

Natural History
Smallest and rarest of Caribbean sea turtles. Heart-shaped gray to green carapace with the indentation behind head. Jaws designed for crushing and grinding. Prey upon variety of crustaceans, mollusks, jellyfishes, seagrasses and algae.

posits between 80 and 100 round white eggs that are slightly larger than a chicken's into this cavity. By laying their eggs above the high tide line, future tides will not erode their nests and expose the eggs.

As a rule, it takes the female between one and two hours to lay all of her eggs. The eggs are soft-shelled and do not break as they are dropped onto the sand. After depositing her eggs, she covers her nest with sand and returns to sea. Females lay up to nine clutches of eggs in a single mating season, and mate every two to three years.

Nesting female Kemp's ridleys band together in huge groups called *arribadas*, the Spanish word for "arrivals." As recently as 1942, *arribadas* with as many as 50,000 Kemp's ridley turtles could be seen along the shores of Rancho Nuevo, Mexico, which lies along the northern coast of the Yucatan Peninsula. This beach is the only nesting site in the world for Kemp's ridleys, a species that has been pushed to the brink of extinction by shrimpers in the Gulf of Mexico. As recently as several years ago, there were estimated to be only about 400 nesting females surviving. In the summer of 1995, 800 nesting females were counted at Rancho Nuevo. Also in 1995, conservation efforts resulted in several females nesting on the Texas shore for the first time in recent history. Scientists had previously released hatchlings on these beaches in an attempt to imprint them as nesting sites in hopes they would return.

The Caribbean coast of Costa Rica is a favorite nesting site of green, leatherback and hawksbill turtles. A beach known as *Tortuguero* (Spanish for "place of the turtle") seems to be the most popular site. From

PETER PRITCHARD/CENTER FOR MARINE CONSERVATION

May through November thousands of turtles lay their eggs in the sands of *Tortuguero*.

A fascinating aspect of the mating and egg-laying ritual that most scientists agree upon is that the hatchling's sex is not determined at the time the egg is fertilized. Instead, the sex is determined by the temperature of the sand that surrounds the egg during the incubation period. As a rule, the deeper any given egg rests in the nest, the cooler the surrounding sand. These eggs produce females, while the shallower eggs which are exposed to higher nest temperatures yield males.

This phenomenon produces a potentially serious problem for sea turtles. An imbalance in the number of males and females can result in places where the shallower eggs are exploited more often by humans and other animals. If the potential imbalance were left to Mother Nature, she would surely solve the problem on her own. But with mankind's intervention in terms of hunting and development of land, along with the introduction of pigs, goats and dogs to some nesting beaches, the resulting exploitation has created an imbalance that tends to yield fewer males.

Incubation time varies from 50 to 70 days. Turtle eggs usually hatch at night. Upon hatching, the newborns quickly head for sea, but life is most unkind to hatchling populations during the early stages of their lives. In fact, many specialists believe that fewer than 10 percent of the newborns manage to survive their first year as they are heavily preyed upon by sharks, other fishes, crabs and birds. Some of those that do manage to survive the onslaught live comparatively long lives. Sea turtles are documented to live at least 30 years, and they are suspected to live to be as old as 50.

It is disheartening to note that all seven species of the world's sea turtles are threatened or endangered. Even with the intense efforts of many conservation-minded orga-

A number of organizations and institutions are working to maintain existing sea turtle populations and to reestablish depleted stocks. The famous turtle farm on Grand Cayman is a leader in the effort.

nizations, the future of sea turtles remains most uncertain. As is the case with so many other species, their predicament is due to a combination of natural forces and the intervention of man. In some parts of the world, the hunting of sea turtles is still legal, and in other places it is often illegal only on paper. Unfortunately, there is usually too little money or effort dedicated to enforcing the law.

The commercialization of many once-isolated nesting beaches has also taken its toll. Artificial lighting from street lights, sidewalks and other sources can confuse hatchlings. When first born, an instinctive orientation to light helps young sea turtles head in the direction of the sea and away from the predators of land. Even faint artificial light can interfere with this instinct.

Entanglement in the nets of shrimp trawlers and ingested plastics are other causes of concern for sea turtles. Plastics, which can look somewhat like jellyfishes and salps, can prove fatal to sea turtles when swallowed.

However, there is some good news. Strong conservation efforts in many places around the world could make a difference in the turtle's survival. The famous turtle farm in Grand Cayman is part of that effort. There, turtles are raised not only for food, but also for stocking.

18

Phylum: *Chordata* Subphylum: *Vertebrata* Class: *Mammalia*

MARINE MAMMALS:
MANATEES, DOLPHINS AND WHALES

*E*ver since mankind has taken to the sea, we have been captivated by marine mammals. The reasons for our fascination are varied, and it is likely that a number of factors combine to create the intense feelings that we have about marine mammals. Certainly we admire many marine mammals for their beauty, grace, entertaining antics and ability to survive in such demanding surroundings. Some of us envy the variety of adaptations that enable marine mammals to perform in the water at a level that humans can only imagine or admire in other creatures. Surely many people feel some collective sense of guilt for the cruelties that our species has imposed on so many species of marine mammals over the years. And it is also likely that many humans feel some sense of kinship with all other mammals, simply because we too are mammals.

In several rivers in Florida, boaters, snorkelers and divers can observe American manatees. These lovable creatures can provide us with entertainment that is rarely surpassed in the underwater world. However, it is paramount to keep in mind that American manatees, like so many species of marine mammals, are an endangered species. So along with our opportunity to observe comes the responsibility not to disturb or harass. Strict regulations regarding manatee encounters have been established by government agencies, and those standards are enforced.

No matter what our reasons are, there is no doubt that those divers who have been fortunate enough to swim eyeball-to-eyeball with a whale, or to have shared a similar experience with a manatee, sea lion, seal or otter, cherish those dives as some of their most memorable.

In the Caribbean, Bahamas and Florida, divers have opportunities to swim with spotted dolphins, bottlenose dolphins, manatees, and occasionally a few other species. A variety of dolphins and whales are also seen on a regular basis from the decks of ships.

The classification of marine mammals includes whales, dolphins, manatees, dugongs, sea lions, seals, sea otters and walruses. Evolutionary specialists maintain that all of these seagoing creatures evolved from terrestrial ancestors. Considerable evidence links marine mammals with their counterparts on land, as the two groups share a number of important characteristics. All mammals are warm-blooded vertebrates; breathe air through lungs, not gills; bear live young which the females nurse through mammary glands; and have hair or fur at some stage of their development, though in some species it is evident only during their embryonic stage.

What special problems does living in the sea pose for air-breathing, warm-blooded creatures? How, for example, do marine mammals avoid decompression sickness (the bends), and how do they maintain their

body temperature? Nature has provided marine mammals with a number of vital adaptations that enable them to avoid the bends even though they make extremely deep dives for extended periods of time. Though the issue is rather complex, key factors are: (1) the heart rate of marine mammals slows significantly when they dive, a trait which reduces the amount of nitrogen introduced to their system; (2) air that would otherwise be trapped in their lungs, allowing for the exchange of gases and the introduction of nitrogen, is pushed toward the throat as their airway compresses with increased depth, thus preventing the absorption of additional nitrogen in the lungs; and (3) circulation to less vital, peripheral body parts which release nitrogen slowly is greatly reduced when the animals dive.

Marine mammals solve the problem of keeping warm in a number of ways. Most have a thick layer of fat that helps insulate them from the cool water temperatures. This layer of blubber varies from species to species. Animals, such as walruses and many whales that live in polar waters, possess thicker layers of fat than manatees, dolphins and whales that inhabit tropical seas. The layer of fat also provides for an energy reserve when food is not available. Sea otters are the only sea mammals that lack a layer of fat. They combat the problem of staying warm by eating incredible amounts of food, and by having some air trapped in their coat, which helps prevent their skin from getting wet.

Reproduction in marine mammals differs in several significant ways from that of land mammals. The gestation period of mammals is longer than that of the lower animals. The longer gestation period allows the embryo to be well developed at birth. In fact, at birth marine mammals are roughly one-third the length of their mother. This advanced stage of development greatly increases the chance for individual survival.

Many marine mammals go without food during their mating season so that the adults can devote more energy and time to guarding, nursing and training their offspring. Fasting also enables some species to migrate the long distances between their feeding and calving grounds in a shorter time because the animals do not have to spend time in the pursuit of food.

The phenomenon known as delayed implantation plays a fundamental role in the reproductive picture of some marine mammals. In many species, sexually mature males and females are together only during the calving and breeding season. Nature has cleverly provided a way that enables these species to calve and mate within a very short time frame. Females are capable of successful copulation within a few hours to a few weeks after they deliver their young. However, the fertilized eggs are not implanted in the uterine wall for several months, hence the term delayed implantation. This phenomenon enables the males and females to gather at a specific time of year, often in specific locations they migrate to, for as short a time as possible. The short time required is important when considering that many species fast during the calving and breeding portion of their annual cycle.

MANATEES

Manatees are described in an order of vertebrates known as Sirenea. This name is derived from the Greek word for sirens, mythical temptresses who lured sailors to their deaths, and its use alludes to the fact that ancient mariners are reported to have mistaken these mammals, which weigh up to 1,500 pounds, for mermaids. Four species are described in the order Sirenea. Three live in waters that are surrounded by the Atlantic Ocean, and the fourth is the Indo-Pacific species known as the dugong. All of these species are com- monly referred to as sea cows.

Only a little over 200 years ago, a fifth species of Sirenean existed in the waters of the Bering Sea. This species was called the Steller's sea cow, which was the largest of the Sireneans, growing to a length of more than 25 feet and weighing up to 9,000 pounds. The species was first discovered by western man in 1741 in an area near the Bering Sea off Alaska. Unfortunately, the meat of Steller's sea cows tasted good to humans, and the downfall of the species began almost immediately. By 1768, only 27 years later, the species became extinct due to overhunting.

It would be nice to say that we have learned from our dreadful mistakes and that other species of mana-

---

AT A GLANCE

MANATEE, AMERICAN MANATEE

Scientific Name
  Trichecus manatus
Habitat
  Shallow water of rivers, bays, estuaries, mud flats, Caribbean off Central America, and Gulf of Mexico. Rarely seen in open sea.
Typical Adult Size
  8 to 13 feet long; 400 to 800 pounds.
Sightings
  Endangered but commonly seen in some areas.
Natural History
  Grayish, sausage-shaped bodies often covered with algae. Usually appear motionless, but capable of swimming close to 12 miles per hour; easily disturbed by divers and snorkelers. Herbivores. Mothers nurse calves for up to two years. Produce one calf once every three years. Sexual maturity at six to ten years.

tees are safe. Unfortunately, some estimates show there may be less than 1,000 Florida manatees remaining.

By far the worst threat to manatees comes from man, and a high percentage of these mammals have lost flippers or other body parts due to collisions with boats and their propellers. The lack of natural predators has led to a lack of fear of just about everything, power boats included, and unfortunately, collisions are common. Despite the fact that manatees are known to live in excess of 30 years, many well-credentialed scientists believe that the accidental death rate and the natural mortality rate of the Florida population exceeds the birth rate. However, Florida has taken considerable steps to reduce the pressure from divers, boaters and commercial development.

In Florida, and in the estuaries and mud flats of several Central American countries, most notably Belize, the species of manatee that is commonly observed is the **American manatee.** They attain a size of 13 feet and 800 pounds, but are not as large as the dugongs of the Indo-Pacific.

Like the other species of manatees, American manatees spend almost their entire lives in shallow water and rarely travel into the deeper waters of the open sea. They never venture forth onto land. Despite living in water, manatees, like all other marine mammals, are air breathers and must come to the surface for respiration. Manatees breathe through large nostril flaps located near the top of their head. This positioning enables manatees to get life-sustaining air at the surface with only a minimum amount of effort.

Like all other mammals, manatees need to maintain a constant body temperature. As a result, American manatees are attracted to the spring-fed, freshwater rivers of Florida because they maintain a constant winter temperature of close to

72°F even when the water temperature dips significantly lower in surrounding waters. Water temperatures in the shallow water estuaries and mud flats off the coast of some Central American countries also maintain fairly constant temperatures within the bounds that are comfortable to manatees.

The grayish bodies of manatees are often colored with patches of green algae, giving some animals a mottled appearance. In some manatees the skin texture is quite rough, and in others, rather smooth. Most specimens have some sparse, coarse body hair. From a purely visual perspective, their skin bears some resemblance to that of elephants.

Manatees have flippers which assist in maneuverability, while thrust is gained by the use of their rounded paddle-like tails. Manatees often appear to be motionless; however, they can sink or rise without apparent effort simply by adjusting their buoyancy. Surprising as it might seem, manatees have been clocked at speeds approaching 12 miles per hour.

Manatees are herbivores, their favorite foods being a variety of seagrasses. They especially love to consume hydrilla, the frilly grass that many boaters despise. In addition, manatees readily feed on water hyacinths and other grasses. Adults ingest as much as 100 pounds of grass per day. With an appetite like that, it is easy to understand how a herd of manatees can easily consume the daily production of a seagrass meadow. Snorkelers and divers who have spent a lot of time in the water with manatees can sometimes locate them by listening for the grinding and crunching noises associated with feeding.

The bristle-covered jowls of manatees are beautifully designed for the task of consuming huge quantities of grasses. When feeding, manatees use their facial bristles to dig into bottom sediment. Then the animals shake their heads vigorously to dislodge any attached sedi-

ment before finally chewing or swallowing the plants whole.

Manatees do not possess incisor-like teeth. Instead, their only teeth are designed for grinding. This adaptation assists them in eating, but their lack of long, sharp teeth leaves sea cows somewhat defenseless. Fortunately, manatees do not have major natural predators in the waters where they reside. In open sea, American manatees are sometimes attacked by sharks, but large sharks are rarely seen in the waters inhabited by manatees.

Nursing behavior is commonly seen. The mammary glands of the female are located under the flippers, so if you see a baby manatee at a mother's flipper, you are obligated to leave the animals alone. The gestation period of manatees is approximately 13 months, and mothers nurse their calves for as long as two years following birth. Each adult female can produce a single calf only once every three years. It is believed sexual maturity is reached between the ages of 6 and 10.

Manatee calves vocalize a lot when being scratched or rubbed. The adults also use high-pitched squeaks and whistles in communication. These audible sounds of pleasure should not be mistaken with the echolocation used by dolphins. The sounds emitted by manatees are not a form of natural sonar, but certainly the sounds do help manatees keep track of one another.

During most of the year, the American manatees that live in the rivers of Florida disperse into small groups, and it is not uncommon to see solitary animals. However, during the colder months of winter, manatees tend to congregate in areas with warmer water such as Crystal River. Located north of Tampa and southwest of Ocala, Crystal River is fed by thousands of underground springs which flow in at a year-round temperature of 72°F. It is in these legendary waters that many snorkelers and divers encounter manatees.

Some manatees seem to enjoy gentle, open-handed stroking on their bodies and necks, but not on their tails. Once a diver has gained a manatee's confidence, it is not uncommon for the animal to roll over, exposing its large underbelly, which manatees love to have scratched in a gentle fashion. It is against the law to pursue, harass or hang onto manatees, but one can remain motionless and allow a curious manatee to approach. That might sound like once-in-a-lifetime odds, but manatees often display a sense of curiosity about humans. Sleeping, eating and nursing animals should be left alone.

Due to the Marine Mammal Protection Act and the endangered species status assigned to manatees, there are strict regulations governing when, where and how divers can legally encounter the animals in Florida. Designated sectors of Crystal River have been denoted as manatee sanctuaries where entry by divers and boaters is prohibited. In other sectors, boating speed limits are strictly enforced.

As one ponders the future of manatees, the words of William Beebe, the first curator of birds at the Bronx Zoo, come to mind. In a quote that is often referenced by naturalists, Beebe stated, "When the last individual of a race of living things breathes no more, another Heaven and another Earth must pass before such a One can be again." One thought that can keep all of us going in the quest to save the American manatee is that despite all the problems, most scientists believe this is a battle that can still be won. Extinction is not inevitable.

CETACEANS

Dolphins and whales are often collectively referred to as cetaceans, a term derived from the name of their order Cetacea, which in turn was derived from the Greek "ceta" for whale. While many laymen separate dolphins and whales into different categories according to size, this popularized classification system has little meaning within the scientific community. Dolphins are actually types of whales, and are described in a separate family (Delphinidae) within the suborder of toothed whales. In terms of classification, most scientists consider whether the animal is a filter feeder or a toothed whale to be far more important than size.

BALEEN WHALES

Most of the ocean's largest creatures are filter-feeding whales. These whales are also known as baleen whales, and some of the larger species are commonly referred to as great whales. Baleen whales use a variety of strategies to feed on dense concentrations of plankton, small fishes and other small animals. Some species scoop small organisms from the sea floor, some skim along the surface, and others rush vertically upward with mouth agape toward their prey. But no matter which strategy they use, all depend upon long fibers or plates, called baleen (once called whalebone), to sieve out their prey. Baleen fibers are horny plates that are arranged along both sides of the upper jaw. The plates, which look somewhat like the fibers of an oversized toothbrush, are made from keratin-like material similar to human fingernails. The baleen plates vary in size from species to species, from less than 12 inches long in minke whales to almost 14 feet long in bowhead whales.

The term great whales probably originated in deference to the enormous size of the larger species of baleen whales such as the blue whales, fin whales and humpbacks. Blue whales attain sizes just over 100 feet long and 120 tons, proportions that make them the largest animals to have ever lived on earth. But clearly not all baleen whales are anywhere close to that size. The term great whales is misleading in some cases, as the larger toothed whales and toothed dolphins, such as sperm whales and killer whales, are as large as the smaller species of baleen whales. Other species of baleen whales includes **sei whales, gray whales, right whales, pygmy right whales, bowhead whales** and **minke whales**.

Baleen whales are placed in the suborder Mysteceti. Most filter-feeding whales inhabit temperate and polar seas, and only a few of these species are commonly encountered in Caribbean waters. These species include **blue whales, fin whales**, and **humpback whales**. Not too many years ago prior to the heyday of whale hunting, blue whales were widespread, though they were probably never considered common. Today blue whales range through all oceans, but they are typically found only in small pods. Blue whales have an overall blue-gray to black color. Their bodies are long and surprisingly slender, but the head is quite broad. Their mouths are almost 20 feet long. Grooved throat pleats allow their throats to expand in accordion-like fashion when they feed.

Blue whales are only rarely seen by divers. From the deck of a boat, one of their key identifying features is the small sickle-shaped dorsal fin which is located well down the back of the animal toward the tail.

Fin whales, often called finback whales, are the second largest of all the whales. Approximately 20 feet long at birth, adults are typically 60 to 80 feet in length. Fin whales are often solitary, and are almost always found in groups of 10 or fewer. Finbacks are usually found in the open sea, but they are also observed in productive coastal waters. They have long, comparatively slender bodies. Perhaps their most unusual identifying character is their asymmetrical coloration. Finbacks are

typically brown to dark gray on their back, and white on their underside. Interestingly, the right side of the jaw and the baleen plates of the right side are white, while those on the left side of the jaw are dark. A light gray chevron-like marking is often present just behind the head. Numerous throat grooves are prominent, and their small dorsal fin is located well back on the body, a feature which can cause initial confusion with blue whales.

Humpback whales have become wellknown as the singing whales. Recordings of their songs are often recognized among the general public as a result of increased public awareness campaigns. Humpback whales have stocky bodies that narrow to a slender tail stock. A typical adult reaches a size of close to 50 feet and 100,000 pounds. Two features make identification comparatively easy. First, the massive bodies of humpbacks are covered with large,

wart-like protuberances, and second, their extremely long flippers can be almost as long as one-third of their overall length. The flipper is almost pure white, both on the top and bottom in Caribbean (Atlantic) humpbacks, while the top of the flippers in Pacific humpbacks is dark like the body.

The songs of the humpbacks have been well-studied in recent years. Scientists agree that the songs play an important part in the communication between whales, but exactly what the role of the songs is remains uncertain. Apparently, not all humpbacks sing, a fact which has contributed to the belief on the part of some scientists that only sexually mature males sing in an effort to outcompete other males in attracting a mate.

Perhaps even more interesting is the fact that the songs evolve over time. All whales in the same area sing the same song, but over the course of time the song changes, and

AT A GLANCE

HUMPBACK WHALE

Scientific Name
Megaptera novaengliea

Habitat
Cosmopolitan. Open ocean from tropical to polar seas. Some calve and breed in comparatively shallow water of Silver Bank off Dominican Republic.

Typical Adult Size
35 to 60 feet, to 100,000 pounds.

Sightings
Seldom seen (endangered), but appear to be making a comeback.

Natural History
Long, white pectoral flippers and large, warty protuberances on skin serve as excellent identifying characteristics. Sometimes known as the "singing whales" due to songs of mature males which are thought to be used to attract a mate. Females often accompanied by escort males. Highly migratory, traveling to polar waters during summer and warmer seas in winter.

it is never the same from year to year.

Humpback whales are often sighted in an area known as Silver Bank near the Dominican Republic, and in the open sea around the Turks and Caicos. Like many baleen whales, humpbacks are considered to be migratory. Their migration routes are not completely understood, but they are generally found in polar waters during summers and in warm tropical waters during the

EYE TO EYE WITH A CREATURE 500 TIMES MY SIZE

From the skiff we had seen several dozen humpbacks over the course of the day. More times than I really care to remember we had slipped into the water as quietly as we possibly could, but all we had to show for our efforts were a handful of fleeting glimpses and tired bodies. We were at the Silver Bank, out of Puerto Plata in the Dominican Republic under the umbrella of the North Atlantic Cetacean Research Center, and had all of the necessary permits and permissions to try to film the whales in the water. The code of ethics, and past history, required that we allow the whales to come to us, if and when they chose. With a large, unconfined animal, any encounter is clearly at their discretion.

We had decided to take a short break after two hours of surface observations in the early afternoon heat, when we encountered a pair of whales, a female with an escort, within a few yards of the mother ship. I was free diving with my long time pal Steve Drogin, and remember telling Steve in a rather flippant fashion that we might as well give it a try because we'll never get a shot of a humpback whale when we are belly up to the bar. I didn't have high expectations, but almost as soon as we hit the water the female turned toward us.

I soon found myself bobbing on the surface directly over her head. More than 50 feet and 100,000 pounds of humpback whale couldn't have been more than three feet below me. Even though I had a Nikonos camera with a wide-angle lens in my hand, I was too close to take a good picture.

All I could see in my viewfinder was a slab of whale. I tried to swim to my right to get a better perspective, but the whale turned as I did. So I went left, and once again the whale turned with me. Suddenly it dawned on me—this was a game and I was the object of the humpback's curiosity.

Moments later the whale shot past me. Then a wall of water from the tail created an enormous splash and the whale disappeared as Steve and I stared at each other in disbelief at the whale's size, grace and power.

Soon the whale turned and came back toward us. Along with Howard and Michele Hall, and Bob Cranston, Steve and I spent the next several hours with the whales, often getting within a few feet of the female's head as we watched her watch us. Their body control is amazing. On a number of occasions I was within inches of the female, so close I could see the barnacles attached to her extending their feather feet into the water column in an effort to feed, but never once did she touch me. A dozen times or more I felt like I could have reached out and touched her, but something inside of me told me that it would be some kind of violation, so I abstained.

The memory of that dive will remain forever etched in my mind's eye. It was humbling, awe-inspiring, exhilarating, highly educational, personal and intimidating all at the same time. But more than anything, it was 100 percent pure fun to feel so alive and to see such a magnificent animal in the wild from such close range. It's a great life!—Marty Snyderman

The tail of a humpback whale can easily be 10 feet wide. The markings on the tails are unique to each whale, and scientists use the markings as a means of identifying individual animals.

winters of the hemisphere in which they live.

Despite their massive size, many whales are extremely wary of divers and snorkelers. In many instances, even large whales go to great lengths to alter their course in order to avoid coming close to divers. But there are exceptions, and occasionally whales become very curious about divers and snorkelers.

Few moments in diving are as memorable and awe-inspiring as those spent staring into the eye of a large whale. Whales generally demonstrate remarkable control over their bodies, repeatedly coming to within inches of divers and snorkelers without ever striking them, though there is a consensus among experienced divers that many whales do not like people to get immediately behind their tail. Many people think the reason for this is that sharks occasionally bite the tails of whales, and having an unfamiliar body behind them makes the whales feel vulnerable.

Sometimes whale calves get excited by divers, and they tend to get a little aggressive in their play. Divers have reported being pushed and bumped by what they described as playful calves. But they were quick to point out that a playful bump from a 15-ton animal can hurt a lot. Whales are wild animals and should always be treated with proper respect.

TOOTHED WHALES AND DOLPHINS

Toothed whales, a group which includes both the toothed dolphins and whales, differ from filter-feeding whales in several significant ways. Certainly one of the most obvious ways is that toothed whales have canine-like teeth as opposed to baleen plates. They feed primarily on fishes, squids and crustaceans as opposed to plankton. Toothed whales have only one nostril, or blowhole, while all baleen whales have a pair of nostrils. When baleen whales spout or exhale, a careful look will reveal two columns of vapor, while only a single column is created by exhaling toothed whales. Toothed whales are described in the suborder Odonteceti.

As a general rule, toothed whales are smaller than baleen whales, though there are some notable exceptions. The largest of the toothed whales is the **sperm whale**. Adult male sperm whales commonly reach a length of 40 feet, and may approach 60 feet. By contrast, a num-

AT A GLANCE

SPERM WHALE

Scientific Name
Physter catadon

Habitat
Open sea in tropical and temperate seas.

Typical Adult Size
45 feet and 80,000 pounds, but males reach 60 feet in length.

Sightings
Commonly seen in some areas, but seldom seen in most parts of Caribbean and associated waters. Estimated world population 1.5 to 2 million animals.

Natural History
Largest of the toothed whales. Large, squared-off head that is almost one-third of total body length. Single blow-hole on left side of head. Feed primarily on fishes, squids and crustaceans captured during dives to as deep as 10,000 feet that last for up to 90 minutes. Often gather in groups called rafts on surface.

BOB CRANSTON

ber of species of dolphins are less than six feet long when fully grown.

Another significant difference between the baleen whales and the toothed whales is that toothed whales are known to use echolocation to navigate and to find their prey. Echolocation is a form of natural sonar that is believed to work as follows: Toothed whales emit sounds from a special organ in the head. A fatty organ called the melon, which is located in the head, focuses the sound waves into directional beams. The sound waves strike objects in the water and are reflected back to an organ called the acoustic window located in the animal's lower jaw. The sound is then transmitted to the inner ear and then to the brain for processing.

Tests have demonstrated that the echolocation system in dolphins is able to distinguish between objects that differ only slightly in shape and density. This degree of sophistication enables the toothed whales to discriminate between prey, potential predators, hazards, other members of their own species, and various other objects.

Divers can often hear the series of high-pitched whistles and clicks emitted by dolphins. These sounds can be heard for considerable distances underwater, and on many occasions dolphins are heard long before they appear within the limits of visibility.

Far too many species of toothed whales and dolphins inhabit the waters of the Caribbean for all to be covered in this text. A brief discussion of a limited selection of Caribbean species follows.

Sperm whales are probably the most widely known of all the whales. They are known to many laymen as the whale named Moby Dick, the cetacean star of Herman Melville's classic. Sperm whales have a shape that makes them nearly unmistakable. They have a large, squared-off head that is almost one-third as long as the overall length of the body. There is a single blow hole on the left side of the head, and the long, narrow lower jaw fits tightly into the underside of the head. The rounded flippers are comparatively small.

Sperm whales have between 18 and 25 long, conical teeth on each side of the lower jaw. These teeth help them snare their favorite prey of giant squid, octopuses and a variety of fishes. Sperm whales are known to make dives as deep as 10,000 feet. These dives can last for as long as 90 minutes as the whales scour the depths for food. Adapted for life in the deep oceans, sperm whales inhabit all open oceans except those in the polar ice fields. They are usually seen on the surface between their dives, "rafting up" in small pods.

A similar yet smaller species known as the **pygmy sperm whale** also inhabits tropical seas worldwide. Reaching a maximum length of only about 12 feet, relatively little is known about pygmy sperm whales. When sighted, they are often mistaken as juvenile sperm whales.

Killer whales are occasionally seen in Caribbean waters. Also commonly called **orcas**, killer whales typically prefer the cooler waters of

AT A GLANCE

KILLER WHALE, ORCA

Scientific Name
Orcinus orca

Habitat
Cosmopolitan. Typically cooler waters of temperate and polar seas, but do inhabit tropical waters. Often seen very close to shore in many areas.

Typical Adult Size
20 feet and 16,000 pounds, but full-grown males, the larger sex, reach length of 30 feet.

Sightings
Seldom seen in Caribbean, but common in many parts of their range.

Natural History
Largest member of the dolphin family. Highly social animals that live in large pods headed by dominant female. Some pods highly migratory (transient pods), some nonmigratory (resident pods). Males possess large, tall dorsal fin. Feed on wide variety of prey ranging from seabirds to blue whales.

temperate and polar seas, but they do range worldwide in tropical seas. Orcas are the largest member of the family of dolphins. Male killer whales are known for their towering dorsal fins. Full-grown males, which are significantly larger than the females, reach a length of close to 30 feet.

The unique coloration of orcas makes identification in the field comparatively easy. Their back and sides are black with the exception of a large teardrop-shaped patch of white behind and above each eye. There is also a variable white saddle-shaped patch on the underbelly. The snout is rounded.

Orcas prey on a wide variety of animals, including seabirds, turtles, fishes, sharks, seals, sea lions, dolphins and even other much larger whales. Orcas are known to be highly efficient hunters that work in cooperative pods of 2 to 20 animals.

When working in cooperative hunting pods, orcas have been documented attacking fully grown blue whales.

While many of the larger species of whales just mentioned are only rarely seen even from the deck of a boat in the waters of the Caribbean, the Bahamas and Florida, it is common for divers and boaters to encounter several species of dolphins. These species include **spotted dolphins**, **common dolphins**, **bottlenose dolphins** and **spinner dolphins**.

Very few diving experiences anywhere in the world are as spectacular as swimming with a pod of spotted dolphins in the crystal-clear waters of the Bahamas. While divers occasionally report encounters with other species and with other pods of spotted dolphins, in recent years the pods that frequent the Little Bahama Bank have allowed re-

AT A GLANCE

ATLANTIC SPOTTED DOLPHIN, PANTROPICAL SPOTTED DOLPHIN, SPOTTED DOLPHIN

Scientific Name
Stenella attenuata

Habitat
Shallow waters near reefs, over sand flats, and open sea.

Typical Adult Size
Males to 9 feet, females slightly shorter and less heavy-bodied.

Sightings
Commonly seen.

Natural History
Juveniles not spotted. Spots appear with onset of sexual maturity. Highly social animals that live in family groups called pods. Live as long as 45 years. Prey upon a variety of crustaceans, squids and fishes. Pods of several dozen to several hundred frequently associated with schools of yellowfin tuna though the nature of the relationship is not well understood.

A spotted dolphin calf swims by its mother. Youngsters lack the spots of the adults.

peated and prolonged encounters. Both scuba divers and snorkelers alike—although free diving usually works best because snorkelers can move faster and seem to keep the dolphins interested longer—have been able to swim eyeball-to-eyeball with these dolphins on a reasonably predictable basis. Encounters with pods of 20 or more spotteds frequently last for over an hour.

On some occasions bottlenose dolphins mix with the spotteds. Other segregated groups of bottlenose dolphins are also seen in small pods on the Little Bahama Bank. Encounters with bottlenose dolphins are typically far less intimate

and they usually last for a shorter time as bottlenose dolphins tend to be more wary of humans.

While all of the intricacies of dolphin societies are not completely understood, it is commonly accepted that some older males serve as guards for the pod. These guards often come in first to give divers the once-over before declaring the waters safe for females and calves, and it is often the same males that seem to herd the females and calves away when they decide it's time for an encounter to end.

The calves suckle for the first year or so of their lives, and during that period their mothers remain close at their side. Spotted dolphins inhabit

tropical and some subtropical waters around the world, and they are usually found over shallow banks in the open sea or in coastal waters where they prey on squids, fishes and some crustaceans. Spotted dolphins are believed to have a natural life span of approximately 45 years.

Years ago when a group of salvage divers who were working on the Little Bahama Bank first reported sighting the pods, the encounters were distant and extremely brief, lasting only a few seconds. The older males rushed in, took a close look and departed. As time passed the encounters became more prolonged and more intimate. Soon the females joined the fray, and over time this pod of spotted dolphins began to allow their young to swim with the divers. It is important to understand that absolutely no food reward has ever been offered by those who first discovered the phenomenon or by those who have followed. The dolphins are there simply because they are curious about divers, and they have some sense that their safety is not imperiled. Those charter captains and crews who visit the dolphin grounds are making every effort to keep the encounters as natural as possible.

As a rule, you will hear the high-pitched whistles and squeaks of their echolocation systems before you ever see the dolphins. And on some occasions that is as close as you will get. But when they choose to grace you with their presence, the moment is truly magic. The sugar-white sand of the Little Bahama Bank creates a very shallow bottom until the edge of the bank plummets into the deep blue waters of the Atlantic and the Gulf Stream. In most cases the diving on the bank is in less than 20 feet of water, and most divers prefer to free dive instead of being burdened by scuba.

Should you decide to join one of the dolphin diving expeditions, you will want to take along your patience. Encounters occur on a regular basis, but by no means are they guaranteed. If the dolphins do not show up, you are faced with the option of sitting on the boat and cruising in hopes that they do, or you can dive on a sand bottom. The sand community is interesting, but most divers do not find it as captivating as coral reefs. There are, however, a couple of very small, but very alive, shipwrecks that are known to area skippers.

If and when the pods of spotted dolphins do show up, they are sure to put on a wonderful show. They often leap out of the water as they approach the boat. Underwater, the dolphins excitedly rush in toward and then away from the divers. During the best encounters the dolphins

will soon slow down and begin to swim around you. The calves of spotted dolphins seem to be especially curious about divers and snorkelers. While spotted dolphins usually do not allow themselves to be touched, it does happen occasionally.

The obvious aquatic skill the dolphins display is remarkable. Even when traveling at high rates of speed, they can turn on the proverbial dime. And even more astonishing, these dolphins can swim within inches of a diver in almost any attitude, and never allow you to reach out and touch them. Specialized nerves in their skin are extremely sensitive to even the slightest pressure wake in the water and allows them to keep close tabs on their surroundings.

Like many other species of dolphins, spotted dolphins interact among themselves constantly. Sexual displays are commonplace. The females often swim upside down exposing their genitals to the males in sexual displays after the males gently bump and rub them. In other cases, the dolphins simply appear to be playing with one another as they pass objects back and forth and chase each other through the water. And somehow after watching these magnificent mammals for some time, you can't help but get the feeling that these animals care deeply for one another. It is very obvious that dolphin societies are well-developed as older animals help look after and protect the young. Spotted dolphins are often associated with schools of yellowfin tuna, and unfortunately they are one of the species that have been victims of insensitive commercial fishing techniques. Exactly what the nature of the dolphin-tuna relationship is remains a mystery. Certainly neither species feeds on the other, but spotted dolphins and yellowfin tuna are often found together.

Underwater encounters with other species such as bottlenose and common dolphins occur throughout

the Caribbean, but on a far less predictable and usually less intimate basis. However, these species, along with spinner dolphins and a variety of other species, are often seen from the decks of boats.

Having been celebrated and admired in art throughout the ages, common dolphins are perhaps the most widely recognized of all species of dolphins. Common dolphins have stocky bodies with a large sickle-shaped dorsal fin, pectoral fins that are comparatively long, narrow and pointed, and they have very strong flukes. Their backs are black from the beak to the area about halfway between their dorsal fin and tail. Their sides are a light hue of yellowish orange and gray. The tail and tail stock are gray, and they display a prominent dark stripe on either side of the head that extends from their blackish beak to their eyes.

Common dolphins are often observed over schools of tuna far out into the open sea, and they are known to hunt for small fishes and squids in extremely shallow water.

While the terms dolphin and porpoise are often used interchangeably, in pure scientific discussions small toothed whales with beaks are referred to as dolphins, as opposed to the larger toothed whales which are called whales, while the typically smaller animals with blunt snouts are called porpoises. Dolphins possess conical teeth, while porpoises have flat, spade-like teeth.

Bottlenose dolphins are characterized by stocky, grayish bodies that fade to a pinkish white underbelly. They are distributed worldwide throughout temperate and tropical seas. They are most often encountered in coastal areas, but are also known to inhabit the waters of the open sea.

While many species of dolphins at times leap out of the water, few species provide the spectacular aerial displays produced by spinner dolphins. Huge pods of spinners are often spotted from a distance of sev-

AT A GLANCE

BOTTLENOSE DOLPHIN

Scientific Name
Tursiops truncatus

Habitat
Open sea and shallows in tropical and temperate seas.

Typical Adult Size
8 to 10 feet, males to 13 feet.

Sightings
Commonly seen.

Natural History
Largest of the beaked dolphins. Cosmopolitan, from coastal waters to open sea, avoiding only polar waters. Highly social animals that live in family groups called pods. Pod size typically between 10 to 25 animals. Prey on wide variety of fishes and crustaceans. "Babysitting" has been reported, during which other adults watch over calf as mother forages for food.

eral miles as the animals repeatedly leap high out of the water. They flip, twist and spin through the air before crashing and splashing back into the sea. Spinner dolphins are extremely fast and agile swimmers. They have comparatively small, slender bodies with a prominent, triangular dorsal fin. The head and upper back are dark gray which fades to light gray along the sides. A dark stripe extends through the beak around the eye and down to the pectoral flipper. Spinners prey primarily on squids and small fishes.

SECTION
V

Enjoying the Marine Environment

19

THE UNTOUCHABLES

So often our fears about the marine environment focus on sharks, barracudas, moray eels and other animals that dominate the legends of sea lore. But if swimmers, snorkelers and divers do encounter problems with unprovoked animals, it is usually not with any of these species. Other than with provoked or baited animals, injuries to humans typically result from touching an animal we shouldn't touch because its natural defense mechanisms are designed to repel or kill. This chapter is intended to help you avoid these injuries. While in some instances we will mention basic first aid practices, this text is not intended to be about first aid.

Speaking in general terms, there are four categories of animals that cause injuries. They are: (1) the **biters**, (2) the **stingers**, (3) the **pokers**, and (4) other **miscellaneous animals**. Eating certain species of marine life can also lead to serious and even fatal injury at times, but food

Opposite page: Moray eels are common residents of many Caribbean reefs. Capable predators, morays are typically shy, reclusive creatures. If left alone, they represent no threat to divers and snorkelers. Remember, however, a number of far more delicate-looking creatures than morays should also be left alone. Look, but don't touch is often a good philosophy to dive by.

Section opener: Savoring a verdant seascape of corals and sponges, including this delicate red rope sponge in the foreground is one of the pleasures of diving. However, a careless kick or dangling console can quickly destroy years of growth.

poisoning is not discussed in any detail in this chapter. We are primarily concerned with how to avoid injuries due to contact with marine animals.

The natural history of the animals mentioned in this section have been discussed in depth in earlier chapters, and those segments should be consulted for additional details. Our goal here is to help you prevent easily avoidable injuries.

THE BITERS

In years past, many of the animals discussed in any kind of a "look, but don't touch" section were creatures like **sharks**, **barracudas**, **moray eels**, **jewfish** and the like. Today we realize that these predators rarely cause any problems for divers unless they are provoked or baited. However, because of their natural capabilities, these injuries may be severe when they do occur.

The real bottom line in any discussion about marine animals that bite is that almost any animal with teeth will bite when provoked, frightened or baited. Injuries from the bites of sharks, barracudas and other fishes are not unheard of, but almost always result from animals being excited by bait or speared fish. Baiting is difficult to control. After all, it is very difficult, if not impossible, to bait one animal without baiting every other creature around it. These animals are included here only as a reminder about the potential problems that can be incurred when bait is introduced into the

water, and to encourage you to give the proper respect to all wild animals.

Perhaps the only real surprise in this section is the inclusion of **octopuses**. Even when lightly handled, octopuses have been known to bite divers. Octopuses have powerful, parrot-like beaks that are capable of penetrating the shells of lobsters, crabs and a variety of mollusks. When they capture their prey, octopuses often inject a toxin intended to paralyze. Though they rarely occur, bites to the hands of humans occasionally penetrate bone, and that can be more serious than first suspected. Medical personnel should be consulted whenever possible in the event of an octopus bite. Bone infections can be intensely painful, serious in nature, and difficult to cure. Properly administered antibiotics can help prevent an otherwise miserable experience.

THE STINGERS

Most animals that sting to protect themselves or to capture their prey are described in the phylum Cnidaria. The cnidarians include **corals**, **sea anemones**, **hydrozoans** (the class which includes **hydroids**, **fire "corals"** and **Portuguese men-of-war**), **jellyfishes** and **sea wasps**. Many of these species are among the most delicate-looking of all marine creatures, and it is certainly fair to say that their looks belie the potency of the stinging cells found within their tentacles. Several species of sponges, especially the **dread red**

Sea wasp.

sponge and the **fire sponge**, and the worms commonly known as **bristle worms** or **fire worms**, are other invertebrates not classified as cnidarians that are also stingers.

Several kinds of fire corals head the list of potent stingers. While they are actually hydrozoans that are commonly called corals, these cnidarians take on several different appearances. Some species overgrow the surfaces of sea fans and other corals, so their shape looks like the surface of whatever they grow on. Still other fire corals are flat and branched, others long and thin, and still other species occur in tall, curved sheets. many are tannish with white tips

Hard corals, such as **brain coral**, **star coral**, **elkhorn coral** and **staghorn coral**, also sting their prey and pose a potential threat to people. In most cases, it is infected cuts that cause problems. Many corals are very sharp, and often divers do not feel the cuts when they occur. If you accidentally bump into a coral head and scrape your skin, be sure to thoroughly clean the afflicted area. The mucous coating of corals often causes infections if the wound is not cleansed. While this type of injury might not sound all that serious, infected coral cuts have taken the fun out of more than one diving vacation. Fortunately, coral cuts can be prevented by not laying on top of, kicking or grabbing corals to anchor and propel yourself along the bottom.

As painful as fire coral and some anemones can be, at least they are usually easy to see and thus avoid. That is not always the case with jellyfishes, Portuguese men-of-war and sea wasps. These animals are often very difficult to see because of their translucent bodies and tentacles.

If you see a jellyfish or a man-of-war, pay attention. As a rule, when you see one there are others nearby. These animals are not good swimmers and they tend to go wherever the prevailing conditions carry them. If you feel you are likely to get stung, the wise thing to do is to exit the water and dive another day or another place.

Sea wasps are sometimes seen during night dives. They tend to migrate toward deep water with the light of day. Occasionally present in large aggregations, sea wasps are virulent stingers. They have translucent, cube-shaped bodies which trail four tentacles. Sea wasps are attracted to bright lights and tend to swarm under them in the top few feet of water. You are also more likely to encounter sea wasps on calm nights than on windy nights.

When night diving, avoid surface swims whenever possible and don't remain on the surface longer than necessary when entering and exiting the water. Some experienced divers recommend wearing a full wetsuit, hood and gloves during all night dives because of the difficulty in avoiding sea wasps and other translucent cnidarians. When returning to the boat after a night dive, if you see any sea wasps, purge your secondary regulator for 20 to 30 seconds while you are directly under the dive ladder before the last 15 feet of your ascent. The stream of bubbles will help clear the area above you.

While the stinging nematocysts of some cnidarians are not capable of penetrating human skin, the best rule of thumb is to avoid contact with bare skin to prevent potential injury to yourself, and to prevent harming the more delicate species.

Reactions to cnidarian stings vary markedly from species to species and from person to person. If stung, apply a topical treatment of meat tenderizer and white vinegar immediately (some people swear by baking soda paste). This will break down the pain-inducing toxins from the stinging nematocysts. **Do not rinse the afflicted area with fresh water. Doing so will trigger any unfired nematocysts that are still on the skin.**

In addition to applying ointment, you should thoroughly wash your wetsuit and other dive gear in salt water to get rid of any unfired nematocysts. In some cases, unfired nematocysts from the tentacles of jellyfish, Portuguese men-of-war and sea wasps adhering to unrinsed gear, especially wetsuits which have remained damp, have been documented to badly sting the user as long as 24 hours after an initial encounter.

Stings from cnidarians can often be intensely painful, but they are rarely serious. However, allergic reactions are not unheard of. As is the case with bee and wasp stings, some people react severely to the stings from fire corals, Portuguese men-of-war, jellyfishes, sea wasps and other cnidarians. It is always a good idea to have a bee sting kit or Benadryl with you whenever you dive. And

of course, you should know how to use it.

The two most common of the stinging sponges are the **dread red sponge** (also called the **touch-me-not sponge**) and the **red fire sponge.** Contact with either species, or even touching your fins or gloves after they have touched these sponges will cause severe itching comparable to that caused by touching insulating fiberglass with bare skin.

The name dread red is probably derived from the color Caucasian skin turns after contact with this sponge. The name is not a reference to the natural color of the species since underwater, touch-me-not sponges actually appear a shade of brown to maroon. The sponges have a rounded, yet irregular, shape. Often hundreds of tiny white worms inhabit dread red sponges, and the presence of the worms can be helpful in identifying the species. Contact with any sponge that is infested with worms should be avoided just to be on the safe side.

Bristle worms are free-living worms that spend their time crawling along reefs and atop gorgonians. Most specimens are 3 to 10 inches long, and their color varies from dark green to vibrant shades of green, orange or red, with numerous tufts of white bristles located along the sides of the body.

It is the calcerous white bristles, or spines, that the animal flares when threatened which causes intense pain in humans. The spines are venomous, and they are sharp as glass, easily capable of penetrating the hardest of calloused hands. The bristles tend to dislodge even when the worms are handled with gloves, and plenty of divers have suffered a potent sting when removing their gloves long after having handled a bristle worm.

THE POKERS

Four groups of animals are classified as potential pokers. They are the **sea urchins**, **scorpionfishes**, **pufferfishes** and **stingrays**. Of these, clearly the main culprit are the sea

Spine of a yellow stingray. Note: Majority of barb is sheathed.

urchins, most notably the **long-spined urchin**. Nighttime is when most divers get stuck by their spines. These big, black pin cushions are usually hidden within the recesses of the reef by day, but they emerge in the evenings to graze on algae. Their needle-sharp spines may reach up to 12 inches in length, and they readily break off when they puncture skin. Furthermore, if you examine a sea urchin spine under a magnifying glass, you will discover that the spines are barbed like a fish hook. The spines have been cleverly crafted by Mother Nature to easily puncture the skin of animals that pose a potential threat to the urchins, but the barbs make it very difficult to remove the spines in one piece.

Hot water, the repeated application of a good drawing salve, and time will usually alleviate any problems. Occasionally spines lodge into joints, and medical attention might be required.

At one time or another, almost every diver has been gouged by a sea urchin spine. If you have not yet had your turn, be thankful, and if you are careful and lucky, perhaps you never will.

Having sharp dorsal spines which can inject powerful venom, **scorpionfishes** are another of the pokers. Masters of camouflage, scorpionfishes are reluctant to flee even if they see you approaching. The best way to avoid a puncture wound from a scorpionfish is to never touch the reef or settle to the sea floor.

The venom of Caribbean scorpionfishes is not deadly, but it can cause severe pain. Immerse the affected area in water that is as hot as can be tolerated, and the heat will quickly destroy the venom. Pain will likely persist for several hours, but in most instances it will subside significantly within an hour or so of being treated.

Occasionally an unfortunate swimmer, snorkeler or diver gets punctured by the barb-like spine of

Long-spine urchin.

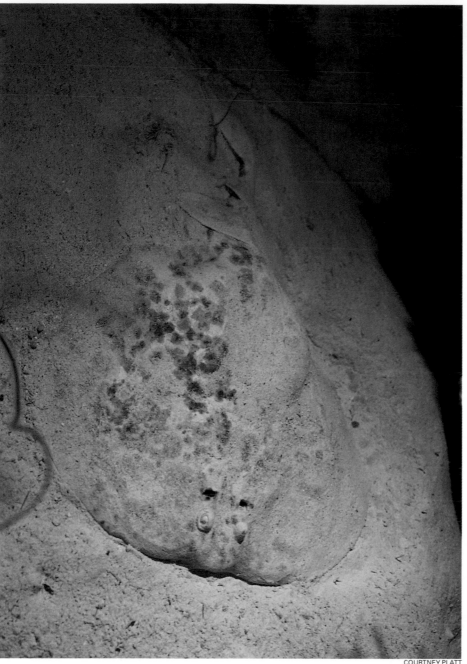

COURTNEY PLATT

Electric torpedo ray.

that is as hot as the victim can tolerate will help break down the toxins and ease the pain, but be sure to clean the wound to help prevent infection.

Balloonfish and **porcupinefishes** are other potential pokers, although they might also be classified as potential biters. Almost always, an injury from a pufferfish or porcupinefish results from divers handling these fishes to get them to take in water, inflate their bodies, and erect their spines. The tips of the hardened spines are sharp and covered with mucus, so any puncture wound should be cleaned thoroughly to prevent infection.

A surprising number of divers have experienced painful bites from frightened pufferfishes and porcupinefishes. They have large, fused teeth, powerful jaws, and a bite that has been known to badly mangle fingers.

Obviously, the best way to avoid being poked or bitten by a pufferfish or porcupinefish is to avoid harassing them in the first place.

MISCELLANEOUS ANIMALS

It only makes sense that contact with electric rays should be avoided. With most species, the shock from an electric ray is not potent enough to cause any serious harm, but the sensation is not something that is likely to be described as pleasant. The most commonly encountered species of electric ray in Caribbean and associated waters is the **lesser electric ray**.

Lobsters and **crabs** occasionally get blamed for causing injuries to divers. Inevitably the injury occurs when a diver grabs a lobster and gets his fingers pinched and cut by the hard, spine-covered exoskeleton, or when he allows a frightened crab to grab a finger with their powerful claws. Clearly the best way to avoid being injured by a lobster or crab is to look, but keep your fingers to yourself.

a stingray. In most instances an unthinking person has tried to handle a stingray, but in some cases someone accidentally steps on a sluggish ray that reacts to protect itself by jabbing the person responsible. Three species of stingrays are commonly encountered by snorkelers and divers in Caribbean waters. They are the **yellow stingray**, **southern stingray**, and **spotted eagle ray**. All have spines located at or near the base of the tail.

The spines are long and jagged, and a puncture wound is usually rather painful. While some toxin might be released, the most serious danger is from an infection which is likely to result from an uncleansed wound. Stingray spines are covered with bacteria and other marine growth, and as a result cleaning any wound is especially important. Soaking the afflicted area in water

20

PRESERVING THE MARINE ENVIRONMENT: WHAT CAN YOU DO?

*I*n recent years in many countries throughout the world, the level of environmental awareness has increased dramatically throughout all levels of society. Education has enlightened us. But even with so many people wanting to do their part, at times the problems can seem overwhelming. It is easy but not necessary to get caught in the trap of thinking "What can little me do to counter the impact of an event as large and destructive as an oil spill?" Obviously, one way to combat the potential negative impact of the industrialized world is to become politically involved on a local level or on a broader scale. But not everyone has the time or the inclination.

Even for those who prefer to operate outside the political arena, there are a lot of ways to contribute to the common cause. Over the years, one of the most important realizations of the environmental movement is that winning this war means winning a lot of small battles on local levels. You can contribute to the overall effort just by doing your part in your daily life.

We are talking about the way you dive—the way we all dive. Just by being a little more thoughtful about our personal habits and actions in the water, we can make an important contribution toward protecting an environment that we all care

Opposite page: Elkhorn coral grows in the shallow waters often between the breakers and the reef. A hardy and fast growing coral, its branching structure helps it endure the continuous pounding of the surf. However, it stands little chance against against careless divers.

deeply about. We are asking you to think about the way you dive—to make an effort to create new habits, change old ones, and become more environmentally conscientious.

"Look, but don't touch" is an excellent guiding philosophy, for the bottom line is that it is far more likely for us to harm the plants and animals of the marine kingdom than to be harmed by those creatures.

Touching, grabbing, poking, petting, leaning on, pulling, moving, etc. can be very harmful, in fact fatal, to many marine animals. Corals, sponges, sea anemones, moray eels, stingrays and myriad other animals can suffer fatal injuries as a result of contact by humans. While the damage is not readily apparent in many cases, our actions can lead directly to infections or other events that can cause their demise.

The real truth is that on a daily basis, some divers somewhere unnecessarily damage the marine environment. We are not suggesting that people quit diving, spearfishing or eating lobster. We are just trying to encourage all divers to join a movement that says "We care, so let's dive in a manner that shows our respect and appreciation for Mother Ocean."

The following suggestions are things you can do during your diving day to help preserve and protect the marine environment:

1) **Try your best to maintain neutral buoyancy**. Almost every diver has, at one time or another, crashed to the bottom because he was negatively buoyant. Every time we crash into coral, we damage, and

in many cases kill, the very animals we have come to see and admire. Try not to crawl along the bottom, but hover neutrally in the water column. Inexperienced divers often insist on using more weight than necessary. If you use less weight, your diving will become easier, you will use less air, and there will be less chance of accidentally crashing into the reef.

2) **Be conscious of your body position all the way to the tips of your fins.** Instructors and divemasters have a saying that goes something like "divers are aware from the neck up." At least they recognize that we are thinking! The problem is that while we do a good job of not bashing into creatures with our heads, as a group we are guilty of doing a lot of unintentional damage with our torso, legs and especially our fins. Spend a few minutes observing unthinking divers and you will often see them smacking the reef, breaking corals, and destroying habitat as they fin madly to maintain their position. If you are a photographer, pay extra attention to what you do with your fins as you leave one subject and move on to your next one, especially when you are working in the tight confines of the reef.

3) **If you accidentally kick something, stop kicking**. Quickly look at your fins and do what you can to avoid creating a path of destruction as you also try not to settle on top of the reef. Divemasters often suggest that you treat the reef like you treat your mother. If you accidentally kick dear ole mom, stop, and try not to do it again!

4) **Tuck your gauges and octopus neatly, though safely, out of the way.** Dangling gauges and hoses dragging along behind you can do a lot of harm.

5) **Pursue your photographic subjects with a sense of appreciation and respect.** Don't allow the pursuit of photography or videography to create a "picture-at-any-price" mentality. Be clever and be patient, but avoid wrestling, exhausting, pinning, stabbing, choking, spearing, shooting or beating your photographic quarry into that perfect pose.

6) **Think about the consequences of touching, grabbing and riding marine life.** The simple act of touching or petting marine creatures often does a lot more harm than we realize. The skin of many fishes, for example, is protected by a coating of mucus. Handling a fish can remove the coating, which often leads to a harmful chain of events, usually starting with an infection. You won't see the damage because the end results don't happen instantly. But fish, corals and a host of other creatures pay dearly from the actions of unthinking divers.

Frankly, we are not sure that a diver does any harm by riding a whale shark for a few minutes. But we are absolutely certain that you can drown a turtle or harass manta rays so much that they won't return to a preferred area. We are equally convinced that some manta rays actually enjoy being scratched, but we also feel certain that often they don't like being grabbed, pinched or manhandled by a horde of divers. Think before you touch, grab or ride.

7) **Never drop or set a boat anchor in a coral reef. Anchors and** anchor chains can do a lot of damage in no time. Tying off to a permanent mooring is best, but when that is not possible, drop your anchor in the sand.

8) **Do whatever you can in a polite and positive way to encourage other divers to become more and more conscientious in their habits.** We don't want to encourage the advent of a ticket-issuing "reef patrol force." We just want to encourage people to treat the marine environment with respect. No one was born with the knowledge of how to do so. All of us have, or probably will, do some damage at some point in time as we dive. It is inevitable. We would simply like to encourage all divers to do what we can to minimize diver damage that can be avoided.

Thank you for caring!

Please think before you touch, grab or ride; it can do more harm than you might suspect. So can a dangling console as in this photograph.

BIBLIOGRAPHY

Auerbach, Dr. Paul S. *A Medical Guide to Hazardous Marine Life.* St Louis, MO: Mosby-Year Book, 1991.

"Bahamas." *The World Book Encyclopedia,* B Vol. 2, p. 28. A. Scott Fetzer Co., 1992.

Barnes, Robert D. *Invertebrate Zoology, 5th edition.* Fort Worth, TX: Saunders College Publishing, 1987.

Bavendam, Fred. "Star Gazing." *International Wildlife,* Vol. 20 (1990), p. 46.

Bonner, Nigel. *Whales of The World.* New York, Oxford, England: Facts on File, 1989.

Boschung Jr., Herbert T., Williams, James D., Gotshall, Daniel W., Caldwell, David K. and Melba. "The Audubon Society Field Guide to North American Fishes, Whales and Dolphins." *Borzoi Book.* New York: Alfred A. Knopf, 1993.

Bramwell, Martyn, ed. *Atlas of the Ocean.* New York: Crescent Books, 1977.

Bulloch, David K. *The Underwater Naturalist.* New York: Lyons & Burford, 1991.

Burgess, Dr. W., Axelrod, Dr. H. and Hunziker, III, R. *Dr. Burgess's Atlas of Marine Aquarium Fishes.* Neptune City, NJ: T.F.H. Publications, Inc., 1988

"Caribbean Sea." *Britannica,* Vol. 2 (1991), p. 867.

"Caribbean Sea." *The World Book Encyclopedia,* C Vol. 3, p. 237. A. Scott Fetzer Co., 1992.

Carson, Rachel. *The Edge of the Ocean Sea.* Boston: Houghton Mifflin Co., 1955.

Castle, Ken, and Frink, Stephen. "Splash: A Guide To The Best Underwater Vacations." *Travel-Holiday,* Vol. 172 (1989), p. 74.

Cleave, Andrew. *Whales & Dolphins: A Portrait of the Animal World.* Leicester, England: Magna Books, 1993.

Cosmopolitan World Atlas. Chicago, New York, San Francisco: Rand McNally, 1987.

Cousteau, Jacques-Yves. *The Ocean World.* New York: Harry N. Abrams, 1979.

Cummings, Stuart and Susan. "The Jewels In The Crown." *Skin Diver,* Vol. 39 (1990), p. 99.

Dunn, Jerry. "Sponges: Living The Simple Life." *National Geographic World",* (1993), p. 27.

Duxbury, Alyn C. and Alison B. *An Introduction to the World's Oceans, 3rd Ed..* Dubuque, IA: Wm. C. Brown Publishers, 1989.

Ellis, Richard. *The Book of Sharks.* New York: Alfred A. Knopf, 1989.
___. "Dolphins and Porpoises." *Borzoi Book.* New York: Alfred A. Knopf, 1989.

Evans, Peter G.H. *The Natural History of Whales & Dolphins.* New York, Oxford: Facts on File, 1987.

"Florida Keys." *Britannica,* Vol. 4 (1991), p. 841.

"Florida, Straits of Florida, Florida Keys." *The World Book Encyclopedia,* F Vol. 7, p. 242. A. Scott Fetzer Co., 1992.

Frehsee, Rick. "Bahamas Dive Guide." *Skin Diver,* Vol. 40 (1991), p. 131.

Frink, Stephen. *Underwater Guide to the Florida Keys.* Key Largo, FL: Blue Water Publishing, 1990.
___. "Shark Junction: Unexso's Thrilling New Dive Adventure." *Skin Diver,* Vol. 39 (1990), p. 60.
___. "Fabulous Florida Keys." *Skin Diver,* Vol. 41 (1992), p. 104.
___. "Fabulous Florida Keys." *Skin Diver,* Vol. 38 (1989), p. 101.
___. "Florida Keys." *Skin Diver,* Vol. 36 (1987), p. 63.

Greenberg, Jerry and Idaz. *Guide to Corals & Fishes of Florida, Bahamas and Caribbean.* Miami, FL: Seahawk Press, 1986.
___. *The Living Reef.* Miami, FL: Seahawk Press, 1979.

Hall, Howard. *A Charm of Dolphins.* San Luis Obispo, CA: Blake Publishing.

Halstaed, MD, Bruce W. *Dangerous Marine Animals.* Centerville, MD: Cornell Maritime Press, 1980.

Harrison, Sir Richard, and Bryden, Dr. M. M., eds. *Whales, Dolphins and Porpoises.* New York, Oxford, England: Facts on File, 1988.

Hauser, Hillary. *Book of Fishes.* Houston, TX: Gulf Publishing, Pisces Books, 1984.

___. *Book of Fishes*. Houston, TX: Gulf Publishing, Pisces Books, 1992.

Hornsby, Al, ed. *Encyclopedia of Recreational Diving*. Santa Ana, CA: PADI, 1988.

Humann, Paul. *Reef Creature Identification, Florida, Caribbean, Bahamas*. Orlando, FL: New World Publications, 1992.
___. *Reef Fish Identification, Florida, Caribbean, Bahamas*. Orlando, FL: New World Publications, 1989.
___. *Reef Coral Identification, Florida, Caribbean, Bahamas*. Orlando, FL: New World Publications, 1993.

Jensen, Albert C. *Wildlife of the Oceans*. New York: Harry N. Abrams, Inc., 1979.

Joseph, James, Klawe, Witold, and Murphy, Pat. "Tuna and Billfish." Tropical Tuna Commission, 1980.

Kaplan, Eugene H. *A Field Guide to Coral Reefs*. Peterson Field Guides. Boston: Houghton Mifflin Co., 1982.

Leatherwood, Stephen, and Reeves, Reeves R. *Whales & Dolphins: Sierra Club Handbook*. Sierra Club, 1983.

Levine, Joseph, and photo, Rotman, Jeffrey L. *Undersea Life*. New York: Stewart, Tabori & Chang, 1985.

Lucas, Steve. "Florida: Skin Diver Guide To The Gold Coast." *Skin Diver*, Vol. 36 (1987), p. 55.

Mannucci, Maria Pia, and Minelli, Alessandro, ed. *Great Book of the Animal Kingdom*. New York: Arch Cape Press, 1982.

Meinkoth, Norman A. "The Audobon Society Field Guide to North American Seashore Creatures." *Borzoi Book*. New York: Alfred A. Knopf, 1981.

Michael, Scott W. *Reef Sharks & Rays of the World: A Guide to their Identification, Behavior, and Ecology*. Monterey, CA: Sea Challengers, 1993.

Minasian, Stanley, Balcomb III, Kenneth C., and Foster, Larry. "The World's Whales." *Smithsonian Books*, 1947.

Murphy, Geri. "Reef Creature Identification: Florida, Bahamas, Caribbean." *Skin Diver*, Vol. 40 (1991), p. 67.
___. "Caribbean Angelfishes." *Skin Diver*, Vol. 41 (1992), p. 23.
___. "Caribbean Moray Eels." *Skin Diver*, Vol. 40 (1991), p. 27.

Quayle, Louise. *Dolphins & Porpoises*. New York: Gallery Books, 1988.

Raven, Peter H., and Johnson, George B. *Biology*. St. Louis, Toronto, Santa Clara: Times Mirror/Mosby College Publishing, 1986.

Robins, C. Richard, and Ray, G. Carleton. *A Field Guide to Atlantic Coast Fishes of North America*. Boston: Houghton Mifflin Co., 1986.

Roessler, Carl. *Coral Kingdoms*. New York: Harry N. Abrams, 1986.

Russo, Ron. "Caribbean Angels Without Wings." *Sea Frontiers*, Vol. 34 (1988), p. 334.

Sefton, Nancy, and Webster, Steven K. *Caribbean Reef Invertebrates*. Monterey, CA: Sea Challengers, 1986.

"Sharks." *Oceanus*, Vol. 24, No. 4 (Winter 1981-82), Massachusetts: Woods Hole.

Snyderman, Marty. *California Marine Life*. Calistoga, CA: Marcor Publishing, 1988.

Steen, Edwin B. *Dictionary of Biology*. New York, Hagerstown, San Francisco, London: Barnes & Noble Books, 1971.

Stevens, John, ed. *Sharks*. Drummoyne, Australia: Golden Press Pty Ltd., 1987.

Stokes, F. Joseph. *Divers & Snorkelers Guide to the Fishes and Sea Life of the Caribbean, Florida, Bahamas and Bermuda*. Philadelphia: Academy of Natural Science of Philadelphia, 1984.

Stoltzenberg, William. "Curiosity Killed The Grouper." *Sea Frontiers*, Vol. 40 (1994), p. 20.

Sumich, James L. *Biology of Marine Life: An Introduction, 3rd Edition*. Dubuque, IA: Wm. C. Brown Publishing, 1984.

Van Gelder, Richard G. *Biology of Mammals*. New York: Charles Scribners' & Sons, 1969.

Voss, Gilbert L. *Coral Reefs of Florida*. Sarasota, FL: Pineapple Press, 1988.
___. *Seashore Life of Florida and the Caribbean*. Miami, FL: Banyan Books, Inc., 1976.

Wallace, Robert. *How They Do It*. New York: William Morrow & Co. Inc., 1980.

Wickler, Wolfgang. *The Sexual Code*. New York: Doubleday & Co. Inc., 1972.

Wilson, Roberta and James Q. *Watching Fishes: Life and Behavior on Coral Reefs*. New York: Harper & Row, 1985.

Wood, Dr. Elizabeth M. *Corals of the World*. Neptune City, NJ: T.F.H. Publications, 1983.

Abdomen. The area of the body located posterior to the cephalothorax in many crustaceans. The tail region in mammals, the area between the thorax and pelvis.

Abyssal realm. The portion of the marine environment in which light does not significantly penetrate. This region includes all water below a depth of 600 feet.

Aerole. The feather-like crown of worms such as feather dusters, which is used both as a respiratory organ and as a feeding apparatus.

Alternation of generations. The alternation of a sexually reproducing generation and an asexually reproducing generation in the reproduction of non-flowering plants.

Amphibian. A cold-blooded invertebrate that lives in water and breathes by gills in the larval stage, and by lungs as an adult. Amphibians are capable of living both in water and on land.

Ampullae of Lorenzini. System of very sensitive nerve-filled pits located near the mouth and head of sharks and some other cartilaginous fishes, which assists these animals in detecting minute pressure changes due to movement of nearby organisms, and which allow them to detect electrical fields emitted by nearby organisms.

Annelid. Member of the phylum Annelida. Annelid worms are known as segmented worms.

Anterior. Toward the forward end or head.

Anthozoan. Any member of the class Anthozoa including sea anemones, jellyfish and corals.

Aphotic. Without light. The aphotic zone of the oceans is the portion that receives little or no light. This region is considered to include all waters below 2,600 feet.

Arthropod. Any invertebrate described in the phylum Arthropoda which includes lobsters, crabs, shrimp, isopods, amphipods, copepods and other crustaceans.

Ascidian. A bottom-dwelling tunicate or sea squirt.

Asexual reproduction. Reproduction which does not involve the union of sperm and egg. Sporulation, budding, fragmentation and fission are types of asexual reproduction.

Attenuated shape. Long and thin with a gradual taper.

Baleen. Long fibers or plates found within the mouths of filter-feeding whales, and which are used to sieve plankton and small fishes from the water.

Benthic. Bottom dwelling. Benthic animals live on or near the bottom, as opposed to pelagic organisms which live up in the water column.

Binomial nomenclature. A naming system for organisms in which each life form is given a scientific name consisting of two words: the first designates the genus and the second designates the species. When correctly printed only the genus is capitalized and both genus and species are italicized.

Bioluminescence. Production of light by living organisms to be distinguished from phosphorescence with which it is often confused by laymen. See phosphorescence.

Biomass. The total mass of organic matter per unit of area. The term biomass is often used when explaining how much food is required to support predators.

Biome. A community or zone that can be distinctively characterized by the plants or animals that live within.

Bivalve. Two shells, as in the case of bivalve mollusks such as scallops and oysters.

Bladder. A sac in animals used as a reservoir for a gas or fluid.

Blowhole. Nostril or spiracle on the top of the head of whales and dolphins through which respiration occurs.

Byssal threads. Tough fibers secreted by the byssal gland located on the foot of many bivalve mollusks. Fibers are used to attach these mollusks to the reef or sea bed.

Calcerous. Containing calcium carbonate.

Carapace. Part of exoskeleton which covers the cephalothorax of some arthropods.

Caudal peduncle. Prominent muscular base just forward of the tail of some fishes such as tuna and mako sharks.

Cephalic lobe. One of the two extendible/retractable projections located on either side of the mouth of manta rays.

Used to channel water and food into mouth.

Cephalopod. Any mollusk in the class Cephalopoda (head-footed) including octopuses and squids.

Cephalothorax. Anterior region of the body of many arthropods. A fused shell covers the cephalothorax of many crustaceans.

Cerata. Projections found on the backs of many nudibranchs. In some nudibranchs, the cerata contain unfired nematocysts from some cnidarians, especially soft corals preyed upon by the nudibranch. Cerata are then used as a stinging defense mechanism by the nudibranch.

Chromatophores. Specialized pigment cells found in the skin of many marine animals such as flatfishes, octopuses and squids. The cells enable these animals to alter their color pattern and hue in order to blend into their surroundings. In some cases chromatophores are believed to be used in intra-species communication.

Ciguatera. Most common type of fish poisoning in humans. Believed to originate with accumulation of dinoflagellates.

Cilia. Minute hair-like processes found along the edge of a cell. Cilia beat regularly and are used in locomotion.

Cirri. Projections growing from the head of certain fishes such as diamond blennies.

Cirripedia. Claw-like legs of crinoids.

Clasper. Structure used by males of all cartilaginous fishes during copulation. Normal males have a pair of claspers which are located on the underbelly.

Class. A taxonomic category below a phylum and above an order.

Cleaner. An organism that removes parasites, dead tissue, bacteria or fungi from the surface of another animal.

Cnidoblasts. Specialized cells found in cnidarians which form and contain a specialized stinging apparatus called a nematocyst.

Coelenterate. Any invertebrate in the phylum Cnidaria including sea anemones, jellyfish and corals.

Cold blooded. Having a core temperature which varies with ambient temperature. Most fishes, amphibians and reptiles are considered to be cold blooded.

Cold biological light. Light produced by bioluminescent life forms.

Colony. A group of living organisms that share a common skeletal case or test.

Commensalism. Symbiotic relationship between two organisms of a different species in which one animal benefits and the other is neither benefited of harmed.

Coral head. Stony structure made up of many living coral polyps which live on calcerous deposits of their ancestors.

Coral reef. Collection of living coral heads.

Coralline. 1) An animal that bears strong resemblance to coral. 2) A type of red algae containing lime. These algaes are often important components of coral reefs.

Crustacean. Any arthropod in the class Crustacea which includes lobsters, crabs, shrimps, copepods, isopods and amphipods.

Ctenophore. Any member of the phylum Ctenophora which includes comb jellies.

Decapod. Any crustacean classified in the order Decapoda including lobsters, crabs, shrimps, amphipods, copepods and isopods.

Delayed implantation. Method whereby some female marine mammals delay the implantation of a fertilized egg into the uterus.

Dermal denticles. The tiny tooth-like structures which make up the skin of cartilaginous fishes such as sharks, rays and skates.

Dinoflagellate. A protozoan described in the order Dinoflagellata having two flagella.

Distribution. The range or area that a species normally inhabits.

Diurnal. Pertaining to the day as opposed to nocturnal. Occurring daily.

Dorsal. Of or having to do with the back or upper surface of the body of an animal.

Echolocation. Biological sonar used by many species of mammals in which the animals send out a series of sounds which are reflected back to the sender off of other bodies, and are then analyzed by the sender to provide information concerning the size, speed, type of object, etc.

Echinoderm. Any marine invertebrate described in the phylum Echinodermata which includes sea stars, brittle stars, sea cucumbers, crinoids and sea urchins.

Ecology. Portion of the discipline of biology concerned

with the interrelationships between organisms, and between organisms and their surrounding environment, also known as environment biology.

Ecosystem. A unit found in nature consisting of all living and non-living forms like tide pools, kelp forests and rivers.

Ectoparasite. Parasite which lives on the skin of another animal.

Elasmobranch. Any fish that is a member of the class Chondrichthyes, the cartilaginous fishes which includes sharks, skates and rays.

Estrus. Period of sexual receptiveness in adult female mammals, also known as the period of heat.

Eviscerate. As in sea cucumbers, act of expelling their sticky stomachs in order to ward off potential predators.

Evolution. Process by which organisms develop over extended periods of time as a result of changes and adaptations.

Excurrent. Outflowing. In sponges the excurrent siphon helps to eliminate wastes and unwanted water, as opposed to the incurrent siphon which takes in water.

Exoskeleton. A protective external skeleton as is found in lobsters, crabs and other arthropods.

Family. A taxonomic category, between order and genus.

Fingerling. A fish as described between the time of the disappearance of the yolk sac and the end of one year.

Fisheye lens. Describes very wide field of vision in fishes. Wide field of vision offers advantages in helping fishes avoid predators. In photography, a lens with a circular area of view and a wide angle of coverage.

Flatworm. Any member of the phylum Platyhelminthes, some of which are marine worms.

Fluke. A horizontal lobe on the tail of a whale. In casual conversation the term tail and fluke are sometimes used interchangeably.

Food chain. Path through which food energy is transferred in nature.

Food web. A group of interlocking food chains.

Flushing. Act of darkening skin by fishes when requesting cleaning services or when being cleaned. Believed to be used to make lightly hued ectoparasites more obvious to cleaner organisms such as gobies and shrimp.

Fugu. Pufferfish flesh served in the Japanese style of sushi. Unless properly prepared, fugu can be very poisonous to humans.

Fusiform. Tapered at both ends. Fishes such as giant barracuda, albacore and blue sharks are said to have a fusiform shape.

Gamete. Any cell which is capable of developing into a complete individual upon union with another sex cell.

Gastropod. Any mollusk described in the class Gastropoda including abalone, other snails, limpets, periwinkles and whelks.

Genus and species. Latin bi-nomenclature used to accurately classify all living organisms. The genus is a subdivision of a family that includes two or more closely related species. When properly written, the genus name is always capitalized and italicized. Species is a subdivision of a genus of two or more closely related organisms. Plants and animals described in the same species are capable of reproducing fertile offspring. When properly written, the species name is always in lower case and is italicized.

Gestation period. The period of time between the implantation of a fertilized egg in the uterine wall and birth.

Gill. Respiratory structure in aquatic animals through which gaseous exchange occurs.

Gill rakers. Projections located on the gill arches of some fishes which serve to prevent food particles from passing through the gill slits.

Gill slits. One of several openings in the wall of the pharynx. In marine animals, the gill slits are separated by arches which bear gills.

Gorgonian. Corals described in the order Gorgonacea which includes sea fans. The skeletal case of gorgonians is comprised in part of a horn-like substance known as gorgonian. A type of soft coral.

Habitat. A natural area such as a tide pool, kelp forest or river that is considered to be the home of many organisms. A biome.

Hard coral. Cnidarians such as brain, elk, star and staghorn coral whose skeletons consist of a calcerous limestone base. It is these corals whose skeletal deposits supply the foundation of coral reefs. A coral reef is built upon the skeletal remains of uncountable hard coral polyps.

Harem. Female animals that mate with a single male, and some of whose behavior the male tries to control.

Hermaphrodite. Animal which possesses the reproductive organs of both sexes. In some hermaphrodites, only one organ (either the male or female) produces sex cells at any given time, while others simultaneously produce male and female sex cells.

Host. Animal involved in a symbiotic relationship which is not likely to derive benefit and which might be harmed.

Ichthyology. Science that deals with the study of fishes.

Ink sac. A rectal gland found in cephalopods that serves to produce and store ink.

Invertebrate. An animal that does not possess a backbone or spinal column.

Iridocytes. Specialized cells found in the skin of flatfish which help enable the fish to closely match the color and pattern of their skin with that of their surroundings.

Isopod. Any crustacean described in the order Isopoda, often observed on fish.

Juvenile. A young or sexually immature organism.

Larva. Immature form of an organism that has been born but is unlike the adult form.

Lateral line system. Concentration of nerves located in grooves along the sides of many fishes. System allows these fishes to detect movement in the surrounding water, and offers great advantages to these species in their effort to avoid potential predators and in capturing their prey.

Life cycle. The complete life history of an organism.

Life history. The complete series of events displayed by an organism encompassing every stage between its origin and death.

Lophophore. Feather-like filtering organ of bryozoan zooid, an individual within a colony.

Luminescence. Production and emission of light without the accompanying production and emission of a significant amount of heat. Bioluminescent organisms create luminescent light.

Mammal. Any vertebrate described in the class Mammalia including man, whales, sea lions, seals, otters, dolphins and manatees. Mammals are characterized by hair and mammary glands which produce milk to feed offspring. All mammals breathe air, have lungs, are warm blooded, and most bear live young.

Mandible. In general usage, the jaw. In arthropods, one of a pair of mouth parts used to cut, crush or grind food.

Mantle. Specialized organ in mollusks which is responsible for secreting the hard shell.

Margin. The edge or border.

Metabolic rate. The rate of chemical or energy changes which occur within a living organism as calculated by the amount of food consumed, heat produced, or oxygen used.

Metabolism. Chemical and energy changes which take place within a living organism due to the activities involved in being alive.

Metamorphosis. A process in which animals such as crustaceans undergo a change in shape or form as the animal develops from a fertilized egg to an adult.

Migration. Mass movement of populations of animals to and from feeding, breeding and nesting areas.

Milt. Seminal fluid produced by the testes of fishes.

Mollusk. Any vertebrate described in the phylum Mollusca which includes a wide variety of specimens such as chitons, abalone, limpets, octopuses, squids, nudibranchs, sea hares, clams, mussels and oysters.

Molt. Act in which a crustacean sheds its shell in order to grow. Also a term applied to the discarded shell of crustaceans.

Mouth brooder. Fish which hold fertilized eggs and/or young in their mouth during the course of gestation/development. Describes the advanced trait of parental care. In many fishes, the mouth brooder is the male of the species.

Mussel. Any bivalve mollusk described in the class Pelecypoda.

Mutualism. Symbiotic relationship in which both animals benefit as a result of the association, and neither is harmed.

Natural history. The study or description of the life of various organisms. A complete discussion of the natural history of an organism would include information concerning the classification, habits, predator/prey relationships, life cycle and distribution.

Natural selection. Process through which natural events determine which life forms will survive and which will perish.

Nematocyst. Specialized stinging cell found in cnidarians, used in defense and/or food gathering.

Nettle cell. Stinging cell found inside the nematocysts of cnidarians.

Notochord. In chordates, a dorsal rod of cartilage that runs the length of the body and forms the primitive axial skeleton in the embryonic stage of all chordates. In most adult chordates, the notochord is replaced by the spinal column. In tunicates, the notochord forms the axial skeleton. In some respects, a notochord is a precursor to a spinal column.

Operculum. Calcified hatch-like plate found in many gastropod mollusks. In fish, the operculum is a flap-like covering over the gills of many species. Used to pump oxygenated water over gills.

Order. A taxonomic category below a class and above a family.

Organic. Having to do with or having been created by living things.

Organic evolution. Process by which various organisms develop, change and adapt over time.

Osmoregulator. An organism that maintains a constant concentration of various salts within the body in spite of the concentrations of the salts in the organism's immediate surrounding.

Osculum. Large central opening of sponges through which filtered water exits.

Oviparous. A specific type of reproduction in which females lay eggs that hatch outside the body of the female. Compare with ovoviviparous and viviparous.

Ovoviviparous. A specific type of reproduction in which females produce eggs encased in a shell which develop inside the body, but the young only receive nourishment from the yolk sac and not directly from the mother.

Parasite. An organism which lives on or in another organism and from which it takes some nourishment.

Parasitism. Symbiotic relationship between two organisms in which one benefits and the other is harmed as a result of the association. The beneficiary is typically referred to as the parasite or symbiont, while the harmed organism is known as the host.

Pectoral. Of or having to do with the chest or breast area of a body.

Pectoral fin. One of the paired, laterally oriented fins of a fish. Pectoral fins are generally forward on the midbody of the fish.

Pectoral girdle. The cartilaginous or bony structure that provides support for the pectoral fins of a fish.

Pedicelariae. Tiny pincer-like organs found on surface of some echinoderms. Often used to help keep skin clean.

Pelagic. Of or having to do with the open ocean. Pelagic organisms live up in the water column as opposed to on the bottom. See benthic.

Pelecypod. Any mollusk described in the class Pelecypoda which includes mussels, scallops, clams and oysters.

Pharyngeal slit. In members of the phylum Chordata, one of a series of openings between the throat (or pharynx) and the surrounding environment.

Pheromone. Type of hormone which is released into the environment by an animal to elicit a sexual response from other members of the same species. Often used as an advertisement that a comparatively immobile organism is going to emit sex cells.

Phoresis. Symbiotic relationship between two organisms in which one organism gets a "free ride" from place to place from another animal. The relationship between remoras and manta rays is described as phoresis.

Phosphorescence. The production and emission of light without the accompanying production and emission of heat.

Photic. Having to do with light.

Photic zone. That region in the marine realm where sunlight is able to penetrate in an amount sufficient to support photosynthesis.

Photosynthesis. Process through which plants convert radiant or solar energy into chemical energy that is stored in the molecules of various carbohydrates.

Phylogenetic. Having to do with ancestral development.

Phylum. A taxonomic category comprising the largest category of the plant or animal kingdom. A phylum is subdivided into classes.

Phytoplankton. Tiny free-floating plants which form the foundation of many marine food chains.

Pinniped. Any aquatic mammal described in the class Pinnipedia which includes seals and sea lions. Pinnipeds have modified limbs that are used as flippers.

Pinnules. Feathery branches which extend outward from the arms of crinoids. Contain tube feet which are used to help trap food.

Placoid cell. A type of scale made of a bony plate that is embedded in the outer layer of skin or in the epidermis of elasmobranchs. Same as a dermal denticle.

Plankton. Free-floating aquatic life forms that tend to float passively, having only limited control over their environment.

Pleopods. Abdominal appendages located under the tail of many crustaceans. Also known as swimmerets. Eggs are attached to pleopods and thereby can be aerated.

Pod. A group of whales, porpoises or dolphins.

Poikilothermous. Cold-blooded; having a core temperature that varies with the surrounding environment.

Polyp. A small, bottom-dwelling form of various coelenterates, animals described in the phylum Cnidaria, which are attached at the base and have a mouth that is surrounded by tentacles. Colonial animals are composed of groups of polyps that live within the same skeletal case.

Posterior. At or towards the tail or back end of the body.

Predation. The act of seeking out and capturing other animals for food.

Predator. An animal which practices predation.

Prey. An animal that is captured and eaten by another animal.

Process. 1) A series of interconnected activities. 2) A projecting outgrowth on a body.

Radula. Plate-like structure that bears rows of tiny teeth. A radula is found in many mollusks and is used as a tool for rasping and chewing.

Reef buttress. Top edge of a reef where the reef drop-off begins.

Regeneration. The replacement of lost tissues or body parts in higher life forms, or the development into a functional individual from a part other than a reproductive cell in lower animals such as sea stars.

Respiration. The exchange of gases between an organism and its surroundings.

Rhinophores. Pair of tentacles found in the head region of some nudibranchs and mollusks. Typically said to be the second pair of tentacles.

Rostrum. A body projection extending forward from the head in manta rays and other animals.

Salp. Common name for several types of free-swimming marine tunicates described in the class Thaliacea.

Salp chain. When a salp asexually reproduces by budding, it often creates a connected group of animals referred to as a chain which consists of the adult with many trailing offspring.

Scientific name. The taxonomic classification known as the genus and species of a given life form. The genus name should always be capitalized and both words should appear in italics.

Sea star. A starfish; term that is replacing the word starfish in some educational circles.

Sea water. Saline water found in ocean basins. Salt contents vary but average close to 3.5 percent.

Sediment. Matter which settles to the bottom.

Sexual generation. In plants that reproduce in a cycle known as alternation of generations, it is the generation which produces gametes, either eggs or sperm.

Setae. Calciferous tufts of free living worms, such as those found on red fan worms.

Shadowing. Term applied to the act in which one species follows, or shadows, a member of another typically larger species for the purpose of gaining protection and/ or food.

Siphon. A tube-like modification of the mantle of some mollusks such as those found in octopuses and squids. Used to forcibly draw in, extract water and direct water to aid in locomotion.

Smoking sponge. Lay term used to describe actively reproducing sponges which are emitting milk-like clouds of sperm and/or eggs.

Soft corals. Cnidarians described in the order Gorgonacea such as sea fans and sea whips. Soft corals contain a horn-like material known as gorgonin used in structural support, but do not lay down a calcerous skeleton, and are therefore, relatively temporary in their physical longevity. They do not make a major contribution to the long term growth of a coral reef.

Speciation. The process by which a new species is naturally formed.

Spicules. Tiny silica needles embedded within some sponges, which help to give structural support.

Spiracles. Excurrent openings found slightly behind and above the eyes of rays, which assist in respiration. Oxygenated water passes through the spiracles over the gills, even when a ray is buried in sand and mud. The term is also used to describe the blowhole of a cetacean.

Spongin. Stringy protein fibers embedded within some sponges. Used to give support.

Stony coral. A coelenterate described in the order Madreporaria. In California waters, solitary corals are often referred to as stony corals.

Subspecies. A subdivision of a species in which interbreeding is possible, but in which slight physiological differences are present.

Substrate. Solid material on which organisms live; the bottom or sea floor.

Swim bladder. Organ found in many bony fishes, which is used to establish neutral buoyancy and thereby help to conserve energy in these fishes. Gases are transferred from the blood supply to and from the swim bladder to control the buoyancy added or subtracted by the swim bladder.

Swimmeret. A slender, branched abdominal appendage found on the abdomen of crayfishes and lobsters. In females, the eggs are carried on the swimmerets.

Symbiont. Organism engaged in a relationship with another organism of a different species, and which is likely to derive benefit from the relationship.

Symbiosis. Intimate relationship between organisms of two different species. Depending upon the specific nature of the association, the relationship is further defined as commensalism, mutualism, parasitism or phoresis.

Taxonomy. The arrangement and classification of plants and animals into categories based on commonly shared characteristics.

Teleost. Any fish with a bony skeleton, a member of the class Oestichthyes.

Tentacle. Any of a number of long, thin, flexible, unsegmented appendages that serve in a sensory, food-getting, locomotive, defensive, attaching, or reproductive capacity.

Terminal. The front end, as in the front of a fish. The mouth of a whale shark is located in the terminal position, while the mouth of a Caribbean reef shark is said to be underslung.

Territory. An area to which animals normally confine their activities. In many cases, the animals vigorously defend the area from intruders.

Torpor. A kind of semi-diurnal hibernation in which

fishes that are active by day rest during the evening.

Trinomial nomenclature. An extension of the binomial system in which a subspecies or a variety is scientifically named with a total of three words, two of which combine to comprise the species name. When properly written, all three words are italicized, but only the genus is capitalized.

Trochophore. Free-swimming larval stage of a marine mollusk.

Trophic. Of or having to do with growth or nutrition.

Trophic level. A particular stage or position within a food chain in which given plants and animals acquire their food.

Tube feet. Part of the water vascular system found in echinoderms capable of creating suction to aid in locomotion, and/or for passing food to the mouth. Sea stars possess rows of tube feet on the underside of their arms.

Uniparous. Bearing one offspring at a time.

Veliger. The more advanced free-swimming larva of some marine mollusks.

Ventral. Of or having to do with the lower surface or underside of a body.

Vertebrate. Any animal having a spinal column, which is described in the subphylum Vertebrata.

Viviparous. A form of reproduction in which the eggs of undeveloped young hatch inside the body of the mother and obtain further nourishment from her as development proceeds. The young are born at a later point in time when development has been completed.

Visceral mass. The main portion of the body of an abalone or bivalve mollusk which is located above the foot and includes the internal organs.

Whorl. A spiral turn or twist in the shell of a gastropod mollusk.

Zooid. Individual animal with a colony of closely associated organisms as in bryozoans.

Zooplankton. Tiny, free-floating animals, many of which play vital roles in the foundation of many food chains.

PHOTO CREDITS

INDEX

A **bold** faced page number denotes a picture.
An <u>underlined</u> page number indicates detailed treatment.

OTHER AQUA QUEST TITLES AVAILABLE

Ask your dive center or book store for other titles by Aqua Quest Publications, publishers of books on dive travel destinations, underwater photography and videography, wreck diving, dive-related fiction, marine life, technical diving and safety. If these books are not available at your local stores, call or write us directly for a catalog of our publications.

Aqua Quest Publications, Inc.
Post Office Box 700
Locust Valley, NY 11560-0700

(800) 933-8989   (516) 759-0476
Fax: (516) 759-4519   E Mail: aquaquest@aol.com